Corporate Warriors

*The Rise of the
Privatized
Military Industry*

UPDATED EDITION

P. W. Singer

CORNELL UNIVERSITY PRESS

Ithaca and London

First published 2003 by Cornell University Press
First printing, Cornell paperbacks, 2004
First printing, updated paperback edition, 2008

Printed in the United States of America

Library of Congress Cataloging-in-Publication Data

Singer, P. W. (Peter Warren)
   Corporate warriors : the rise of the privatized military industry /
P. W. Singer.
        p. cm. — (Cornell studies in security affairs)
Includes bibliographical references (p.   ) and index.
   ISBN-13: 978-0-8014-7436-1 (pbk. : alk. paper)
   1. Defense industries.   2. Military-industrial complex.
3. Privatization.   4. Defense industries—United States.
5. Military-industrial complex—United States.   6. Privatization—
United States.   7. United States—Military policy.   I. Title.
II. Series.
   HD9743.A2S56 2003
   338.4'7355—dc21

                                        2003000456

Cornell University Press strives to use environmentally responsible
suppliers and materials to the fullest extent possible in the publishing of its books. Such materials include vegetable-based, low-VOC
inks and acid-free papers that are recycled, totally chlorine-free, or
partly composed of nonwood fibers. For further information, visit
our website at www.cornellpress.cornell.edu.

Paperback printing   10 9 8 7 6 5 4 3 2

Contents

Preface

I t was only indirectly that I first stumbled across the phenomenon of private companies offering military services for hire. I had never heard of such a thing, until I joined a U.N.-supported project in 1996, researching the postwar situation in Bosnia. As we interviewed regional specialists, government officials, local military analysts, and peacekeepers in the field, it soon became evident that the entire military balance in the Balkans had become dependent on the activities of one small company based in Virginia, (Military Professional Resources Incorporated)—MPRI. I visited the firm's regional offices, located in a nondescript building along the Sarajevo riverfront, where the firm coordinated the arming and training of the Bosnian military.

The members of the firm were polite and generally helpful, but the ambiguity between who they were and what they were doing always hung in the air. They were employees of a private company, but were performing tasks inherently military. It just did not settle with the way we tended to understand either business or warfare. However, there they were, simply doing their jobs, but in the process altering the entire security balance in the region. I was struck by this seeming disconnect, between the way we normally view the world of military affairs and the way it actually is, and wanted to learn more. I spent the next years following just that path, interviewing hundreds who either work in the industry or are close observers of it and even spent a period working at the Pentagon, helping to oversee one of the firm's contracts.

In the time since, both the industry and the firm I visited have certainly grown up. MPRI was recently bought by a Fortune-500 firm, while other companies offering military services have been discussed in many of the world's most prominent newspapers, radio, and TV outlets.[1] Beyond the general media, the idea of private businesses as viable and legitimate military actors has also begun to gain credence among a growing number of political analysts and officials, from all over the political spectrum.[2] Their activities have caught the attention of legislative officials in a number of countries and led to the submission of several bills covering their actions.[3] An international forum of African heads of states advised their use in certain situations, as did the commander of the U.N. operation in Sierra Leone.[4] Even Sir

Brian Urquart, considered the founding father of U.N. peacekeeping, advocated the hire of such firms.[5] Another sign of emerging market maturity is that a new industry trade association, International Peace Operations Association (IPOA), recently formed to lobby on behalf of military firms.[6]

The essential point is, that in the time since my first encounter with what I began to think of as "Corporate Warriors," this private military industry is no longer so small or obscure. However, for all its growth, our understanding of it still remains greatly limited.

WHAT IS MISSING?

Part of why the military industry remains an enigma is that although numerous newspaper and magazine articles have been written on the activities of such firms, most have been long on jingoistic headlines and short on earnest examination. Within academia, there have been a few articles and reports that have introduced and described some of the firms, but the broader field remains largely uninformed.[7] Most studies of the firms have been generally descriptive rather than integrative. None have addressed the industry broadly or comparatively and our knowledge of the industry still has not been advanced in any systematic manner.[8]

The reason is that the limited research done so far on military firms has focused on case studies of individual companies or of single conflicts where they were present, most often in Africa where they made their first appearance. Analysts have also tended to treat the more "mercenary" type as miniature armies in isolation. They have not placed them in a context with either similar companies that offer other types of military services or with general business models. A typical description is the erroneous statement that the client list of these firms is "limited to weak states with corrupt leaders."[9]

The result is a vacuum of established facts and a lack of understanding of this industry or the firms within it. "There are no universally accepted definitions of even the most widely used terms."[10] No framework of analysis of the industry exists, no elucidation of the variation in the private military firm's activities and impact, no attempts at examining the industry as a whole, and no comparative analyses.

Equally dangerous is that much of what has been written about these firms is noncritical, with very little examination of the industry from an independent perspective. The topic is exceptionally controversial, with people's livelihoods, reputations, and even perhaps the industry's ultimate legality dependent on how academia and policymakers meld to understand it. Unfortunately, the small amount of qualitative analysis that has been done is often highly polarized from the start, aimed at either extolling the firms to the extent of even comparing them to "messiahs," or condemning their mere existence.[11] In turn, these biased findings are often misused by the firms or by their opponents in pushing their own agendas.[12]

Thus, years after my first contact with the industry, the entire topic still remains murky to the general public, not only in the arena of known facts about the firms and their operations, but also in the lack of explanatory and predictive concepts and independently assessed policy options. This book is intended to resolve these issues, both the growing vacuum in theoretical and policy analysis of the industry, and the limitations of prior approaches.

THE STRATEGY OF ATTACK

The objective of this work is not simply to create a compilation of facts about individual firms operating in the military field. As significant as it would be finally to collect the often incongruent information about the industry into one place, the creation and implementation of an overall analytic architecture is more important. This book organizes and integrates what we know about the firms in a systematic manner, allowing for the development of underlying theories that can guide us in the future.

To build an objective system of understanding of this industry and its place in world affairs, my plan has been to leverage lessons from fields as disparate as international relations theory, security studies, political economy, comparative politics, industrial analysis, and organizational behavior. In addition to focused examination on the firms themselves, the study also draws from corollaries both within the military arena and from parallels in industries with similar structures, and similar privatization experiences. My aim thus has been to establish an understanding of the private military industry and its implications that has both depth and breadth, to find generalizations that can be fleshed out and corroborated with historical reference.

A brief word about data availability is necessary. The topic of privatized military firms remains largely unexplored for a variety of reasons: the relative newness of the phenomenon, its failure to fall neatly into existing theoretic frameworks, and, most important, the character of the business itself. Because these firms' operations are almost always controversial and secrecy is often the norm, research is difficult. Although many are seemingly quite open about their operations (when it is in their best interests to present a positive public image), many others try their utmost to cover up the scope of their activities or try to intimidate those seeking to write about them. For this reason the reader will notice the copious footnotes to demonstrate where each bit of information came from. A number of these firms walk a fine line of legality, with potentially illegitimate clients, business practices, and employees with dark pasts. Some firms are also often at the center of dangerous covert or semicovert operations that many clients, including the U.S. government, would rather not have discussed.[13] Combined with the lambasting some firms have received in the press, many in the industry remain suspicious of outside writers and are usually only willing to speak off the record.[14] Likewise, although government activities are open to examination under laws such as the Freedom of Information Act, the company contracts are protected under proprietary law, often making their activities completely deniable.

This secrecy can be an advantage to this line of business, and may in part explain its boom. The aura of mystery, however, somewhat curtails outside study. Thus, this work should be read with these limitations in mind. I have done my utmost to weed out the rumors from the facts and provide an objective analysis of the industry, indicating whenever appropriate what is confirmed and what is suspected. At the very least, it is the most complete overview of the private military industry available in the public domain.

This study has been written with the conscious decision to speak to three different audiences. The first is the academic world. I hope that this project helps scholars and students (whether they study security issues, international relations theory, political economy, or regional studies) gain greater insight into the privatized military phenomenon, not only its emergence, but also its importance. I also hope that the study dares academic readers to reexamine their theoretical presumptions. We should take a look beyond the dusty histories in the library and ensure that our understanding of the world is still in line with the momentous reality of an international system replete with players such as these firms.

The second audience is the world of policy. Every day, individuals working in the field of foreign affairs and defense matters (whether in the government, the military, international organizations, humanitarian groups, or even the press) respond to crises and conflicts that touch on matters intimate to this new industry. Many even deal directly with the firms on a contractual basis. It is worrisome that both real and potential clients, and even those charged with regulating the industry, still operate in a relative void of information and unbiased analysis. My intention is that this project may serve as an objective resource to policymakers, unlocking in a clear and useful manner the complexities of the industry, presenting both its possibilities and dangers, and the full measure of the dilemmas it raises.

Last is the general reader. Although the aim is a work of substance, I also hope to serve the individual who really doesn't care about the fate of neorealism or may never contract with one of these firms, but is simply looking to learn about a fascinating topic. The stories, personalities, and possibilities that emerge from this new industry are truly beguiling. Politics and warfare are fundamentally exciting stuff. Of greater significance, they are also matters far too important to be left to the so-called experts.

For their generous financial support, my appreciation goes to the Belfer Center for Science and International Affairs (BCSIA) at Harvard University, the Olin Foundation, the Brookings Institution, and the MacArthur Transnational Security Program.

For their advice and guidance through the process, my gratitude goes to my committee, Professors Sam Huntington, Bob Bates, and Graham Allison of Harvard University. I cannot think of a more distinguished group. They not only provided valuable direction, but also gave the freedom necessary to explore new ideas. I must also thank others working in the international relations field who inspired and supported me along the way, including Elizabeth Cousens, Michael Doyle, Martin Indyk, Iain Johnston, Colonel Greg Kaufmann, Bear McConnell, and Anne Marie Slaughter. The support of two communities of scholars are also greatly appreciated, the International Security Program at BCSIA, ably led by Steve Miller and Steve Walt; and the "virtual" private-military discussion community, organized by Doug Brooks of the IPOA and South African Institute of International Affairs, which helped put me into contact with scores of industry executives, employees, and analysts.

For their helpful suggestions in editing and improving various versions of the text, I am indebted to Gavin Cameron, Scott Corey, Laura Donohue, Robert Fannion, Bryan Garsten, Neal Higgins, Sean Lynn-Jones, Ben Runkle, Allan Singer, David Singer, Adam Sulkowski, and Jeff Wilder.

And, lastly, my appreciation to my friends and family for their love and support that made this journey possible. But, most of all, my thanks to Susan Morrison-Singer, not only for your essential technical assistance, but also for suffering through years of me talking about such delightful topics as rebels in Sierra Leone and mercenaries in Colombia. You are my best friend and my total love.

PETER WARREN SINGER

Washington, D.C.
April 1, 2002

I. THE RISE

ONE

An Era of Corporate Warriors?

"Of course, nobody seriously recommends that the military be privatized. . . . If death and disaster on a considerable scale are inevitable
products, the rule seems to be that this responsibility is the business of
the government."

—David Sichor, *Punishment for Profit*

Sierra Leone is a former British colony located in West Africa. It is
roughly the size of South Carolina. It is also, by almost any measure,
the worst place on earth to live. The country ranks dead last on the
United Nations' Human Development report, which rates the quality of life
and future prospects of the nations of the world. The infant mortality rate
is 164 deaths per thousand births. Only 30 percent of the adults in the country are literate. The average life span is just 37 years.[1]

More important, Sierra Leone is an exemplar of the desperate position
that weak states found themselves in at the close of the twentieth century.
Since the end of the Cold War, it has known little but conflict and chaos. In
1991, a violent rebellion began in its hinterlands. Although initially small in
scale, the weak government was unable to halt it. The fighting quickly
evolved into one of the most vicious civil wars in history. The group that
started the rebellion, the Revolutionary United Front (RUF), quickly became notorious. It not only openly admitted that it targeted civilians with
murder, rape, and torture, but it also highlighted its use of child soldiers to
carry out its attacks. The group's particularly heinous calling card was the
amputation of captured civilians' arms.

By 1995, absolute anarchy reigned in Sierra Leone. Roadside ambushes,
nighttime massacres of villages, and machete mutilations had become the
norm of life and death. After four years of fighting, the situation was critical
for the government. The diamond mines that had fueled the local economy
had been lost. Rebel control of the countryside also cut off the agricultural
trade. The government's military was in complete disarray, fighting an ineffective, losing battle. Many of its underpaid soldiers had even joined the
rebels or targeted civilians on their own. Locals took to calling them "sobels"
(a combination of "soldier" and "rebel"), as the two pillaging sides were almost indistinguishable. When the rebels approached within 20 kilometers

of the capital city of Freetown, fears that the war would end in a general massacre grew. Most foreign nationals and embassies hurried to evacuate the
country. The situation appeared hopeless.

Almost immediately, though, the circumstances completely reversed. A
modern strike force quickly deployed and hammered the rebel forces with
precision air and artillery attacks. These were quickly followed up by helicopter assaults and advances by mechanized infantry units. The rebels were
taken completely by surprise and, in just two weeks, were driven away from
the capital city. Using novel tactics and superior weapons, the new forces
fighting for the government then retook the major diamond-producing areas. This action restored the much-needed revenue source. Soon afterward,
the main rebel stronghold was destroyed by ground assault. In a final coup
de grâce, the RUF's jungle headquarters were located and eliminated. Over
a few short months, the once-dominant rebels had been crippled and forced
back into the bush. Such a degree of stability had been achieved that Sierra
Leone was finally able to hold its first free elections in 23 years, bringing into
power a civilian-led democracy.

At first, the rebels had no clue as to who had stepped in to save the government of Sierra Leone. The helicopters and armored vehicles that had attacked them revealed no national flags or insignia. Many of the soldiers even
had their faces blackened with paint, to further mask their identity. Moreover, there were no obvious candidates to aid the government. It had no
close allies in the region; none of the great powers were interested in this
tiny African state; and the overextended UN was incapable of intervening
even if it had wanted to—and it did not. This mystery did not last long,
though. It was soon learned that the soldiers and pilots who had turned the
tide of battle were not members of any nation's army. Rather, they were employees of a private firm based in South Africa, called Executive Outcomes.

At roughly the same time, about 4,000 miles away, the war in the former
Yugoslavia was also entering its fourth year. The new states of Croatia and
Bosnia-Herzegovina were both former republics that had broken away from
Yugoslavia in the wake of the Cold War. Their struggles for independence
were not to be easy. Serb minorities within each fledgling state fought to rejoin the former Yugoslavia, now dominated by Slobodan Milosevic's nationalist Serb party.

Having originated as a conglomeration of local militias, police forces, and
paramilitaries, the new militaries of the Croat and Bosnian governments
were generally amateurs at best. Short on weaponry, training, and established institutions, they had begun the war by suffering a series of demoral-
izing defeats. Much of their territory was soon in the hands of their
respective Serb minorities, who had been supported by the professional Yugoslav army. The terrors which ensued inside the captured areas, often
played out on the world's television screens, were given the dark label of

"ethnic cleansing." In the face of inaction by the international community, more than 200,000 people died and 3,000,000 more were left as refugees.

After the initial fluidity, the battlefield had soon stalemated, with the superior weapons and training of the Serbs grinding out against the numeric edge of the Croats and Bosnian Muslims. By 1995, a rough ceasefire had been brokered in Croatia. In Bosnia, the fighting raged on.

This all changed in the spring of 1995. The Croats launched a surprise attack they called "Operation Storm." The offensive displayed a professionalized force that took the Serbs unawares. The Croat's ragtag militia had been secretly transformed into a modern Western-style army.

Military observers described it as a textbook operation—a NATO textbook, and said that whoever planned the offensive would have received an "A plus" in NATO war college.[2] As a journalist described it, "The lightning five-pronged offensive, integrating air power, artillery and rapid infantry movements, and relying on intense maneuvers to unhinge Serbian command and control networks bore many hallmarks of U.S Army doctrine."[3] Besides the planning, the execution of the offensive was also exemplary. According to European military officers who witnessed the attack, the initial Croatian river crossing into Serb-held territory was a "textbook U.S. field manual river crossing. The only difference was the troops were Croats."[4]

This coming-out party for the new Croat army was the turning point of the entire war. The Serbs, who had rarely been on the defensive in the past, were stunned at the Croatian military's new cohesion and effectiveness. The offensive overwhelmed the local opposition in Croatia and then steamrolled into western Bosnia, turning the Bosnian Serbs' flank. Within weeks, the overall war, in both Croatia and Bosnia, was over. The reversals on the ground, combined with the renewal of NATO air strikes, had finally forced the Serbs to the negotiating table after four years of failed attempts.

The easy manner in which the Croats were able to reshape the balance of power in the Balkans remains a source of dispute. The question at the center of the debate is not about the aid of a foreign state or other institution, though. Rather, it is the exact role of a private company based in Alexandria, Virginia—Military Professional Resources Incorporated (MPRI)—which is known to have advised the Croat military during this period. The general belief in the region is that the training and advanced military planning assistance the firm provided to the Croat army was instrumental. While the firm's public line is ironically to deny that it played any part in Storm's success, the Croats certainly were happy customers and openly credit the company as the reason behind their victory. Individual MPRI employees also take credit for the firm's role in the success.[5] In fact, at the following peace conference in Dayton, Ohio, the Bosnian Muslims made their signature conditional on receiving help from the same group that was rumored to have advised the Croat force. Otherwise they would not accept the peace agreement.[6]

Just a few years later, war in the Balkans would once again break out. Decades of Serb abuses in the mainly Albanian province of Kosovo culminated in a Kosovar uprising. The civil war soon turned ugly, with numerous massacres. Many feared a new genocide. Unlike in previous years, however, this time Western nations vowed not to stand idly by, and in the spring of 1999, NATO launched an air campaign to force the Milosevic government to the negotiating table.[7]

Despite the benevolent cause, the military campaign was not popular in the United States. The public was far more concerned with domestic issues than another Balkans war, making a reserve call-up politically difficult. Supporting such an operation would also be a strain to an already overextended U.S. military. The situation was made even more difficult when Milosevic's forces launched an ethnic-cleansing campaign, driving hundreds of thousands of Kosovars across the border, seeking to use the refugees as a weapon to lash back at the West. Humanitarian groups were unprepared for the hordes of displaced families, and concerns arose as to who would house and feed them.

It was a tough conundrum. How could the U.S. military find a way to provide the logistics for its forces, without calling up reserves or the National Guard, while at the same helping to deal with the humanitarian crisis that the war had provoked?

The solution to this problem turned out to be quite simple: the U.S. military would pass the work on to someone else, in this case to a Texas-based construction and engineering firm. Instead of having to call up roughly 9,000 reservists, Brown & Root Services was hired. Not only would the firm construct a series of temporary facilities that would house and protect hundreds of thousands of Kosovars, but it would also run the supply system for U.S. forces in the region, feeding the troops, constructing their base camps, and maintaining their vehicles and weapons systems.

The privatized effort was one of the quiet triumphs of the war. The humanitarian crisis was avoided and U.S. forces would go on to force the Serbs out and later keep the peace in Kosovo. All the while, they were fed, housed, and supported by Brown & Root. General Dennis Reimer, the Chief of Staff of the U.S. Army at the time, would personally thank the firm for its crucial job well done. "Part of the reason for that progress [the peacekeeping missions' achievements] is the support from Brown & Root. Everywhere I visited I saw the results of your efforts. I just wanted to express my appreciation for all that you have done and for the contributions of the people employed by Brown & Root. In my mind, this [the Kosovo operation] is a great success story, and Brown & Root has played a key role."[8]

THE PUBLIC MONOPOLY OF WAR . . .

These three episodes are more than simple illustrations of the recurrence of violent conflict after the end of the Cold War. Rather, they are indicators

of a profound development in the manner that security is both conceptual-
ized and realized. For in each conflict, a critical factor behind the turn of
events was a private firm being hired to offer military services, hardly the traditional means of winning wars.

To understand the importance of this development, a bit of background
on services and government responsibilities is required. Traditionally, the
government provides all its citizens with certain services, which are generally paid for through taxation. This takes place in what is known as the public sector. In contrast, in the private sector, individual citizens, now known
as consumers, purchase needed goods and services in an open market, paying with their own discretionary funds. This market is made up of private
firms motivated by profit. Thus, the distinctions between these two sectors
are the sources of funding, the nature of the relationship between provider
and user, and the employment status of the deliverers.[9]

The division of the world into public and private spheres is at the center
of the long debate over what government's role should be. Ever since the
rule by kings was replaced by the bureaucratic state in the seventeenth century, there has been a give-and-take between the public and the private, with
the line between the two constantly in flux. In fact, the debate about where
this line should fall has been described as one of the "grand dichotomies of
western political thought."[10]

Sometimes governments have found it expedient to transfer some of
their public responsibilities to the private sector. They may do so because of
issues of cost, quality, efficiency, or changing conceptions of governmental
duties. Health care, police, prisons, garbage collection, postal services, tax
collection, utilities, education, and so on are all examples of services that
have been shifted back and forth between being viewed as essential public
responsibilities of the government to something best left to the private market.[11] The terms "outsourcing" and "privatization" are used interchangeably
to describe this relocation of service provision, often in the same breath.[12]
Both are generally accepted practices; indeed, the economic concept behind them can be traced back as far as the founding economist Adam Smith's
writings in the 1700s.[13]

One area where the debate over public or private never ventured, though,
was the military, the force that protects society. The production of the goods
needed to wage war long ago became the domain of the market. But by the
time the state had been accepted as the dominant means of government,
the service side of war was understood to be the sole domain of government.[14] In fact, providing for national, and hence their citizens', security
was one of the most essential tasks of a government. Indeed it defined what
a government was supposed to be.[15]

The result is that the military has been the one area where there here has
never been a question of states outsourcing or privatizing. Even the most
radical libertarian thinkers, who tend to think that everything else should

be left to the market, made an exception of the military. All viewed national defense as something best carried out by a tax-financed, government force.[16] As such, for the last two centuries, the military profession has been seen as distinctive from all other jobs.

> The military is very different from any other profession and is unique specifically because it comprises experts in warmaking and in the organized use of violence. As professionals, military officers are bound by a code of ethics, serve a higher purpose, and fulfill a societal need. Their craft sets them apart from other professionals in that the application of military power is not comparable to a commercial service. Military professionals deal in life and death matters, and the application of their craft has potential implications for the rise and fall of governments.[17]

In short, since states started to replace rule by kings and princes in the 1600s, military services have been kept within the political realm under the control of the public sector. One of the great political scientists of our time, Samuel Huntington, summarized this distinction, "Society has a direct, continuing, and general interest in the employment of this skill for the enhancement of its own military security. While all professions are to some extent regulated by the state, the military profession is monopolized by the state."[18]

. . . AND THE PRIVATIZED MILITARY FIRM

The story does not end here, however. Instead, it is the present breakup of this public monopoly of the military profession that is the focus of this book. The importance of the three episodes presented here is that they illustrate how the public–private dichotomy in the art of war, which was once solidly fixed, is now under siege. The firms who took part in these operations are distinct in that their business involved outsourcing and privatization heretofore unimagined. The debate about the public and private sectors has moved farther than it ever has before—to military services themselves.

The companies behind these episodes are a new development known as Privatized Military Firms or PMFs. They are business organizations that trade in professional services intricately linked to warfare. They are corporate bodies that specialize in the provision of military skills, including combat operations, strategic planning, intelligence, risk assessment, operational support, training, and technical skills.[19] By the very fact of their function, they break down what have long been seen as the traditional responsibilities of government. That is, PMFs are private business entities that deliver to consumers a wide spectrum of military and security services, once generally assumed to be exclusively inside the public context.

The idea that private companies could perform these military functions sounds fanciful enough. MPRI advertises itself as possessing "the greatest corporate military expertise in the world." The very possibility of such a claim, invoking the mixture of the public military and the private modern business corporation, would have seemed not only paradoxical but even preposterous just a few years ago. In the post–Cold War era, though, this cross of the corporate form with military functionality has become a reality. A new global industry has emerged. It is outsourcing and privatization of a twenty-first-century variety, and it changes many of the old rules of international politics and warfare.

THE GLOBAL PRIVATIZED MILITARY INDUSTRY

What is even more shocking is that not only does this new industry of privatized military firms simply exist, but it has become global in both its scope and activity. Beginning in the 1990s, PMFs have been active in zones of conflict and transition throughout the world. They have been critical players in several conflicts and often the determinate actor. They have operated from Albania to Zambia, often with strategic impact on both the process and outcome of conflicts. As illustrated in Figure 1.1, their operations are not restricted to any one geographic area or type of state. PMFs have been active on every continent but Antarctica, including in relative backwaters and key strategic zones where the superpowers once vied for influence. Moreover, their operations have become integral to the peacetime security systems of rich and poor states alike. Their customers also are ranged across the moral spectrum from "ruthless dictators, morally depraved rebels and drug cartels" to "legitimate sovereign states, respected multinational corporations, and humanitarian NGOs."[20]

For many, this industry may be a bit of a shock. A quick tour around the globe is perhaps needed to reveal the full extent and activity of PMFs.

Africa

On a continent where weak state structures and the legacy of civil conflict combine to create a truly insecure environment, PMFs are almost pervasive.

The war in Angola illustrates. More than eighty firms offering military services have come to participate in the conflict in one role or another.[21] Almost all of these firms' employees are former soldiers from around the globe. They include ex-U.S. Green Berets, French Foreign Legionnaires, South African paratroopers, Ukrainian pilots, and Ghurka fighters from Nepal. As explored later in chapter 8, the Executive Outcomes firm was one of first PMFs in Anglola, being hired in 1993 to retrain Angolan army forces and then lead them into battle. Its employees also flew the Angolan air force's aircraft and launched commando raids against UNITA command centers. Another firm, International Defense and Security (IDAS) has been particularly instrumental to the Angolan government in its defense of cor-

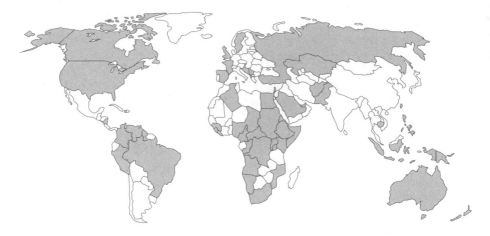

Figure 1.1. The Global Activity of the Privatized Military Industry, 1991–2002. Areas where firms are confirmed to have been active are in gray.

porate diamond fields and blocking the primary supply route of rebel forces.[22] In addition to direct combat activities and military training, other firms have provided a range of military services, including aerial reconnaissance and intelligence (Airscan) and demining (Ronco and DSL).[23] Rebel forces, in turn, have used private companies to gain military advantages of their own. Private experts have provided tactical training and specialists to staff the rebels' artillery and tank forces. Reportedly, in exchange for offshore oil concessions, Ukrainian companies also provided UNITA with a small air force of Mig-27 and Mig-21 jet fighters and Mi-24 attack helicopters.[24]

Similarly, PMFs played a multiplicity of roles in the war in the Democratic Republic of Congo (what was once known as Zaire), also for all the sides. In the mid-1990s when his regime began to fall, long-term ruler Mobutu Sese Seko began negotiations with MPRI and Executive Outcomes for aid against the rebellion led by Laurent Kabila. Neither firm took on the contract, as the regime was on its last legs and seemed unlikely to be able to pay. Another company, Geolink, did ultimately assist the regime, but was unsuccessful.[25] Mobutu's regime fell, and Kabila, who reportedly had been assisted by the Bechtel company, took over power.[26]

Kabila's new government was quickly threatened by shifted coalition of rebel forces. His adversaries included former Mobutu supporters, who contracted with the Stabilco firm, the national armies of Rwanda and Uganda, who were assisted by another Johannesburg-based military intelligence firm, and Angolan UNITA rebels, still supported by mercenaries and PMFs of their own.[27] Seeking help from all corners, Kabila hired Executive Outcomes, which supplied his government with air combat support, electronic warfare assistance, and security protection.[28] Other intervening states such as Zimbabwe were supported by air supply firms, such as Avient, who reportedly also operated fighter jets and attack helicopters for their clients.[29]

Angola and Congo are no exceptions. Instead, private military activity is rampant across the continent. In its war with Eritrea, Ethiopia leased a wing of jet fighters from the Sukhoi firm, along with the pilots to fly them, the mechanics to maintain them, and the commanders to plan out their strikes.[30] In Sudan, Airscan reportedly has operated with at least two other firms to help to protect oil fields from rebel forces.[31] Other companies, including Executive Outcomes spin-off firms, are performing similar functions in the fighting in Algeria, Ivory Coast, Kenya, and Uganda. In the Liberian war, International Charter Inc. (ICI) and Pacific Architects and Engineers (PAE) provided military aviation and logistics support to the ECOMOG peacekeeping force.[32] When faced with an army mutiny in late 2002, the government of Ivory Coast is rumored to have hired Sandline to help put down the revolt.[33] The governments of Cameroon, Nigeria, Equatorial Guinea, and Congo-Brazzaville all have contracted with private firms to help reorganize and train their militaries. In other fields, Mechem, Mine-Tech, and SCS handle the dangerous but important task of demining operations in postwar states like Mozambique.[34]

The use of PMFs in Africa is also not just limited to governments or MNCs, however. Private firms have reportedly worked for rebels in both Senegal and Namibia as well as in Angola, providing military training to antigovernment dissidents. In Burundi, Hutu rebels are alleged to have received arms, training and operational services from South African PMFs, including Spoornet, while Dyncorp offers logistical support to the rebel alliance in Sudan. Even the quasi-state of Puntland (it is unrecognized by the international community), which has emerged from Somalia's ashes, contracted out its coastal patrol to the Hart Group.[35] Aid groups have also been getting in on the act. Faced with poaching that threatened the northern white rhino in the Congo, the World Wildlife Fund received a bid from Saracen for military-style protection of the game preserves, while the aid groups Worldvision and ICRC hired Lifeguard to protect their facilities and staff in Sierra Leone.[36]

Europe

The extent of activity on the African continent, though, must not mislead one into thinking that the PMF industry is only a regional phenomenon. In addition to the previous examples of Croatia and Bosnia, MPRI had a similar military restructuring program in Macedonia. Its military training centers also influenced the Kosovo conflict next door. When previously serving in the Croatian Army, the commander of the Kosovo Liberation Army (KLA) rebels, General Ceku, received MPRI training. Many of his soldiers are also rumored to have attended the firm's training centers in Bosnia. The firm is also reportedly waiting in the wings to provide advisory services in Kosovo, once the KLA is allowed to become the official defense force of a future Kosovo entity.[37]

The activity of PMFs, though, extends outside the Balkans. There are many British and French-based military firms (Eric SA, Iris, Secrets, Sandline, etc.). London is one of the unofficial hubs of the industry. Other operators on the European continent include Cubic, which is helping to restructure the Hungarian military as it works to reach NATO standards, and the International Business Company (IBC), based in Germany, which offers troop training and weaponry.

The British military exemplifies the current trend toward military outsourcing and gives the sense of the penetration the industry is making into the European market. Already private firms run many essential services for British forces, often in areas where one would not expect a company to be in charge. A typical example is that a private firm has begun training the Royal Navy in operating and maintaining its newest nuclear-powered submarines.[38]

The British defense ministry announced an initiative in 2001 that will take military privatization to the next level. Labeled the "sponsored reserves" system, the plan authorizes the entire transfer of key military services to private companies, including the Royal Navy's aircraft support unit, the Royal Army's tank transporter unit, and the Royal Air Force's air-to-tanker refueling fleet, all of which played vital roles in the 1998 Kosovo and 2001 Afghan conflicts. The costs for the refueling contract alone is expected to run more than $15 billion.[39] Also in the works is the privatization of the Defence Evaluation and Research Agency (the British equivalent of the American DARPA (Defense Advanced Research Projects Agency), which is in charge of the development and assessment of military technology.[40] The Blair government has even floated the idea of privatizing future troop donations to UN peacekeeping missions.[41]

The Former Soviet Union and the Middle East

To the east, an explosion of private military activity has accompanied the fall of the Berlin Wall. The deterioration of order in post-Soviet Russia provides a dramatic illustration.[42] Besides the nearly 150,000 employees of private security firms that operate inside Russia, several new companies have ventured onto the international market to provide military expertise for hire. This has resulted in thousands of ex-Soviet soldiers working in the PMF field. A notable example is the Moscow-based Alpha firm, founded by former elite KGB Special Forces personnel, which entered into a corporate linkage with the international Armorgroup firm.[43] Elsewhere, contract soldiers have been active in Chechnya, fighting alongside regular forces, and in defending strategic facilities in Azerbaijan, Armenia, and Kazakhstan.[44]

It is fairly likely that with the uncertain security environment in Central Asia and the plans of several international conglomerates to begin exploiting area oil reserves, the privatized military industry will next move into this region. The pipelines for these oil fields are planned to run through some of the most conflict-ridden areas in the world, including Chechnya and Georgia. One is even planned to go through Afghanistan. The combination of the extremely weak state structures, corruption, high-value natural resources, unpredictable local armed units, and the firms' unique capabilities and past experience in guarding pipelines and other commercial assets in Africa and Latin America (for many of the very same multinational companies) makes for a sure recipe of military industry expansion in Central Asia.

Military firm activity is also quite significant in the Middle East. Several prominent firms are based in Israel, such as Levdan, which was active in Congo; Ango-Segu Ltd., which was reportedly in Angola; and Silver Shadows, which worked in Colombia. More significant, perhaps is the near absolute reliance of some of the Persian Gulf states on private firms. Saudi Arabia, where the industry practically runs the national armed forces, offers a graphic illustration.[45] Vinnell trains and advises the Saudi National Guard, which functions like a praetorian guard to the regime, protecting important strategic sites. The firm has more than 1,400 employees in country, many of whom are ex-U.S. Special Forces, working on a contract estimated to be worth more than $800 million.[46] Vinnell is not the only PMF in Saudi Arabia, however. BDM provides logistics, training, intelligence, and comprehensive advisory and operation services to the Saudi Army and Air Force; Booz-Allen Hamilton runs the military staff college; SAIC supports the navy and air defenses; O'Gara protects the royal family and trains local security forces; and Cable and Wireless provides training in counterterrorism and urban warfare.[47] There are similar setups in the other Gulf States, such as in Kuwait, where Dyncorp supports the air force and MPRI runs a training center.[48]

Asia

A great deal of private military activity has occurred in Asia as well. The 1997 Sandline intervention into the Papua New Guinea conflict, which resulted in a mutiny by the local army, is the most notable. But PMFs have also been active in many other Asian states. The Taiwanese military has hired military advisory services from firms such as MPRI. In Nepal, a number of ex-Gurkha soldiers, who fought for the British and Indian armies under contract, have formed PMFs of their own, such as Gurkha Security Guards. In Cambodia, COFRAS, a French firm, provides demining services.[49] In Burma, the French firms ABAC, OGS, and PHL Consultants are all rumored to have helped train the local military and assist it in actions against rebels. In the Philippines, Grayworks Security provides military training and counterterrorism assistance to the government.

Indonesia is one of the dominant states in Southeast Asia, but, in turn, also has had extensive experience with PMFs. It used Executive Outcomes to carry out commando operations, while many other firms were used to support the international intervention into once Indonesian-held East Timor.[50] These included UN-employed intelligence and security firms and Dyncorp, which provided helicopter and satellite network communication support. The Indonesian government also hired Strategic Communication Laboratories, a firm that specializes in psychological warfare operations, to help it respond to outbreaks of secessionist and religious violence.[51] Offshore, violent attacks on commercial shipping in the South China Sea are on the rise. As a result, private firms such as Trident have also begun to take on antipiracy duties.

Illustrated by its own reliance on logistics outsourcing during the East Timor operation, Australia is the country at the forefront of the trend toward use of PMFs within Asia. Like Britain, it has announced a plan to turn over the entirety of certain military services to private companies.[52] Perhaps most interesting, though, is Australia's privatization of military recruiting. Raising an army has long been a daunting numbers game for governments. In response, "In a management decision that would surely leave Karl von Clausewitz, the 19th-century Prussian military philosopher, speechless, Australia's military has outsourced its recruitment functions to Manpower, a U.S.-based temporary staffing group."[53] Experts believe that this sort of privatized military recruiting will be the way of the future; indeed, Britain and the United States have also begun to turn over military recruiting tasks to similar firms.[54]

The Americas

Last, PMFs have also been quite active in the Americas. At least seven U.S.-based military companies are active in the ongoing conflict in Colombia.[55] Many claim that these private contractors, such as Dyncorp and EAST Inc., ostensibly hired by the U.S. State Department to help in the antidrug effort, are actually going well beyond such tasks, including engagement in counterinsurgency operations for the government.[56] On the other side of the conflict in Colombia, an Israeli military firm, Spearhead Ltd., is rumored to have provided combat training and support to the drug cartels and antigovernment militias.[57] Large businesses and landowners have also hired private forces to protect their properties in the midst of the conflict.[58] British Petroleum (BP) even directly contracted a battalion of soldiers from the Colombian military, who were advised by the Armorgroup military firm.[59]

The industry is also quite active elsewhere in the Western hemisphere. The Canadian military has made logistics outsourcing moves similar to those of Australian and British forces. It also has contracted with civilian firms to provide electronic warfare (EW) training and various other air combat support services.[60] In Haiti, former soldiers of the army now serve as private forces for the elite families who run the political system, while Dyncorp has taken over the training and deployment of the new Haitian National Police.

Dyncorp even maintains an "on call" list of Spanish-speaking personnel, in case the firm is ever hired to staff a mission in a post-Castro Cuba.[61] One of the more tragic incidents with PMFs operating in the Americas made the news in May 2001, when a CIA surveillance plane mistakenly directed Peruvian air force planes to attack a passenger plane carrying American missionaries. The crew running the surveillance systems were employees of Aviation Development Corp., a PMF that had been subcontracted by the agency.[62]

As in Colombia, Mexican drug cartels have also been rumored to receive similar private military assistance. Such private experts have begun providing military tactics and countersurveillance techniques to the cartels, helping them both to monitor and counter law enforcement activities and also protect cartel leaders from rival organizations. U.S. intelligence has already detected one private military training camp in Mexico, where the cartel forces of the Arellano Felix organization were trained on a variety of equipment, from rocket-propelled grenades and heavy machine guns to encryption devices and night vision and radio intercept systems.[63] Elsewhere in Mexico, several corporations have hired their own private armies, including most notably the Jose Cuervo distillery. Fed up with an inadequate government response to sophisticated raiders, the famous tequila maker employs a 125-person, military-style unit, deployed to protect its valuable agave fields.[64]

Ironically enough, despite being the dominant power on the international scene today, the United States may make the most extensive use of the privatized military industry. Indeed, from 1994 to 2002, the U.S. Defense Department entered into more than 3,000 contracts with U.S.-based firms, estimated at a contract value of more than $300 billion.[65] The areas being outsourced are not just minor ones such as military food services (although 1,100 Marine Corps cook positions were privatized in 2001), but include a variety of areas critical to the U.S. military's core missions.[66] At a time when downsizing and increased deployments have left U.S. forces stretched thin, private firms have provided the United States with an array of services: security, military advice, training, logistics support, policing, technological expertise, and intelligence. In the last few years, the U.S. Department of Defense has outsourced everything from depot and base upkeep to more than 70 percent of army aviation training. The maintenance and administration for such strategic weapons as the B-2 stealth bomber, the F-117 stealth fighter, the KC-10 refueling aircraft, the U-2 reconnaissance aircraft, and numerous naval surface warfare ships are all privatized.[67]

Such firms operating alongside U.S. forces have become nearly ubiquitous. When the Russian nuclear sub *Kursk* exploded, it was a civilian, contracted surveillance ship that first observed it.[68] Airscan protects USAF and NASA launch facilities, while BDM provides training in infowar, special operations, and intelligence and has also provided interpreters and translators for the U.S. military for operations in Somalia, Haiti, Bosnia, Central Asia, and the Persian Gulf. Betac has been associated with the U.S. Special Operations Command and reportedly assisted on clandestine operations throughout the world.[69] MPRI provides force management for the U.S. Army, doctrine development for Training and Doctrine Command (TRADOC), and, perhaps most surprisingly, operates the ROTC program in almost 220 universities.[70] Like the British forces, the U.S. Navy and Marine Corps have also begun to explore the possibility of outsourcing air-to-air refueling operations (to Omega Air Inc.), while the U.S. Navy and Air Force have hired ATAC to provide and fly adversary aircraft during their military training exercises.[71] Even the computing and communications at NORAD's Cheyenne Mountain base, where the U.S. nuclear response is coordinated, has been privatized, in this case to OAO Corp.[72]

The Pentagon has also outsourced a large part of its external military assistance programs, with MPRI, DFI International, and Logicon being the major players. The United States recently established the African Center for Strategic Studies (ACSS) to help African states improve their national security planning and defense budgeting. The program is similar to the military schools established for Europe, Asia-Pacific, and the Americas. But unlike those, which are operated by the U.S. military, the development and implementation of the ACSS curriculum is run by MPRI.

The result is that while contractors have long accompanied U.S. armed forces, the wholesale outsourcing of U.S. military services since the 1990s is unprecedented. Industry personnel were present to a limited extent on the frontlines during the Gulf War. Since then, though, reductions in military forces coupled with high mission requirements and the unlikely prospect of full mobilization, mean that the requirement for outside support has seen exponential growth, multiplying by a factor of five.[73]

Every major American military operation in the post–Cold War era has involved considerable levels of support and activity by private firms offering services that the U.S. military used to perform on its own.[74] The operations in Kosovo illustrate this trend. Before the conflict, Dyncorp supplied the military observers who fulfilled the American portion of the international verification mission. Once the air war began, besides the logistics and engineering support, private firms also supplied much of the information warfare aspects of the operation.[75] In the follow-on KFOR peacekeeping operation, firms serve the same roles and also supply personnel for the international policing efforts. In fact, when a shortage of surveillance aircraft left the U.S. forces in the Balkans without their critical "eyes in the sky," they even outsourced their aerial intelligence-gathering function. The U.S. Army hired Airscan, a Florida-based company that provides similar services in Colombia, Angola, and Sudan.[76]

Indeed, if any operation should have been a purely military one, it would have been the response of the United States to the terrorist attacks of September 11, 2001. Although the military enjoyed broad support among the American public, and any previous concerns about casualties were set aside, private employees still played a variety of roles in the war in Afghanistan. They deployed with U.S. forces on the ground (including serving in the CIA paramilitary units that fought alongside our Afghan allies), maintained combat equipment, provided logistical support, and routinely flew on joint surveillance and targeting aircraft. Even the noted Global Hawks, the Air Force's most advanced unmanned surveillance planes, were operated by private employees.[77] In the subsequent peacekeeping operations in Afghanistan, the industry has stayed active in these areas and beyond. For instance, the European troops of the International Security Assistance Force (ISAF) were flown in on Russian-made military transport planes leased out by a London firm, while Afghan president Hamid Karzai is protected by a DynCorp security force, made up of roughly forty ex-U.S. special forces troops.[78]

In the following antiterrorism operations elsewhere around the globe, PMFs played similar roles. For example, in early 2002, the United States deployed a military training contingent to the former Soviet republic of Georgia, to help root out radical Muslim terrorists who had taken over the Pankisi Gorge. Although led by a U.S. Army officer, the rest of the training team was actually staffed by PMF employees.[79] In fact, for those Taliban and al Qaeda members unlucky enough to be caught, they can plan on spending their next years housed in a military prison at Guantanamo Bay, built not by U.S. soldiers, but by Brown & Root for $45 million.[80]

In sum, the examples listed in this quick tour—many of which will be discussed in the following chapters—provide only highlights of the extent of the privatized military industry. They are intended only to illustrate it breadth, not its entirety. The amazing aspect is that military firm activity could have been even much greater, if one also considers the very real contract offers that did not come to fruition. For example, Nigerian dissidents reportedly offered Executive Outcomes $100 million to help train and lead a rebellion against the Abacha regime.[81] The Kosovar rebels reportedly were also interested in the similar services of Sandline. Closer to home, the Mexican government negotiated with Executive Outcomes for help in quelling the Chiapas rebellion. The list goes on and on. The "what ifs?" that these contracts provoke illustrate just how extensive the change is in the manner one goes about creating military capability.

THE BOTTOM LINE AND THE REST OF THE STORY

The provision of security has long been recognized as the most important function of government. By the start of the twentieth century, state control over the means of violence had been institutionalized through a process that spanned centuries.[82] But as long as it took to develop, this cartelization of state power has proven to be short-lived.

An overall global pattern is emerging, one of growing reliance by individuals, corporations, states, and international organizations on military services supplied not just by public institutions but also by the nonsovereign private market. The changes that this phenomenon portends are tectonic. The emergence of a privatized military industry may well represent the new business face of warfare.

My assertion is not that the state or the public military profession are disappearing. It is a far more complex story. For in many areas, the power of PMFs has been utilized as much in support of state interests as against them. By removing absolute control from government, however, and privatizing it to the market, the state's hold over violence is broken.[83] With the growth of the global military services industry, just as it has been in other international areas such as trade and finance, the state's role in the security sphere has now become deprivileged. The start of the twenty-first century has begun to see the Weberian monopoly of the state slowly break down.[84]

What makes this industry worthy of study is not just the fact that private companies have begun to move onto the battlefield, but also the scope, location, and criticality of their role in the prosecution of warfare. Not within the last two centuries, at least, has there been such reliance on private soldiers to accomplish tasks directly affecting the tactical and strategic success of engagement.

In sum, radical changes in military relationships are emerging, and so we need radical reassessments. With the creation of an industry of privatized military firms, states, institutions, organizations, corporations, and even individuals can quickly lease military capabilities of the highest level off the global market. As will be explored in the following chapters, this opens up a world of possibilities, in both policymaking and theory building. The industry is not only significant but also quite fascinating.

TWO

Privatized Military History

Trade must be driven and maintained under the protection and favour of your own weapon. . . . Trade can not be maintained without war, nor war without trade.

—Jan Coen, Governor General of the Dutch East Indies Company

Hiring outsiders to fight your battles is as old as war itself. Nearly every past empire, from the ancient Egyptian to the Victorian British, contracted foreign troops in some form or another. Likewise, the popular literature and entertainment of nearly every age is replete with their stories.[1] In some eras, these private entrants into conflicts were individual foreigners, brought in to fight for whichever side bid the highest, known as "mercenaries" in common parlance. In other periods, they came in the form of highly organized entities. For both, the important factor was their goal: private profit, derived from the very act of fighting.

The following chapter explores the history of private actors in warfare, thus laying the groundwork for understanding the present private military firm, or PMF, industry. It examines their activities, their significance, and the conditions under which they have prospered. Of particular interest is that these past military entities often mirrored, or in some cases even initiated, the development of the prevailing business forms in general society—trading and military groups organized along tribal or cultural lines, the very first companies and written contracts, the rise of individual entrepreneurs, intricate joint stock ventures, and so on.

An important realization of this retelling of military history, from a privatized perspective, is the amazing constancy of such actors in every era. Our general assumption of warfare is that it is engaged in by public militaries, fighting for the common cause. This is an idealization. Throughout history the participants in war were often for-profit private entities loyal to no one government.

In fact, the monopoly of the state over violence is the exception in world history, rather than the rule.[2] As Jeffrey Herbst has written, "The private provision of violence was a routine aspect of international relations before the twentieth century."[3] Nonstate violence dominated the international system in the past and was very much marketized. Indeed, when one takes a broad view of history, the "state" itself is a rather new unit of governance, appearing only in the last four hundred years. Moreover, it drew from the private violence market to build its public power.

Private military organizations particularly thrived in periods of systemic transition. Governments were weakened, powerful military capabilities (often superior to local capabilities) were available on the open market, and transnational companies were often the most efficiently organized actors. In short, much of privatized military history is reminiscent of the post–Cold War world today.

PRIVATE WARRIORS IN ANCIENT HISTORY

Men specializing in warfare were likely created at the very first divisions of labor among humankind.[4] The constant of conflict in human society meant that specialists in it could gain their livelihoods by marketing their relative efficiency in the use of force. They could do so locally or search elsewhere for better markets. The consequence is that the foreign soldier hired for pay, the mercenary, is an almost ubiquitous type in the entire social and political history of organized warfare.[5]

At an early date in human history, they organized themselves, because of the great advantages of scale in the use of violence.[6] Although the organization of military groups in the ancient era varied in place and time, it typically was tymocratic (money-based). The earliest urban civilizations concentrated weapons in the hands of certain groups based on economic status. Most early governments were unable to develop specialized administrative structures or regular armed forces.[7] Instead, trained soldiers were a premium resource, and thus foreign units were valued for the expertise they could add to any ancient army. These early hired units, like other business ventures of the time, were generally ordered along tribal or cultural lines.

The earliest records of warfare include numerous mentions of outside fighters being employed to fight for ancient rulers. The first official historic reference is of mercenaries who served in the army of King Shulgi of Ur (ca. 2094–2047 B.C.E.). The battle of Kadesh (1294 B.C.E.) is the first great battle in history of which we have any detailed account. In this fight, where the Egyptians fought the Hittites, the army of Pharaoh Ramses II included units of hired Numidians.[8]

The rest of ancient history is replete with stories of hired, foreign troops. Even the Bible tells their tales. The Pharaoh chased the Israelites out of Egypt with an army that included hired foreigners, while David and his men (when they were on the run from Saul) were employed in the Philistine army of Achish.

Although a few of the Greek city-states, such as Sparta, relied on citizen armies, it was a general practice for ancient Greek armies to build up their forces through the hire of outside specialists. The most notable included units of Cretan slingers, Syracusan hoplites, and Thessalian cavalry.[9] Several naval units, including those that fought on behalf of Athens in the Persian wars, were also privately outfitted. Xenophon's famous "Ten Thousand" was a unit of out-of-work Greek soldiers who were hired to fight in a Persian civil war (401–400 B.C.E.). When their employer, a contender for the Persian crown, was killed in the initial battle, they were stranded without pay and had to fight their way back across Asia Minor. Their story became the basis for what is considered one of the first novels in history, an entirely new form of literature.[10]

The Macedonians honed their craft fighting on behalf of the varied Greek city-states during the Peloponnesian War (431–404 B.C.E.). They soon defeated their old clients in the following wars of King Philip. By the end of its conquest of the Persian empire (336 B.C.E.), the army of his son Alexander the Great had evolved from a largely Macedonian force into one primarily made up of hired soldiers. It also contracted a navy of 224 ships from the Phoenecians. The successor Hellenic empires similarly guaranteed their security by recruiting foreign units rather than using native forces.

In the following period, the Carthaginian empire was almost entirely dependent on mercenary troops and saw both the benefits and the costs. At the conclusion of the First Punic War (264–241 B.C.E.), the hired army, which had not been paid and was threatened with disbandment, revolted, in what was known as the Mercenary War. The rebels were only put down when the Carthaginians were able to hire other mercenary units. In the next war, however, the Carthaginians returned to a contracted force with great success. Hannibal's army of hired, expert soldiers crossed the Alps and dominated the Roman citizen army in the Second Punic War (218–202 B.C.E.). It was never defeated in battle but ultimately was unable to overcome Carthage's inferior material position. The war was essentially lost when Rome took Carthage's silver mines in Spain, meaning that the city-state could no longer afford to maintain a large hired army.[11]

Although early Rome was distinguished by its citizen army, it too was highly reliant on mercenaries. Even during the Republic period, it relied on hired units to fill such specialties as archers and cavalry. They were usually recruited from the economically backward areas of the ancient world. For example, Rome recruited Numidians, Balearics, Gauls, Iberians, and Cretans during the Punic Wars. As the empire grew, the scope of these hired units gradually expanded, as it became relatively harder to recruit native Romans into the force. At the end of the third century C.E. the imperial army was more Germanic than Roman.[12] Likewise, the rulers of the follow-on Byzantine empire also came to depend on the military expertise of foreigners to fight their battles. These foreigners included the noted Varangian Guard, Byzantium's most elite force, which was made up of hired Norsemen.[13] Its Muslim opponents often included hired units as well, including the famous Mamalukes, who would eventually take over the rule of Egypt and other places.[14]

THE MIDDLE AGES: A RETURN TO OPEN MILITARY MARKETS

After the fall of the Roman empire, Western Europe sank into the Dark Ages and any semblance of a money-based economy faltered. In a world with little or no governance capabilities, feudalism, the system of layered obligations of military service, became the mechanism by which armies were created.

Despite the social underpinnings of the feudal system, hired soldiers were an integral part of any medieval army. They often filled out the more technical services that short-term feudal forces could not supply. The first private military organizations that appeared in the period were bands of skilled workers who rented themselves out to the highest bidder. Often, they specialized in some particular weapon, such as the crossbow, which was considered not fit for gentlemen, but required too much skill and practice for peasant levees.[15] Later in the period, early firearms and cannon also shared the same characteristics. The profession of artillerymen even formed an international business guild, replete with its own patron saint and jealously guarded professional secrets.

The problem of the feudal military system was that the entire process was extremely inefficient. Rulers had limited, unspecialized forces on call for only short periods of the year. Most important, they were beholden to their own lieges for troops, despite the fact that their lieges were often the very opponents that they needed to put down. Thus, feudalism's social constraints on military service helped lay out the rationale for rulers to turn back to relying on hired units.

By the thirteenth century, the revival of an urban-based commercial economy in Europe began to put money in people's hands again. Particularly important was the growth of banking. Trading companies emerged in this period, and several Italian towns even turned themselves over to private investors to run.[16] It was in this changing context that the *condotta* (contract) system blossomed. This arrangement, by which military services were contracted out to private units, initially was driven by business guilds that saw it as reasonable and economical to avoid mobilizing all of society and keep the most efficient citizens (themselves) from the waste of warfare.[17] The recourse to hired units was also supported by the nobility, who feared the power of an armed populace and thus preferred mercenaries.

As in almost all developments in the Middle Ages, the Italian cities took the lead in reintroducing the practice of contract units. Venice began by hiring out salaried rower-soldiers for its navy during the Crusades (1095–

1270), and the evolution to hired ground forces was not far off. The city soon developed a sophisticated system designed to prevent its contracted forces from gaining too much power. Potential usurpers were carefully supervised by dividing contracts among several mutually jealous captains. Honors were also bestowed on loyal and successful leaders and their place arranged within Venetian aristocracy, so as to integrate them into the old political order.

Interestingly, Florence, which was otherwise one of the more progressive cities, was unique in the Italian cities by lagging far behind the trend toward private units. Its humanistically trained magistrates, such as Machiavelli, were instead dazzled by Roman Republican institutions.[18] For a brief period, they built up civic militias, sacrificing military efficiency in their faithfulness to old traditions. After their city militia continually lost to smaller mercenary armies, Florence too began to employ hired units.[19]

The process was not limited to Italy, though. The nature of warfare in the period meant that the quality and skill of soldiers mattered much more than sheer numbers.[20] Across Europe, rulers began to charge *scutagium* ("shield money," the cost to equip a fighting man) instead of requiring the annual turnout of actual feudal hosts. These sums were then used to hire mercenaries. By the end of the fourteenth century, privately organized units had largely taken over the field of battle from their feudal predecessors. The way to form an army now consisted of "commissioning" (the term still used today to denote the rise to an officer rank) a private individual to raise troops, clothe them, equip them, train them, and lead them. In exchange, the organizer received payment and a potential share of any goods seized in the conflict.[21] Many of the military campaigns launched in Aquitaine, Brittany, and Normandy in the period were actually some of the first great "joint stock enterprises," in which private investments were ventured in expectations of future shares.[22]

The growing market and availability of hirable soldiers meant that war on a large scale began to be waged more frequently.[23] By the 1300s, Italy, Spain, and France were the scene of almost constant conflict, and the overwhelming presence of warfare soon permeated all aspects of life.[24]

THE VERY FIRST "COMPANIES"

The proliferation of private military forces coincided with rising conditions of instability. These included extreme changes in political orders or when standing armies were reduced at the end of a war, which particularly characterized the Hundred Years War period (1337–1453). Over the years of on and off again campaigning in the war, there was a loosening of a rigidly defined order.

The absence of centralized control created a situation optimal for the private soldier. While originally many soldiers hired themselves out as "free lances" (the origin of the modern business term), sooner or later the money ran out or that phase of the war came to an end. In either case, the soldiers were left without employment. Having no homes or careers to return to, many of these soldiers formed "Companies" (derived from "con pane," designating the bread that members received). These were organizations designed to facilitate their employment as a group or, at the very least, provide one another sustenance and protection. They would travel together in search of work, usually in the form of new campaigns to fight, and support themselves along the way by blackmailing towns and villages.

The evolution to the name "Free Companies" was intended as a challenge.[25] In feudalism, the entire society was fastened to a set place in the strict hierarchical ladder. However, the period saw the development of a larger military class than either the countryside or the available local wars could support. If their own principalities were not at war, these impoverished soldiers broke their feudal bonds and went in search of employment, prepared to put their swords at the disposal of the highest bidder.[26] In turn, the free companies magnified the failings of the feudal system and helped bring about the complete collapse of the old order. Feudal ideals of noble birth, land as the basis of authority, the church as an unassailable structure, and loyalty and personal honor as the only motives for fighting were each undermined by the fact that the dominant military actors of the period were private companies of freelance soldiers.[27]

The free companies evolved from temporary organizations, essentially bands of soldiers whose primary aim was to protect themselves and exploit local populations, into permanent military and economic organizations that were systematically in the pay of one or more localities.[28] Over time, the agreements that they signed with their employers became highly detailed, specifying the length and terms of service, number of men, and pay. The *condotta* developed into a document of great care, drawn up by the equivalent of modern-day lawyers.[29]

The companies also developed deliberate marketing strategies, intentionally spreading tales of their fierceness and cruelty. The rationale was to create brand awareness of a sort among potential employers and also deter opposition on the field. One company leader wore on his breastplate "Lord of the great company, enemy of God, of pity, and mercy." Another was proud to tell of how he had once found two of his men arguing over a young nun. With Solomon-like judgment, he decreed "half each" and cut her in two.[30]

The men of the companies were generally loyal, but just to their unit, not to their home country or employer. Contrary to popular images, the hired companies were not interested in killing per se and instead generally conducted themselves within the accepted professional strictures of warfare when facing other military forces. Since their preoccupation was with money, they concentrated on taking prisoners, which would generate handsome ransoms. This often led to subdued and prolonged battles. At its highest form, battles between the free companies became something of an art form. Encounters were subtle affairs of shock and maneuver, characterized by feints and surprises, with the bulk of forces held in reserve until the decisive moment. Company leaders had the caution of true professionals, underscored by their heavy personal investment in their own workforce.

Despite the focus on the economics, Machiavelli's scornful accusation of the free companies fighting only "bloodless battles" is not borne out by the facts.[31] The majority of the bloody battles of the Hundred Years War were decided by the companies. Whenever the fighting paused and there was no longer employment, the various companies then roamed France at will and pillaged and burned those towns that would not pay for their protection.

In France, the king once attempted to wipe out the free companies, but the assorted units united into one army and crushed the king's feudal army at the battle of Brignais (1362).[32] The defeat was a terrible shock to the government and created an intense panic throughout the country at what the companies might do next. However, the companies could hardly believe what they had done. Having no real political agenda, their unity of purpose quickly evaporated. Each went back to its individual job searches, and the joint private army dissolved. Eventually, the French kings mounted new campaigns against Spain and Hungary just to find the private units some employment and get them out of the country.

By the late 1300s, though, many free companies had already crossed the Alps into Italy in search of more constant employment. Italy rapidly became the prime marketplace for the companies for two reasons: the large number of warring states and the extreme wealth for the time. Despite their limited geographic size, the many Italian states were actually the great powers of the day. They had extreme wealth, which was importantly not tied to land, but rather was in the form of tradable capital. This was linked to the predominance of cities in their social structures, with the added implication that the local citizenry was considered productive and not to be wasted on the battlefield.[33]

The companies soon controlled the battlefields of Italy, putting their swords into service for anyone willing to pay and making life hell for those who would not. Among the most prominent was the Great Company, an organization nearly 10,000 strong. From 1338 to 1354, it ran what was essentially an Italy-wide protection racket. Other notable companies included the primarily English White Company (immortalized in Sir Arthur Conan Doyle's novel by the same name) and the Grand Catalan Company, which would later move to Greece and rule Athens for more than sixty years.[34]

By the end of the fourteenth century, the foreign companies' success in the field led local Italian nobles to mimic their operations. Gradually, the foreign companies lost their dominant positions to local enterprises, which were at an advantage on their home turf. The new form was known in Italy as *condottieri*, after the name of the contract. These came in all sizes, from small hired bands to the large private armies of families such as the Gonzagas or Colonnas. Other condottieri leaders, such as the Viscounti and Sforzas, became politically dominant in the cities that employed them, eventually seizing control from their employers.[35]

Back in France, the original generating point of many free companies, a number remained active in the border wars that lasted through the period. Their dominance was only ended when King Charles VII was able to exploit the despair they caused French merchants. In 1445, he got the growing bourgeois class to agree to a special tallage. He used these funds to put a number of companies on regular pay and then crushed the remaining companies in France. He then kept his companies on long-term hire (rather than just for the campaigning season), creating the first standing army seen in Europe since the Dark Ages. The result is that the modern French army had its origins in the Germans, Scots, and Italians of the free companies.[36] The French king's primary rival, Duke Charles the Bold of Burgundy, was so frightened by this regular force that he quickly imitated it, starting a process across Europe. Unfortunately for him, his new regular army was squandered in an expedition against the fiercely independent Swiss cantons.

THE SWISS AND THE LANDSKNECHTS: BEYOND MERE BUSINESS RIVALS

The next phase of private economic actors in warfare began ironically enough as a battle for political freedom. The Swiss forest cantons united to resist foreign rule in 1291, forming the Swiss Confederation. Fiercely independent, each town supplied what were essentially citizen-militia, organized into units of pikemen. The Swiss pike square, which was in many ways the reinvention of the ancient Greek phalanx, ended the dominance of the mounted knight on the European battlefield. Armed with 18-foot pikes and massed in a square formation, the units could stop a cavalry charge cold and then steamroll any other infantry opposition when they got up momentum. The pike square's effectiveness depended on discipline, coordination, and a powerful self-confidence, each of which the tough Swiss mountaineers had in ready supply.

At the battles of Sempach (1386) and Näfels (1388) the Swiss won great military victories against Austrian invaders. Sempach, in particular, sent shockwaves through Europe, as a force of only 1,600 Swiss pikemen defeated the 6,000-strong Austrian army. These battles dealt major blows to noble rule, as they showed the knight to be on the way out. The Swiss followed these victories with defeats of the Hapsburg emperor (1446) and then Charles the Bold's force at the battle of Morat (1476).

For the next century, mercenary work became something of a national industry for the Swiss. The Swiss innovation was not just in their tactic of the pike square, which dominated the battlefield, but also in learning to export their special skills. They transferred their experience in warfare (gained at no cost to their employers) from their own poor, infertile, and overpopulated mountain regions to better-off conflict zones.[37] The system was fairly simple. The men of a given valley or village would emigrate as a group, in effect an organized, cohesive combat unit, and hire themselves out to anyone willing to pay for their services.[38] Like the previous free companies, the first Swiss units crossed south into Italy and found great riches in the ongoing fighting there, inspiring others to follow suit. The canton governments tried to regulate the business but essentially laid down only one rule: that Swiss regiments not fight each other. When they did find themselves on opposite sides, whichever group had first received the contract was allowed to stay on the field, leaving the other employer truly in the lurch.

The Swiss mercenary units soon earned an unrivaled reputation for their skill and courage and would serve for hire in other armies for centuries to come. Much of the time, the Swiss had a particular business understanding with the crown of France. The French king relied on them to make up the bulk of his infantry and also his personal bodyguard. Swiss regiments served in the French force until just after the Napoleonic Wars. Even today, the Swiss mercenary tradition lives on. The Pope is protected by the Swiss Guard, the evolution of a regiment hired in 1502 to fill out the forces of Pope Julius II.

Similar to the present environment, the barriers to entry for organizing a military unit were quite low, so successful ventures were rapidly copied and marketed. A particular case in point is that of the landsknechts, mercenary organizations from South Germany and Austria. Upon seeing the success of their neighbors, similar business enterprises were soon organized in these areas, often with the sanction of the Hapsburg ruler.

The most common foe of the landsknechts were Swiss mercenary units, who held a special contempt for them, feeling they were poor copies, who had essentially stolen their brand. Unlike most battles between hired forces, no quarter was given when these two types fought. The main difference of the landsknechts from the Swiss units was that they were not so socially organized. They were generally recruited with no regard to hometown and were drawn from a broader social spectrum. German nobility did not scruple only to raise and organize the units, but also served in the ranks. Thereafter, to "trail a pike" became a perfectly acceptable form of activity for the nobly born in Germany and later England.[39]

Although they had started out as inferior fighters, by the end of the period, the landsknecht companies begin to outclass their traditional Swiss rivals. For the landsknechts, war was a purely business proposition and had no ties to domestic social institutions; thus, they more easily adapted to the changing requirements of war. Whereas the Swiss remained highly specialized, using just the pike and edged weapons, the landsknecht organizations diversified, adding artillery units and then personal firearms. The market supremacy of the Swiss finally came to an end at the battle of Bicocca (1522). A much smaller contingent of landsknechts killed over 3,000 Swiss mercenaries, using earthworks, attrition, and the newly developed arquebus guns. It was this flexibility that allowed some landsknecht companies to endure into the period of Thirty Years War and beyond.[40]

MILITARY ENTREPRENEURS AND THE THIRTY YEARS WAR

By the seventeenth century, the conduct of violence was a capitalist enterprise that was little different and in fact highly intertwined with other industries. Indeed, "war became the biggest industry in Europe."[41] As such, wealth and military capability went hand in hand; or, as the French put it, "Pas d'argent, pas de Suisses."[42]

European armies of the period often were simple amalgamations of hired mercenary companies, all with their own specialties. "Albanians" (a general term for Eastern Europeans and Greeks) were valued as light cavalry. The Scots and Gascons were often found as mercenary infantry (the Gascons had a tradition as crossbowmen and adapted nicely to firearms). The Swiss pike units stayed in the market (though no longer dominating), as did the German landsknechts and reiters (cavalry pistoleers). For the most part, "patriotism" was a meaningless concept to the average soldier of the period.

Particularly prominent in the business of war was the new class of military entrepreneurs. These were individuals (sometimes bourgeois, sometimes petty nobles) who recruited and equipped military units at their own cost and then leased them out, akin to pieces of property. This private trade in military units allowed rulers to wage war on a considerable scale, while avoiding the need to make major reforms in their administrative and fiscal systems. Among the more prominent military entrepreneurs were Louis de Geer, an Amsterdam capitalist who provided the Swedish government with a complete navy (sailors and commanders included); Count Ernest Mansfield, who raised an army for the Elector Palatine in 1618 and then put his sword at the hand of the highest bidder; Bernard von Weimar, who raised armies first for Sweden and then for France, and most famously, Count Albrecht von Wallenstein, who through the military business became the wealthiest man in all of Europe.[43]

Wallenstein converted his personal estates into a vast complex of armories and factories, and his army soon conquered most of what is now Germany and the Czech Republic. His was not just a powerful army but also "the biggest and best organized private enterprise seen in Europe before the twentieth century. . . . Its structure mirrored that of contemporary society."[44] Much like a modern-day corporation, all the force's officers had financial stakes in the operations and each counted on rich returns on their investments.

Although the concept of individual brokers dominating the trade of war is a bit jarring to our current notions of a national military, in fact the "state" is a fairly new emergence in the overall flow of history. It was not until the seventeenth century that the use of official armies, loyal to the nation as a whole and not to the specific rulers or houses that led it, took hold in Europe. The Thirty Years War (1618–1648) was in many ways a turning point for these historic tides.

During that war "by and large, the military forces of every country consisted of mercenaries," and almost all the battles were fought completely by hired units.[45] In fact, the entire military outlay of the warring sides was often little more than *solde*—the stipend paid to mercenaries for their clothing, food, arms, and powder.[46] Even in the army of Gustavus Adolphus, which revolutionized maneuver warfare, hired foreigners made up 90 percent of the total.

These units took to living off the land, leaving the countryside devastated in their wake. The system worked best if the hired forces were used in offensive operations in foreign provinces; if not, the fiscal costs saved by contracting-out were offset by the higher social costs to the employer resulting from the burden that such units placed on local populations.[47] Leaders made sure to keep them away from their homelands whenever possible.[48]

The ultimate result of the Thirty Years War, however, was that the concept of sovereignty won out against that of empire. The Hapsburg family's power, which had personified the rule by personal empire, was broken, and individual national units began to encroach on its rule. The war had been so devastating that the only conceivable resolution was to let each nation decide its own internal matters. The following Peace of Westphalia in 1648 solidified the emergence of the state by enshrining the importance of sovereignty over affairs within borders.

THE STATE TAKES OVER THE MILITARY MARKET

It was in this context that hired armies of foreigners began to be replaced by standing state armies made up of citizens. The ultimate inflection point of this change were the Napoleonic wars starting at the end of the eighteenth century. Although hired troops were present through the 1700s, this period saw the wars of kings finally evolve into the wars of people.

Although individual combat skill had mattered more than numbers in the earlier periods, the level of warfare began to increase, in order to take advantage of new economies of scale on the battlefield. The basic cause was that continued technological development of firearms provided a major reduction in the required length of training. Whereas weapons such as crossbows and the early handguns and arquebus needed years of preparation, an individual could become an effective musketeer after a fairly short period of training.[49] Thus, large numbers of soldiers could be more readily acquired by the conscription of citizenry than by outside hiring. The musket then became a dominant battlefield weapon. It was less costly in terms of bringing forces unto the field and more effective in massed infantry formations. The consequence was that the "the decline of mercenary warfare coincided with the emergence of large armies as the scale of warfare began to increase."[50]

The mass army that began to take the field was both a cause and an effect of the organizational form of the state. Numerical advantage now mattered more. So states with large armies could expand territorially, which made their power even greater. This expansion, along with the costs of maintaining now larger standing armies, required the ability to extract resources efficiently, which led to the practice of taxation.[51] This, in turn, required the dramatic growth in size and power of the centralized state apparatus. Small kingdoms and other nonterritorial political entities, such as the German principalities and the Vatican, simply could not compete and either disappeared or receded into other nonmilitary arenas.

An added simple economic rationale was that the constant costs of disbanding and then later reenlisting hired forces were often prohibitive, as were the costs of relying on outside entrepreneurs, whose reliability was questionable. In the closed campaigning seasons, foreign contract soldiers also often found other, less acceptable ways of making a living. They were no longer extracting wealth from unvalued peasant lieges. With the emergence of states, their living off the land now harmed the prosperity of their employers' new tax bases.[52]

Eschewing private forces was also a functional response to international demands, both strategic and normative. After the victories of French revolutionary forces against the hired professional forces of Austria and Prussia, states realized that they could no longer keep the old, militarily inefficient system, even if meant turning over some power to the public. After the shock of defeat and occupation after the battle of Jena (1806), Prussia completely revamped her forces into citizen armies and was quickly able to return to the war and help defeat the French forces. Once this path became an international model, it provided the new commonsense starting point for how other militaries should be designed using citizenry.[53] Although the domestic tradeoff was risky to their security as rulers, the adoption of a citizen army was seen as the internationally efficient and necessary outcome for those states that sought to survive.[54]

It is evident, though, that the practice of war also changed as a response to changing notions of nation-state identity.[55] As the Enlightenment took hold, ideas of the social contract, the prestige of natural science, and rationalism provided a new way of thinking about the relationship of state to soldiers and citizenship to service. Unlike in earlier centuries, when feudal arrangements and then military companies prevailed, people were more willing to fight as citizens than as subjects. Those who fought for profit, rather than patriotism, were completely delegitimated under these new conceptions.

As part of this process of recasting exactly what was a state, weak nations also began to assert claims regarding the impermeability of their borders. But in claiming that their sovereignty was more substantial than in the past and intervention in their domestic affairs was illegitimate, they "could no longer buy an army or navy from the international system."[56] They had to be able to show they could defend themselves without having to hire external help.

Finally, the new connections between citizen and state also meant that citizens were perceived as representatives of their home state. As citizen armies became the new norm, states also began to pass neutrality laws, which prohibited their citizens' enlistment in foreign armies. The rise of this institution of neutrality was also driven by state rulers' interest in controlling their power over society. As part of their monopolization of the authority to deploy forces, they had to accept responsibility for violence emanating from their own jurisdiction. This helped to dry up the supply of private foreign forces, as rulers could no longer distance themselves from actions of their citizens while still professing neutrality.[57]

In short, by the 1700s, the entire structure of war had begun to evolve in the direction of the impersonal, bureaucratic state. While Queen Elizabeth I had to enter into commercial contracts with her own subjects in order to raise a navy to stop the Spanish Armada in 1588, a hundred years later such a system was unimaginable. By the 1700s, the conviction began to grow that if rulers went to war for personal profit they were little better than criminals.[58] The state's increasing monopoly over the business of war was also felt overseas. Before, states could fight in Europe, while their colonial businesses could still stay at peace or vice versa. By the mid-1700s, this had changed, another result of the extension of state power. A further illustration of the shift from private wars was the different treatment meted out to prisoners. Captured soldiers were once seen as private property, with ransoming being part of the economic rationale behind military enterprises. By the Seven Years War (1756–1763), this practice that had guided tactics in earlier periods was anathema.[59]

The French Revolution and ensuing Napoleonic wars (1789–1815) signaled the end of hired soldiers playing a serious role in warfare, at least for the next two centuries. The citizen revolt and the decades of war that followed heralded a new era for military, political, and social history. Nationalism and the power of a society at arms proved to be overwhelming forces, particularly in the hands of skilled generals such as Napoleon and Blucher.

More important, the state apparatus had finally begun to evolve into an efficient and capable means of governance, weakening the power of actors outside its control.

MERCENARIES IN THE AGE OF REASON

This phase-out of private units was gradual and incomplete, however, lasting well into the 1800s and the Concert of Europe. Many professional militaries remained highly disassociated with the nation they served. Wellington's army at Waterloo, for example, had large numbers of hired units from the German states, and as late as the Crimean War in 1853, the British hired 16,000 Swiss and German soldiers.[60] Likewise, private business ventures still played a variety of large-scale military roles in regions outside the European state system, including contracted units that fought during the breakdown of Chinese Imperial rule and the charter trading companies.[61]

The typical European army of the 1700s reflected this mix and was truly a multinational force. Hired foreign forces constituted from 25 percent to 60 percent of all land forces. Venetian diarist Marin Sanuto referred to the armies of his time as "Noah's Ark Armies," in that they contained at least two of every kind. Likewise, the prize system of payment meant that the navies of the period were also filled out with outsiders. For example, one-third of the Dutch navy was French; there were also more French than Italians in the Genoese navy; in the Russian navy only 10 percent of the officers were Russian; even up to the late Victorian period almost half of the Royal Navy was non-British.[62]

For some soldiers in this period, being a mercenary was an economic necessity. After the 1688 "Glorious Revolution" in England, when Protestant William of Orange drove out Catholic James II, many of James's forces fled to France and formed units within the French Army. Similar experiences occurred after failed rebellions in Ireland and Scotland, with the most notable exile mercenary unit being the Irish Wild Geese regiment that worked for French and Spanish kings.[63]

The most vaunted army of this period, the Prussian army, exemplified the prevalence of mercenaries. Even by the end of Frederick the Great's rule in the 1790s, more than half of the soldiers in its army (over 200,000) were hired foreigners. These included the corps d'elite unit of 7-footers, who were specially tracked down over Europe for their height, regardless of their nationality.[64] The fact that more than 80 percent of all royal revenues went to this outsized and almost foreign army accounted for the often-quoted quip by the Marquis de Mirabeau that "Prussia is not a state with an army, but an army with a state."

A new development in the military market in the 1700s was the entrance of states as business competitors. That is, many of the economically weakest powers in the period needed a way to build up their budgets. So, they took to hiring out their own militaries to fight others' wars. The most notable was Hesse-Kassel in Germany, which was almost completely subsidized by the contracts its army had with the Netherlands, Venice, and England.

During the American War of Independence, the British government did not have the troops both to maintain its worldwide colonial obligations, including holding down ever-simmering Ireland, and also defeat the numerous American patriot forces. Its allies, such as Russia, refused to loan it troops to put down what they saw as an internal peasant revolt. So Britain turned to the international market, primarily the German principalities. In all, 29,875 hired German troops crossed the Atlantic. Approximately two-thirds were from Hesse-Kassel, so the formations were all called "Hessians" by the Americans. (Some of the more prominent figures on the American side were also contracted foreign soldiers, such as Baron Von Steuben, whose military training at Valley Forge is credited with turning the Continental Army into a true fighting force.)[65]

As history shows, the Hessian experience did not turn out as their British employers anticipated. Rather than intimidating the American rebels into submission, news of the contracts signed with the German states was one of the factors that fomented the Declaration of Independence by the colonies.[66] Once deployed, the Hessians acted with barbarity in the early fighting in New York, helping to galvanize undecided colonists against the British. In turn, Washington's men defeated Hessian detachments at Trenton and Princeton (1776), energizing the American cause. In fact, many of the Hessian troops found that life in America compared quite nicely to Germany and by the end of the war roughly a third of the force deserted.

The general point is that although the historic trends were building against it, the mercenary trade remained a fully legitimate practice well into the 1700s. As such, the military labor market was internationalized. All states used hired units in some form or another and many were completely reliant on them. Indeed, the system was so globalized that one German noble (Count Wilhelm zu Schaumburg Lippe Bueckburg) even established an international military academy, where officers of all nations could receive training, pool their experience, and pass on the rules of the game to the next generation.[67]

The interesting aspect is that contract armies endured throughout this period not because of their military efficiency but rather because of political expediency. Frederick the Great's military may have been completely dependent on them, but he was of the opinion that soldiers for pay had "neither courage, nor loyalty, nor group spirit, nor sacrifice, nor self-reliance."[68] He also conceded that an army of patriotic citizens would be more effective and cheaper than his own. Like the rest of European rulers, however, he was unwilling to risk the redistribution of political power that conscription would force.

THE CORPORATE FREE HAND: MILITARY BUSINESS VENTURES
OUTSIDE THE STATE SYSTEM

Private businesses also began to take on military roles outside of governments through the charter company system. In this arrangement, joint-stock companies were licensed to have monopoly power over all trade within a designated area, typically lands newly discovered by the Europeans. Such preference was given not only for political reasons (for rulers to reward domestic supporters or to give national ventures an advantage over foreign competitors) but also because a prior monopoly advantage was thought necessary to counter the uncertainties of engaging in risky, large-scale activity in distant lands.

The two most noted of such ventures were the Dutch East India Company and the English East India Company. The Dutch company formed in 1602 and was granted privileges in its charter that no Dutch citizen operating outside the company could trade in the Indian Ocean area. Similarly, the English East India Company started with a stock offering in 1599. It was granted exclusive trading rights by the English crown in the same area.[69]

While nominally under the control of their license back home, abroad, the charter ventures quickly became forces unto themselves. They not only dominated the business networks (monopolizing trade in spices such as nutmeg, cloves, cinnamon and pepper, tea, and, later, silk, Chinese porcelain, gold, and opium) but also acted to ensure their own military protection.[70]

Thus, it was not uncommon for private charter companies to take on the trappings of a state. They became quite curious institutions where all the analytical distinctions between economics and politics, nonstate and state domains, property rights and sovereign powers, and the public and private broke down.[71] Indeed, the Dutch company's charter explicitly provided for its own broad powers of war and other forms of sovereignty.[72] As the company was described in the *Universal Dictionary* in 1751,

> One of the reasons why the Dutch East India company flourishes, and is become the richest and most powerful of all others we know of, is its being absolute, and invested with a kind of sovereignty and dominion. . . . [it] makes peace and war at pleasure, and by its own authority; administers justice to all; . . . settles colonies, builds fortifications, levies troops, maintains numerous armies and garrisons, fits out fleets, and coins money.[73]

Such firms not only posted huge profits by controlling the trade between East and West but also controlled armed forces and territory that dwarfed those of their home states. The English East India Company hired a mix of British, German, and Swiss mercenaries, as well as local Sepoy units. By 1782, the company's army was over 100,000 men, much larger than the British army at the time. The Dutch company also grew from its modest beginnings and soon had more than 140 ships and 25,000 men permanently under arms (mostly Japanese mercenaries and hired German units).

The key, though, was that the areas where the charter companies took on military functions all fell outside the established order of the European state system. The growth in the power of the trading companies came at the same time as the collapse of local governance structures in what were considered colonial areas (such as the fall of the Mogul empire). The companies arrived in the midst of local chaos with superior technology and organization (parallels to PMFs today). The resulting actions they took to protect their own interests—building forts, establishing markets, recruiting local mercenary armies—soon led to their political control of the entire Indian subcontinent.[74]

The initial activities of the trading companies illustrate how they used their military operations to force out trade competitors.[75] The English company's first entry into the Indian market was in the form of naval intervention to aid the Mogul emperor against Portugal. The company's ships sank most of the Portuguese fleet in the region. In doing so, it secured the Mogul's alliance and exclusive trading privileges. It later did the same in the Persian Gulf region. The only problem was that the company's actions were in direct opposition to the English government's diplomatic aims back in Europe. The company had been directly told by King James I to avoid unprovoked attacks on the Portuguese as he needed their alliance, but it chose the path of profit instead. The Dutch approach was similar. They militarily eliminated Portuguese and Spanish markets and also aimed at new areas, such as what is now Indonesia. If local leaders refused to trade with them, they were punished with bombardment and invasion.

Military activities were an essential part of trading companies because they helped improve profits. As their forces grew larger and all the untapped markets had been opened, however, they increasingly came into full-blown conflict, particularly on the Indian subcontinent. In 1757, prompted by revenge for the "Black Hole of Calcutta" affair (after the fall of their trading fort to the local Bengal leader, who was allied with the French East India Company, 63 men of the EIC were locked in a 14-by-18-foot prison cell where they died), the English company moved to take all of the Indian trade by force. It defeated the Dutch company in a land and sea battle in 1759 and drove out the French in 1761. The French company dissolved, but the Dutch company lasted another half century, still controlling markets in Java and Borneo.

Surprisingly, the firms' engagement in warfare did not hurt their bottom lines but instead proved quite rewarding. For example, news of the English East India Company's capture of the French fort of Chandernagorre in 1757 drove its stock price up 12 percent in the London market.[76] The overseas enterprises opened up by the firms' military prowess were undeniably lucrative. After 1634, the Dutch company paid a regular annual dividend that fluctuated between 12 percent and 50 percent on the initial investments.[77]

Nonetheless, the outsourcing of trade controls to private companies had unintended consequences, particularly as the firms often engaged in activities that were contrary to their home government's national interests. Similar to the previous example of the English East Indies Company attack on the Portuguese garrisons in India despite specific government orders, the Dutch West Indies Company involved the Dutch government in an ill-judged and prolonged land war with Portugal in Brazil. Even worse, when Portugal sued for peace, the company lobbied hard against the treaty. Its directors argued that the company had profited handsomely by the war, and thus it should be continued.[78] Business rivalry in India was also a primary cause of the Dutch-English wars of the 1660s.

Ultimately, though, the trading companies began to weaken as the political environment stabilized. Times changed, and the firms became victims of their own earlier successes. As one English politician of the time put it, "The affairs of this company seem to have become much too big for the management of a body of merchants."[79] Likewise, as their rivals disappeared and local rulers no longer required constant deterrence, the large military investments the firms had made stopped paying off. (Eventually, sustaining company-owned forts, armies, and so on took from 50 percent to 70 percent of the Dutch firm's revenue.)[80]

By 1799, the Dutch East India Company had begun to lose money and dissolved during the crisis of the Napoleonic Wars. The English East India Company lasted longer, but in the 1830s the British government broke its monopoly on trade with India. The company became financially insolvent, but was kept in existence by the British crown to function as the government of India. The simple reason was that no one could quite agree on how to replace the firm's rule. This compromise ended in 1857, when the firm equipped its army with the new Enfield rifles. A rumor spread that the cartridges were greased with beef fat—thus defiling any Hindu, and the company's Indian regiments mutinied. Eleven thousand Europeans were massacred in the "Sepoy Mutiny." Now powerless, compared to its earlier position, the firm was forced to call in British Army troops to save itself. The shocked British public seized on the company as a scapegoat. In 1858, the British government called in the firm's £100 million debt. It seized the company's territorial possessions as collateral payment. Thus the British empire's "Jewel in the Crown" was actually bought in a bankruptcy sale.

The length of the charter companies' histories is striking, particularly when one compares them to the longevity of most states. The Dutch East India Company lasted 194 years; the Hudson's Bay Company, 200 years; and

the English East India Company, 258 years. Even afterward, the historic con-
tinuities of companies at arms in nonstate areas such as sub-Saharan Africa
continued. During the rubber boom in the Belgian Congo at the turn of the
twentieth century, the entire system was militarized, with each rubber company having its own contracted forces.[81] Rhodesia was ruled by a private
company until 1924, and large parts of Mozambique were controlled by the
Niassa and Mozambique Companies until the 1930s.

THE INDIVIDUALIZATION OF THE PRIVATE MILITARY MARKET

By the twentieth century, though, the charter companies were largely gone,
and the state system and the concept of sovereignty had spread across the
globe. With them, the norms against private soldiers began to build in
strength as well. Having once been large integrated enterprises, the primary
player in the private military market became the individual ex-soldier, what
we now conceive of as mercenaries. Such men would hire themselves out on
an informal basis, usually to rebel groups or businesses operating in weak
state zones, such as Latin America, China, and, later, Africa. Many were
swashbucklers in the mold of a by-gone era, interested more in the adven-
turer's lifestyle than any long-term results. Once at the center of warfare, by
the start of the twentieth century, the international trade in military services
was marginalized and mostly pushed underground.

The heyday of these mercenaries was during the decolonization period
in the 1950s and 1960s. They were most notable during the war in the
Congo from 1960 to 1964, where private units hired by mining firms fought
in support of the Katanga secession. These groups were known by the nick-
name "Les Affreux" ("The Terrible Ones") and included such notorieties as
the Irish-born commando "Mad" Mike Hoare, and Frenchman Bob Denard.
Denard would later lead a series of violent coups in the Comoros Islands and
the Seychelles from the 1970s on; his last coup attempt was as recent as
1995.[82]

Colonial interests who wanted to remain influential in their old stomp-
ing grounds funded these mercenaries. There was also a strong link to the
South African apartheid regime. The use of mercenaries thus became a symbol of the racism that hindered the self-determination of the new states, further strengthening international opinion against private actors in warfare.[83]

Nonetheless, the modern individual mercenary remains a player in warfare even today. For example, more than 30,000 Russian mercenaries have
fought in the various wars in the former Soviet Union and more than 2,000
Russians fought in the former Yugoslavia.[84]

Some governments continue to hire foreign soldiers on a limited basis.
The French government maintains the Foreign Legion as one of its elite
forces, while Gurkha regiments, made up exclusively of Nepalese citizens,

serve on behalf of the British and Indian governments.[85] The United Arab Emirates relies almost exclusively on soldiers hired from Oman, Yemen, Jordan, Pakistan, and Great Britain.[86] Likewise, the Solomon Islands hires soldiers from Fiji and Great Britain.[87] Thus, the mercenary trade no longer dominates, but it certainly is still present.

THE OVERALL HISTORY: PATTERNS OF PRIVATE MILITARIES

In looking back at the history of private actors in warfare, a few patterns become evident. The first is that the demand for hired troops has been linked to whatever is the prevalent nature of warfare. When quality mattered more than quantity, the activity and significance of mercenaries was typically higher, primarily because skilled professionals were superior to ill-trained or citizen soldiers. When quantity was the dominant factor and conscripts could be just as effective, hired troops' role in major wars declined.[88]

The second is the complementary relationship of mass military demobilization in one zone to new wars in other weaker state zones. These are also likely to be areas where the effects of quality would be felt more. The result is a supply and demand dynamic of warfare that has prevailed over and over again.[89] One can even map out the flow of conflict by the movement of demobilized or defeated military officers as far back as the the end of the Peloponnesian War and the rash of ancient wars that followed elsewhere in the Mediterranean world.[90] Similarly, the Spanish expansion into the Americas and Italy was driven by a surplus of soldiers created by the end of the Reconquista.[91] Disenfranchised, losing sides drove much of such surpluses. After their failed revolts in the late 1700s, many Poles fought for America, France, and even Haiti. Latin American independence from Spain was driven by foreign veterans of the Napoleonic Wars. The U.S. army in the Civil War benefited from officers fleeing the failed 1848 revolts in Europe. After World War I, veterans flocked to the wars in China and later Spain, while after World War II, a large number of Germans ended up fighting for their old adversaries in the postcolonial wars (for example, more than 80,000 Germans, mainly ex-Waffen SS, served with the French in Vietnam and Algeria).[92]

The third pattern is that private military actors thrive in areas of weak governance. This may be when a large number of states are in close proximity but militarily unable to secure their own territory. Or, it may be when a large, ramshackle empire is under ineffectual central control and torn by political and ethnic divisions.[93] In either situation, private military forces, particularly those efficiently organized along business lines, proved able to become major players in sustaining and benefiting from violent conflicts.

The final pattern is the frequent linkages between private military organizations and other business ventures. In some periods, the lines between the two were indistinct, while in others there was clear differentiation. What-ever the form of the business alliance, synergies often resulted, enabling both military successes and greater profits. The advantage of such ties con-tinued to be relevant well into the early twentieth century, again primarily in weak state areas.[94]

There is, however, a more important concluding point to take away from this tour through privatized military history. As the myriad of examples il-lustrate, the "contemporary organization of global violence is neither time-less nor natural."[95] At numerous stages in history, governments did not possess anything approaching a monopoly on force. Instead, rulers were of-ten highly reliant on the supply of military services from business enter-prises. Private actors, such as free companies, contracted units, military entrepreneurs, and charter companies played key roles in state-building and often served governmental interests. These organizations also had the ten-dency to become powers unto themselves, however, and often grew superior in power to local political institutions, particularly in areas of weak gover-nance.

In sum, the lines between economics and warfare were never clear-cut. From a broad view, the state's monopoly of both domestic and international force was a historical anomaly. Thus, in the future, we should not expect that organized violence would only be located in the public realm.

THREE

The Privatized Military Industry Distinguished

> That era, the era of Mad Mike Hoare, Black Jacque Schramme, and Bob Denard, is finished . . . "We are an international business like any other business," a pin-striped, bespectacled and utterly harmless looking corporate head told us. . . . "We go where we are wanted and where people can pay our fees."
>
> "Soldier of Fortune—the Mercenary as Corporate Executive,"
> *African Business,* December 1997

Although certain parallels exist between the past private military organizations and even present-day mercenaries, the current wave of PMFs has some fundamental differences. In the wake of globalization and the end of the Cold War, the private military market has expanded in a way not seen since the 1700s. It has also been religitimated to an extent, or, at least, opened back up to allow a nearly public trade.

The essential difference is the corporatization of military services. PMFs are structured as firms and operate as businesses first and foremost. As business entities, they are often linked through complex financial ties to other firms, both within and outside their industry. In fact, many of the most active PMFs, such as Armorgroup or Vinnell, are openly part of broader multinational corporations.[1]

MERCENARIES: A LESS THAN IDEAL TYPE

No clear consensus has been reached on how to define mercenaries. In the public imagination, they are the men depicted in such films as "The Wild Geese" or "The Dogs of War"—freelance soldiers of no fixed abode, who, for large amounts of money, fight for dubious causes. The very word "mercenary" has certainly acquired an unflattering connotation. In the general psyche, to be "mercenary" is to be inherently ruthless and disloyal.[2]

However, this judgment does not provide a usable definition of the practice of selling military services. *Webster's Dictionary* provides a more formal description, defining a mercenary as "a soldier hired into foreign service."[3]

However, this characterization is too broad, as it also includes any foreign units serving within national forces, such as the French Foreign Legion, and any number of volunteer soldiers who received stipends, such as the International Brigade that fought in the Spanish Civil War. One would be hard pressed to include such forces in the same vein as Les Affreux, extolled in the early issues of the trade magazine *Soldier of Fortune* (who would seem to be the prototypical mercenary type if there ever was one).

The Geneva Conventions perhaps provide the best general description, defining a "mercenary" as a foreign person who, despite not being a member of the armed forces in the conflict, is specifically recruited in order to fight and is motivated essentially by private gain. However, the legal designation that this international law draws from has its flaws. Due to political compromises among the signatory states, the negotiating parties later added overly specific descriptions that limited the definition of mercenaries. The conventions were amended to define mercenaries as only operating in international conflicts (some state parties wanted to use them internally), when, obviously enough, hired foreigners can and do fight in internal conflicts.[4]

For our purposes, a more analytic and balanced definition of a mercenary must involve several critical facets. There is general agreement that mercenaries are individuals who fight for employers other than their home state's government. Equally important is the fact that their motivation for fighting is economic gain; this "cash nexus" is what distinguishes a mercenary from a volunteer soldier.[5] The classicist Y. Garland expanded on this by defining a mercenary as a professional soldier whose conduct is dictated not by membership in a political community, but above all by the desire for gain.[6] The mercenary's loyalty is only governed by his contract, not by any greater or permanent cause or duty. Unlike other soldiers, they are neither serving country, nor protecting family or home, nor fighting for a greater force that they believe in; they simply harbor an open commitment to war as a professional way of life.[7] That is, their occupation entails a certain devotion to war itself, in that their trade benefits from its existence. Although soldiers often serve to prevent wars, mercenaries *require* wars, which necessarily involves their casting aside a moral attitude toward war.

As a result of this differing motivation, mercenaries are distinguished from other foreign soldiers by their independence as well. For them, there is no "military servitude," which the soldier-turned-poet Comte de Vigny defined as an essential part of professional soldiering.[8] Mercenaries are under no obligations other than to their own economics. Unlike those who serve within national armies, they can leave military life whenever they choose. Their relationship to the cause they fight for is that of employee and nothing more. This distinguishes them from the more formal foreign units, such as the Gurkhas and the French Foreign Legion, that are integrated into national forces and whose members are held under the powers of military law.

The manner in which mercenary forces are recruited and then organized is another useful, distinguishing factor. The mercenary trade operates outside legal parameters. Thus, recruiting by modern-day mercenaries is done obliquely. For example, in setting up a mercenary force for operations in the Congo in the 1960s, Mike Hoare found his soldiers by posting thinly veiled classified ads in newspapers.[9] The result of this inefficient system is that recruiting for mercenaries often pulls in a true mixed-bag of soldier. Hoare, for example, openly complained that in his mercenary force "there was too high a proportion of alcoholics, drunks, booze artists, bums and layabouts, who were finding it difficult to get a job anywhere else and thought this was a heaven sent opportunity to make some easy money."[10]

A further consequence is that, on occasions where mercenaries are ordered into units, their organizations are completely ad hoc. Few mercenary soldiers will have worked together, and there is little or no joint training, doctrine, or coordination. They tend to operate in loose, small units. Being neither legally nor contractually bound, they also have a limited hierarchy, making command inherently weak, particularly given the minimal controls any leader could place over a force that has only the weakest of short-term obligations.

The end result of this extemporized grouping is that modern mercenary formations are limited in their capabilities. Most are unable to provide anything other than direct combat support at the small-unit level and some limited introductory military training. They certainly do not have the skills, capital, or established methods and capabilities to provide complex multiservice operations as do PMFs. Military support, such as logistics or engineering, are also outside their scope, as well as large-scale or long-term training and advisory packages. Nor are they diversified organizations. They are limited in their ability to operate in more than one geographic setting at a time and generally restricted to one customer at a time. Likewise, they remain highly dependent on their host communities for logistics and support. The end result is that mercenaries provide marginal aspects of military outsourcing, but certainly not the complete transfer of responsibility that privatization entails.

MERCENARIES TODAY

As discussed in chapter 2, the private military market was delegitimated by the end of the 1800s for both material and normative reasons. The practice of hiring foreign soldiers was universally condemned and legislated against, culminating in the Geneva Conventions that withdrew from mercenaries the legal protections that soldiers enjoyed in warfare. Essentially, the mercenary

Table 3.1
<hr>

What Makes a Mercenary?

Seven essential characteristics distinguish modern-day mercenaries from other combatants and military organizations:

Foreign: A mercenary is not a citizen or resident of the state in which he or she is fighting
Independence: A mercenary is not integrated (for the long term) into any national force and is bound only by the contractual ties of a limited employee
Motivation: A mercenary fights for individual short-term economic reward, not for political or religious goals
Recruitment: Mercenaries are brought in by oblique and circuitous ways to avoid legal prosecution
Organization: Mercenary units are temporary and ad-hoc groupings of individual soldiers
Services: Lacking prior organization, mercenaries focus on just combat service, for single clients

<hr>

trade was criminalized. Many freewheeling mercenaries and filibusters (irregular military adventurers), who had operated with complete license in the past, found themselves proscribed and even prosecuted in their home states.

However, as also explored in chapter 2, this did not mean that the private soldier was eliminated. Rather, the trade proved quite durable. It simply devolved to the individual level and went underground. Despite the supposed legal bans, mercenaries were active combatants in wars throughout the 20th century, particularly in those areas considered peripheral by leading state powers. Except for their short-term successes in the Congo in the 1960s, however, their impact on these conflicts was marginal, and no established state military forces relied on their support.

Even today, mercenaries are present in contemporary warfare even though they have met with limited success. The simple reason for the persistence of mercenary activity is that in many areas governance and legal systems have broken down, giving enterprising ex-soldiers both room to maneuver and demand opportunities for their skills. The profit motive predominates for most, and the rewards are quite lucrative. In the Kosovo war, for example, the going rate for professional soldiers to help the rebel KLA group was a reported $4,000 per month, while private fighters on the Serb side were given a free license to pillage and loot the countryside; many left with truckloads of stolen consumer goods. Latin American drug cartels are also rumored to pay highly for military specialists willing to work for them.[11]

In fact, the present pattern of mercenary involvement in conflict is as high as any other time in the last century, rivaled in scope and pervasiveness only by the decolonization period in the 1960s.[12] Mercenaries today operate around the globe, based in numerous countries. As an illustration, Ukrainian mercenaries alone are rumored to have been active in fighting in Abkhazia, Algeria, Angola, Bosnia, Chechnya, Croatia, Dniester, Guinea, Kosovo, Liberia, Nagorno-Karabakh, Sierra Leone, Tajikistan, and Zaire. In many of these wars, they have served on both sides.[13]

Nevertheless, the entire process of the black market trade in military services remains inefficient. The impact of such individual operators in contemporary conflicts has been limited at best. Few can be credited with having any great influence on the ultimate outcome or even the continuance of the conflicts in which they became involved. Moreover, although mercenaries were active in many wars, no client military forces have grown dependent on their presence.

An episode in the last days of the Mobutu regime in Zaire in 1996 illustrates quite sharply the limits of ad-hoc, individual mercenary activity, particularly in comparison to that of PMFs. Faced with a growing rebellion, Mobutu turned to what was essentially a legacy of the past. He hired a motley collection of poorly skilled white mercenaries, mostly Bosnian Serb war veterans, right-wing French radicals, and Ukrainian pilots. The force became known as the "White Legion" and was organized by many of the same leaders who had fought for Mobutu in the 1960s, now just thirty years older.

However, this second coming of "Les Affreux" met only with defeat. The opposition of the 1990s was quite different than in the 1960s. The 1990s rebel force they fought was bigger, more heavily armed, and not prone to running away at the first shots fired. The thrown-together mercenary units were highly unprofessional (many of the Serbs serving while drunk throughout the period and many of the French lacking any military experience) and dissolved under limited pressure. Mobutu's regime fell soon thereafter.[14] For success, military ventures must have the professionalism and capabilities that come from prior organization and doctrine. For privately organized enterprises, often this requires links not only to past military experience but also to larger business ventures.

PRIVATIZED MILITARY INDUSTRY: MORE THAN JUST MERCENARIES

If traditional individual mercenary activity still continues around the globe, what then distinguishes the new privatized military industry? Some critics of the industry assert that there is no distinction. One of the more prominent, Abdel-Fatau Musah, has gone so far as to claim that "private military companies are nothing but the old poison of vagabond mercenaries in new designer bottles."[15] Such opponents of PMFs focus on the economic motivations that direct both individual mercenaries and the firms in the military industry. Others have also found equally limited variation. For example, the United Nations has a designated special rapporteur delegated to monitor mercenary activity. This official has claimed that the only essential difference between mercenaries and PMFs was that states are the ones doing the hiring of the firms.[16]

The problem is that such characterizations are normative judgments rather than analytic evaluations and not very factual ones at that. They are limited in their scope and underlaid by motivations either to eliminate the PMF industry or bring it under the control of antimercenary laws. Moreover, neither description is an accurate reading of the situation. Economic motivations might drive both individual mercenaries and PMFs, but many other critical distinctions alter both the two types of operations and the manner that these motives manifest themselves. Likewise, the claim that state hire is the only difference is flatly wrong. It misses both the fact that states have employed mercenaries in the past and continue to do so in the present, and that the private military industry serves a much more diverse clientele than just states.

PMFs are unlike either the individual mercenaries of the 1960s or those freelancers still active today. Although sharing similarities, they are also distinct from the contracted units of past centuries, such as the Swiss or the Hessians, or even the charter trading companies. Instead, they represent the next evolution in the provision of military services by private actors, parallel to the development of the modern business organization. A more complete, and less normative, assessment of the phenomenon finds that it is the *corporatization* of military service provision that sets them apart.

The newest wave of private military agents are commercial enterprises first and foremost. They are hierarchically organized into registered businesses that trade and compete openly (for the most part)and are vertically integrated into the wider global marketplace. They target market niches by offering packaged services covering a wide variety of military skill sets. The very fact that a coherent industry made up of these companies is identifiable provides evidence of their distinction.

Several distinguishing characteristics follow from this corporatization. In a sense, each provides business advantages that help explain the shift toward the firm as the mode of organization. The first ramification is that PMFs are organized in business form. This is in contrast to either the ad-hoc structure of individual mercenaries forming loose units or the social makeup of many of the historic contract units (such as the Swiss regiments that were local militias marketed abroad). PMFs are ordered along pre-existing corporate lines, usually with a clear executive hierarchy that includes boards of directors and share-holdings. This creates a tested, efficient, and more permanent structure that can compete and survive in the global marketplace.

The second implication is that this new private military actor is driven by business profit rather than individual profit. PMFs function as registered trade units, not as personal black-market ventures for individual profit or adventure. As firms, they can make use of complex corporate financing, ranging from sale of stock shares to intra-firm trade, meaning that a wider variety of deals and contracts can be worked out. For good reason, individual mercenaries tend only to trust payments in cash and, in turn, cannot be trusted for anything beyond the short-term.

The key is that it is not the person that matters, but the structure that they are within. Many PMF employees have been mercenaries both before and after their employ, but their processes, relationships, and impacts within local conflicts were completely different.

The third distinguishing characteristic of the privatized military industry is that the arena they compete on is the open global market. That is, unlike the activities of the White Legion or similar mercenary units, PMFs are considered legal entities bound to their employers by recognized contracts and in many cases at least nominally to their home states by laws requiring registration, periodic reporting, and licensing of foreign contracts.[17] Rather than denying their existence, private military firms are registered businesses and, in fact, often publicly advertise their services—including many even having corporate websites on the Internet.[18] This status differentiates them not only from mercenaries, who had to hide from the law, but also from past entities, such as the charter companies, that did not coexist with any state law, but rather made their own laws.

New military firms also provide a much wider offering of services and, importantly, to a much wider variety of clients. As the head of Sandline was proud to note, firms in the privatized military industry are "structured organizations with professional and corporate hierarchies . . . We cover the full spectrum—training, logistics, support, operational support, post-conflict resolution."[19] This provides another differentiation from past private military organizations. The goal of PMFs is service provision rather than the exchange of goods—a key distinction from the charter companies. Although one sector exclusively focuses on combat services like contract units and military entrepreneurs, another distinctive development is that PMFs provide military services outside the tactical sphere. Moreover, many are diversified enough to work for multiple (and a wider variety of) clients, in multiple markets and theatres at once—something none of the prior private military actors could do. As previously noted, those that have hired PMFs include other multinational corporations; state regimes—both foreign and the home bases of the firms; international organizations; and even nongovernmental organizations.

The corporate approach and the openness of this market also create more proficient recruitment patterns. Unlike the black market, word-of-mouth recruiting forms used earlier (such as the veiled classified ads, the village crier approach that the landsknecht recruiters used, or the *zielverkoopers* ["soul sellers"], who for a bounty tricked ignorant farmers into becoming employees to charter companies), public application processes are used by most PMFs, and they work from established databases that attempt to cover the available employee pool.[20] Firms screen potential employees for valued skill-sets and tailor their staff to specific mission needs. In addition to the efficiency gains, the resultant output is usually more effective. While mercenary units operate as collections of individuals, the personnel within PMFs are organized within the defined structures of a corporate entity. They are specifically grouped so as to operate with a set doctrine and greater cohesion of activity and discipline.[21]

Finally, the firms differ in their relations outside the industry. In addition to the contractual arrangements made with their customers, many are tightly linked with greater financial holdings and conglomerates. They either trade on the open market, and thus have institutional owners, or exist within broader corporate structures that offer a variety of services. Vinnell, for example, began as a construction firm that helped build the Los Angeles freeway and Dodger Stadium, but has since moved almost completely into the military service field, providing tactical advisory and support to the Saudi regime. More important, it is just one branch of the much larger BDM company. In turn, the Carlyle Group, an investment firm that includes on its board such prominent figures as former Secretary of State James Baker and former Secretary of Defense Frank Carlucci, owned BDM.

Such ties provide a whole new level of both legitimacy and connections for PMFs. In addition, they allow the firms greater access to financial capital and also to have on call other corporate resources. The only previous entities that came close to this breadth of resources were the charter companies. However, as noted previously, their ultimate focus was on trade in goods, rather than provision of military services. In addition, charter companies only operated outside of state controls, rather than working with states.

Table 3.2

How Are PMFs Different?

Organization:	Prior Corporate Structure
Motives:	Business Profit-Driven, Rather than Individual Profit-Driven
Open Market:	Legal, Public Entities
Services:	Wider Range, Varied Clientele
Recruitment:	Public, Specialized
Linkages:	Ties to Corporate Holdings and Financial Markets

WHAT IF IT'S ALL JUST A FRONT?

It must also be noted that the flip side of the mercenary-PMF comparison has also been argued. A few claim that the firms are not private entities at all, but rather are simple "front companies" for the reigning world powers, that is, covert public entities with political rather than economic motivations.[22] Such firms have existed in the past, including, most famously, the corporations set up by the CIA in the 1960s such as Air America, Civil Air Transport, Intermountain, Air Asia, and Southern Air Transport.[23] Many such hidden operations likely continue today.

However, the fact that front companies still exist does not mean that each and every PMF is a front for covert operations. Many PMFs are public entities owned by financial institutions and individual stockholders, allowing a measure of transparency not enjoyed by front companies of the past. The wide variation in their clientele and contracts also illustrates how the PMFs of today focus on taking advantage of disparities in military capabilities, rather than the pure strategic considerations that guide companies operating covertly for states. Many of the services that the industry offers, such as logistics, are simply too mundane to necessitate covert control. In addition, while the past front companies operated only in limited hot-spots for their governments, firms in the privatized military industry have worked for all types of customers and entities, in all types of places, sometimes including those contrary to their home governments' wishes. There are also pricing structures and competitive practices in the private military market that never characterized front companies. Finally, their financial independence and business motivations have even led some PMFs to defraud their own governments, in a way quite different from what any front for a bureaucracy would consider.[24]

Many PMFs do maintain close ties to their home governments, often because of the business advantages. Many PMFs (such as Vinnell, Betacls or Dyncorp) also are rumored to have worked on covert operations for governments. As a result, the accusations of conspiracy will continue, as any ties would obviously be hidden and difficult to disprove. The key, however, is that just because a firm is hired by a customer does not mean that it becomes part of them institutionally. In fact, the very rationale for many firms' success may rather be their willingness to undertake these tasks while still remaining independent from government administration, Thus, PMFs provide the advantage of an extra layer of cover from public scrutiny and congressional oversight. In a sense, certain PMF sectors have supplanted the need to set up front companies.[25]

FOUR

Why Security Has Been Privatized

"The best minds are not in government. If any were, business would steal them away."

—Ronald Reagan

The privatized military industry is not just a flashback to historic private military agents. Nor is there any one simple cause behind its emergence. Instead, it is distinctly representative of the changed global security and business environments at the start of the twenty-first century.

The end of the Cold War is at the heart of the emergence of the privatized military industry. The standoff between the two superpowers ordered international politics for half a century. When the Berlin Wall fell, an entire global order collapsed almost overnight. The resultant effect on the supply and demand of military services created a "security gap" that the private market rushed to fill.

There were two other necessary factors to the emergence of the industry, however. Both are long-term trends that underlay the transfer of military services to private entities and the reopening of the market. The first factor comprises the broad transformations that have taken place in the nature of warfare itself. These have created new demands and new market opportunities for PMFs. The second factor is the "privatization revolution," which provided the logic, legitimacy, and models for the entrance of markets into formerly state domains. The confluence of these momentous dynamics led to both the emergence and rapid growth of the privatized military industry.

THE GAP IN THE MARKET OF SECURITY: CHANGES IN POST–COLD WAR SUPPLY AND DEMAND

The end of the Cold War produced a vacuum in the market of security, which manifested itself in numerous ways, feeding both the supply side and the demand side. Global threats became more varied, more capable, and more dangerous, while the traditional responses to insecurity and conflict were at their weakest. This transformation fed into a larger phenomenon of state collapse and resulted in new areas of instability. Massive military demobilizations, in turn, provided a large pool of labor for the PMF industry and cheapening of start-up capital.[1]

With this vacuum, the firms are eager to present themselves as respectable bodies with a natural niche in the current, often complicated new world order. As Colonel Tim Spicer, an industry executive, comments, PMFs consciously aim to fill the security void of the post–Cold War world.

> The end of the Cold War has allowed conflicts long suppressed or manipulated by the superpowers to re-emerge. At the same time, most armies have got smaller and live footage on CNN of United States soldiers being killed in Somalia has had staggering effects on the willingness of governments to commit to foreign conflicts. We fill the gap.[2]

Released Conflicts

The first force driving the privatization of military services has been the massive increase in global levels of conflict since the Cold War's end. In part, these wars are a consequence of a power vacuum that is typical of transition periods in world affairs. In the previous period, the two superpowers provided order and stability and strictly controlled trouble spots. Conflicts certainly did occur, but those that threatened to spread were kept in check and many internal revolts were either deterred or quickly clamped down. This is no longer the case.

While many hoped for a "new world order" of global peace after 1989, the real order that came about was that of "peace in the West, war for the rest."[3] A particular outgrowth was the dramatic increase in the number of conflicts occurring inside countries. The incidence of civil wars has doubled since the Cold War's end and by the mid-1990s was actually five times as high as at its midpoint. The broader number of conflict zones (i.e., places in the world at war) has roughly doubled.[4]

There have been three patterns to this expansion in global violence. The first is the implosion of states. By the time the Cold War ended, many states, in particular client or postcolonial states, were financially fragile, patriarchally structured, and lacked systems of accountability; in short, they were highly dependent on external props.[5] Once these buttresses were removed after the superpowers pulled back, local rulers were unable to live up to their side of the social compact and the state apparatus simply atrophied. Lacking strong public institutions and infrastructure, the weakest, such as Somalia and Sierra Leone, essentially dissolved from the pressures within. Others, such as in the Balkans, suffered from ethnic tensions, once frozen from above, that were released with the breakup of the Soviet empire.[6]

The result of such failures of governance was conflict and a reordering of the state system, which opens up new spaces for private military actors to operate. Transnational criminals, economic insurgents, warlords for profit, armies of child soldiers, and brutalized civilians are all found in these zones of conflict and lawlessness.[7] The virtual absence of bureaucratic state institutions also means that outsiders take on a wider range of political roles conventionally reserved for the local state apparatus, including that of security.[8] In turn, the external world is unable to decouple from such areas, as there remain vested interests, both political and economic, and concerns about threats that might emanate from stateless zones. Thus, outside powers too, often turned to private firms for security, in lieu of using the local state.

Second, in spite of the overall trend toward more internal wars, many countries are beginning to fight across borders once again, as in the case in Congo and Ethiopia-Eritrea. This stems from a collapse of the security balance that was maintained by the superpowers. Today's local leaders are no longer restrained in their foreign policy by external checks. Many perceive that they now have the ability to take matters into their own hands.[9] With weak forces and no outside benefactors, however, they too have looked to the private military market to fill out their forces. For example, most of the states that intervened in the DRC necessitated support from PMFs to deploy their armies.

Finally, a third factor has been the remarkable growth in the influence of international markets, assisted by the opening of economies at the Cold War's end. This "globalization," however, while it has rewarded many, has not produced a homogenous world economy or culture. Instead, it has left many behind.[10] From the 1.3 billion who live in poverty to the 800 million presently starving, the dimension and magnitude of global human insecurity is stunning in all its measures.[11]

Most important, the brunt of such social problems has fallen on the youngest segments of the population, who now supply the foot soldiers for wars.[12] A substantial proportion of the children around the world are undereducated, malnourished, marginalized, and disaffected. The excluded constitute a huge reserve for the illegal economy, organized crime, and armed conflicts. As the world population continues to swell from the present 6 billion to 9 billion by 2025, this situation will worsen as greater pressures toward resource scarcities and resulting conflict grow.[13]

In sum, the end of the Cold War removed the controls over the levels of conflict while also releasing unresolved tensions and new pressures; the period since has seen a resultant massive increase in instability.

The Rise of Non-States in Violence

Facilitated by the opening of the world economy and new stateless zones, the rapid change in the global security paradigm also led to the emergence of new conflict groups, not bound to any one state.

Where it once appeared that war was the exclusive domain of governments and their militaries, this is no longer true. Dangers emanate from an array of sources, not exclusively from the military forces of states. The lines between civilian, soldier, guerrilla, terrorist, or criminal have become more blurred than ever, and small numbers of individuals can now embody greater threats than entire armies. Perhaps there is no greater indicator of this than the recent U.S. war on terrorism, where the most powerful state in history found itself under attack from an amorphous terrorist network not linked to any one state. In fact, the advance that Osama bin Laden brought to terrorism was its privatization, essentially acting as a venture capitalist for terror cells at a time when state sponsorship dried up.[14]

These new conflict actors range from terrorist organizations like al Qaeda to transnational drug cartels. The increasingly borderless world system has played a part. It may help world trade flows, but its negative result is that conflicts are engendered by the ease of criminal economic transactions and new availability of illicit supplies. Many of the internal conflicts that have popped up since the Cold War are in fact criminally related assaults on state sovereignty by non-state actors (for example, in Colombia, Liberia, Sierra Leone, and Tajikistan). Such 'stateless' zones not only breed greater conflict but also local actors whose very existence is defined by violence.[15]

A striking part of the emergence of non-state conflict groups is their growth in independent power. In Colombia for instance, neither the drug cartels nor the rebel FARC movement have any outside patrons, but both have been able to build notable military capabilities.[16] As a result, the local military is unable to enforce sovereignty over its own nation.

The growth of these non-state conflict groups shows no sign of abating, and the activity of these groups has opened up the market for PMFs both on the supply and the demand sides. Some firms have gone to work for non-state conflict groups, helping them in their quest to gain greater military capabilities. Rebel groups in Angola, Sierra Leone, and DRC and international criminal syndicates have all received military help from private companies, which have provided specialized military skills, such as training, and the use of advanced military technologies.[17] Their state opponents, in turn, have also hired PMFs.

As noted in the previous section, the PMF industry benefits from the business opportunities that open up as a consequence of the actions of these new conflict groups. Despite the risks associated with conflict zones, foreign MNCs are increasing their involvement in these areas, particularly in mineral exploration and production. There has been a corresponding increase in their tendency to rely on private military help to reduce the risks to their investments.[18] Thus, the market for PMFs is stimulated by both the emergence of non-state conflict groups and the failure of the world community to regulate them.

Labor: The Market Flood of Soldiers

Another major shift on the international market of security was the deluge of ex-soldiers onto the open market because of downsizing and state disappearance after the end of the Cold War. Thus, the private military labor pool for both conflict groups and private firms broadened and cheapened. Akin to the financial effect of changes in the interest rate, these developments affected both the demand side and the supply side.

The half-century of the Cold War was a historic period of hypermilitarization. The end of it sparked a global chain of downsizing, with state militaries now employing roughly 7 million fewer soldiers than they did in 1989. The cuts were particularly strong in the former Communist Bloc, as the Soviet state and many of its clients' forces essentially disappeared. Most of the Western powers have also drastically reduced the sizes of their military establishments. The U.S. military has one third fewer soldiers than at its Cold War peak, while the British Army is as numerically small as it has been in almost two centuries.[19] The end of the apartheid regime in South Africa and concurrent reforms in neighboring states also resulted in similar changes in their military structures.

These massive demobilizations produced an oversupply of dislocated military skilled labor. Complete units were cashiered out and a number of the most elite (such as the South African 32d Recon Battalion and the Soviet *Alpha* unit) loosely kept their structure and formed private companies of their own. With the shrinkage of state militaries have also come fewer opportunities for advancement and promotion within ranks; so it is not just a matter of getting rid of conscripts, but also the downsizing of professional, careerist soldiers. The result is a sharp increase in military expertise available to the private sector.[20] Moreover, as public security apparatuses broke down, it was not just the line-soldiers who were now left jobless. It is estimated that nearly 70 percent of the former KGB also entered the industry.[21]

Another important aspect of the cutbacks in state military organizations is the functional areas in which they took place. A great part of the cuts were in back-end support areas. For example, the U.S. Army Material Command alone was reduced by 60 percent.[22] However, force op-tempo (the frequency of military deployments) grew much greater than anticipated, causing a gap in the ability of the United States to support the many of its new post–Cold War interventions.[23] This gap has been the genesis of the multibillion dollar military logistics outsourcing sector.

Tools: The Market Flood of Weapons

Military downsizing has meant that not only trained military personnel glutted the world market but also that the resources and tools for large-scale violence were brought into the reach of all types of private actors. Massive arms stocks have become available to the open market. Machine guns, tanks, and even fighter jets can be purchased by any customer.

The most common and cheapest weapons on the market are usually ex-Soviet equipment, sold off directly by Russia or dumped by satellite states that had disappeared, downsized, or reconfigured their militaries to meet Western standards. One such example was the literal auction of the old East German Army after reunification in 1990.[24] The new unified Germany did not want the East's old weapons and chose to put its entire stock on the market. The result was essentially a huge yard sale of weaponry, where nearly every weapon in the East German arsenal was sold, most of it to private bidders at cut-rate prices. Missile attack boats went for $200,000, while light machine guns went for $60.[25]

As scores of other countries followed this example, sophisticated weapons systems flooded the market. The result is that anyone with enough cash can find a private supplier of almost any type of weapon at a bargain price.[26] In Africa, a T-55 tank, retrofitted with the latest reactive armor, costs $40,000, less than a SUV.[27] In Colombia, the FARC has used its cocaine profits to purchase enormous quantities of weapons and then have them delivered to Colombia in huge Il-76 transport planes, once owned by the Soviet Air Force.[28]

Not only has the military market shifted but the military balance between state and society has also been fundamentally altered. Until the closing decades of the twentieth century, even the weakest state forces were almost guaranteed to be able to maintain internal order because they controlled the primary weapons of war. Now many private forces have the most sophisticated weapons systems available to them, including fighter aircraft and advanced artillery, and can even outgun state forces.

A linked trend contributing to the boom in conflict has been the proliferation of inexpensive light weapons. The typical analyses of world threats focus on the most complex and expensive systems, but light weapons (which include rifles, grenades, machine guns, light mortars, land mines, and other portable systems) are the weapons most often used in contemporary warfare. They produced 90 percent of all casualties in the 1990s, mostly civilians.[29] In West Africa alone, 2 million people were killed by small arms in the 1990s.[30]

After 1989, millions of light weapons were declared surplus and dumped on the world market. Much of the stocks ended up in the hands of arms brokers and gunrunners, who have no compunctions about their final destination or use.[31] At the same time, manufacturing has continued apace. There are an estimated 550 million small arms floating around the globe, such that there is no place that small arms are not startlingly cheap and easily accessible. In Uganda, for example, an AK-47 can be purchased for the price of a chicken. In Kenya, it can be bought for the price of a goat.[32]

The consequence is that governments no longer have control over the primary means of warfare, which was once key in the formation of states.[33] Now, private conflict groups can present greater threats. In turn, private firms can tap the same arms market to build their own force capabilities, often in direct response.

The Decline of Local State Governance

The easy availability of both sophisticated weapons systems and inexpensive small arms is representative of a broader weakening of the state in many parts of the world.[34] Since the seventeenth century, the bureaucratic state has been the most important and most characteristic of all modern political institutions. At the turn of the twenty-first century, however, the majority of states in the world are either combining into larger regional communities or falling apart internally.[35]

The essential reason is that many states have simply been unable to live up to their side of the sovereign promise. Their borders are less secure, national markets are less relevant, and central bureaucratic authorities, from legal systems to banks, cannot maintain control from within while still staying competitive on the international level. The underlying factors behind this are manifold. For example, technology, which was such help in building the state after the Middle Ages, has now empowered other organizations that lack sovereignty.[36]

In the developing world, an important catalyst in this process has been the decline in external support to weak states. Those states that depended on Soviet aid and support found this fountain dry up entirely and immediately. Foreign assistance from the West also fell after the end of the Cold War.[37] Finally, there were new global macroeconomic policies that had a disastrous effect on state capacity. In particular, structural adjustment led to increasing micro-management by donors and the imposition of managerial structures that externalized much decision making.

The outcome is the striking weakness of the majority of states in the present world system. To describe them as truly sovereign players is simply erroneous. Most are so enfeebled as to be incapable of carrying out their most basic functions. The majority have GNPs that cannot compare to the leading corporations or even the budgets of large cities or universities in the United States. Large parts of such countries as Angola, Afghanistan, Sudan, and Congo have actually never been under true state control. In others, such as Liberia, the only semipolitical authorities are the principal agents of the state's very destruction.

Indeed, in much of the developing world, the security environment is shaped by the very weakness of the state. Most borders are permeable, with only sporadic and weak control of the flow of people and goods. This blurs the distinction between external and internal security problems.[38] These failed states are breeding grounds for instability, lawlessness, and ethnic and religious turmoil as well as havens for terrorists and criminal leaders. The major threats of today come not from major states projecting power but from weak or failed states projecting instability. It's no coincidence that such zones bereft of real government were primary refuges for Bin Laden and his ilk in al Qaeda.

In sum, many states are less willing and less able to guarantee their own sovereign autonomy. Instead, they have increasingly delegated the task of securing the life and property of their citizens to other organizations, including PMFs.[39] The irony is that this new wave is a reversal of the processes by which the modern state originally evolved. To gain military power, regimes do not need to follow the old path of developing their economy or efficient state institutions to tax for military forces. Rather, they must simply find a short-term revenue source, such as granting a mining concession, to pay a private actor.[40]

The Decline of the Local Military Response

A specific manifestation of weakened local state capacities is the poor condition of most militaries in the developing world, particularly in Africa. Many public armed forces are ill-trained, ill-equipped, and often understaffed. As a result, they often have been unable to guarantee the security of their country. "In short, the principal forces of order are in disorder in many countries at a time when the legitimacy of central governments (and indeed sometimes the state) is in doubt."[41]

The causes of the poor conditions of militaries in the developing world are manifold. The immaturity of the forces and the proclivity of corrupt leaders either to misuse their militaries for domestic coercion or to perceive them as a threat and intentionally enfeeble them are two of the root causes.[42] In addition, militaries in the developing world became dependent on superpower security assurances, rather than focusing on their own capacities and resources. When this external military aid dried up, local forces were incapacitated.[43]

Few militaries in the developing world have high professional standards, and many are hampered by politicization, poor management, and lack of civilian oversight. As with other state institutions, the militaries are also often compromised by ethnic imbalances, and corruption.[44] Many states also use the military as an employment program to take in the uneducated, illiterate, or sickly. Training levels are very low as well. For example, "In most African armies, indiscipline, economic problems and laxity in management have relegated training to the back seat. It is not unusual to find entire brigades who have not fired a rifle since their basic training."[45]

The result is that even if they are able to buy sophisticated equipment, many developing state militaries simply lack the skilled personnel to operate and maintain it. When one examines their true capabilities, the raw numbers of weapons they own become meaningless. Mozambique, for instance, possesses 43 fighter jets, 6 helicopter gunships, and 12 naval vessels, but it has so poorly maintained its fleets, that it "doesn't have one boat that floats or one plane that flies."[46] Thus local militaries have a great need for outside specialists to maintain and operate these systems. They also tend to lack the capability for sustained strategic mobility; few have advanced command, control, intelligence, airpower, naval power, or logistics support systems.[47] All these shortfalls are debilitating whenever the countries face complex security challenges and lead to the need for PMF assistance.

As an example, Nigeria is widely considered to have one of the more effective militaries in Africa and has been cultivated by the United States to operate as a regional enforcer. However, the Nigerian force has been so debilitated by years of corruption that its ministry of defense does not even know how many troops are in it. Unit commanders earn paychecks based on the number of personnel they oversee; therefore, many inflate the number of soldiers they actually command and pocket the difference.[48] This is only the tip of its problems. The navy has 19 admirals and 34 commodores, but can put to sea only 9 vessels. An external audit of the Nigerian military (interestingly performed by MPRI) found that 75 percent of the force's equipment was faulty or out of commission.[49] Many soldiers were without basic equipment such as helmets, canteens, and, in some cases, badly needed eyeglasses. There was also little to no active training.[50] Likewise, South Africa's army is estimated to have only 3,000 truly combat-ready personnel and four operational tanks.[51]

On top of these weaknesses, there is a growing danger to militaries that will be exceptionally insidious and destructive: AIDS (Acquired Immune Deficiency Syndrome). By the year 2005, it is estimated that more than 100 million people worldwide will have become infected. While it is an obvious major public health problem, AIDS constitutes a military issue, as well.[52] As a U.S. State Department report warned, the AIDS epidemic is "gradually weakening the capacity of militaries to defend their nations and maintain civil order."[53] Infection rates are particularly high among young military populations in developing states, such that state armies are being gutted. Estimates of current infection rates among African armies, for example, include 50 percent of all troops in Congo and Angola, 66 percent in Uganda, 75 percent in Malawi, and 80 percent in Zimbabwe.[54]

The result is that there has been an overall decay of state armed forces in developing regions. Given the increasing inadequacies of local military and security forces, compared to the rising challenges, it is no surprise that national and corporate leaders would choose to bring in help from whatever quarter is available, including even the private sphere.[55]

The Decline of Outside Intervention: Great Power Unwillingness

Another important factor in the opening of the military market for private firms is the declining willingness of outside powers to intervene in these more numerous outbreaks of violence. Weak local state capabilities did not matter as much during the second half of the twentieth century, as both superpowers and former colonial states who had interests in developing regions. They regarded the periphery as a strategic battleground and often intervened to aid a client state. Now, however, much of the world's conflict zones no longer fit into the strategic calculus of major states.[56]

There are three general factors that have altered the climate under which the United States and other major industrial powers decide whether to intervene into these zones.[57] The vast majority of potential interventions are discretionary, in that they are not about their own strict survival. Second, western military structures are still largely designed for major total warfare and are often inappropriate for limited interventions. Finally, for a variety of reasons, many of these states have developed a marked intolerance for casualties in conflicts that do not directly threaten the core of the nation.[58] While the U.S. public was willing to accept casualties in the Afghan campaign as it viewed it as a necessary fight, the same was not true for operations elsewhere, such as in Somalia or the Balkans, where the case for intervention was not so clear. In the words of former U.S. senior diplomat Dennis Jett, "Ever since Somalia, putting U.S. troops at risk [in discretionary interventions] has not been an option. . . . The criticism for losing people in an African civil war is going to be a lot harsher than for not committing troops to that situation."[59] Within the new Bush administration, this tendency toward avoiding commitments was only further reinforced.

This dynamic also means that reserve activation to fulfill staffing requirements is more politically sensitive than ever. Thus, even when forces do deploy, support tasks that had been handled by reserves must increasingly be turned over to the private market.[60] The end sum is that when terrorists strike directly at the United States, it is easy to ramp up unified public backing for troop deployments; when a small African state sinks into chaos, the support is simply not there.

It is important to note that this pullback is not just an American phenomenon but also characterizes former colonial powers, who in the past had regularly intervened in African and Asian states. For example, France's self-styled role as the "gendarme of Africa" has changed greatly. The number of French troops based in Africa decreased by more than 40 percent in the 1990s and will be further reduced by another 75 percent in the next few years.[61] As one French general notes, "'The post-colonial era is over."[62]

In short, intervention requires the willingness to make real sacrifices, but such readiness is no longer in limitless supply. This opens greater leeway for PMFs to operate. Just like nature, the security market abhors a vacuum.[63]

The Decline of Outside Intervention: UN Inability

In the initial optimistic burst after the Cold War, it seemed that the UN would take over this international stabilizing role from the superpowers. These ambitions reached their peak with the UN Secretary General's 1992 document *An Agenda for Peace*. However, operational disappointments in Bosnia, Somalia, and Rwanda then acted to curb UN activity. Indeed, whereas 82,000 UN peacekeepers were in the field in 1993, by 1995, it was down to 8,000 and as low as 1,000 in 1999.[64] Now, the UN no longer even undertakes peace enforcement operations. In addition, the dominance of the Security Council by Western powers has meant that certain conflicts, such as that in Bosnia, tend to receive greater attention than those outside of Western interest areas, such as Liberia.

Several factors prevent the UN from effectively playing a stabilizing role. First are past and present financial strains, primarily from member states' failure to pay their dues. Debts to the organization, including the over two billion dollars that the United States owed in arrears, increased at the same time as the costs of peacekeeping went up by a multiple of fifteen, hampering effectiveness in the field.[65]

Second, the UN is clearly not an organization designed for fighting wars. The department that oversees the operations in the field is highly politicized, underfunded, and understaffed (it has 400 personnel total, half the size of the UN's department of public information). Its staffing process also results in a short supply of true military professionals skilled in the areas they oversee. The process of defining, planning, assembling, fielding, and supporting the operations in the field is thus hindered. The fact that the UN is a voluntary organization also acts as a straitjacket of sorts. It is usually difficult to find states willing to send forces to conflict zones. Thus, UN missions are too often left with the second-rate militaries that do not have the training, equipment, or will to carry out the necessary missions.[66]

Finally, the voluntary processes also mean that assembling and deploying a force is often painfully inefficient and slow. For example, six months after the UN Security Council had authorized the peacekeeping force for Sierra Leone, most of the force still had not arrived.[67] Moreover, coalitions of the willing involve bringing together troops from scores of states that have differing training and capabilities.[68] This often results in the lowest common denominator of force effectiveness. Sometimes, internal rivalries and dissension break out. In the Sierra Leone operation, for example, the Nigerian deputy commander of the force twice refused direct orders from his Indian mission commander to deploy his troops into combat.[69]

The result is that the UN is hamstrung in its ability to intervene properly to stop conflicts and stabilize zones of violence, equally leaving the gap in the market to PMFs. Some have even likened the UN's position to the medieval papacy, in that it still has moral authority, but has been forced to swerve from one financial crisis to the next and is forever negotiating with constituents who refuse to pay debts.[70] As chapter 11 explores further, there is a possibility that, like the papacy, it too will look to contract out to private military agents.

The Decline of Outside Intervention: Regional Organization Failings

Regionalism is emerging as one of the more important trends in international relations today.[71] Many thus believe that regional organizations have the potential to supplant the UN's role and allow states to join forces and police their own neighborhoods. Indeed, operations in Liberia, East Timor, and Kosovo indicate that the UN is increasingly farming out peace enforcement tasks to regional organizations.

While they certainly carry the potential to deal better with increasing conflict and instability, there do remain several problems with regional subcontracting. As the Congo war illustrates, local members of regional organizations often have their own interests in local conflicts. Eleven African states have participated in the fighting in the Congo and in the aftermath could hardly be expected to serve as neutral outside parties. Just like the UN, regional groupings also reflect the strengths and weaknesses of their member states. Some, most notably NATO, are made up of wealthy states with well-armed and highly trained armies. The remainder, usually in the areas that need them the most, often fall below the minimal standards for effective conflict management. Thus, Kosovo gets 50,000 superbly equipped peacekeepers while Sierra Leone, seven times its size, had to make do with an under-equipped 9,000-person force. Most regional forces also lack the back-end transport and logistics to support their operations, often leading them to turn to PMFs for this backing if they do deploy.

By the end of the 1990s, there were attempts to bolster the ability of certain regional organizations to undertake stabilizing operations. For example, one was the African Crisis Response Initiative (ACRI), a U.S.- government-funded program, actually administered by MPRI. It provided peacekeeping training to certain African states.[72] Programs like ACRI, though, have been limited in effectiveness primarily because of the small number of units they train and the underlying institutional problems that remain unresolved.

TRANSFORMATIONS IN THE NATURE OF WARFARE

Despite the market opening that these shifts in supply and demand have created, there are two underlying trends, without which military service privatization is unlikely to have occurred or certainly would have been lessened in scope and impact. The first of these is that warfare itself is under going revolutionary changes. Massive accumulations of soldiers, machinery, and money were once required to take full advantage of the tools of conflict. In fact, this necessity lay at the heart of the triumph of the state form.[73] However, changes in the nature of weapons technology mean that small groups now possess the ability to wield massive power. The result is that "The steady concentration of power in the hands of states, which began in 1648 with the Peace of Westphalia, is over, at least for awhile."[74]

At the high intensity level of warfare, the requirement of advanced technology has dramatically increased the need for specialized expertise, which often must be pulled from the private sector. The flip side is that the motivations behind warfare and its impact on the roles of militaries also seem to be in flux. Low intensity conflict, primarily taking place in global areas of transition, has often lost its ideological motivations and instead has become criminalized. In sum, warfare is undergoing several key transformations—diversification, technologization, civilianization, and criminalization—each of which creates opportunities for private firms to play increasing roles.

Non-State Empowerment

The first change in warfare covers the diversification in military power to outside of the state's hands. The rise of violent non-state groups was covered in the previous section, but the essential point is that the growing power of non-state groups, particularly in relation to most state forces, will entail massive changes in the dynamics of warfare.

One of the things that made nation-states the most effective organizations for waging warfare in the industrial age was the overwhelming expense of troops, equipment, and supplies. Only those entities that could mobilize large amounts of money, flesh, and material could succeed at it, and thus the state was gradually able to weed out its institutional competitors.[75]

Technological and financial developments, however, have made it possible for smaller organizations to wage war. With the open military market capabilities, financing is often the only limiting factor, such that private, illicit, and commercial organizations can now find ways to match state armed forces. Despite losing state sponsors at the Cold War end, the rebel UNITA group in Angola, for example, was able to finance the private construction and maintenance of an entire mechanized field army through a nearly $2 billion diamond trade.[76] Well-financed actors are thus able to buy state-of-the-art talent that gives them an edge. Moreover, by contracting out their armed actions, they lessen the risk to themselves.[77]

It is important to note that the strengthening of actors other than states is not just about weapons but encompasses the entire spectrum of warfare. In many fields, such as microelectronics, software engineering, and biotechnology, the civilian sector has already become more advanced that the military. Intelligence of the quality available to state agencies is increasingly available on the open market. Already, commercial satellites are providing high-resolution images for sale, heretofore the exclusive province of the intelligence agencies of the superpowers.[78] Likewise, key military technologies such as GPS and FLIR are commercially accessible.

One noteworthy area is the new importance of information warfare (IW), which involves such diverse activities as psychological warfare, military deception, electronic combat, and both physical and cyber attack to mislead and break down opponents. The hi-tech, low personnel requirements of IW is tailor-made for non-state organizations, especially when taking on nation-states. Almost 100 non-state groups are developing information warfare capabilities. There are equally many private information warriors, who, for the right price, will develop and conduct information attacks on behalf of clients.[79]

The result is a potential complexification of conflict itself. Some analysts argue that the most complex struggles of the twenty-first century will pit networks of private actors against states, who in turn will rely on private support.[80] The idea of a foe with a single national center of gravity of the sort Clausewitz outlined is past. Indeed, as Michael Mandelbaum writes, "Guerrillas, terrorists, members of private militias—even malevolent computer hackers—seem to be displacing the formally trained, well-equipped, publicly funded soldier."[81]

The Requirements of Technology

For those who wish to stay at the leading edge of military capabilities, there is a growing need for technical expertise, increasingly from private sources. A new aspect of twenty-first-century warfare has been the strategy of information dominance, which especially entails a greater requirement for private assistance. This echoes past periods of warfare, described in chapter 2, where quality mattered more than pure quantity. There are similar effects on the demand for private military experts.

Throughout history, technological advances, both military and nonmilitary, have been important in warfare.[82] However, modern technology has taken on a Janus face of sorts.[83] While past military technological leaps were only effective when grouped inside large systems amenable to state control (such as railroads or cannonry), new technologies such as the Internet and telecommunications reach full effectiveness only when they are decentralized and allowed to transcend borders.

The "Revolution in Military Affairs" (RMA) is the general term coined to describe this trend within modern warfare. The RMA claims that the new technology, in particular the integration of information technologies, is creating a multiplicative rise in the lethality and mobility in munitions.[84] While large states can take great advantage of the RMA, as the success of the U.S. forces in Afghanistan against the tribally organized Taliban illustrates, this technical change can also erode some of the traditional advantage that states hold in armed conflict. For instance, as the world's most "wired" nation and thus dependent on information infrastructure in a military, economic, and social sense, strategic information warfare could be particularly problematic for the United States.[85] Non-state groups may even be superior to formal militaries in this arena, due to their decentralization. They may also be better equipped. The head of the NSA recently noted that their flexibility, combined with the faster pace of industrial development, means that non-state groups often have access to superior technology than U.S. governmental agencies.[86] Indeed, in several U.S. military war games, small units of hackers, hired off the private market, have proven capable of gaining access to critical military systems and disrupting entire military operations.[87]

Strategic information warfare is particularly important to the PMF trend, as thus far the private sector has proven to be better than the military in its key aspects.[88] Private firms might not only be able to match state armed forces in this new sphere of warfare but also already draw a great deal of business from it.[89] Industry analysts predict that spending on information war assets will continue to grow and that firms in this sector are located in what they refer to as "the sweet spot" of the market.[90]

Privatization and Civilianization

These changes lead directly into the next major alteration in the nature of warfare, that many military functions can and are being transferred to civilian specialists. As the civilian role in warfare has become greatly heightened, it is increasingly difficult to draw any precise line between military and nonmilitary occupations.[91]

Most of the information systems used by the world's modern military forces are designed, developed, and managed by civilians, primarily for civilian purposes, and make extensive use of the civilian information infrastructure.[92] The result is that, as one analyst notes, "The U.S. Army has concluded that in the future it will require contract personnel, even in the close fight area, to keep its most modern systems functioning. This applies especially to information-related systems. Information-warfare, in fact, may well become dominated by mercenaries."[93] Indeed, an article in the U.S. Army's professional journal has already advised that the U.S. military "hire specialized PMCs for specific offensive information campaigns, providing a surge capability instead of attempting to maintain limited-use, cutting-edge skills in the regular force, far removed from its core activity."[94]

Illustrated by major U.S. military exercises at Fort Hood and Fort Irwin, the "Army of the Future" will require huge levels of battlefield support from private firms. To allow these exercises even to occur, companies such as Hughes and TRW have to send hundreds of employees into the field to act as trainers, repairmen, troubleshooters, programmers, and hand holders to military personnel. Indeed, as James Adams, an industry expert, writes, "the whiz kid programmer may be the surrogate warrior of the future."[95]

It is not just an issue of information warfare or battlefield support though. Areas as diverse as weapons testing, aerial refueling, and the highly technical maintenance of F-117 and B-2 Stealth bombers are all private now. The simple fact is that the weapons systems required to carry out the highest levels of conflict are becoming so complex that as many as five different companies are often required to help just one U.S. military unit carry out its operations.[96] As one defense analyst put it, "We're using the most advanced technology in the history of the world to wage wars and sometimes the people who built it are the only ones who know how to fix it."[97]

This civilianization of warfare flies in the face of the traditional laws of war. Civilians were once assumed to be noncombatants and thus immune from targeting wherever possible. This immunity, however, was predicted on their not being an inherent part of military operations. The digitized battlefield and the new "surrogate warriors" places this immunity at risk.[98]

The Criminalization of Conflict

The changing reality of the warrior ethos is another aspect of the transformation of contemporary warfare, termed by some as a breakdown in the "Warrior's Honor."[99] In "high-intensity warfare," that is, the large-scale military operations carried out by western powers, combat has become more technological and more civilianized. At the same time, in the majority of conflicts carried out in the developing world, it has become messier and criminalized. What is interesting is that both involve the monopoly of war being taken away from public professionals.

In many of the ongoing wars around the globe, the traditional rationales behind the initiation, maintenance, and continuation of war are under siege. The profit motive has become a central motivator, equal or greater to that of political, ideological, or religious inspirations.[100] Or, as one military analyst puts it, "With enough money anyone can equip a powerful military force. With a willingness to use crime, nearly anyone can generate enough money."[101]

While economics has always played a role in conflict, the end of the twentieth century saw a new type of warfare develop, centered on profit-seeking enterprise. It was organized mass violence, but of the type that also involved the blurring of traditional conceptions of war (what Clausewitz defined as violence between states or organized groups for political purposes), organized crime (violence by privately organized groups undertaken for private purposes, usually financial gain), and large-scale violations of human rights.[102]

As discussed in chapter 2, private forces often fought in the past, but usually the conflicts they linked into had a broader motivator. The military entrepreneur Wallenstein, for example, may have been motivated by personal greed, but the Thirty Years War he fought in was about broader religious and political dynamics. Today, the fighting in a number of conflicts around the globe lacks this broader cause and is now driven by multiple logics of resource appropriation, from seizing mineral assets and protecting the drug trade to simple looting. This new criminalized mode of war holds true from places as disparate as Tajikistan and Colombia. In Sierra Leone, the key matter in the ten-year war was not over who was in place in the capitol, but who had control over the country's diamond fields. Similarly, in describing the war in Congo, where foes and allies alike battled over diamond and Coltan mines, one local observer noted, "People are fighting for money. Everything that happens, it's about money."[103]

While many of these wars are fueled by new conflict entrepreneurs and local warlords, the broader end of the Cold War also played a part in this shift. When outside superpower patronage ceased, the calculus of existing guerrilla and opposition groups took a more market-oriented direction. Rather than stop fighting, it just made them realize that their war economies had to change and that they had to find their own financial resources.[104] In short, if these groups wanted to survive, income generation (pure plunder, the production of primary commodities, illegal trading, and so on) had to become an essential activity. A particularly lucrative area for conflict groups has been the international drug trade. For example, 70 percent of opposition groups' funds in Tajikistan are from drug income, while Colombian guerrillas take in an estimated $800 million a year.[105] Far from being irrational or a breakdown in a system, war then becomes an end not a means, an "alternative system of profit and power."[106] Many of these bands then continue violent activities long after the original rationale for their formation has lost meaning.[107]

This criminalization of wars creates new dynamics that are relevant to the PMF trend. It leads to marked differences in the manner that forces conduct themselves, often in ways that are counterintuitive to what a conventional military doctrine would prescribe. For example, many of the wars see large measures of cooperation among supposedly warring sides. In Sierra Leone, for example, the RUF received much of its arms from the government and ECOMOG troops it was supposed to be fighting.[108] The obsession with private gain also causes forces to act in a less than strategic manner, when viewed in the conventional sense. For example, rebel forces in such wars tend not to attack military installations or strategic chokepoints, such as airports and harbors, but rather hit targets that they can loot.[109] The combination of these criminal goals and increasingly less professional, "soldierless" forces also leads to a variation in strategies toward civilians. Unlike Mao's traditional insurgency strategy, these new or reconstructed groups aim at terrorizing and pillaging the population, rather than winning hearts and minds.

All of these factors make criminalized war messier and more intractable. They are also more amenable for other profit-motivated entities, such as PMFs, to become involved. As these wars have become more and more prevalent, the role of a private firm in warfare is also harder to dispute, particularly when their professionalism stands in sharp contrast to local irregular forces, who are motivated by profit just the same.

THE POWER OF PRIVATIZATION AND THE PRIVATIZATION OF POWER

The openings created for private actors in the wake of the post–Cold War market shift and transformations in the nature of warfare were underscored by the third critical trend: the new power of privatization.

While Keynesianism and the welfare state were once dominant economic guiding principles, the close of the twentieth century saw a gradual shift to a belief in the superiority of the marketplace in fulfilling organizational or public needs. Underscoring this swing was the success of privatization programs in Europe, Latin America, and the United States, and the striking failure of command economies in the Soviet bloc. At the same time, the business strategy of outsourcing became critical to the rejuvenation of several industries.

These compared successes and failures provided important antecedent conditions for the growth of the privatized military industry. They not only shifted economic power, opened minds, and shattered worldviews but also offered important avenues for rethinking past practices.[110] The idea that the marketplace should be the solution gained not only legitimacy but, in fact, became the de facto international model for efficient governmental and business practice. Thus, when leaders faced new challenges and thought about how to improve their operations, whether in garbage collection, prisons, or in military support, they began to look to the private sphere. In short, "if any economic policy could lay claim to popularity, at least among the world's elites, it would certainly be privatization."[111] As more and more functions were externalized by states, it was less of a stretch for them to consider doing so in the military domain.

The Privatization Revolution

Governmental outsourcing is certainly a movement with momentum. The last decades of the twentieth century were marked by a cumulative externalization of state functions across the globe.

The tidal wave of global privatization began in Britain with the election of Margaret Thatcher in 1979. The Thatcher government undertook a vociferous and comprehensive program of denationalization and privatized many state industries. Although it met with great resistance and rancor in its initial stages, the move was soon considered a resounding success in helping to turn around the entire British economy.[112]

The British example provided a model for other nations seeking to resurrect struggling economies and through the 1980s and 1990s many followed suit. Privatization as a guiding norm soon spread around the globe.[113] International financial institutions, like the World Bank and IMF, played a critical role in turning this ideology into a normative reality. For both lender agencies and the governments that fund them, privatization represents the willingness of rulers to turn their backs on state patrimonialism.

As the Soviet bloc collapsed, nearly every state in it transitioned to a democratic regime and the accompanying market economy by privatizing its massive state industries. For postcommunist states, privatization of state industries signaled the end of a socialist conceit and the first step in the transition to liberal democracy. Indeed, within the West's conceptual universe, the idea of democracy is now closely linked to that of privatization.[114]

In sum, the 1990s saw unprecedented levels of privatization.[115] By 1998, the rate of global privatization was roughly doubling each year.[116] This "privatization revolution" went hand in hand with globalization; both trends embraced the notion that comparative advantage and competition maximize efficiency and effectiveness.[117]

In response, many internal elites tended to relinquish their social duties and focus on safeguarding their own economic fiefdoms, furthering the trend toward outsourcing.[118] For example, Indonesia, Liberia, Sierra Leone, and Congo are all failing states that contracted out public tax collection to private firms.[119] The general result is that the involvement of companies, often foreign, in the provision of public services became even more pronounced around the globe. The recent period has seen the snowballing of such externalization to the point that, in many arenas, the state bureaucracy has been completely displaced. This has been particularly so in the developing world. In a number of such states, outside groups run nearly every formerly public field, from public health to human rights monitoring.[120]

The effects of this privatization wave were felt both deeply and widely. A growing number of previously "untouchable areas" of government, from prisons to postal systems, became private. In the United States in the 1990s, hundreds of billions of dollars worth of formerly governmental activities were taken over by private companies. This move was pushed from the left by the Clinton administration's "national performance review" and from the right by the pro-privatization Republican majority in Congress.[121]

That political trends toward privatization would then cross into the realm of security should not be so shocking. In fact, many of the first targets of privatization were national defense manufacturing industries. With falling procurement budgets and rapidly escalating costs of research and development, a number of governments sought to preserve vital defense industries through marketization. Examples include Thomson-CSF and Aerospatiale in France and British Aerospace and Rolls-Royce. The result has been a privatization and globalization of defense technology and production.[122]

The privatization of protection, embodied by PMFs, has quickly become linked to this expansion of market-based solutions. As Mark Duffield writes, "Wherever patterns of privatization have evolved, all have created the demand for private protection. Indeed, the one thing that has characterized the expansion of global markets in unstable regions is the increasing use and sophistication of private protection to assure the control of assets."[123]

The Outsourcerers

This global trend to outsourcing also appeared in the corporate realm. As companies sought to reconfigure for the challenges of the global information age, the business strategy of outsourcing took hold and further influenced PMF legitimacy and expansion. As one trade group argued, "Outsourcing is the new shape of business. The changes that are taking place are tectonic."[124]

The particular genesis for the adaptation of outsourcing in the United States was the perceived challenge in the 1980s from what was known as "Japan, Inc." Faced with declining competitiveness with Asian rivals, many businesses sought to raise their efficiency by focusing on "core competencies." Their strategy was to outsource activities not critical to their mission.[125] This approach proved successful, and many credit it with the rapid turnaround of what used to be seen as industry dinosaurs, including IBM, AT&T, and Chrysler.[126] The seeming lesson of outsourcing was that it was *the* way to revitalize and grow a business.

Outsourcing soon became a dominant business strategy and a huge industry in and of itself. Global outsourcing expenditures topped $1 trillion worldwide by 2001, doubling in just the three years between 1998 and 2001.[127] Furthering the popularity was the fact that many of the most successful businesses of the new economy used the strategy. Of the 300 largest international companies, 93 percent outsourced some function.[128]

Many defense leaders directly pointed to general industry's success and advocated the emulation of business practices by the military. Initially, this was begun in areas where the military was simply repeating what was already available in the private sectors, such as data processing or health services.[129] Over time, however, the feeling grew that in the search for efficiency, no area should be discounted.[130]

Domestic Corollaries: Private Security

In many ways, the privatization of the military is just a more aggressive aspect of a larger trend of privatization. Essentially the state is abandoning its commanding heights; all of its most characteristic institutions are in decline—state-owned institutions, social security, justice, education, and now internal and external security.[131]

Indeed, the parallel to military outsourcing is already manifest in the domestic security market. The private security business is "a growth industry par excellence worldwide" and one of the fastest growing economic sectors in many countries.[132] The background to this industry's boom has several characteristics. Like the PMF industry, the growth of private security in the domestic sense is directly connected to the scaling down, and subsequent withdrawal, of the public police from many of its functions. Likewise, governments themselves have driven much of the private security boom. In the United States, for example, nearly one-third of all active private security guards are employed by the government.[133]

There has been a dramatic growth in the U.S. security industry since 1990. The amount spent on private security is 73 percent higher than that spent in the public sphere, and three times as many persons are employed in private forces as in official law enforcement agencies.[134] Linked with this trend, "gated communities" are now the norm in residential construction, with more than 20,000 such communities in the United States; in fact, four of every five new communities in the United States are guarded by private forces.[135] As one defense analyst wryly points out, "You already see more and more people hiring private security firms to keep the Third World away from suburban America."[136]

Aside from formal policing work, private security firms are taking on a wider variety of other homeland security functions once performed by governments. For example, industry leader Wackenhut runs prisons in thirteen states in the United States and in four foreign countries. It also provides SWAT teams that protect nuclear weapons facilities in South Carolina and Nevada from terrorist threats.[137]

The same trends are taking place around the globe. In South Africa, the ratio of private security personnel to uniformed police officers is approximately four to one. In the UK and Australia, it is two to one.[138] Private security personnel within Britain (roughly 250,000) actually outnumber the British army. In parts of Asia, the private security industry has grown at 20 percent to 30 percent per year. Even in communist China, some 250,000 guards are employed by the private security industry.[139] Perhaps the biggest explosion of private security is the result of the near complete breakdown of public agencies in postcommunist Russia, with over 10,000 new security firms opening since 1989.[140]

Private Triumph and the Public's Fall

The ultimate outcome is that government is no longer the preferred or even the default solution for public concerns. Although some argue that the trend toward privatization is part of a more general societal fragmentation, resulting from the deterioration of communal connections, the move is better described as a normative shift in worldview.[141] The failings of government provision, when compared with a number of seemingly successful privatization and outsourcing strategies, facilitated the questioning of established thinking. Not only was government increasingly put under the microscope, but the use of private actors gained new legitimacy. Privatization and outsourcing, even in the security realm, have thus entered the menu of formulated options. In many cases, they became the only institutional pathways open.[142]

A striking aspect of this shift in worldview is the fate of the word "public" itself. In Ancient Greece, where the distinction between public and private was first invented, it was the public domain that was lauded. Indeed, the Greek word for "private"—*idios*—is the base of our word "idiot."[143] Today, the situation is a polar opposite. "Public"—in such terms as "public schools," "public housing," or "public transportation"—is synonymous for many with second-rate or cheap. At the same time, there has been a reevaluation of public servants. In what's been called the "Fall of the Public Man," the commercial world has been judged superior and is more respected.[144]

Thus, in current conceptions of governance, the superiority of market-based solutions is near testament. U.S. Army General Barry McCaffrey, later the nation's "drug czar" in the 1990s, perhaps captures the prevailing sentiment best. When asked his opinion on the hiring of PMFs in Colombia, he responded, "I am unabashedly an admirer of outsourcing. . . . There's very few things in life you can't outsource."[145]

Thus the privatized military industry is just the next logical step in this global trend of privatization and outsourcing.[146] It is simply a more aggressive manifestation of the market's move into formerly state-dominated spheres. As one observer opined, "If privatization is the trend these days, the argument goes, why not privatize war too?"[147]

II. ORGANIZATION AND OPERATION

FIVE

The Global Industry of Military Services

"The times now require you to manage your general commerce with
your sword in your hands."

—The director of the East Indies Company to his employees

The identifying marker of the privatized military industry is their offer of services traditionally falling within the domain of national
militaries (combat operations, strategic planning, military training,
intelligence, military logistics, and information warfare). Although a number of firms, Sandline and MPRI for example, are eager to trumpet their
martial aspects, many others, understandably enough, do not openly identify themselves as military players. Some, such as Vinnell or Booz Allen, are
relatively hidden as divisions within larger corporate structures. Others,
such as Armorgroup, identify themselves as lying outside the military field,
using the more legitimate-sounding moniker of "private security firms."
Their claim is that they provide only passive services for private clients in
domestic situations. However, they are far different from the security
guards that work at local shopping malls. A number of such "private security firms" are neither quiescent in their operations, nor are the settings in
which they operate either peaceful or even civilian in nature. From offering training in special-forces tactics to providing armed units designed to
repel guerrilla attacks, both their services and their impact are definitively
military in nature.

As the agent behind these services is a corporate one, we can perform the
same type of industrial analysis that is used to understand market structures
in other, more seemingly innocuous business fields. Due to the focus on a
few firms rather than the broader industry, no one really has done so before.
The benefit of such an industrial analysis is not only to clarify the function
of the military market and its constituent firms but also to glimpse into their
likely evolution.

INDUSTRY STRUCTURE

The privatized military industry is not a capital-intensive sector, particularly
in comparison to such traditional industries as manufacturing or, more per-

tinently, a public military structure; this is a critical feature of the industry. The barriers to entry into the private military service market are relatively low, as are the economies of scale. Although national armed forces require substantial and regular budget outlays to sustain themselves, all one requires for a low-level PMF is a modicum of financial and intellectual capital.

For the PMFs that operate on the battlefield, the necessary tools of the trade are readily available and often at bargain prices from the international arms bazaar. Many contracts are designed so that the client is responsible for providing the weapons or other logistical needs of the firm; the PMF just supplies the personnel. If this is not the case, a number of firms have been able to make gains by handling the purchasing on behalf of the client, for an added charge. This increases their significant profit margin.[1]

The key to the PMF industry structure is that the labor input is relatively cheap and widely available, both on international and local markets. The continuing supply drive behind the labor pool is the comparatively low pay and prestige in many state militaries. Employees of PMFs tend to be paid anywhere from 2 to 10 times as much as in the official military and police. Thus many of the public force's best and brightest are lured away. In developing regions, local militaries also tend to lack consistency in their pay, while in developed regions many ex-soldiers are drawn into the industry by the prospect of combining their public retirement pay with a full private salary. Occupational stability and corporate rewards (including stock options in the more established firms) are further draws.

However, it is only when organized in a corporate structure that this workforce is able to realize its potential; individually, they provide much less added value to customers. The fact that the costs of training have already been born by state institutions means that these costs are borne elsewhere in society. Whereas a state's military might invest hundreds of thousands of dollars to recruit, train, and retrain each individual soldier, PMFs can quickly pull the same services from the open market for a fraction of a cost. This means that, although the industry can often be quite manpower intensive, with some operations employing hundreds and even thousands of operators, their marginal revenue from each operator is even higher.

There is an added implication of this labor-capital mix. Since the barriers to entry are so low, corporate branding and reputation are the keys to moving into a position of dominance in the market. This may come from the reputation that employees carry over with them from past military experience, such as MPRI selling itself based on the past battlefield achievements of its employees while in the U. S. armed forces. Or, it may come from the successes of the firm itself and resulting high customer retention rates, such as with Armorgroup.

VIRTUAL COMPANIES

An interesting feature of the burgeoning private military industry is that many of its firms operate as "virtual companies." Similar to e-commerce or temp-worker firms that save by limiting their expenditure on fixed ("brick and mortar") assets, these firms do not maintain large numbers of permanent employees, in military parlance "standing forces." But rather they use databases of qualified personnel and specialized sub-contractors.[2] Most employees are then brought in once contracts are signed, on a case-by-case basis. Any tools of the trade (typically weapons systems and other military equipment) are not held in stock but rather are bought or leased rapidly from the international market, also on a case-by-case basis. Such global resource allocation builds greater competence in contracting with less operational slack. In business terms, the implication is that, compared to state militaries, the firms are also more "boundary spanning." That is, a greater portion of their organization is task-focused and in contact with the client's needs, which also builds greater efficiency.

An added consequence of these lowered fixed costs is that it allows global location. Although it might be advantageous to base in areas rich in potential recruiting or clientele (such as MPRI's and Vinnell's headquartering near the Pentagon), this is not a necessity. In the unregulated electronic world, potential employees can be contacted and recruited from almost anywhere and databases and contracts can all be maintained on-line. Akin to the practices of the financial services world, a number of firms such as Sandline, maintain offices in central locations such as London and Washington, D.C., but are actually registered in more corporate-friendly environs such as the tax havens of the Bahamas or the Caymans.

The virtual nature of the structure also provides the potential for a short but profitable organizational half-life. Companies can rapidly dissolve and recreate themselves whenever the need arises (whether due to potential regulation, prosecution, or even the need to shed a poor brand name). The close of Executive Outcomes in December 1998 is the outstanding example of this. When domestic regulation became an issue, the original firm based in South Africa transformed itself into several firms located outside of the country. The virtual form means that, if the local risks become too high, the company simply can "move on."

This fluid structure is a major reason why many PMF advocates are able to make a claim that PMFs, as a rule, do not work against the interest of their home states.[3] Although this assertion is actually debatable (as later chapters explore), the fact remains that if a firm decides to place its headquarters in a particular place, it probably has already calculated that it is not going to have difficult regulatory problems with that particular home government.[4]

If it were to make a move contrary to its home state's interest that threatened retaliation, it likely would be savvy enough to locate elsewhere first.

INDUSTRY EMPLOYEE POOL: THE VALUE OF "EX"

The typical employees of the military services are as global and as varied as its services. Coming from all over the world—Angola, Canada, Israel, Nepal, Ukraine, the United States, the U.K., and Zimbabwe, they are specialists in anything from reconnaissance and aerial insertion to logistics management or training dogs for demining. They range from jungle fighters with over 20 years of combat experience to 'desk jockeys' who possess only administrative skills. But one thing tends to unite all the workers of the PMF industry— almost everyone is a former soldier. The field is perhaps unique among industries in one's former profession is integral to one's present job. The very name "ex-"—ex-Green Beret, ex-Paratrooper, ex-General, and so on— defines the employee base of the private military industry.

For the most part, PMFs tend to hire former personnel of national militaries. Some firms such as MPRI only recruit from their home military, whereas others such as Armorgroup are truly multinational in employee base. Employees may have been anything from the lowest-ranking enlisted personnel to the highest-ranking flag officers. A few firms also recruit from nonstate organizations and rebel groups (Executive Outcomes, for example, brought in veterans from the African National Congress), but the bulk of the personnel in the industry have served for at least some time in the public military. This propensity may be in slight decline, however, in the information and electronic warfare subsector of the industry, as computing skills are more important in these areas than pure military background.

One lure is that the military industry offers recently retired personnel a relatively easy, even natural, transition stage into private life. An employee of a London-based PMF described the motivations that led him to join the industry. "I joined the Army at 18 and left at 42. What else could I do but be a soldier? . . . What choice do I have?"[5] This should not imply that the employee pool in the PMF industry is only aged vets forced into retirement since at the typically young age of recruits, a soldier could put in over 20 years of military service and still be just 38 years old at his or her retirement. Also, many soldiers around the world leave their forces before formal retirement age, due to some dissatisfaction with the service, or if they are downsized for political reasons. As a result many PMF employees are in their twenties and early thirties. Even those "graybeards" (as one interviewee referred to himself) who do retire because they are too old for public service, still can provide their invaluable experience to client forces lacking in military background or leadership.

Likewise, just because its pool of employees is generally drawn from people who have exited the military, the industry is certainly no lesser in skill. In fact, it might even be the opposite. In this era of downsizing, lower comparative pay, and diminishing prestige, private industry is quite able to pick and choose, and even lure many of the best and brightest away from state militaries. In economic terms, the industry is able to "labor poach" and select who its wants and needs. Not counting stock options or insurance, an enlisted soldier equivalent might make as much serving in a single day in a PMF combat team as they could in a month in the public military, providing quite an incentive.[6] In fact, the British special forces have recently launched an unprecedented recruitment drive, as many of its soldiers are being enticed away by private military firms offering more than double their yearly pay.[7]

That almost everyone in the industry is an "ex-something" has a twofold advantage. The costs of training and evaluation have been accrued elsewhere at the state's expense rather than that of the firm, which now benefits from them. This means that the cost of investment in employees' skills, including the most specialized of military proficiencies that took years and tens of thousands of dollars of public spending to develop, is almost negligible for the PMF. This is a huge comparative advantage in relation to public agents. As far as ongoing human investment, the firm must typically only invest in the upkeep of relevant skills and how best to harness them inside the organization.

The firm also has a preset screening advantage paid for by the public military. The employees' service commendations and advancement will indicate their performance capabilities, as will the screening requirements of the units and armed forces in which they served. In comparison, a state army must recruit generally and then hope that some percentage of its training expense will pay off. This is part of the reason why some firms such as MPRI use only members of their old national forces; they already know how to evaluate them. It is also why veterans of special-forces units or other highly regarded units like the Gurkhas continually pop up in the PMF employee pools. In addition to their potential psychological proclivities to be drawn toward these demanding and adventurous careers, these soldiers have already passed the most difficult of job skills tests.[8]

The previous job experience of a private firm's employees also has the aforementioned advantage in brand marketing. Promotional literature and company websites often offer as much information on their employees' public military records as they do on what the firm itself has done in the past. In the end, the structure of the industry means that most of the firm's value-added to a client is its employees; hardware can be acquired from almost any source, but appropriate expertise is hard to come by. Accordingly, firms are eager to recruit based on the prominence or reputation of an employee or the units in which they served, as the final payoff to the firm will be much greater. At the command level, some firms make up a veritable 'who's who' of a nation's ex-military establishment. MPRI's parade of stars is the classic example (see Chapter 8), but it is certainly not the only firm that plays to the cachet value. For example, Levdan's commander in Congo was a former Israeli general, while other members included the office chief for Israeli intelligence and the son of the Israeli Army's Chief of Staff.

In addition to the marketing benefits, recruitment for prominence has a veiled payoff as well. Such officers are more likely to be trusted and respected when selling to foreign clients. Back home they also can call on a pre-existing network of contacts that feed them privileged information and contracts.[9]

MARKET COMPOSITION: SIZE AND RETURNS

There is no doubt that the provision of military services is a growing industry. For over a decade, the expansion of the sector has been acyclical, with the revenue pattern continually moving upwards. In other words, economic and political crises are fueling demand from outside the sector. Still in its infancy, the industry is yet to experience the typical maturity plateaus or even overall recessionary declines that occur in most industries. The industry is booming globally and adapting to the changing nature of war.

Unfortunately, the lack of full transparency in the industry prevents exact data collection. Best estimates are of annual market revenue in the range of $100 billion, indicating its health and power.[10] By the year 2010, the industry is expected to at least double in revenue.[11]

Moreover, the boom in the industry has a self-promoting effect. Successful operations are often publicized and the visibility of its activities nourishes perceived insecurity among those that are not currently beneficiaries. This feeds back into further demand across the private military industry as a whole. For example, the Sierra Leone leadership hired Executive Outcomes after it read about the firm's successful Angola operations in the news media. Another structural benefit to the PMFs is that client dependency grows each time they outsource or privatize functions. The client loses expertise and capabilities and becomes more reliant on the PMF. This is part of the reason behind the great traction in the industry.[12]

Accordingly, staggering economic gains have been made in investments in the PMF industry. In the 1990s, publicly traded companies in the field grew at roughly twice the rate of the Dow Jones industrial average.[13] Although not on the level of some of the most high-flying Internet stocks (many of which crashed), the rate of return to investment in this sector has often been astounding—and without the stomach churning volatility. For example, during the 1990s an investor who bought stock in Armor Holdings would have had a rate of return roughly 10 times better than if they had put their money in the Standard and Poor's 500 index.[14]

The result is that although much of the military-industrial complex on the production side suffered from downsizing and consolidation at the end of the Cold War, the military services industry blossomed. In fact, it has offered a means for large military-oriented companies, such as TRW or Northrop Grumman (with its Logicon services division), to maintain profitability in time of shrinking public contracts. For example, by making ventures into the service side of the business, the middle-tier firm L-3 grew into the 23rd largest defense business in the world.[15] Similarly, through the billion dollar contracts its BRS subsidiary had in support of U.S. military operations, Halliburton was able to smooth out the overall downturn in the general oil-services industry in the mid-1990s.

Because they remain uncategorized by any formal measure, the exact number of PMFs that have entered the market is difficult to establish and it most definitely remains in constant flux. The global number is estimated to be in the mid-hundreds. In London alone, there are headquartered at least 10 firms that have overseas contracts thought to be worth more than £100 million (roughly $160 million). These firms have more than 8,000 ex-British soldiers on their books as employees. Similarly, at least several dozen firms based in the United States specialize in providing tactical and consultative military services.[16] Another 60 such firms work in the demining subsector.[17] If one broadens the counting of PMFs to include back-end military support firms, or diversified firms, the number multiplies.

Smaller organizations that primarily operate overseas, are thought to be even more numerous, but are harder to track. Many are chartered all over the world in corporate friendly locales and are often little more than a letterhead and a Rolodex file or database of willing employees. In Africa alone, close to 100 of such private firms come and go. Examples include: Omega Support, Southern Cross Security, Panasac, Bridge Resources, Corporate Trading International, Longreach PTY Ltd., and Strategic Concepts.[18]

Due to the industry's youth, there still appears to be significant market space open for new companies. For example, there are about 250 firms in the U.S. military training market. When measured in terms of revenue generated, the major firms dominate. Lockheed Martin has the largest market share at 18 percent. L-3/MPRI has 10 percent, and CAE Electronics has 8 percent.[19] However, although each grew their business between 1997 and 2000, the three market leaders still lost 8 percent of their total market share. This indicates the growth of greater competition within this subsector.

Thus, the privatized military industry is still in its relative infancy, but it appears that the true boom lies shortly ahead. The reason for this optimism is that the potential client base is only now being tapped, meaning that the market is far from saturated.

MARKET DRIVERS: LUCRATIVE CONTRACTS AND GROWING CLIENTS

Contracts in the military services field range from under $1 million to well in the $100 million or more range. Moreover, business agreements in this industry often include hidden perks, side deals, spin-off earnings, and secondary contracts that can multiply formal contract figures by four or five times in actuality.[20]

The largest contracts are those linked to supporting the operations of the most advanced militaries. Brown & Root has received over $2 billion as part of recurring contracts with the US Army in the Balkans. In 1996 alone, BDM had over $1.5 billion in military service contracts. Forty-five percent of SAIC's overall revenue (roughly $1 billion) came from national security contracts with the U.S. military.[21] It must be remembered that these figures are not from the sale of weapons systems, as the traditional corporate-military relationship would presume, but from the provision of military-related systems operators and support.

The smaller fish in the market, often the most "virtual" and fly by night, compete for contracts closer to the low end of the spectrum. These are generally measured in the hundreds of thousands of dollars. For example, Onix International, made up of ex-New Zealand SAS soldiers, rescued a businessman held hostage in East Timor for $220,000.[22] Examples of other such small businesses, "micro-caps," PMFs include Stabilco, Secrets, Security Advisory Services Ltd., and Special Projects Services Ltd.[23]

Although governments and their militaries remain the obvious employers of the industry, the clientele of the military service industry also is growing to include: multinational corporations, non-governmental organizations, and the UN and other regional and international organizations. These clients represent untapped areas and the next likely market drivers.

Multinational Corporations

In previous decades, the biggest risk faced by multinational corporations operating in poor countries was nationalization and seizure of their assets by the local government. In the 1960s and 1970s, for example, BP and Exxon lost oil fields in Venezuela and Iran, and the firm Anglo-American lost its mines in Zambia.[24] More recently, however, such formalized expropriations have become rare.

Instead, the real risk to investment located in the developing world is from violence directed at their employees or facilities. The U.S. State Department lists 74 countries in which physical security is a problem, of which 34 endure actual civil war or rebel insurgency. In many of these places, multinational corporation facilities are often at the epicenter of conflicts. For example, oil industry facilities and pipelines are the focal point of fighting ranging from Algeria to Azerbaijan and mining corporation sites are contested in Congo, Sierra Leone, and Angola.

The dangers of operating in these zones are quite high. In Colombia, for example, rebels attacked corporate pipelines and other oil industry facilities 985 times between 1986–1996; in 2001 alone, the 480–mile Limon Covenas pipeline was bombed 170 times.[25] After September 11, the risks of operating in the Arab world are seen to have similarly intensified.[26] The result is that doing business in conflict zones is often perceived as a true gamble. Or, as The Economist notes, "The world viewed from the boardroom is a nasty place."[27]

The easier solution for these multinational corporations would be to pull back from risky areas and limit operations to safer confines. However, in addition to the lost sunk costs, to do such would be to miss out an investment bonanza. High political-risk areas are among the last frontiers of market expansion; as such, the best business opportunities are often in the most unenticing places.[28] The outcome is that in spite of the increasing dangers, foreign companies are investing huge sums into areas at conflict and reaping huge profits. In particular, natural resources such as oil, natural gas, diamonds, gold, and bauxite all must be pulled out of the earth wherever located, regardless if in a peaceful stable country or a raging conflict zone.[29]

The investment boom in the world's most dangerous places has generated a concurrent increase in demand for PMFs' services. As the managing director of the firm Sterling Lines, Hugh Brazier, notes, "Companies are becoming far more reliant on providing their own security because they can't rely on foreign governments to protect them."[30] PMFs therefore provide an accessible means for companies not involved in security issues to manage their political risks abroad.

As such, PMFs act as "investment enablers," providing clients with robust security that make otherwise extremely risky investment options safe enough to be financially viable. In the midst of conflict, they create localized stability that reduces costs and increases investment values. For example, Halliburton received over $200 million to develop oil well services in the rebellion-ridden Angolan Cabinda enclave. Without the protection guarantees against rebel attacks provided by the PMF Airscan and its local joint ventures, this contract would be worthless.[31] If the PMFs were not providing protection, it is unlikely that the multinational corporation would be willing to take the risk.

The result is huge outflows of money from these multinational corporations to PMFs. In Algeria, where Islamic terrorists are battling the government, oil firms spend close to 9 percent of their operational budgets on military-style protection. Similar measures are in place in Colombia, where fighting off leftist guerillas, narco-terrorists, and paramilitaries keep the security costs for multinational corporations at around 6 percent.[32] As in the broader industry, the military services that multinational corporations pay for run the full gamut of possibilities. PMFs have provided other corporations with everything from armed commando units to logistics services. Air Partner, a British firm, even recently launched a "global evacuation service."[33] The firm offers to whisk multinational corporation employees to safety from any conflict predicament, meaning that when a crisis emerges, expatriates and their families no longer have to rely on the Marines arriving offshore in time.

Humanitarian Operations: International and Non-Governmental Organizations

Another "pot of gold" market for PMF contracts that is tremendously appealing to PMFs is work for groups with humanitarian agendas, such as the agencies of the United Nations or even nongovernmental organizations.[34]

Already, PMFs provide important services to humanitarian operations. For example, it was the emergence of international institutions and nongovernmental groups as new clients that caused the mine-countermeasures market to boom. Demining operations have been contracted out in nearly every U.N. operation, with the overall world market reaching $400 million annually.[35] Minetech and the Executive Outcomes offshoot Saracen provide such operations in Angola, for example. Portions of the police and logistics functions in peacekeeping operations have also been outsourced to such firms as Dyncorp. Likewise, nongovernmental aid groups often face extreme humanitarian disasters, such as the need to feed and house hundreds of thousands of refugees during the crises in Kosovo and East Timor. In these cases, they also looked to the industry for military-style surge capacity in the area of supply and engineering.

There is also a potential role for PMFs to provide the security for such operations. Aid agencies and nongovernmental organizations can always be found in danger zones. The industry offers the nonprofit sector a cost-effective means of reducing their security risks. A number, such as Worldvision in Sierra Leone and UNHCR (United Nations High Commission for Refugees) on the Afghanistan border, have hired PMFs for protection and security advisory.[36] In a sense, the firms create a counterpart to their help to multinational corporations, becoming here what one might consider "aid enablers." Indications are that this client sector will boom in the very near future. Faced with increasing attacks, the United Nations, for example, hopes to raise its annual budget on security for its relief and refugee agencies by 300 percent.[37]

Adding U.N. aid agencies and other humanitarian organizations to their client list would clearly benefit the privatized military industry. A fundamental problem in the past has been that many of the clients most willing to hire PMFs, weak states, are also those least likely to fulfill payment. In contrast, recurring institutional support from international and nongovernment organizations would help diversify and solidify the revenue flow of the industry. An added bonus is that humanitarian operations tend to run toward the long term, meaning extended and thus more profitable contracts.

Of course, greater employment by nongovernment and international organizations would have to be predicated on the companies gaining greater public legitimacy. Already edgy about using private military services and being dependent on donor support, these organizations are drawn toward hiring the more reputable, higher-end firms. Firms that target this particular client sector might try to discontinue their engagement with sketchier clients, such as authoritarian governments, or expand into new sectors, in order to appear to have cleaner hands. For example, Blue Sky is a security consulting firm that tries to distinguish itself by claiming to be formed specifically to act as an "ethical" firm. In turn, many see the recent expansion by Armorgroup into the more innocuous sector of humanitarian demining as a part of a gateway plan to gain greater credibility within the international community and further burnish its image.[38] It is important to note, however, that a shift by such firms away from working for unprincipled clients would simply create a gap in the market. The demands of these clients would remain, only to be filled by companies less concerned with appearances.

MARKET TRENDS: GLOBALIZATION, CONSOLIDATION, AND NORMALIZATION

The overall military services market is quite dynamic. Although as late as the mid-1990s no truly global companies existed, this seems to be the direction that much of the market is now moving toward.[39] Initially being made up of a limited number of firms offering limited military specialties, the PMF industry is expanding to offer a wider range of sophisticated services.

As the businesses respond to marketplace demands, a rapid consolidation into diversified transnational firms is taking place. PMFs are essentially following the standard business techniques for market engineering used by other types of firms. Many are either partnering up with equals or acquiring smaller market participants with niche market and technologic specializations. The reason for this consolidation centers on brand marketing and subspecialization seen as necessary by the leading firms to compete on the global scene. Broader-based firms can more easily offer the wider range of services that are seen as necessary for complex security situations. Already having social capital and established records in their brands, diversification also allows the bigger international companies to increase their market share rapidly. Of course, this is all to the detriment of smaller specialized or local firms.

The merger of the British firm Defense Service Limited with Armor Holdings exemplifies the trend toward consolidation and diversification. Using primarily ex-SAS personnel, DSL originally offered security training and consultation to governments and multinational corporations operating in conflict zones. It did everything from guard embassies and oil and mine installations in Angola (where its employees numbered well over 1000) to training special-forces units in Indonesia, Jordan, Mozambique, the Philippines, and Uganda. Over time, it slowly expanded its operations by acquiring other similar companies using ex-SAS personnel, such as Intersec and Falconstar.[40] In turn, Armor Holdings, a United Stated-based firm that started out in the body armor business, acquired DSL in 1996. Intent on building up its "risk management services," with a growth through acquisitions-strategy, it created the new Armorgroup division, with DSL at its core. It then began filling out these service-side offerings. Over the last four years, Armor has acquired 20 new companies, bringing under its control an array of military-related services, ranging from mine clearance to intelligence.

With the realization that the Internet is vast unregulated environment weakly controlled by governments and thus a ripe market, Armor also has begun to expand its "virtual security" offerings; it recently purchased both IBNet, which does Internet surveillance and competitive intelligence gathering, and NTI, staffed by former U.S. Air Force personnel, which does computer security and investigations for both state agencies and Fortune-500 corporations (including CNN, Yahoo, and E-Bay). As the threats of Internet crime and cyberterrorism continue to grow at an exponential rate, Armor's new stake in the virtual security field will likely become increasingly valuable.[41]

Another Armor acquisition was that of the Alpha firm, based in Moscow. Alpha is essentially a privatized unit of "Alpha," the most elite Soviet special-forces organization, an equivalent of the U.S. "Delta Force." The "Alpha" unit was known as "the Spetnaz of Spetnaz," as its members were recruited from the best of other Soviet elite forces.[42] For Armorgroup to add the legacy of this unit was a significant gain in both capabilities and reputation, particularly for operations in former Soviet states.

Such corporate alliances and acquisitions allow Armorgroup to maintain a truly global presence. It has over 5000 personnel located in over 40 subsidiaries based in over 50 countries. A typical example of one of its subunits is Defense Systems Colombia (DSC), previously a subsidiary of DSL and now within Armorgroup Latin America. DSC has over 350 personnel, most of whom are ex-Colombian military, including its general manager, who was the former commander of the Colombian army. It provides protection within Colombia from rebel attacks, primarily to multinational corporation facilities.[43]

The success of Armor's acquisitions strategy was demonstrated when it

was named among *Fortune* magazine's 100 fastest growing companies in
1999 and 2000.[44] Overall, Armorgroup's contracts have grown by nearly
400 percent in the last 4 years, almost entirely through referrals. Some subunits have been even more successful (such as DSC, which grew 750 percent
from 1997 to 2000).[45] As one financial analyst notes of Armor, "They have
also demonstrated a very capable ability to integrate the companies they've
purchased . . . The market they're participating in is incredibly fragmented,
with little end in sight to their acquisition opportunities."[46]

Armor is just one example of the merger mania in the military services
field, but as a market leader, its strategic vision has set the tone. Other recent mergers include that of Securicor and Gray Security. Gray, in turn, owns
the mid-tier military firm Teleservices, active in the Angola conflict.[47] Group
4 Falck is a Danish firm that has gone on a buying spree, most recently purchasing Wackenhut. In the summer of 2000, MPRI was purchased by L-3
Communications, a firm specializing in communications and security support services. L-3 was created in 1997 by the merging of business units spun
out of the defense manufacturers Loral and Lockheed Martin.[48]

These acquisitions are also important in that they may very well be part
of a process of industry "normalization," a process by which the emerging
privatized military industry becomes considered no different than any other
industry. When L-3, which is listed on the New York Stock Exchange, purchased MPRI, one of the most prominent PMFs, there was no controversy
whatsoever, including no outcry from either individual stockholders or the
investment institutions that control the majority of its shares. As one executive of MPRI jokes, "Anyone with a 401(k) retirement plan is probably an investor in our company."[49]

SPECIALIZATION AND REPUTATION: LIMITS TO
CONSOLIDATION AND GLOBALIZATION

Although the move toward corporate military conglomerates is in full effect,
some sectors of the field remain highly specialized. This is due to concerns
of reputation that cut in both directions. A number of firms that engage in
humanitarian operations, such as the demining companies Ronco or Mine-
tech, focus only on their singular specialty, despite the fact that they recruit
many of the same ex-military personnel as larger, more diversified firms.[50]
Although still military in nature, demining is considered more acceptable
than such areas as combat training or strategic consulting, because it involves
weapons' removal, rather than use. In order to keep their humanitarian-
minded clients happy, many demining firms do their utmost to disassociate
themselves from the rest of the PMF industry and the "mercenary" label. The
fate of these firms remains to be seen, as the diversified PMF conglomerates
move into their sectors.

Reputation concerns also limit consolidation in an opposite manner. Outside of global tier companies, a market niche remains for more aggressive, smaller firms that can cut informal deals that these bigger transnational firms cannot. Such companies have less regard for their corporate image and can more easily insinuate themselves in the political network of unseemly regimes. They also can utilize the barter system of payment that larger firms with scrutinized accounting practices would not be able to employ. Such PMFs are the firms that are most likely to go "rogue," as explored further in chapter 14.

Some transnational firms try to have it both ways. They have a central global brand, but also attempt to take advantage of the benefits of such smaller organizations by rapidly spawning new firms once they gain entry into a local market. The associations that built around Executive Outcomes was an example of this, whereby soon after deployment into a country it would create a network of smaller local firms. Led by former employees, these spin-offs specialized in different services, ranging from security protection to airlift. Some even moved out of the military services field and returned to general industry, entering the telecommunications and even vacation/resort business. Having seized local market share, these new firms would remain even after the original PMF's operations had ostensibly ended. In Angola, such 'stay-behind' firms associated with Executive Outcomes reportedly included Shibita Security, Stuart Mills, Saracen, and Alpha 5.

The result of this marriage of local specialization and transnational branding is a flexible network, loosely linking each new market into an overall corporate structure. There are three key advantages of this system. First, it reduces the already limited capacity of domestic regulators back in the central firm's home country to monitor its activities. Second, the web of related businesses provides an added flow of corporate rewards to PMF employees. Third, the overall network can be mobilized by the transnational firm whenever it needs a surge capacity for larger operations in one spot.[51] This modern structure is akin to what economic historian Frederick Lane described in the development of "differentiated enterprises" in colonial areas, where the military end of an enterprise created trade opportunities for other corporate units.[52]

However, the PMF industry may not completely mimic the development of such colonial industries. In fact, a new change in the market is that PMFs from less developed countries have recently emerged. For example, demining firms based in Africa are slowly gaining market share in the sector, to the detriment of those from richer states. Minetech, based in Zimbabwe, has quickly become one of the industry leaders, winning over 130 contracts around the world, worth more than $1 billion. The irony is that a PMF based in an area that has recently suffered from war may even have a comparative advantage—because of the war's effect on labor pricing and experience.

It remains to be seen however how these firms will evolve. These firms can provide relatively inexpensive military services that may be able to undercut established Western firms.[53] As many clients may be under significant budgetary restrictions, clear price differentiation may be significant in their decisions on which PMF to hire.

Thus, it is a possibility that future industry clients will have an even broader private military service menu to choose from. Bargain price solutions from developing-region PMFs may duel with the latest technical panacea offered by Western-based firms. Competitive issues will mean that the more successful PMFs will likely be those that move toward product integration rather than pure cut-rate price or pure technological expertise; that is, the strongest competitors will be those that can best balance cost efficiency and quality.

However, another likelihood emerges. Just as has happened in other emerging industries, smaller locally-owned firms may be gobbled up in their embryonic stages, before they threaten the larger transnational conglomerates. The market seems to have a tendency toward consolidation and the larger international firms will be able to make quite attractive offers at the outset to induce the best smaller firms to link up. Armorgroup's franchise system may be the model for this expansion.

SIX

The Privatized Military Industry
Classified

> The panoply of services defies classification, but they all involve the export of private military expertise in some fashion.
>
> Juan Carlos Zarate, "The Emergence of a New Dog of War"

The firms that participate in the military industry neither look alike nor do they even serve the same markets. They vary in their market capitalization, number of personnel, firm history, corporate interrelationships, employee experience and characteristics, and even the geographic location of their home base and operational zones.

The single unifying factor for the privatized military industry, though, is that all the firms within it offer services that fall within the military domain. But even these services themselves are quite diversified. While firms such as EO and Sandline offer direct combat services, Saladin Security and Armorgroup offer military training and assistance located primarily off the battlefield. Levdan offers assistance with military weapon procurement (that is, where to get the weapons one needs), while MPRI provides consulting and strategic analysis (how to employ such weapons in the most effective manner). Asmara and Network Security Management bid services in the secretive field of intelligence, while Brown & Root operates in the more innocuous privatizing of military logistics.[1]

Accordingly, a true problem for understanding the overall military industry and generating a theory about it is that this internal variation has largely gone unexplored. A general belief among the existing studies of PMFs is that there is no clear method to break the industry down into its constituent parts.[2] Furthermore, understanding of the privatized military industry is seriously hampered by the fact that few generally accepted definitions exist, even of the most basic terms.[3] A new taxonomy of the industry is needed, one that is not only more logical, but also attuned to the unique business-military cross that defines the industry.

ILL-DEFINED AND INDETERMINATE: THE CURRENT INDUSTRY TAXONOMY

A few attempts have been made at classifying PMFs as groups, rather than thinking about them only on a case-by-case basis. The typical analytic division has been to distinguish firms by the general level of their activity. Some firms are termed "passive" in their operations and those that are "active." A number of analysts and some of the firms themselves use this classification.[4] For example, companies that engage in combat operations or seize territory, such as Executive Outcomes, are placed in the "active" category, whereas those that defend territory or provide training and advice, such as MPRI, are placed in the "passive" category.

Unfortunately, this categorization has been unsuccessful from either an analytical or theoretical perspective. The original basis for dividing companies into "passive" and "active" boxes was more for simple convenience (and biased self-definition by the firms themselves), rather than as a taxonomy designed to yield explanatory and predictive implications. Hence, theoretic development remains stymied, with no clear policy prescriptions, no new findings, and no new research questions about the differing impacts of the firms have been drawn from it, nor were ever planned to be.

The ultimate problem is that "passive" and "active" firms are conceptually interchangeable, as are their results. The hire of either type of firm can have quite strategic effects and help alter the entire course of the war, contrary to their monikers. To place different firms within this active-passive division also often requires impossible dexterity and usually is dependent on one's perspective. One person's active firm is another person's passive one.

For example, firms, such as Armorgroup or Southern Cross Security, which offer area defense and installation security within conflict zones, are often conceived as "passive." Rather than attacking forces or seizing territory, they simply create a zone of security around a client's assets. However, both their operations and the impact that their hiring has on the outcome can also be conceived as very active. Rather than being simple security guards in the domestic conception, such firms stake out the control of zones and fend off military attacks, sometimes using military-style force. Due to the nature of most internal conflicts and wars, the facilities that such firms deploy to guard are often strategic centers of gravity. Their market entrance, even as a "passive" firm thus has strategic impact. For example, some firms protect corporate sites that serve as primary funding sources for sides in civil wars or lie across critical lines of communication, as with the Belgian firm IDAS in Angola.[5] In cases such as these, their hire and resulting defense of these sites is actually perceived as aggression by the other side.

Some theorists try to circumvent this difficulty by determining the passivity of a firm by whether its employees are armed or unarmed. This is often the distinction used to separate "private military companies" from "private security firms." Although this does set a more clear line of differentiation, the passive-active division is still the crux of the system and it still does not work. Many firms that describe themselves as "security" companies often perform military roles, with military consequences.[6]

The underlying basis of the distinction is built on dubious assumptions. In addition to "armed versus unarmed" being an antiquated division in an era when a person pushing a computer button can be just as lethal as another person pulling a trigger, whether a firm's employees actually operate weapons or not does not determine their ultimate role or impact on a conflict. In the instances of both Croatia and Ethiopia, private consultation and training were critical enabling factors to successful, war-ending military offenses. Yet, the firms that offered these services would be defined as passive, simply because their employees were unarmed and too high-level to be wasted on the battlefield. This division also counterintuitively lumps firms that offer military officers for hire or provide training in offensive military doctrine along with those that offer logistics or supply-chain management. The services obviously differ, but the passive/active distinction does not recognize why.

The final problem is that the active/passive, private security/military monikers are really normative determinations within an economically motivated setting. For good reason, no other industry classifies its sectors this way, as the categorization typically degenerates into a biased way of distinguishing the "good" passive/private security firms from the "bad" active/private military firms. For the most part, firms are quick to claim themselves as passive, for obvious reasons. They then have a better claim to legitimacy and less reason to fear regulation.

Other attempts at dividing the industry have used boundaries drawn from general political science. One suggested delineating line was whether the firm was purely international or domestic in orientation.[7] In today's global world, this division is artificial and antiquated. It ignores not only the multinational characteristics of the industry (in both its basing and operations), but also firms' rapid ability to transfer and recreate themselves across state borders. A firm that one day is considered international could quickly close shop and then open domestic affiliates the next day, much in the manner that Executive Outcomes did. Moreover, most wars today are internal, so it is unclear what is gained by this national borders distinction.

Another potential classification system is drawn from offense-defense theory (ODT); that is, whether the firm's services are designed to bolster or to deter aggression.[8] Leaving aside the general problems with ODT's failure to deliver on both its explanatory and predictive claims in regular military affairs, when applied to the military service industry, this theory quickly suffers from the same problems as the active-passive distinction.[9] Just as almost any weapon or doctrine has both offensive and defensive implications depending upon one's perspective (that is, which end of the gun barrel one is facing), so too can the firms that enable their use. An added problem with this system is that the critical factor in classifying the firms then would lie outside the industry. How to determine the firm's type would depend on the client's motivation for the hire for a specific contract, rather than anything intrinsic about the firm.

TIP-OF-THE-SPEAR TYPOLOGY

The solution to this dilemma is to recognize the duality that is at the very nature of the privatized military industry. At its base level, the industry is driven by both military and economic fundamentals. A successful typology of its constituent parts must take into account both elements.

In the military context, the best way to structure the industry is by the range of services and level of force that a firm is able to offer. the industry. The useful analogy from military thought is the "Tip of the Spear" metaphor.[10] Traditionally, units within the armed forces are distinguished by their closeness to the actual fighting (the "front line") that result in implications in their training levels, unit prestige, roles in the battle, directness of impact, and so on. For example, an individual serving in a front-line infantry unit (that is, in the "tip") possesses completely different training experiences and even career prospects than one serving in a command or a logistics support unit.

Using this concept, military organizations break down into three broad types of units linked to their location in the battle space: those that operate within the general theater, those in the theater of war, and those in the actual area of operations, that is, the tactical battlefield.[11]

What is most interesting, though, is that organizing the private military industry by the services offered by equivalent military unit types more or less mirrors the distinctions made among firms within general corporate industry. The type of services that a firm offers and where they are located within the client's organization is how one categorizes the normal business outsourcing industry. Outsourcing firms are also broken down into three broad types (service providers, consultative firms, and noncore service outsourcing). Thus, the-tip-of-the-spear distinction—by military unit location— is analogous to how outsourcing's linkage with business chains also break down. This further illustrates the utility of a typology drawn from both contexts, as then cross-field parallels and lessons can be drawn.

The privatized military industry is thus organized into three broad sectors: *Military Provider Firms, Military Consultant Firms,* and *Military Support Firms.* The benefit of classifying the PMFs with this typology is that one can then explore not only the variation within the industry but also the variation in firms' organization, their operations, and impact. Broader statements can

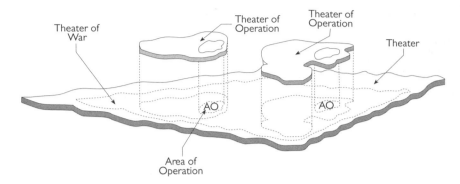

Figure 6.1. Military Theater Organization
From Dept. of the Army, *Contracting Support on the Battlefield,* FM 100-10-2. April 15, 1999.

be made about overall firm types, rather than being forced to rely on simple judgments that only apply to one specific firm. The result is a system of classification that not only reflects the unique complexion of the military service industry, but also, ultimately, yields theoretically informed findings that cross the political and business arenas.

The proviso of any such typology, however, is that it is a conceptual framework rather than a fixed definition of each and every firm. Some firms are clearly placed within one sector. However, similar to other industries and equivalent military functions, other firms lie at the sector borders or offer a range of services within various sectors. Moreover, with ongoing global consolidation into ever larger multinational PMFs, there is a potential growth in the number of these firms, such as Armorgroup, that cross sectors. Despite this, the framework remains robust. Such sector-spanning firms usually still divide down into internal divisions that fit within the defined sectors. As later chapters explore, the ensuing impact of a contract is determined by the sector that it would fall under.

MILITARY PROVIDER FIRMS

"Military Provider Firms" are defined by their focus on the tactical environment. In a military sense, such firms provide services at the forefront of the battlespace, by engaging in actual fighting, either as line units or specialists (for example, combat pilots) and/or direct command and control of field units. This purchaser/"provider" split is drawn from common business terminology. It defines those firms that supplement the client's core activity at the implementation level of the business chain, often having direct contact with the customer base.[12]

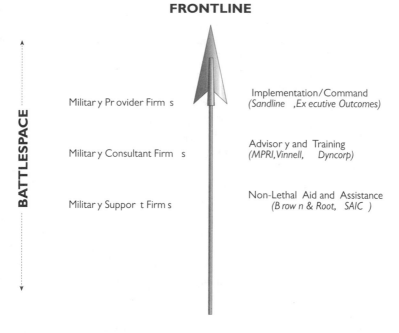

FRONTLINE

BATTLESPACE

Militar y Pr ovider Firm s

Implementation/Command
(*Sandline ,Ex ecutive Outcomes*)

Militar y Consultant Firm s

Advisor y and Training
(*MPRI, Vinnell,   Dyncorp*)

Militar y Suppor t Firm s

Non-Lethal Aid and Assistance
(*B row n & Root, SAIC*)

Figure 6.2. "Tip of the Spear" Typology
Firms distinguished by range of services, level of force.

Executive Outcomes, Sandline, SCI, and NFD are the classic examples of this type of privatized military implementers, having run active combat operations in Angola, Sierra Leone, Papua New Guinea, Indonesia, and elsewhere. Firms that fill specific military specialties on the battlefield, such as Airscan's capability to perform standoff military reconnaissance for the U.S., Colombian, and Angolan governments or Sukhoi's air force leased out to Ethiopia, are also included in this category. Some nonmilitary corollaries to firms in this sector include sales brokerage firms such as Advantage Crown and Kelly Clark, that represent multiple manufacturers who have outsourced their retail force, or "quick fill" contracting firms that work in the computer programming industry.

Typical clients of firms in the provider sector tend to be those with comparatively low military capability, faced with immediate, high threat situations. Firms within this sector tend to offer clients two types of contracts, providing either a) overall unit packages, or b) specialized "force multipliers." In the first case, the firm provides the client a stand-alone tactical military unit. Although firms often provide small combat teams, sometimes they provide large-scale, combined-arms units that could operate independently on the battlefield. In Sierra Leone, Executive Outcomes deployed a battalion-sized unit on the ground, supplemented by artillery, transport and combat helicopters, fixed wing combat and transport aircraft, a transport ship, and all types of ancillary specialists (such as first aid and civil affairs). In this type of situation, the firm is not supplementing the client's pre-existing forces, but rather providing an alternative or even replacement to them. Some firms make the marketing analogy to the changes in the computing industry (the operations of Dell in the late 1990s as compared to the IBM of the 1980s). Rather than selling only the hardware, they also deliver a workable package, containing all the elements the client needs to make use of modern military technology, that is, the hardware, software, personnel, installation, training, and implementation.[13]

Although these firms deploy units that are often much smaller in manpower relative to their client's adversaries, their effectiveness lies not in their size, but in their comprehensive training, experience, and overall skill at battlefield judgment, all in fundamentally short supply in the chaotic battlefields of the last decade.[14] Utilizing coordinated movement and intelligent application of firepower, their strength is their ability to arrive at the right place at the right moment. The fundamental reality of modern warfare is that in many cases such small tactical units can achieve strategic goals.[15] It must be remembered that their combat adversaries are often light on military training and may even have a core cadre that is also small in number. Charles Taylor launched his rebellion in Liberia with only a few dozen men, as did Sankoh in Sierra Leone and Kabila in Zaire/DRC. Equally small numbers of top-level military experts, added to the opposing sides, could have been more than enough to tilt the balance at the early stages of these wars.[16]

However, it is more common for military providers to offer the second type of contract, as "force multipliers." The firm's employees play active roles alongside those of the client, but in a way designed to make the overall combination more effective. Typically, their employees provide either specialized capabilities too cost-prohibitive for the local force to develop on its own (such as flying advanced fighter jets or operating artillery control systems), or they may be distributed across the forces of the client, in order to provide general leadership and experience to a greater number of individual units. In the first case, using a firm to fill out specialty roles may provide a local force the combined arms capability that it would otherwise lack, or provide an edge in one critical combat domain—such as gaining control of the air. It is important to note that even clients with relatively strong militaries might choose this option of hiring private specialists from the provider sector, in order to have the very best of all fields.[17]

In the second case, of specialized "force multipliers," the effectiveness of the generalists is not found in their numbers, but in their skills at battlefield assessment, management, and coordination. At the tactical level, provider firm's employees can act as mini-generals, providing the expertise that is often lacking.[18] As their client's forces are often marginally trained and disciplined, the addition of a few highly skilled personnel to 'stiffen the backs' can have dramatic impact, akin to past colonial armies that mixed tribal levees with trained officers.[19] Another more recent example is the impact that a small number of U.S. special force personnel had when distributed among Northern Alliance forces in Afghanistan.

A final note regarding firms in this sector must be made. As is explored later, this is the most controversial sector of the private military industry. Provider firms also tend to be the most "virtual" in structure, with the concurrent advantages of quick restructuring and transferability. They tend to attract the most negative public attention and are at greater risk of external regulations being implemented that may prove damaging to their business.

For this reason, understandably, most firms within this sector are quick to deny that they offer tactical military services, often claiming just to be military advisers (one is reminded of the descriptions of the U.S. military's early role in Vietnam). In many cases, however, the reality does not reflect their claims. As a former major from the British Parachute Regiment, who now works for such a firm, tells, "If we do operate in civil wars, we are there as 'advisers' or 'trainers.' But, of course we are on the frontline, and the excuse is so that we can see if our training is working."[20] Others claim to only be providing "security" or "guarding facilities." But, as noted earlier, this security entails military-style protection, from military threats in the midst of war. As a result, identifying the specific firms within this sector is often a daunting task. It is certain, however, that as long as a demand for military provider services exists, some PMFs will agree to engage in active combat.[21]

MILITARY CONSULTING FIRMS

Firms that provide advisory and training services integral to the operation and restructuring of a client's armed forces characterize the second sector within the military services industry. They offer strategic, operational, and/or organizational analysis. They have engagement with the client at all levels, except at what businessmen would describe as "customer contact." That is, they do not operate on the battlefield itself. Although their presence can reshape the strategic and tactical environment through the re-engineering of a local force, it is the client who bears the final risks on the battlefield. This is the critical distinction from firms in the provider sector. The impact of consulting firms, however, is not any less than those in the other sectors. Their employees may not engage in direct combat activities, but in modern warfare, the application of knowledge and training are often just as valuable as the application of firepower.[22]

Examples of firms in this sector include Levdan, Vinnell, and MPRI. The best nonmilitary corollaries to this type are management consultants, with similar sub-sector divisions. For example, some nonmilitary consulting firms, such as McKinsey or Bain, focus on the high-level strategic side similar to MPRI, whereas other subsector firms such as Arthur Anderson tend focus on the more technical aspects, similar to what Dyncorp does in the military sector.[23]

The typical client of a military consulting firm tends to be in the midst of military restructuring or aiming for a dramatic increase in its capabilities. Their needs are often not as immediate as those who hire firms in the provider sector, but the contract requirements are often more long-term, as well as more lucrative.

The primary advantage of using outside consultants is access to and delegation of a greater amount of experience and expertise than almost any standing public military force in world can match. For example, MPRI has behind it the skill-sets of thousands of ex-officers, including four-star generals. The addition of such a brain trust to any force can provide a powerful military advantage.

The "commander's estimate," as it is known in military parlance, is at the crux of firms' offerings in the military consulting sector. In essence, the client is seeking the firm's expert military advice. The typical consultant contract specifies a situation facing the client —be it how to recapture a rebel province, or how to restructure a military. The firm then analyzes what might be done to solve the predicament.[24]

An important intra-sector distinction is then between firms that offer pure analysis and those that offer the consultation and training linked to these recommendations (but not implementation—the distinction with the provider sector). In an ideal setting, the firms would provide unbiased evaluation in this initial estimate. But since there often exists the possibility of further contracts down the road, many military consultancy firms are motivated to make recommendations that seek to steer future business their own way. In common business terms, this is described as gaining "traction" with a client, through the establishment of a long-term relationship. The aim is for repeating contracts.[25]

Hence, the irony of contracting with consulting sector firms is that sometimes their hire, although originally intended to build a self-sufficient force, may have the reverse effect. By turning over critical self-evaluation tasks, the client can become increasingly hamstrung in its own decision-making processes. It gains no experience from its own activities and becomes increasingly more reliant on the firm's expertise. Familiarity also breeds a greater trust in the hired company as an honest broker. Although this can be a positive development, it also enhances the firm's opportunity to later press the need for additional contracts.[26] These new contracts may or may not be necessary, but as the client's dependence grows, it will be less able to decide on its own.

A number of firms in the military provider sector, such as Sandline, have made public moves toward transforming themselves into consulting firms because of the greater legitimacy and profit margins within in the military consulting sector.[27] The line between advising and implementing, however, sometimes can be quite fuzzy; often, if a trained soldier has been hired to teach, it is difficult to duck out of the way when the opportunity comes to put training into practice.[28] During the Gulf War, for example, employees of Vinnell accompanied their Saudi National Guard units into combat at the battle of Khafji.[29] Thus, firms that self-identify as military consultants may not always be such, and close observation of their actual activities may be required.

MILITARY SUPPORT FIRMS

Firms that provide supplementary military services characterize the third sector of the industry. These privatized functions, include nonlethal aid and assistance, including logistics, intelligence, technical support, supply, and transportation. As with what has occurred with supply-chain management in general industry, the benefit of this type of military outsourcing is that these firms specialize in secondary tasks not part of the overall core mission of the client. Thus, they are able to build capabilities and efficiencies that a client military cannot sustain. The client's own military, in turn, can concentrate on its primary business of fighting. The most common clients of such support firms are those engaged in immediate, but long-duration interventions, that is, standing forces or organizations in need of a surge capacity.

The military support sector is not only the largest in scope and revenue, but also the most varied in subsectors. Interestingly, it is also the sector least explored in the context of military privatizing.

Often misunderstood as just traditional "contractors," military support sector firms are typically not included in analyses of the privatized military industry. The simple reason is that their often mundane operations appear less "mercenary." However, as with their equivalent support units in the military, although they do not participate in the execution or planning of combat action, they fill functional needs critical to overall combat operations. Like the troops serving in the support units that these firms are hired to replace or supplant, military support sector employees are also still open to combat threats. One side's rear area is another side's deep battle.[30] The difference is that in the past, whenever their duties took on a role more integral to the military, contractors lost their civilian status and were replaced by official military units, such as the Seabees, the U.S. Navy construction battalions in World War II.[31]

Whereas the firms in the provider and consulting sectors tend to be akin to what economists term 'freestanding,' that is, originally established for the specific purpose of utilizing domestic advantages to serve targeted external markets, military support firms often are more like traditional multinational corporations.[32] Typically, they have either expanded into the military support market after reaching a level of dominance in their original business ventures elsewhere, or found it to be an external area where they could maximize previously established commercial capabilities. For example, Ronco was once a development aid company that has since moved into demining. BRS originally focused on domestic construction for large-scale civilian projects, but has since found military deployment support and logistics a profitable area in which to leverage its prior expertise and resources. BRS augmented U.S. forces in Somalia, Haiti, Rwanda, Bosnia, and most recently secured a $1 billion dollar contract in support of KFOR in Kosovo.[33] This last figure illustrates that firm revenue tend to grow in size as one moves up the industry typology. Other military support sector firms include Boeing Services, Holmes, and Narver. Parallels of general support sector firms include companies such as Marriott-Sodexho that offers institutional facilities management and, of course, general supply-chain management firms that many military support sector firms are modeled after.

The military's core task is generally perceived as combat, so it is far from surprising that the primary areas for support sector firms has been in the more mundane combat support sectors. Although it was once seen as unsuitable for privatization, the military logistics role—transporting and supplying the troops on the battlefield—has been notable for the extent of this sort of privatization. Part of the reason for this lies in the greater number of multinational operations (which have the inherent problem of national differences in equipment and procedures), in regions with weak local infrastructures. The other part is a result of downsizing and elimination of logistics units, as forces try to squeeze the fat out of their organizations.[34] During the Gulf War, private U.S. firms undertook almost the entire logistics and maintenance support for the Saudi army.[35] In more recent overseas deployments, the U.S., British, French, Canadian, and Australian militaries have all outsourced major parts of their logistics to private military firms.[36] Indeed, the Canadian armed forces recently privatized its entire supply chain, including weapons maintenance and transportation, to the British firm, Tibbett and Britten. Other clients of the firm include Wal-Mart and the Gap, such that critics jokingly termed the outsourcing plan "Warmart."[37]

Just because it is increasingly being outsourced, however, one should not doubt the importance of logistics to overall military operations. In the very words of official U.S. military doctrine, "Since the dawn of military history, logistical capabilities have controlled the size, scope, pace, and effectiveness of military operations . . . Logistical capabilities must be designed to survive and operate under attack; that is, they must be designed for combat effectiveness, not peacetime efficiency."[38]

The privatizing of rear-area or supplementary military functions, though,

` has not been limited to logistics. Firms active in the support sector run the gamut from Ronco and Special Clearance Services that clear land mines to Strategic Communications Lab, a firm that provides psychological operations (PSYOPs). As with the other subsectors in the industry, the expansion and development of information technology has enhanced military opportunities for private firms.

Some of the more intriguing subsectors of the private military industry have been that of privatized intelligence and information warfare. At all levels of warfare, these functions, which involve gaining knowledge about an opponent, while denying them knowledge of oneself, are critical to military success. Thus, they traditionally have been restricted to the most trusted institutions of the state. However, a growing assortment of private firms now offer these services, many of them formed by intelligence analysts and operators made superfluous since the end of the Cold War. Although it sounds somewhat shocking that private firms could undertake such roles, in a sense their growth is a throwback to the past. For example, during the American civil war, the Pinkerton detective agency (now part of Securitas A.B.) was the primary intelligence organization for the Union side; that is, until the Union considered the area serious enough to develop its own spy forces.[39]

Part of the rationale for this outsourcing is that the commercialization of high technology has meant that the intelligence capabilities limited to the superpowers just a few years ago are now available to any willing buyer. Localized reporting that once could only be accessed at great risk by being smuggled across borders is now readily available on the Internet, as can the reams of state statistical data that was once the sole provenance of intelligence agencies . Many private intelligence firms market organized databases of these materials.

That a great deal of information comes from open sources does not change its importance. According to former CIA Director James Woolsey, about 95 percent of all intelligence comes from open sources; the other 5 percent is from covert sources, in the case of the United States, predominantly satellite surveillance.[40] Even in this area, the proliferation of civilian earth observation satellites and improvements in image analysis techniques mean that the private market is already eroding the great power monopoly.[41] After the terrorist attacks of September 11, the CIA and U.S. Air Force even began contracting out some of their high resolution, satellite photography for operations in Afghanistan to Space Imaging and Digital Globe, two companies based in Colorado.[42]

Indeed, it appears that the private intelligence subsector (meaning the retrieval of information concerning an enemy or possible enemy or an area) is at the initial stage of a huge boom. For many nations and political groups, most of their intelligence analysis and operations are gradually being outsourced to private firms and consultants.[43] In Australia, for example, even the decision concerning who within the government receives national security clearance is made by a private intelligence firm, Business Risk Services.[44] The results may be surprising improvements in effectiveness and efficiency. In 1995, for instance, the CIA held a public competition to see who could gather the best information, most quickly, for a specified policy scenario (in this case, a possible intervention into Burundi). The winner was not a team from one of the various U.S. government and military intelligence agencies. Rather, the winner was from a Washington-based company, Open Source Solutions; in fact, the CIA's own team finished last.[45]

Information warfare is another fertile ground for private firms. In addition to governments, who both increasingly utilize, and are at risk from, politically motivated information warfare attacks, private corporations are also players in the unregulated cyperspace. The stakes are quite high and we are already seeing the beginning of what one might conceive as corporate conflict.[46] In 1999 alone, the Fortune 1000 companies sustained losses of more than $45 billion from thefts of their proprietary information through suspected corporate-sponsored hacking, better known as "Netspionage."[47]

The result is a new breed of support sector companies that carry out the maintenance and protection of the lines of communication off the battlefield.[48] Solutions to problems in cyberspace are primarily technical, but also involve military specialties and approaches, such that many of the top firms have a distinctly military-related background and mentality. As an illustration, the firm I-Defense has worked with the defense ministries of both the United States and Great Britain, the National Security Agency, and the CIA. I-Defense executives include James Adams, a leading thinker on changes in warfare, Sir Michael Rose, a retired British general who commanded the 22nd SAS regiment and the UNPROFOR operation in Bosnia, and Kurt Campbell, a former U.S. Assistant Secretary of Defense.[49] In fact, the firm has already established agreements with major corporations such as Microsoft, Citigroup, and Itochu, an indicator of further cross-industry ties likely to occur between PMFs and beyond.[50]

SEVEN

The Military Provider Firm: Executive Outcomes

> The [end of the] Cold War left a huge vacuum and I identified a niche in the market.
>
> —Eben Barlow, Founder of Executive Outcomes

Executive Outcomes (EO) is the company in the privatized military industry that is perhaps the best known. From the murky apartheid past of its founders to its slick corporate advertising, it is not an exaggeration to say that Executive Outcomes has become emblematic of the overall phenomenon of corporate armies. It is also the most celebrated player in the implementation subsector, conducting openly public military operations all over the globe. As such, Executive Outcomes embodies much of what any definition of a military provider firm is all about. The irony of all this notoriety is that Executive Outcomes formally dissolved itself in early 1999 and thus is no longer open for business (more on this later).

Beyond the direct military impact the firm had on numerous wars, its range of political and business links made it a viable power in Africa and beyond. Although its corporate mission was similar to other PMFs, EO's defining organizational characteristics lay in its origins in the elite forces of the apartheid-era South African Defence Force (SADF) and its tight business links to other mining and oil corporations. Its success was partly due to this integration into a larger economic holding. This allowed both (the PMF and its association of companies) to intervene into areas where governments and other companies feared to go.

With its ability to organize and deploy an elite fighting force in a matter of days, Executive Outcomes was not only the most notorious example of a military provider firm in its purest form, but, as even its most fierce critics admit, one of the most effective. The firm also truly captures the dilemmas and complexities that mark the provider subsector. At the very same time that EO was accused of being "a mercenary army of racist killers," humanitarian groups, such as the "Children Associated with the War" organization in Sierra Leone, were formally thanking it for its work.[1]

ORGANIZATIONAL CHARACTERISTICS

Executive Outcomes was founded in 1989 by Eben Barlow, a former assistant commander of the 32nd Battalion of the SADF and then agent with the South African Civil Cooperation Bureau (CCB). Such innocuous unit names belie the fact that the 32nd Battalion was one of the most elite strike forces in South Africa's bush wars with its neighbors in the 1970s and 1980s. Known as the "terrible ones" by its opponents, the 32nd was honored at the time for having the highest kill ratio of any unit in the SADF, but later accused of egregious human rights violations by the South African Truth Commission.[2]

Equally, the CCB was anything but a mild civil organization. It was discovered in 1990 to be the front for a covert assassination and espionage unit, used to eliminate enemies of the apartheid regime abroad.[3] While in the CCB, Barlow, who is recognizable by his one green and one blue eye, was assigned to Western Europe. There, he was in charge of spreading disinformation against Nelson Mandela's African National Congress (ANC), for example, releasing propaganda in England that the ANC was working with IRA terrorists. He was also responsible for setting up front corporations to evade sanctions and sell South African weapons abroad. During this time, Barlow is suspected to have made many of his corporate world contacts that would later prove useful for EO. The sophisticated manner in which Executive Outcomes was linked within a complex structure of multinational holdings, purposefully created to mask its operations and the exact involvement of its allied firms, also seems to be a result of his CCB expertise. Thus in many ways, Barlow was the modern heir to Albrecht Wallenstein—an innovative military mind, whose genius lay in recognizing business opportunity and creating a new organizational methodology of warfare.

Most of Executive Outcomes's personnel, excepting some specialists, such as Ukrainian pilots, tended to share this background in the SADF special forces.[4] They were drawn from elite units as the Parachute Brigade, the Reconnaissance Commandos, and 32nd Battalion. These elements were the leading forces in South Africa's efforts to undermine its neighbors, carrying out covert operations in Mozambique, Namibia, and Angola. Other personnel were reputedly part of Koevoet, a police counterinsurgency unit that is known to have committed many atrocities in the Namibian war, including the torture and killing of prisoners.[5] When the apartheid regime ended, most of these units were summarily disbanded, leaving thousands of veterans available for work (close to 60,000 soldiers left the SADF in total).

These veterans became the base of EO's employee pool. Many joined the firm for financial reasons, as salaries were quite attractive, ranging from $2,000 to $13,000 per month (dependent on experience and expertise). The average pay was about $3,500 a month for soldiers, $4,000 for officers, and

$7,500 for aircrews, all importantly paid in more stable U.S. dollars.[6] Such salaries were a huge lure, as they came out roughly to five times that of equivalent duties in the South African military and ten times that of the average soldier in other African militaries (who are rarely actually paid). Executive Outcomes was also innovative in being among the first PMFs to standardize the provision of life insurance and full medical coverage to all its employees.[7]

Despite the financial enticements, many employees in the firm also cited psychological explanations for joining up. When they returned home from fighting the former regime's dirty wars, they received what they saw as rough treatment by the South African transitional government. Where their services had once been lauded, now it was a source of embarrassment to the South African state. The disavowal of their activities and failure to honor their losses stung those soldiers. Instead of seeing themselves as evil, they saw the operations in the border wars as a service to their nation. In the interim, however, the South African "nation" had become more broadly defined.

As such, there was also a profound sense of "post-apartheid redemption," that drew the veterans to the firm.[8] EO personnel prided themselves in using the same skills they had learned in the SADF to protect local civilian populations, who in some cases they once had targeted in their public duties. In fact, during their operations in Sierra Leone, local civilians treated them like heroes. When they entered some towns, crowds would gather and begin chanting and cheering. A quote from one local woman captures the respect felt for the EO employees, "They saved us. They are saints!"[9] For the former defenders of apartheid—one of the most despised political systems ever devised—it was a novel experience.[10]

Using ex-SADF personnel had several advantages for the firm. It ensured common training, a pre-existing hierarchy, and extensive combat experience in low intensity conflict and counter-insurgency operations. The company proudly advertised that it had over 5000 years of combat experience, far more than most armies can claim.

Executive Outcomes drew its forces from this ex-SADF pool of experience on a contract-by-contract basis. The original recruitment was mainly word of mouth, which also provided a check on personnel quality. The only constantly employed unit was at the Pretoria headquarters that served as a command center and kept a 24-hour radio watch. EO maintained no standing force in the barracks, but rather kept a database of immediately available personnel. It claimed it could call over 2,000 men on very short notice. Notably, approximately 70 percent of EO personnel were black Africans, which goes against common assumptions of it being a white mercenary company. The 32nd Battalion, from which the firm drew many of its employees, actually included numbers of Namibians and Angolans, who had an equally hard time returning to their home communities after the changes in government.

However, critics were right in pointing out that the officer-level positions of EO were primarily white.

EO promoted itself as providing five key services to clients: strategic and tactical military advisory services; an array of sophisticated military training packages in land, sea, and air warfare; peacekeeping or "persuasion" services; advice to armed forces on weapons selection and acquisition; and paramilitary services.[11] Training packages covered the entire realm of military operations, including everything from basic infantry training and armored warfare specialties to parachute operations.

EO'S CORPORATE NETWORK

Based in Pretoria, Executive Outcomes was officially just one subsidiary within a larger South African holding company/venture-capital firm, Strategic Resources Corporation (SRC). Its leadership, however, was also on the SRC board, indicating their greater influence in the broader organization. In addition to Executive Outcomes, SRC reportedly owned approximately twenty other companies associated with the military firm's operations, including the PMFs Lifeguard and Teleservices, which guarded Branch Energy mining concessions, and Saracen, another security provider in Uganda and Angola.[12] These firms are essentially stay-behind asset protection companies. As a general rule, they arrived after EO's departure, but concurrent with the arrival of Branch-Heritage mining operations. These firms then employed some of the same EO personnel who were willing to stay on in-country. Thus, EO could claim that it had officially ended its military operations and withdrawn from a country, while still maintaining a local presence. Engineering and logistics companies (such as Falconeer and Bridge International that supplied U.N.-related organizations) were also within the spokes of the SRC holding.

However, the SRC umbrella was a much more intricate corporate network, as an apparently close relationship existed (though denied officially) between the SRC umbrella holding in South Africa and the Branch-Heritage Group, a financial holding registered at the Plaza 107 building in London. In 1993, Executive Outcomes was also registered in England (where the laws against mercenaries were much more lax than in South Africa) with this holding. Branch-Heritage Group's senior director is Anthony Buckingham, a charismatic businessman and also a former SAS veteran known for his behind the scenes influence throughout Africa. Buckingham was at the center of both EO's first big contract in Angola and also Sandline's inception.[13]

Branch-Heritage Group includes a number of mining and oil concerns located around the world, and, not surprising, has investments in almost all the areas where Executive Outcomes has conducted major operations. Its businesses also then hired stay-behind security companies from the SRC holding company. Branch-Heritage has also been reputedly associated with Jupiter Mining in Guinea.[14] An apparent umbrella organization, Diamondworks, reportedly was the overall holding firm for all the Branch Energy firms. Diamondworks is registered on the Canadian stock exchange for public trading. A further indication of linkage is that many of the leading personnel from Branch-Heritage, Executive Outcomes, and Sandline have also served in some capacity for Diamondworks, including at the executive level.

It is thought that an unofficial part of a contract that Executive Outcomes made with cash-strapped countries was the provision of resource concessions to its related companies. Country resources were privatized into partially state-owned and partially Branch-Heritage-owned companies, which then, in turn, paid for Executive Outcomes' or its subsidiaries' security services. The companies deny this and claim that the relations between the SRC firms and Branch-Heritage mining firms were simply that of "good friends."[15] However, Branch Heritage certainly had a privileged position in the areas where EO operated, reportedly having a right of first refusal on lucrative mining claims and many of the director positions in ostensibly separate firms had the same persons filling them.[16]

To further complicate matters, the Branch-Heritage Group in London also owns the PMFs Sandline International and Ibis Air Air. Although Sandline was legally constituted in 1996 and is registered in the Bahamas, it was formerly known as Plaza 107 Ltd., and has its headquarters in the same building as the others in the London-based holding (and even reportedly once mistakenly used the Branch corporate letterhead).[17] Sandline's original director was Timothy Spicer, a retired British colonel in the Scots Guards, who previously had served as the spokesman for the UNPROFOR peacekeeping operation in Bosnia. Sandline also had a Washington office, headed by Col. Bernard McCabe, retired, a former U.S. Green Beret. At times, Sandline's operations have been almost impossible to differentiate from those of the other firms in the SRC holding. Many of the same personnel and equipment were used in both Papua New Guinea (where Sandline claimed to sub-contract Executive Outcomes employees) and in support of the ECOMOG peacekeeping operation in Sierra Leone (the firms supplied pilots for Nigerian Alpha jets and its own helicopter gunships).[18] Sandline also has publicly admitted to providing a "backup unit" for intervention on behalf of its "associate company" Lifeguard (the very same EO stay-behind firm that is part of the SRC).[19]

Another firm that is an integral part of the EO story is Ibis Air, which could be described as essentially the private air force of Executive Outcomes. It was a separate holding in the umbrella group, but was so closely bound to the firm to be almost indistinguishable to outsiders. Ibis Air accompanied EO in its most significant operations, tending to be leased out in a separate contract to EO or to the client/state that had hired EO. Its directors notably included Lafras Luitingh, the former recruiting director of the SADF Reconnaissance Commando unit and then of Executive Outcomes itself.

The links with the Ibis Air gave Executive Outcomes the ability to lift and deploy a fighting force anywhere around the globe. This is a capability that most state militaries lack. The aircraft directly owned by Ibis Air reportedly included at least two Andover military transport aircraft, two or three used 727 passenger jets (that it bought from American Airlines for $550,000 total), a number of Russian Mi-17 armed transport helicopters, Mi-8 cargo helicopters, Mi-24 attack helicopters, a squadron of Swiss-made Pileuas training aircraft converted to fire air-to-ground rockets, and Mig-23 advanced jet fighter-bombers. It also had the capability to lease and operate any type of combat aircraft available on the world market, which allowed it to surge out in a hurry. For example, during the height of the Angola and Sierra Leone operations in 1995, Executive Outcomes/Ibis Air reportedly operated about 20 helicopters.[20] EO/Ibis Air pilots have also flown Su-25 close-support bombers and Mig-27 ground-attack fighters that were loaned out to the firm by the Angolan air force. The Angolan air force had the hardware from its former Soviet patrons, but lacked the combat skills to use them effectively.

The linked capabilities provided by Ibis Air (despite it formally being a separate company) gave Executive Outcomes a decided advantage in the battlefield. It became part of company policy that all operations have the support of at least one attack helicopter and a medical transport plane on standby—certainly not a normal *Fortune* 500 business strategy, but a wise one, considering the circumstances of its business.

As illustrated by Ibis Air's inventory/order of battle, Executive Outcomes preferred to use ex-Soviet weaponry, often bought by the client to EO's specifications. These weapons were cheap, due to Cold War overproduction, and easy to obtain, usually from Eastern European dealers. In particular, the Soviet Mi-24 "Hind" attack helicopter, armored with titanium and equipped with four-barreled Gatling guns and a 40mm grenade launcher, was one of the most effective and intimidating weapons that the firm had in its operations. In addition to the Migs and Hinds, EO also made use of former Soviet armored vehicles in mechanized ground attacks, including BMP-2 infantry fighting vehicles and BTR-60 armored personnel carriers. Although the firm moved light, the ability to employ such heavy equipment whenever necessary was a characteristic of Executive Outcomes; during its Sierra Leone operation, it even had a freighter stationed off of Freetown's harbor.[21]

HISTORY OF MAJOR OPERATIONS

As the political winds changed in South Africa, Barlow left the state military and formed Executive Outcomes in 1989, originally as a counterintelligence consultancy firm. The company was registered in South Africa and took as its corporate symbol the paladin chess piece, from the 1960s U.S. television series, *Have Gun, Will Travel* (about a freelancing gun for hire in the Old West). Its first contracts were to provide covert espionage training to the SADF special forces units, as well as security provision, training, and "the gathering of market-related information and marketing warfare" to such major corporate clients as the diamond firm DeBeers.[22]

EO soon realized that it had discovered a growth industry. Word of mouth spread about its effectiveness and, by 1991, the firm had started running operations outside of South Africa. These initial efforts included: mine security efforts; infiltrating and penetrating organized crime smuggling syndicates; and operations for a South American government (rumored to be Colombia), conducting clandestine counter drug raids that it termed "discretionary warfare."[23] The contract that would bring EO into the forefront of the field, however, was in Angola, ironically enough where many of its employees had just spent the previous decade fighting.

Angola: Demonstrating the Power of the Private Firm

Angola is a nation blessed with natural resources and as such should be a country with a thriving economy. It is Africa's second largest oil producer after Nigeria, with recent discoveries suggesting it could soon become the largest. It is the sixth largest supplier of imported crude oil to the United States.[24] The tragedy, however, is that instead of benefiting from this wealth Angola has been at war for the last three decades. The result is that the country ranks 160th among the world's nations in terms of quality of life.[25]

The war in Angola can be traced to its abrupt independence from Portuguese colonial rule in 1975. At this time, several hundred thousand Portuguese—virtually the entire educated population—abandoned the country, but not before stripping it of everything of value, including, in many cases, even taking their doorknobs.[26] The new Angolan nation was thus left with few citizens trained in statecraft, industry, or agriculture, but a ready supply of warring guerilla armies. Then, for the better part of the next quarter-century, the superpowers, their proxies, and white minority governments in the region stoked the conflict by injecting cash, arms, and military personnel. The Soviet Union and its allies supported the communist Movimento Popular da Libertacao de Angola (MPLA) party that was able to seize the government, while the United States and the South Africans supported Jonas Savimbi's National Union for the Total Independence of Angola (UNITA), which continued the rebellion from the hinterland. At differing times, the war took on conventional and guerilla war aspects, as the conflict flowed back and forth between the state army, the Forcas Armadas Angolanas (FAA), and Savimbi's rebel UNITA force.

Many of EO's employees had been involved in the Angolan conflict in the late 1980s, while serving in the SADF. On numerous occasions, the SADF intervened to prevent UNITA's defeat and also to punish Angolan support of rebels fighting apartheid rule in Namibia and South Africa. However, by the time EO became involved in the Angolan conflict, the tide of war had turned. The end of the Cold War had left the Angolan government without external support, as many of its Soviet-bloc allies now ceased to exist. By 1993, UNITA had advanced from its bases in the interior to the government's coastal bastions. The regime was on its back heels.

The critical turning point occurred in March 1993, when UNITA captured the oil facilities in the coastal town of Soyo. These specific fields were critical in two ways: the oil resources were an essential government source of finance and the facilities in question were owned by Sonogal, the state oil company, and Branch-Heritage Oil, the same company in the overall umbrella owned by Tony Buckingham. UNITA would not allow the companies to remove their oil and drilling equipment, that they were leasing for $20,000 per day, and the FAA did not have the capability to recapture the site without blowing up the valuable equipment in the process.[27]

The exact details of the initial contact are not public, but what is known is that this is the point that Executive Outcomes first made its mark in the Angolan conflict. The firm was hired to recapture the town of Soyo (and Sonogal and Heritage Oil's valuable assets along with it) on behalf of the Angolan army. An EO unit of about 80 men quickly launched a commando assault that, after fierce fighting, seized the installation from the UNITA rebels.

The Soyo operation provided the first demonstration of the firm's true combat capabilities. Not knowing that the commandos were actually former SADF soldiers, who had fought alongside them earlier in the war, UNITA claimed that white mercenaries were fighting for the government. The oil companies initially responded that the men were actually just "security guards" defending the site, which was a rather remarkable claim, considering that UNITA was in control of the facility at the time. However, the truth of the operation soon came out and EO took public credit.

The Soyo operation and the fact that EO became quite open about its involvement in the battle sent shockwaves around the region. Observers were amazed both at the company's overall combat effectiveness and that it was now fighting alongside the Angolan government, which had been the fiercest enemy of the private firm's employees when they were serving in a previous public capacity. It created layers of suspicions. Many back in the South African military establishment saw this as disloyal. Equally, the Angolan army was suspicious of their new allies. UNITA, in turn, felt betrayed by its former South African compatriots.

The importance of the Soyo battle was that it demonstrated that a private firm could play an integral role in a conflict, by providing military services for hire to the highest bidder. This point was solidified when, as soon as EO's men withdrew from Soyo, UNITA retook the facility from the Angolan army. Without the PMF, the Angolan government was back to square one.

In light of this and continuing losses suffered by the FAA, EO was offered a $40 million, one-year contract in September 1993 to help train the state army and direct front-line operations. It was at this same time that most observers felt the government was teetering on the edge of defeat. Reportedly, both Buckingham and Simon Mann (a former British officer, now in the mineral business) played key roles in brokering the deal, which occurred at the personal behest of the Angolan president.[28] EO was reportedly paid by state monies that had originally generated from Ranger (a Canadian mining firm associated with Buckingham). In turn, the funding firms allegedly received payment in oil and mining concessions.[29]

With EO direction, the Angolans re-established the 16th Brigade, which ironically, had been shattered by the South African military in the 1980s. The 5,000 troops and 30 pilots of the brigade were trained in new tactics and skills, ranging from motorized infantry to engineering and artillery. The frequent shared battle experience of the Angolan troops and their South African instructors, though on different sides of the battlefield, meant that past mistakes could be discussed and corrected.[30] EO personnel, who totaled approximately 500 men, along with their air assets, later fought alongside of and operationally commanded the force. In addition to retraining and fighting along with the 16th Brigade, EO also supplied aircrew that flew Angolan air force combat aircraft, and special forces that conducted commando operations against UNITA command centers.[31]

With tactical assistance from Executive Outcomes air assets, that struck at UNITA troops concentrations and launched raids all over the countryside, the joint EO/FAA force became the spearhead of a government counter-offensive. It met with great success and retook all the major Angolan cities and most resource areas. UNITA was forced out of its bases in the northwest and cut off from arms and food supplies. EO and the FAA ended up securing the entire oil region of Angola and much of the diamond producing areas. Importantly, these victories solidified the government's ability to make arms purchases and payments abroad, key to rebuilding the rest of its army.

Beaten back and stunned by the new tactics, which included deep penetration air-ground assaults and night attacks never used before in the conflict, the UNITA rebels agreed to a peace accord in Lusaka in November 1994. In a seeming recognition of EO's effectiveness, UNITA made a condition to its signature that the company leave the country (Savimbi had already promised to execute any captured EO "mercenaries," but never got the opportunity). As the peace agreement was tenuous, the company's contract with the Angolan government continued on for a year. But, after personal lobbying by U.S. President Clinton, it was ended in December 1995.[32]

In the aftermath of the contract's termination, a U.N. peacekeeping operation deployed, but was unable to secure the peace and fighting resumed (in what was to become a recurrent theme with EO). The war continued for several more years (at the time of writing a new peace accord had been signed in the wake of Savimbi's death), but the government, controlling the resource-rich zones that EO helped secure, was in the superior position.

Although some critics say Executive Outcomes's success in Angola has been overstated, it is evident that it played a determinate role in ending that stage of the war. The company's arrival coincided with the exact turning point in the government's war effort. It not only contributed training and tactical advice, but also played a critical active role in operations that exploited UNITA's weaknesses and destroyed its morale. EO provided the Angolan army with crucial military expertise that it lacked, giving it a distinct edge over its opponent.[33] As a UNITA soldier stated at the time,

> We used to know we could sleep well at night. In this recent war, new tactics meant that fighting continued at night and that light infantry units led by these Executive Outcomes guys would come deep behind our lines. We could no longer rest. It weakened us very much. It is the new tactics in which they trained the FAA [the Angolan government army] that made the difference. They introduced a new style of warfare to Angola. We were not used to this.[34]

Defense strategists agreed with the soldier and credit EO with being an essential component in reinvigorating the FAA and turning the war's tide.[35] Both Savimbi's demand that the firm leave and the resurgence of the war after it had left also provide indicators of just how important the firm was to changing the war's dynamics.

Sierra Leone: The Firm Saves the State

About the same time that the situation in Angola had begun to wind down for Executive Outcomes, things began to completely fall apart for the government of Sierra Leone.

Akin to Angola, the sad irony is that Sierra Leone should be one of the richest countries in Africa. It is endowed with vast amounts of the highest-grade diamonds in the world, in-ground kimberlites.[36] In fact, diamonds as large as 103 carats have been discovered by children foraging; single mines, such as the one Executive Outcomes was later able to secure for Diamondworks, can produce over 200,000 carats per year.

Instead, none of Sierra Leone's wealth has benefited its populace. The post-colonial regime led by Siaka Stevens, quickly devolved into a one party kleptocracy. Stevens intentionally weakened his military, so that it could not threaten him and his coterie, who were enjoying the fabulous wealth of the country while the rest of the country languished.[37] As noted in Chapter 1, by the 1990s, the country ranked last in the U.N. Human Development Report.[38] The reason for this lie in its underdevelopment, corrupt governance, and the terrible civil war that resulted.

The fighting in Sierra Lone began in March 1991, when a small group of fighters led by Foday Sankoh crossed the border from Liberia, fighting under the flag of the "Revolutionary United Front" (RUF). The RUF had originally been founded by a group of exiled students opposed to Stevens's rule. Sankoh was a bitter, poorly schooled, but charismatic former army corporal, who had trained in Britain in the 1950s. Having been kicked out of the army for suspicion of being involved in a coup, he became a commercial photographer. Fairly unsuccessful at that, he joined the RUF and quickly took over the group's military wing. He soon forced out the politically-minded student leaders. Sankoh then made integral connections while training at a revolutionary camp in Libya in the 1980s.[39] He made the acquaintance of Charles Taylor, an escaped convict from a jail in Plymouth, Massachusetts, who was an aspiring rebel leader in neighboring Liberia. Some years later, in 1991, Taylor's bid for power in Liberia had stalled when the Nigerian-led ECOMOG intervention force stepped in. Significantly, the Sierra Leone government had supported this operation and even allowed Freetown to be used as a base. In response, Taylor provided his old friend in the RUF with money, arms, and mercenaries to launch a campaign across the border to de-stabilize Sierra Leone.

Sankoh's attacks more than succeeded in that respect. The rebels were quick to demonstrate their brutality, decapitating the leaders of border communities and putting their heads on stakes. Although lacking any clearly defined political agenda, their willingness to use violence against the regime took advantage of the cleavages that split Sierra Leone (between town and country, and between the repatriated-slave elite and indigenous peoples). It appealed to those most dispossessed and alienated by the failure of postcolonial Sierra Leone. The RUF also built out its force by abducting children and forcing them to kill on its behalf.[40] The organization soon cut a swath of terror across the countryside, with its signature atrocity being the amputation of limbs.[41]

The government's ability to resist the RUF was undermined by its very corrupt nature. The army had been largely ceremonial, completely unprofessional, and recruited from among the same alienated youths as the RUF. Consequently, there was little resistance and towns and villages quickly fell to the rebels.

The military then tried to build up its forces in a fairly unwise manner, rapidly enlisting criminals and street kids (often as young as twelve). When this force deployed, the new soldiers lacked the most basic military training and many had never even fired their guns. The conscripts' daily ration of marijuana and rum did not help matters much either, and the government's military soon dissolved into a looting force that tended to target the civilian populace instead of the rebels. Reputedly, it also killed a number of its own senior officers when they rebuked them following defeats in the field.[42] "There were no coherent front lines, no political causes, and for the terrorised public, no place was safe. What had begun as a civil war had become civil chaos."[43]

The government then hired the Channel Islands-based Gurkha Security Group (GSC) to train its army and bring some sense of order. GSG was primarily made up of ex-Gurkha fighters (Nepalese nationals who served in British regiments, renown for their courage and use of the knife) and had experience guarding corporate assets during the wars in Mozambique and Angola. However, before the firm could make much headway, GSG suffered heavy casualties in a rebel ambush in February 1995. Importantly, it lost its local commander in the battle Bob Mckenzie (an American veteran of Vietnam, Rhodesia, and Croatia). Mckenzie was apparently then eaten by the rebels and his body emasculated, as a warning to other would-be interveners. Forewarned, GSG broke its contract with the government and left Sierra Leone.[44]

By April 1995, the rebel RUF force had advanced toward the capital. The sense of doom at the impending slaughter was such that embassies began to evacuate the city. Grasping at options (the U.N., U.K., and United States had all declined the government's request to intervene) the beleaguered regime hired Executive Outcomes. The contract was for approximately $15 million dollars and called for the defeat of the RUF and their clearance from the capital region and several key industrial sites.

Ironically enough, the leader of the government, Valentine Strasser (a 26-year-old army captain, who had taken over after the former president fled), had first heard about the company from articles in *Newsweek* and *Soldier of Fortune* magazines, illustrating how the firm's public approach worked to its benefit. It is also likely that EO was hired on the recommendation of the ubiquitous Anthony Buckingham, whose Branch-Heritage mining company had operations in Sierra Leone. The government could not afford to pay EO's startup fee, so Buckingham agreed to bankroll the operation in exchange for future diamond mining concessions in the Kono region (a calculated risk, as the area was rebel-held at the time).[45]

The original one-year contract called for a total of 160 EO personnel to be deployed on the ground. It was later supplemented by contracts for additional manpower that brought the total costs to $35 million, about $1.5 million per month for the 21 months that the firm was in the country. Given that the contract aim was to reestablish the government's control over the economically productive parts of the country and that it was a fraction of the overall military budget, it seemed a pretty good deal to the government.[46]

Executive Outcomes deployed the same month, with most of its troops flown directly from Angola (no passports or visas required). The force brought its own aircraft and was matched up with uniforms, weapons, and armored vehicles, provided by the government. Within nine days, the EO force had not only stopped the rebel advance, but sent them back 126 kilometers into the jungle interior, mainly through the skillful employment of helicopter gunships that had not been used in the conflict previously. Originally, the rebels were clueless as to what had hit them; the white, EO personnel blackened their faces and their equipment carried no distinguishing markings. But once it was figured out that the South African firm was behind the turn around, a reward of $75,000 dollars in diamonds was offered for anyone who could shoot down one of EO's helicopters.

EO originally had a three-month plan to win the war, but was surprised at the ease with which they drove back the poorly trained RUF. EO veterans of that campaign said that although they had some difficulty defeating UNITA in Angola, the RUF had been "child's play."[47] In the process of the initial operation to clear the capital, EO inflicted losses of several hundred killed and over 1,000 desertions on the rebel force.[48]

The firm's soldiers then began training a separate unit of army troops to operate with them. They also organized and trained units of a local tribal militia known as 'Kamajors' ("hunter" in the local Mende dialect). These were professional forest hunters knowledgeable about the jungle. The superstitious Kamajors also believed in juju (voodoo) fetishes, such as the magical ability of certain shirts to repel bullets, and some openly practice cannibalism, eating the heads and hearts of enemies killed in action.[49] The military training of the Kamajors would become significant later, as it created an additional armed force in Sierra Leone not tied to the government. The Kamajors' rise to power has since complicated domestic politics in Sierra Leone and also provides an illustration of the unintended consequences PMFs can have on conflicts.

After clearing the capital area, EO forces then moved on the Kono diamond fields in the eastern part of the country, which they retook in just two days, and were a critical prize as a source of ultimate payment (as in the Angolan operation). After that, the RUF's stronghold in the Kangari Hills was taken. It was seized in a ground assault bolstered by an additional 200 EO personnel, flown in from South Africa specifically for the operation and paid for in an additional, second contract.

Whereas the previous style of warfare prior to EO's arrival had been roadside ambushes and quick withdrawals, EO strategy mandated the constant pursuit and punishment of the rebel force, whenever it came into contact. It also made use of air and artillery assets and sought to engage the RUF in stand-up battles that the rebels were loathe to face. The firm ultimately pushed the RUF back to the border regions. Effectively defeated, the RUF agreed to negotiate with the government for the first time.

In February of 1996, such a measure of stability had been achieved that a multiparty civilian presidential election was conducted in Sierra Leone. (In the interim, a new leader, General Julius Bio, whom EO preferred to Strasser, had taken over the Sierra Leone government. The firm did not carry out, but did approve of the coup, as Bio was considered easier to work with.) Despite RUF opposition to the voting process, the elections brought into power Ahmed Tejan Kabbah, a former U.N. administrator. When the RUF pulled out of the peace agreement in October, EO went back into the field and destroyed its headquarters in the southeast of the country. In November, the RUF leader signed peace accords, which, as in Angola, mandated EO's withdrawal as a condition of signature.

After signing, "Sankoh conceded that, had EO not intervened, he would have taken Freetown and won the war."[50] At a total cost of $35 million dollars (significantly, just one-third of the government's annual military budget), the fighting in Sierra Leone had ceased and over one million displaced persons returned to their homes. Suffering less than 20 total casualties, including those from accidents and illness, the private firm had succeeded in bringing stability to two endemically conflict-ridden states.

However, the stability that Executive Outcomes engendered on the battlefield was not long lasting. Facing opposition from the international community for continued employment of the firm and expecting the deployment of a U.N. peacekeeping force, President Kabbah terminated the firm's contract early. Executive Outcomes left in January 1997. Due to renewed RUF opposition and the failure of any donors to supply the necessary $47 million bill, the expected U.N. force did not deploy and a Nigerian-led ECOMOG force entered the country in its place. At the same time, the Sierra Leone military began to agitate under civilian reforms.

EO had warned Kabbah that their premature departure had left the way open for another coup, predicting that one would occur within 100 days (company intelligence sources had ensured that at least two previous coup attempts had been forestalled). The firm then offered the president a new deal, to equip a 500-man paramilitary force and provide a private intelligence unit to protect the civilian cabinet. Either due to misguided trust in the capabilities of the regional organization's peacekeepers, the feeling that EO's contract price was too high, or simple indecision, Kabbah never replied to the company's offer.[51]

"This proved a mistake that crucially changed the balance of military force and upset whatever basis had existed for political accord"[52] EO's warning came to fruition; the coup came on the 95th day after it had left. In a bloody attack led by mid-level army officers who had been secretly cooperating with the rebels, Kabbah's civilian government was toppled in May 1997. The coalition of renegade soldiers and RUF fighters then terrorized the capital city, Freetown, pillaging homes and businesses in a practice they called "Operation Pay Yourself."[53] Mass killings and general chaos returned. The ECOMOG force pulled back to its camps. Government and U.N. officials sought protection in the offices of the EO-associated security companies, such as Lifeguard, that had stayed behind to guard mining properties. The general populace, however, was left unprotected.

This episode would lead to Kabbah's hire of Sandline International several months later to bring his regime back to power. Sandline used many of EO's tactics to destabilize the illegal military regime that followed the coup, in particular, training and equipping Kamajor units to act against the coup leaders. It also tactically assisted and advised the Nigerian-led intervention force in its drive to oust the combined coup/RUF force from the capital city in March 1998.

Sandline reportedly was promised $10 million to advise Kabbah's countercoup efforts and rebuild the Kamajor militia, flying in over 300 tons of weaponry. The financier this time was Rakesh Saxena, a former Thai banker. At the time, Saxena was under house arrest and awaiting extradition from Canada for his role in the BCCI bank defrauding (and reportedly embezzling $100 million from the Thai national bank). Saxena had several business interests in Africa and hoped to parley his support for Kabbah in exchange for diamond concessions in the Kono region.[54] It is unclear as to why EO was not brought back in, but possible explanations include the legacy of a negative relationship between Kabbah and EO, or a reluctance to use the highly publicized firm by Western governments that had privately sanctioned the countercoup strategy. In the end however, the same stockholders of the Branch-Heritage/SRC/Executive Outcomes consortium stood to benefit.

Sandline's operations in support of the countercoup were successful, with the coup/rebel force being driven from the capital. The aftermath, however, proved embarrassing to the Western powers. The firm's shipment of arms to the region was held to be in violation of the U.N. arms embargo. The British custom's agency launched legal proceedings and raided the firm's offices. Sandline responded that its operations had been with full knowledge of the British Foreign Ministry. This was originally denied, but then later proven true. The ensuing "Sandline Affair" nearly cost the job of British Foreign Minister Robin Cook, who at the time had been advocating an "ethical foreign policy."

Years after the government terminated its contract with EO, Sierra Leone has yet to recover. The fighting continued on until the RUF collapsed under the combined pressure of a rebuilt Sierra Leone Army, incursions by the Guinean army, and a revitalized U.N. force. Elections were finally held again in 2002. In the interim, however, roughly 10,000 civilians have been killed by the same RUF organization that the firm had once defeated in a quick and easy fashion.

EO'S SECRETS TO SUCCESS: SKILLS AND SPIN-OFFS

Executive Outcomes had operations in Uganda, Kenya, South Africa, Indonesia, Congo, and a number of other states. But the Angolan and Sierra Leone episodes capture the impact that an effective military provider firm can have in altering the process and outcome of a conflict. The reasons for EO's particular success lay in its proficiency in counterguerilla warfare and its location within a larger corporate structure.

In each major operation, the firm fought against numerically superior opponents. However, it was able to defeat them through masterful operations that took advantage of the other sides' weaknesses. The only known unsuccessful EO operation was in the Congo, where the firm was not defeated in battle, but rather betrayed by the government that had hired it.[55]

The firm had a unique expertise in low-intensity conflict, drawing from its years of experience. It recognized that the concept of front lines was meaningless in such wars and aimed to keep the enemy force constantly off balance, wherever it was located. Surprise long-range helicopter assault operations against targets deep within enemy territory, supported by the ground attack aircraft, became a hallmark of EO operations, as did the use of pinpoint suppressive fire with mortars and follow-up pursuit of ambushes. It also was innovative and adjusted to changing situations by using ad-hoc tactics not found in the books, options perhaps less possible in a public military. Other keys to success included the strict discipline of the force and the cohesive identity it was able to maintain, even when operating in chaotic zones. This is ironic considering the contractual basis of the private force. However, a unifying factor was past experiences and the unique common language; Afrikaans was spoken by all, including the black Namibians and Angolans who had previously fought alongside the SADF. The difficult language also meant that the firm's opposition was unable to understand any EO messages they intercepted.

For the most part, EO had no great weapons advantage against it foes. It armed itself with equipment purchased on the open market, to which these foes could also access. However, as with other firms in the provider sector, EO did benefit by introducing some new technologies to the fighting or by using old, off-the-shelf ones in a novel manner.[56] The firm initiated night fighting and made the first employment of infrared night-vision gear in its conflicts. It also made devastating use of napalm, cluster bombs, and fuel air explosives (FAEs).[57] FAEs are bombs that, on detonation suck out oxygen in a massive fireball, killing all life within a one square mile radius, made recently famous in their use in Afghanistan against Taliban cave complexes.

However, many feel EO's greatest strength was the firm's superior employment of military intelligence. In each case, it built a profile of enemy operations, which were then broken down through targeted air strikes and helicopter assaults. Both radio intercepts and aerial reconnaissance intelligence were used in this effort. In Angola, the challenge of gaining familiarity with the enemy was aided by the earlier experience of fighting alongside UNITA, while in Sierra Leone, the Kamajors also helped in their role as scouts.

What also set Executive Outcomes apart is a skillful use of its broader corporate networks. As heirs to a long-established security establishment, the firm possessed connections and skills that gave it advantages over rivals, in particular its experience with clandestine operations, underground networks, front companies, and sanctions busting.[58] Overall, some 80 companies are reported to have been associated with EO in some capacity and each worked to the firm's benefit.[59]

A unique legacy of EO operations were the spin-off subsidiaries that it left behind, even when its contract expired. As noted, it is rumored that the company was indirectly paid through mining concessions that were sold off to related corporations. These firms then hired back some of the original EO force as continued local security, providing reward to employees and a ready military force on call. For example, approximately 100 of the 285 EO personnel in Sierra Leone, including the former local commander, stayed behind to work with Lifeguard, a sister company in SRC.[60] Many of these firms' employees remained on EO's books and could be mobilized as needed, giving the firm a quick surge capacity that it could pass on to its clients.[61]

This "security-led" approach to mining allowed the Branch-Heritage group to beat out rivals, such as the global giant DeBeers, in gaining diamond rights.[62] EO was aware of critiques of the seeming multiplication of subsidiary companies, but replied that it was just providing two commodities that are scarce resources in Africa—physical security and economic expertise.[63]

In order to quell its mercenary image and expand its economic reach, the firm also made an effort at expanding its civilian role, working up plans for a hotel resort in Angola and even a cellular phone network. Other firms in the holding company offered medical services, civil engineering, water purification, and hospital construction. The premiere military provider firm even set up water filtration networks and free medical dispensaries in Angola and Sierra Leone and also distributed Bibles to local populations.[64]

THE END AND FUTURE OF EXECUTIVE OUTCOMES

On January 1, 1999, Executive Outcomes disbanded. In its press release, the firm tried to put a positive spin on the demise stating, "African countries are busy working out solutions in Africa. . . . Let's give them a chance." It went on to cite "the consolidation of law and order across the African continent" as a reason for the company's purported obsolescence.[65] However, given the number of conflicts still ongoing across the continent, these explanations rang a bit hollow.

Despite the efforts to burnish its image, the past came back to haunt EO. It was never able to shake its link to the apartheid-past of its founders and clients found it easier to hire a competitor, including even one of its spin-off firms, that did not carry as much negative publicity. They could get the same services without the complications. Linked to their history in the apartheid regime's defense (with many of the firm's employees or former units being mentioned in the ongoing Truth and Reconciliation councils deliberations), the new South African government had been embarrassed by EO's activities. As a result, domestic legislation was begun in 1997 that sought to regulate the new trade in private military services. Under the provision of the "The Regulation of Foreign Military Assistance Bill," a company such as EO was compelled to seek government authorization for each contract.[66] Despite the fact that law was essentially unenforceable and had a problematic definitions concerning the scope of its powers, the firm evidently decided that staying local was not worth the effort. There were also reports of internal disputes among the executives.[67]

As a result of these factors, EO, which had been the defining firm in the military provider sector chose to cease operations. At the time, many analysts took this to mean that such military provider firms that offered implementation and combat services were no longer viable.[68] However, they could be no more wrong.

Rather than truly ending its business, it appears that EO simply devolved its activities, illustrating perhaps the final advantage that private firms have, even in death. As a corporate entity, nothing bound the organization known as Executive Outcomes to any one place or even to that name. That the company closed it offices in Pretoria does not mean that its spin-offs or "affiliates" also closed their businesses. A number of the firms once associated with EO, such as Sandline, Lifeguard, Alpha 5, Saracen, and Cape International, are all still active in the military provider sector, each operating in more corporate-friendly locales. Likewise, a number of new provider firms, headed and staffed by former EO personnel, such as Southern Cross and NFD Ltd., have all opened up since EO's close. There have also been reports of other firms using the old EO connections for recruiting.[69] The end result is that although Executive Outcomes technically closed, in another sense it simply globalized.

In the broader analysis, EO was a true innovator in the overall privatized military industry, providing the blueprint for how effective and lucrative the market of forces-for-hire can be. The Executive Outcomes name itself may be a thing of the past, but the business of providing tactical military assistance is alive and well. The demand for this sector remains and so does the supply. The firm's reputation lives on, as well. As one PMF executive commented, "If EO was still around and put out word tonight that it has a contract for 3,000 men, without providing any further details, Pomfret [the South African military base town, where the firm used to recruit] will be a ghost town tomorrow."[70]

EIGHT

The Military Consulting Firm: MPRI

> We've got more generals per square foot here than in the Pentagon.
>
> —Gen. Harry E. Soyster, retired, MPRI executive

Military Professional Resources Incorporated (MPRI) is one of the most well known players in the military consulting sector. In fact, it is also one of the more prominent firms in the wider private military industry, primarily due to its operations in the former Yugoslavia, where it helped alter the entire course of the war.

The firm's defining characteristic is that its employee pool draws from the highest levels of retired U.S. military personnel. Their collective experience offers the firm's clients both strategic expertise and intimate ties to U.S. policy. Originally, MPRI planned to tap into the domestic military market that opened up as the Pentagon downsized at the end of the Cold War. The opening of the global market of military services, however, has instead led it to take on an increasing array of international operations, in many settings where the U.S. military is prohibited.

Although there is a general uneasiness at the concept of retired American military personnel trading commercially on skills and contacts developed while in public service, those within MPRI say that the firm is distinguished by its professionalism and loyalty to U.S. foreign policy goals.[1] MPRI also makes pointed comparisons with other firms in the field, seeking to make clear its location within the military consulting sector.

> EO has been directly involved in combat; MPRI claims to work only in a training capacity. A senior MPRI employee compared the two companies thus in July 1997: "when a fire is raging a government may call in EO. But when the fire has been put out, we . . . install the necessary precautions to ensure it won't start again." Others believe the distinction to be less clear-cut. A U.S. State Department official notes, "The only difference is that MPRI hasn't pulled the trigger—yet."[2]

ORGANIZATIONAL CHARACTERISTICS

MPRI was founded in 1987, when eight former senior military officers of the U.S. military incorporated the company under the business-friendly laws of

Delaware. The firm's headquarters are located in an office block in Alexandria, Virginia, which the company literature pointedly notes is just a short distance from the Pentagon, implying a continuing close relationship. By 2002, a local staff of about 40 handled contracts and administration, while about 800 MPRI personnel were deployed in the field. The firm's annual sales had grown to the $100 million range.

The key asset of the company (as with Executive Outcomes) is a carefully managed database of former military personnel, among whom the company can replicate every single military skill. As of 2002, over 12,500 personnel are on-call and the list grows by hundreds each year. MPRI recruiting is accomplished in a more standard business manner than EOs, mainly through trade journal advertisements and by means of its corporate website. Roughly 95 percent of this pool is former U.S. Army personnel, which helps maintain corporate cohesion of procedures.[3] About half of the officers in the database reportedly have combat experience and/or PhDs.[4] As with EO, no standing force exists, so that personnel selection is specifically tailored to each contract's requirements.

The original CEO of MPRI was Vernon Lewis, a former army major general, who previously had founded Cypress International (a war matériél supply firm). The board of directors includes fourteen others, mainly retired generals and admirals. The 23 original founding employees had over 700 years of combined military experience. More recently, Carl Vuono, a retired four-star general, who was Chief of Staff of the Army during the Gulf War, took over as president of the firm.

Hierarchy within the company broadly appears to reflect former seniority of rank within the military, a shared trait with other firms in the Type I and II sectors. Prominent in its international divisions are Crosby "Butch" Saint, former commander of the U.S. army in Europe, and Harry "Ed" Soyster, a retired lieutenant general who served as the head of the Defense Intelligence Agency (DIA). Soyster also acts as the unofficial spokesperson for the company. Jared L. Bates, a retired three-star general, heads the national group that handles domestic operations. Other MPRI personnel comprise former professional soldiers of every grade, including a number of retired career noncommissioned officers, who make up the backbone of every army. In this category MPRI has over 200 retired Sergeant Majors, among the most respected soldiers in the entire force.

A particular aspect of MPRI that stands in contrast to that of Executive Outcomes, is the close ties it has been able to maintain with its home government. The fact that MPRI is exclusively made up of retired U.S. military personnel tends to give the U.S. government an overt amount of trust in the firm. The company, in turn, is careful both to nurture this relationship constantly and also to leverage it for its own client base. Company executives maintain close contact with former colleagues still in public service, who, in many cases, are their former subordinates. These relations in turn, provide the firm with a steady flow of business recommendations and information.

This gives MPRI a decided advantage over corporate rivals. For example, a number of its international contracts were first established through direct referrals from U.S. officials. The Colombian government chose MPRI after Brian Sheridan, U.S. Assistant Secretary of Defense for Special Operations Low-Intensity Conflict (SOLIC), recommended the firm to its Minister of Defense.[5] Similar occurrences are known to have happened in Croatia, Bosnia, and Nigeria. Likewise, the firm has admitted that it has often been able to access U.S. intelligence reports "at very high levels."[6]

The concern of such ties, however, is that it defeats the notion of competition that underlies the advantages of privatizing services.[7] These extremely close ties to the U.S. military establishment, although beneficial in some ways, have also raised some questions about whether MPRI is simply a private extension of the U.S. military. Soyster's tenure as head of the DIA coincided with the use of private arms dealers to equip U.S. allies abroad such as the contras in Nicaragua and mujahedeen in Afghanistan. At the same time that MPRI was working with the Croat military, these same dealers were active in arming the force, in violation of the UN weapons embargo.[8] Such links led officers from other European forces stationed in the NATO force in Bosnia to question how one would know if a MPRI employee was really a retired officer, or still active with the DIA, and whether it made a difference in the end.[9]

Equally, many feel that MPRI operates as just another mechanism to "reward the alumni" after retirement. For example, among its top personnel who worked in the Balkans are James Chambers, a former Lt. General who was once director of U.S. contingency operations in Bosnia, and John Sewall, another former general who was the Pentagon's special advisor to the Bosnian-Croat federation.[10] That both Chambers and Sewall worked on the same areas in both their public and private capacities raised eyebrows among regional observers. However, MPRI denies any wrongdoing and simply sees itself as tapping a national resource in the form of the retired American military community. Utilizing this pool of expertise, it claims to be able "perform any task or accomplish any mission requiring military skills (or generalized skills acquired through military service), short of combat operations."[11]

Domestically, MPRI has worked on numerous contracts for the U.S. military, doing everything from conducting analyses and simulations, running training exercises, to helping administer the ROTC and Staff College programs. All of these contracts, which were once handled by the military, illustrate the extreme confidence the U.S. government has in the firm.

On the international level, MPRI is also quick to point out that it only works on contracts approved by the U.S. government. This has had the interesting effect of its public client pool being determined by the changing winds of post-Cold War U.S. foreign policy. In 1995, for example, the firm made a bid to work for longtime ally Sese Seko Mobutu in Zaire, but due to policy shifts, it was rejected by the State Department, illustrating that the private firm's inclinations are not always in line with all branches of the U.S. government. Later in the same year, the company made several attempts to work with the Angolan military. These were taken by many in the region as a bellwether that the United States had also officially switched its support from the UNITA rebels (whom the CIA had armed during the Cold War), to backing the Angolan government, which had gained the support of Western oil companies.

In contrast with the purely domestic focus at its inception, the international part of MPRI has become a growth force for the business. The firm originally began these efforts by teaming up with several traditional defense manufacturers to assist foreign clients on new weapons introduction and integration. However, the military skills training and advisory contracts with other governments are what soon attracted the most attention. The services MPRI offers its foreign clients include doctrinal development, restructuring defense ministries, advanced war gaming, training on every type of weapons system, and military instruction down to squad-level tactics. The most senior-level personnel, such as the former chiefs of service and theater commanders-in-chief, also provide military leadership seminars to the higher-ranking military officers of foreign states.

The packages that MPRI offers make it possible to completely restructure a military from the bottom up and become compatible to NATO-level standards. In all aspects, the training mimics the exact type of instruction that the MPRI personnel provided U.S. military personnel when they were on active duty. The result is that in imparting to foreign forces 'the American way of warfare,' the firm is bringing to the military field the same dynamics that work in any other field of international trade, transferring knowledge capital from areas of high supply to those of low supply.

In sum, the military skills and expertise that MPRI can offer a client are perceived to be extremely high and thus in great demand. Its performance record demonstrates that with MPRI consulting and training, a nascent army can be transformed from a militia into a modern effective fighting force, much more rapidly than otherwise. Bosnian Prime Minister Muhammed Sacirbey reportedly said that having MPRI work for his government was 'the next best thing' to official U.S. military assistance.[12]

However, it must be noted that all is not perfect in the world of the premiere military consulting firm. MPRI is unique in that it is the only firm in the private military industry that has yet, at least by 2002, been mentioned in a war crimes tribunal. Its role in Croatia raised such concerns that the International War Crimes Tribunal meeting in the Hague contacted the Pentagon for information about the firm.[13] The firm is also unique in being the only PMF that has a website dedicated to reporting its alleged abuses (not very subtly titled www.mprisucks.com).[14] Some allegations on this site (including those posted by current and prior firm employees), consist of the standard accusations that the firm is more interested in contract renewal than efficient performance, but other allegations claim that the MPRI divisions outside the United States have shown disregard for both local laws and U.S. fair employment practices (including sexual harassment, preemptory firing, etc).[15]

HISTORY OF MAJOR OPERATIONS

MPRI began its business by exclusively operating within the United States and soon had work at military installations across the nation. Its initial contracts included providing new equipment training for U.S. active and reserve forces (for example, it was in charge of introducing the M2/M3 Bradley fighting vehicle into the Army National Guard) and support to the Army Staff and War Colleges. Since then, it has expanded its role such that it has become one of the primary corporate advisors and consultants to the U.S. military, in most cases to functions that had never been privatized before.

Two domestic contracts deserve special mention. In 1996, the Army began the process of privatizing the Reserve Officer Training Corps (ROTC). In this unique program, former Army personnel were hired by MPRI to work at colleges as professors of military science and administrative noncommissioned officers (NCOs), roles formerly filled by active military personnel. The firm initially ran a pilot program at 15 universities and has since expanded to taking over ROTC in more than 200 universities. Although they are actually private-sector employees, these MPRI instructors still wear uniforms.[16] Despite these attempts to shield the corporate role, the irony still remains; the next generation of U.S. Army leaders will be introduced to the force through the services of a private firm. Indeed, with a pilot program just launched to privatize regular recruiting to MPRI and Resources Consulting Inc., the same may hold true for future U.S. armed forces enlisted personnel as well.[17]

The other domestic contract that warrants discussion was with the Training and Doctrine Command (TRADOC) in 1997. In this case, MPRI was asked to develop and write the Army's field manuals on how to deal with acquiring and managing contractors in a wartime environment. The ultimate products were FM 100–10–2, *Contracting Support on the Battlefield*, and FM 100–21, *Contractors on the Battlefield*, which provide the tactics, techniques, and procedures for the management and control of commercial support of military operations.[18] In essence, a private company wrote the rules that gov-

Table 8.1

MPRI Domestic Contracts with the U.S. Military
- Organizational support of the U.S. Army Force Management School
- Instructors to the U.S. Army Combined Arms and Services Staff School at Fort Leavenworth (that basic branch officers attend as part of their professional military education program)
- Instructors to the Command and General Staff College (CGSC), that all higher-level officers attend
- Tactical training and war gaming support to the Combined Arms Support Command (CASCOM)
- Organization assessment & development for the U.S. Army Staff, the U.S. Army Space and Missile Defense, the U.S. Army Office of the Director Information Systems for Command, Control, Communications, and Computers (OSDISC4), the Joint Forces Command (JFCOM), and the Office of the Secretary of Defense
- Simulations development and support for the Defense Advanced Research Projects Agency (DARPA)
- Mentoring, expert support, and senior leadership seminars for various individual units of the Army and the wider Department of Defense
- Strategic planning and staff augmentation support to the U.S. Army Matériel Command (AMC), the George C. Marshall Center, the Joint Warfighting Assessment Center, U.S. Army Deputy Chief of Staff for the Operations and Critical Asset Assurance Program, Joint Program Office
- Military doctrinal support to the Army's Training and Doctrine Command (TRADOC) development of Information Superiority concepts Joint Venture Program (Force XXI) Army Experimentation Campaign Plan, and the Quadrennial Defense Review
- Logistical planning, as a principal subcontractor to the LOGCAP process.

---

ern how the U.S. Army would interact and manage other such companies. Despite being written by a firm within the industry, the manuals fail to recognize the full implications of the new form of contracting that has developed in the privatized military industry. Instead, they only cover the more traditional contractors and ignore the new policy and legal issues raised by PMFs such as MPRI.

Taking the International Market by "Storm"

MPRI has obviously been quite successful in garnering contracts within the U.S. domestic military services market. The firm's notoriety and growth within the military consulting sector, however, is due to its successful expansion into the global market. The first international contracts the company had were seminars on the lessons of the Gulf War it developed and held for the Taiwanese and Swedish militaries in 1991. It followed these with a minor operation in Liberia to train Nigerian peacekeeping forces in the ECOMOG operation on the use and maintenance of military vehicles that the U.S. government had supplied. The company also had a five-year contract with the U.S. State Department to administer the shipping of over $900 million worth of donated medical supplies and food to the former Soviet states.

However, it was in the former Yugoslavia that MPRI gained international brand recognition. Under a contract with the State Department, 45 MPRI personnel served as border monitors for the UN sanctions against Serbia from 1994–5. More important, it was also during this period that the company was first contracted by the Republic of Croatia to help its military's transition into a professional force.

Croatia had been one of the first republics to break away from Yugoslavia in 1991, but with an under-equipped militia force, it had suffered greatly when its Serbian minority in the Krajina region rebelled with the support of the Yugoslav army. At the time of the MPRI contract, a UN-monitored ceasefire line requiring suspension of hostilities had been established between the Croat forces and the Krajina Serbs (who had gained control of a large swath of territory that lay astride the main lines of communication for all of Croatia).

With the war also going badly for the Serbs opponents and the UN peacekeeping operation languishing, the basic goal of U.S. policy in the region became to bring the situation to an endgame. The concept was to turn the Croats into the U.S.'s "junkyard dog"; that is, to strengthen them into a regional enforcer and ally them with the Bosnians, in order to balance Serbian power.[19] This endeavor was solidified in the Washington Agreement in 1994, that linked together the conflicting Muslim and Croat elements inside of Bosnia. However, for the concept to have any effect, the amateur armies with whom the United States had sided required bolstering. This would be a difficult challenge because of a 1991 UN arms embargo that prohibited the sale of weapons to any of the warring parties.[20] Military training and advisory were also prohibited by this international embargo, which the United States had approved in the Security Council.

It was at this time that the Pentagon referred the Croatian Defense Minister to MPRI.[21] Once the Washington Agreement allowed a State Department license to be given (in September 1994), the Croat government signed MPRI to two separate contracts. The first was the long-range management program, intended to provide the Croatian Ministry of Defense with "strategic long-term capabilities" and was to be led by recently retired Major General John Sewall, who had just served as the Pentagon's point man in the region.[22] After a survey team assessed the situation, the program officially began in January, 1995. A second signed contract provided for the design of a Democracy Transition Assistance Program (DTAP) that officially began in April, 1995. DTAP is run out of the "Petar Zrinski" military school in Zagreb, and officially provides for the classroom instruction in democratic principles and civil-military relations to officers previously accustomed to the Soviet model of organization.[23] Neither contract is claimed by MPRI to involve any other type of military training.

The officially expressed policy behind the contracts was that they would help transform the Croatian army into a more professional, NATO-style force that would be a suitable candidate for the Partnership for Peace program. However, in August of 1995, the Croat forces launched a massive offensive, called "Operation Storm," whose scale and sophistication caught everyone in the region off guard. In a shocking fashion, the Croat army revealed that it had transformed from a ragtag militia into a highly professional fighting force. The Krajina Serb defenses crumbled and, within a week, the entire territory was seized.

Quietly pleased with the results, the U.S. government downplayed that the offensive had both violated the UN cease-fire and created 170,000 new refugees. In addition, numerous reports of human rights violations surfaced in the wake of the offensive, including the murder of elderly Serbs who had stayed behind.[24] The International War Crimes Tribunal has since indicted the Croat commanders of the offensive, who may or may not have received instruction and guidance from MPRI or Pentagon planners.[25]

Operation Storm, besides being the first major victory of the war against the Serbs, was to be the crucial turning point of the war in former Yugoslavia. The Bosnian Serbs lost their last active ally, and the Croat army then linked up with the Bosnian government army and drove into their enemy's western flank. In the course of the offensive, the Croatians regained all but 4 percent of their land and also came to occupy 20 percent of Bosnia. The beleaguered Serbs agreed to a cease-fire and the Dayton Agreement was signed in November, 1995. Observers present at the negotiations in Dayton, Ohio, relate that the Bosnian government made an important precondition to their signature: the provision of a similar program to train and equip their own military.[26]

Although MPRI categorically denies any involvement in Operation Storm or related training, the dramatic overall improvement in Croat strategic and tactical skills over the same span is difficult to ignore. As one analyst notes,

> No country moves from having a ragtag militia to having a professional military offensive without some help. The Croatians did a good job of coordinating armor, artillery and infantry. That's not something you learn while being instructed about democratic values.[27]

Despite MPRI's officials' denial that "they could have got a battle plan just as well from Georgetown University, as from MPRI," the absolute success of

Operation Storm definitely carried a Western-style imprint that appears to bear evidence of MPRI's assistance.[28] In particular, it made sophisticated use of war maneuver techniques to destroy Serbian command and control networks. These were quite different from the outmoded Warsaw Pact military tactics the Croats had used earlier in the war and more reminiscent of the U.S. Army's *Air-Land 2000* doctrine that the firm was expert in.

In fact, analysts were quite complimentary of the job that they ascribed to MPRI in advising the Croat force. The British colonel in charge of the UN observer mission in Krajina at the time stated, "It was a textbook operation, though not a JNA [Yugoslav army] textbook. Whoever wrote that plan of attack could have gone to any NATO staff college in North America or Western Europe and scored an A-plus."[29] Another defense observer directly linked the increase in the Croat's battlefield prowess to MPRI's training, crediting the firm with being a "vital element in the shift of political balance between the warring parties of Croatia and Bosnia."[30]

Indeed, the commonly accepted belief is that the MPRI operation started in October 1994, rather than later in January 1995, and included training not only in democratic principles, but also in basic infantry tactics (such as covering fields of fire and flanking maneuvers,), and medium-unit strategy and coordination as well.[31] Suspicions of the firm's involvement in the planning of the operation were further raised when a Croat liaison officer later informed the local press that, in the weeks before the offensive, MPRI's CEO, General Vuono, had secretly met on Brioni Island off the coast of Croatia with General Varimar Cervenko, the Croat officer who was the architect of the campaign. In fact, in the five days prior to the offensive, local press reported that Vuono and his men had at least ten meetings with Croat officers involved in the operation.[32] They were likely too busy at the time for coursework on democratic principles.

Although the extent of MPRI's involvement is still in dispute, the final results are not. Prior to MPRI's hire, the type of operation undertaken in "Operation Storm" was beyond the ability of the Croatian army.[33] Even if specific assistance in the offensive was not given, it is extremely possible that MPRI training exercises given to their Croat clients, such as wargaming, were tailored to such a contingency. At the very least, the U.S. leadership techniques and military organizational advice that MPRI does admit to having provided, did help the Croatians in their advance. After MPRI began training, a dramatic organizational and attitudinal transformation occurred in the Croatian forces, lifting military morale and discipline.[34] As one MPRI employee noted, "We were not there very long—if the Serb-Croat War had been fought in 1999 our fingerprints would have been all over it. But as it was, even in the brief time we were there, we made something of a difference, if only in the confidence we helped instill."[35]

In the wake of this success, MPRI won its next high-profile contract, administering "Train and Equip," the Dayton-inspired program to build up an integrated Bosnian Federation military. After a supposed seventeen-week bidding competition with two larger, rival American firms in the advisory sector (SAIC and BDM), MPRI was hired in May, 1996, to advise the Bosnian force during its reorganization and professionalization process. The difficulty inherent in this official version is that as early as December, 1995, it was widely known that MPRI would be the firm that would administer the training and preparatory work began before May.[36]

The overall contract was valued at approximately $50 million and carried provisions for yearly renewals. The program was titled the Military Stabilization Program and differed from the contracts with the Croats in that it had official provisions for combat training. Along with a $100 million surplus arms transfer program, the program was intended to help create a balance of power within Bosnia, which it was hoped would prevent future Serb aggression.

The payment method for MPRI's role in Bosnia's Train and Equip Program is indicative of the complexity of the firm's role. Although the contract itself is directly between MPRI and the Bosnian government, the firm was actually paid with money donated to Bosnia by moderate Islamic countries such as Saudi Arabia, Kuwait, Brunei, United Arab Emirates (UAE), and Malaysia. However, it was a U.S. official at the State Department (initially Ambassador James Pardew) who officially administered both the program and the financial account into which the money was deposited. In no other example of governmental privatizing, at either the federal, state, or local level, does such an example occur of having the purchaser, provider, contractor, and regulator in so many different personas.

The original Program Manager for MPRI's operation in Bosnia was retired Major General William Boice. Boice's particularly relevant experience to the situation in Bosnia was that he was the former commander of the U.S. Army's 1st Armored Division (making for some nice potential contacts with his former unit, which had provided the initial core of the NATO peacekeeping force that was in charge of administering the local security situation at the time in 1996). Headquartered on the third floor of a non-descript former university building in downtown Sarajevo, the MPRI operation in Bosnia consisted of approximately 175 personnel, who would develop and conduct an expansive training and advisory regime that Boice described as "a unique program in the history of the United States."[37]

The tasks that MPRI was contracted to accomplish were wide-ranging, numerous, and at the core of Bosnian military capabilities. As stated by Ambassador Pardew at the time,

> They will assist in the establishment of the Ministry of Defense and the Joint Command. They will perform a mission analysis and force structure development. They will be involved in the selection and integration of weapons

into the Federations forces. They will develop an integrated logistics system; assist with command and control; assist in the development of training policy; assist in the conducting of unit training. They will establish a combat training center, or centralized training center for all forces. They will establish individual training programs; create a simulation center for staff training. They will help in the development of personnel management education and force development programs, and they will assist in operational planning and strategic concepts for the defense of the Federation.[38]

The program began with the restructuring of the Bosnian Ministry of Defense and a combined logistics system. This was much more difficult a task than in Croatia, as MPRI was essentially trying to bring together two separate armies (the Bosnian Muslim ABiH and the Bosnian Croat HVO) under one organization. This tense dynamic presented recurring difficulties for the program that still remained unsettled five years later. Concurrent with this army reorganization, MPRI built a training school and computer simulation center near Hadzici, as well as established a field combat simulation center near Livno that had been designed to mirror the force training grounds in the United States (complete with an "OPFOR" enemy training unit). The 60-kilometer by 18-kilometer (roughly 40-mile by 12-mile) training grounds are especially realistic as they still contain gutted villages abandoned by Serbs during the previous round of fighting.[39] MPRI followed essentially a 'pebble in the pond' approach; that is, the students who have passed through the school are then expected to impart their knowledge throughout the Bosnian force.

MPRI's activities are expected to vastly improve the combined Bosnian army's performance as a fighting force. The training and, in particular, the simulation centers will certainly add to the Bosnian soldiers' individual skills. When combined with a more professional leadership advised by MPRI planning experts, the overall effect should multiply the Bosnian military's effectiveness on the unit- and overall-force levels. The MPRI model of training has proven effective in the Balkan region, and, with the involvement of their experts in the planning of Bosnian strategy, could prove to be even more so in the future.

One concern, however, is that the program may actually work all too well. European allies strongly opposed both the Train and Equip program and the hire of MPRI, and publicly condemned both. The general feeling on the ground among these forces was encapsulated by one Norwegian peacekeeper in Sarajevo, who imparted that he found the whole concept "disgusting."[40]

Critiques fell in two general categories: that rearming one side was poisonous to the evenhanded atmosphere required of international peace implementation and that, rather than simply balancing the Serbs' power, the Bosnians will be tempted to use their new-found weapons and skills to aggressively take back lost land.[41] It is generally agreed that due to their early losses, the Bosnian Muslim side has the greatest incentive to restart the war in order to regain lost territory, this time on its own terms. Many regional observers feel that if the NATO force were to withdraw at this time, the Bosnians might take advantage of internal Serb division and attempt to seize disputed territory. MPRI's response to this is that it is only teaching defensive strategies and limited counterattack tactics. However, the distinction with offensive tactics is slight. As a Bosnian officer training at the Livno grounds commented, "We'll be able to learn the rest by reading between the lines."[42]

MPRI Expands Around the World

MPRI has continued to stay active in the Balkans. Following the Bosnian contract, it set up a smaller-scale program for the new Macedonian state's military and border patrol. As the Kosovo war heated up just across the border, MPRI's local connections were quite useful to U.S. policymakers. Although not directly involved in the war itself, MPRI also influenced the fighting through its programs elsewhere in the region. As noted in chapter 1, both the rebel Kosovo Liberation Army's (KLA) commander and a number of its officers are known to have received MPRI training in the Croat and potentially the Bosnian contracts. The firm is certainly in the running to provide the same sort of start-up advisory assistance to a new Kosovar army, if the province's independence is ever recognized.[43] In turn, the Macedonian contract later came under fire when a local Albanian revolt occurred; some of the rebel leaders, fighting against the national army that MPRI was advising, were also rumored to have gone through MPRI training during the Croat contract.[44]

Having established its reputation in the Balkans, the firm aggressively moved to expand its international operations. In the Middle East, it has begun operations that support force integration for the Saudi Arabian military, including threat analysis; force management, establishing requirements, force development and design, acquisition, resource management, and force integration; as well as other key considerations, such as doctrine, leader development, logistics, and staff organization. Since 1999, MPRI has also been active in Kuwait, providing force-on-force training at the company- and battalion-task force levels.

Beginning in 1996, talks were reported to have occurred between MPRI and the government of Sri Lanka, involved in a war against the Tamil "Tigers." The negotiations reportedly involved a contract providing training and assistance to the military's special forces.[45] Allegedly, an officer soon to retire from the U.S. Delta Force was considered to lead the operation. However, the Sri Lankan government backed out of the negotiations for causes unknown.[46] The interesting part is that the State Department begrudgingly had granted a license to MPRI, despite initial disapproval due to the extensive allegations of human rights abuses by the Sri Lankan Army (which had thus made it ineligible to receive official U.S. military assistance).

MPRI has also made numerous forays into the African market. In 1996, MPRI negotiated a $60 million contract with the Angolan government to provide a similar training program to its military and police forces. EO had bid for the contract but lost out, despite most observers feeling the South African firm was far better suited for the conflict situation in Angola.[47] The NATO model is perceived to be of limited value in Africa (particularly in comparison to the proven EO approach).

The likely rationale behind MPRI gaining entrance into Angola ran in two directions. For the United States, it would provide enhanced influence over the local situation, whereas the Angolan government saw it as a way to bind the United States closer and further isolate UNITA, the Angolan rebel force. Political advantage seems to be the real impetus behind the deal, rather than MPRI's specific training program and expertise.[48]

However, the contract has yet to come to fruition for a variety of reasons. These initially included disagreements over the duration and cost of the contract. Renewed fighting between the government and UNITA also complicated MPRI's role. Reports had the firm and government finally coming to agreement in November 1999. However, by the next year, they had once again faltered. It may be supposed, if the rumors are true, that the key sticking point is not the actual contract numbers, but rather the absence of extra bonuses (i.e., bribes) for the Angolan Army officers involved in the contract negotiations.[49]

MPRI was eventually able to successfully enter the African market through two regional programs. The first is the African Crisis Response Initiative (ACRI), a seven-nation training program established in 1996 to create effective, rapidly deployable peacekeeping units. The idea is to build a compatible African force, trained to U.S. standards, that can operate jointly in the event of humanitarian crisis or in a traditional peacekeeping operation. To date, more than 5,500 African troops have been trained under the program, with MPRI supplying the administration and much of the training.[50] MPRI also provided similar services to the African Center for Strategic Studies (ACSS), a senior level U.S. government program designed to train African officers and civilian defense officials in national security strategy and concepts of civil-military relations. ACSS is structured along the same lines as the regional programs at the George C. Marshall Center in Germany and the Asia-Pacific Center in Hawaii, but is the only one administered by a private firm.[51]

More recently, MPRI has also engaged in contracts with Nigeria and Equatorial Guinea. Until the civilian elections in 1999, Nigeria had mostly been ruled by a revolving set of generals. The resulting theft and corruption hit a high point with the late General Sani Abacha, who stole more than $2 billion from the Nigerian state in the 1990s. The MPRI program involves the restructuring of the Nigerian military to reflect its new regional responsibilities and bring it under better civilian control. In the initial stages of the project, MPRI was paid by the U.S. Agency for International Development (better known for funding nutrition, education, and economic reform initiatives than PMFs) to conduct a survey on what was needed to "reprofessionalize" Nigeria's military.[52] As often occurs in the general consulting sector, the firm was then contracted to implement the very recommendations it originally had advised. The danger of this is, of course, that competition might have produced a more efficient process; but, nonetheless, MPRI was hired to begin the next phase in April 2000, for just over $7 million (with the Nigerian and U.S. governments splitting the costs).

In July 2000, the firm followed the Nigeria contract by working with the regime of Equatorial Guinea to assist in the design of a "National Security Enhancement Plan" and the formation of a coastal defense force. The contract raised a number of political questions about the firm's exact fit with U.S. foreign policy goals, however. The contract had initially been rejected by two separate State Department offices, holding it up its signing for two years.[53]

The State Department's concern was that Equatorial Guinea, most of which is an island off the coast of western Africa, is one of the most tightly closed and repressive societies still remaining after the end of the Cold War. Its government is a strict military dictatorship, headed by Obiang Nguema, who seized power in 1979 by deposing and murdering his uncle. MPRI's new client was a human rights violator of the most extreme kind, accused of political killings, election fraud, and questionable monetary practices. Any gathering of ten or more people in Equatorial Guinea is considered illegal and citizens have been jailed and tortured for violations as minimal as possessing photocopies of foreign newspaper articles.[54] The government even once threatened the U.S. ambassador with death, for trying to save local political prisoners.

The concern is that MPRI's contract will allow this government to strengthen its grip on power. The two closest allies of the firm's new client are North Korea and Cuba; so, in addition to the human rights concerns, aiding the regime in any way may not be in the U.S.'s best strategic interest. Regardless, the contract was pushed after high-level MPRI lobbying convinced U.S. policymakers that if it was not allowed to do the job, some other foreign (in this case, French) PMF would.[55]

During the same period, MPRI also began work in Colombia, South America, officially as part of "Plan Colombia," a $7.5 billion strategy to eradicate the cocaine trade. As in Nigeria, MPRI was at the initial analytical stage (being paid $850,000 for six weeks of assessment work) that helped the Colombian government devise the three-phase action plan to be implemented when the aid package was fully funded. Once again, it had pre-positioned itself to garner the more lucrative ensuing contract.[56] It was successful in this and, by the summer of 2000, MPRI employees were working full-time in Colombia under an initial $6-million contract.

The project, headed by a retired U.S. Army major general, was designed to aid the Colombian military in its development and reform. Ostensibly, the contract was only supposed to aid Colombia's counternarcotics operations, but certainly spilled over into counterguerrilla campaign effectiveness. MPRI worked with the armed forces and the Colombia national police in the areas of planning, operations (including psychological operations), military training, logistics, intelligence, and personnel management.[57] In a similar manner to the situation in Bosnia, the firm was paid by foreign-aid money that has been channeled through Colombia's budget. So delicate was the process of this money flow, as well as the exact nature of MPRI's work in Colombia, that an ongoing debate ensued within the U.S. State Department as to whom exactly MPRI worked for in this case.[58]

Unlike the operation in Croatia, however, the MPRI contract in Colombia did not end on a positive note for the firm. The contract was terminated prematurely in May 2001, after Colombian military leaders expressed dismay that the company had staffed its Bogotá office with no Spanish speakers and provided advisors with little expertise in the type of low-intensity conflict that the state was engaged in (a recurring theme, indicating that much like the force it evolved from, MPRI's services are perhaps better suited for traditional conflicts). "Finally, Colombian officers felt patronized by retired American generals who hadn't seen combat in years."[59] MPRI was still paid for its services, however.

THE FUTURE OF MPRI: HOW CORPORATE CAN A MILITARY COMPANY GO?

MPRI's operations illustrate how the privatization of military services has worked in many ways to the advantage of government. The private firm was able to go where U.S. military troops could not officially become involved and succeeded in furthering American foreign policy goals. Direct participation could thus be denied and there was no limiting public oversight or debate. The end result is that MPRI provides the potential of a privatized policy mechanism, at less cost and lower political risk.

Drawing from these advantages, MPRI has established a secure location for itself in the military consulting sector. Along the way, it has also made a great deal of money. The extent of its profitability seems to have been recognized by the fact that other firms soon sought a piece of the action. In July 2000, L-3 Communications (NYSE:LLL) acquired the issued and outstanding stock of MPRI. Other than releasing that it was purely monetary purchase, terms of the transaction were not disclosed.[60]

A spin-off from Loral and Lockheed, L-3 is a leading supplier of military training services, secure communications services and products, avionics products, microwave components and telemetry, instrumentation, space and wireless products. Like MPRI, its primary customer is the U.S. Department of Defense and selected U.S. government intelligence agencies, but it also serves aerospace firms (including making the infamous "black boxes" that record accident data on planes), commercial telecommunications, and cellular customers. L-3's CEO, Frank Lanza, explained L-3's rationale in adding the military firm to its group,

> MPRI is a growth company with good profit margins and competitive advantages that no other training business can match and its services are complementary to our products. In addition, the company is at the forefront of two positive defense industry dynamics. The U.S. military is privatizing many functions to reduce its increasing operations and maintenance budget and to compensate for its expanding national security commitments and declining manpower. MPRI is also active on the international front, as changing political climates have led to increased demand for certain services . . . These programs tend to expand and to lead to other opportunities.[61]

The purchase of MPRI by L-3 represents a major step both in the development of the firm and the overall military consulting sector. Public capital groups assisted the merger and now MPRI is part of a consortium that trades on the public stock market. In a sense, it thus provides an added stamp of legitimacy to the firm's activities that it did not have when it was privately held.

At the same time, it puts the MPRI under all sorts of new pressures and scrutiny. The firm is even less responsible to the government, now that it is owned by institutional investors (including foreign ones), who are concerned more with the bottom line than with U.S. strategic interests. A particular concern is the need to maintain constant growth to support L-3's current high stock valuation. As MPRI tries to maintain its place as the preferred consultant to the U.S. military this could introduce more tensions, similar to the conflicting motives at play between firm and government in the Equatorial Guinea contract.

Now more solidly established in the corporate sector, one can also expect that the firm's work environment and practices might be altered. New growth pressures might mean that former military rank will have less impact on placement in the firm's executive hierarchy. Likewise, new service areas are being introduced to target a broader array of clients, particularly in the corporate sector. Notably, these require less specialized military expertise, and include a new public affairs competency and a new privatized law enforcement program.

The public affairs group provides training and advisory services to clients ranging from the U.S. Department of Defense Information School to the 2002 Salt Lake City Olympic Committee. It also provides consultant reviews of Hollywood scripts that require military subject matter expertise. The law enforcement program, "The Alexandria Group," is headed by a retired F.B.I. Assistant Director and provides support to national, regional, and local law enforcement organizations and special investigations capabilities to any client, public or private. This section has become a growth area in the wake of the September 11 attacks in 2001 and increased U.S. homeland security spending.[62] However, as these operations expand, nonmilitary voices will have a greater role in MPRI.

The purchase by L-3 and addition of such new programs would seem to provide MPRI with additional areas of profitability. At the same time, such changes could lead to an interesting turn of events. They might represent the beginning of the PMF's "civilianization." Whatever the outcome, the future of MPRI appears bright.

NINE

The Military Support Firm: BRS

Keep up with the new things or you'll obsolete yourself before you know it. Anybody can do the easy things. Look for the harder jobs if you want to keep ahead.

—Herman Brown, Co-Founder of Brown & Root

Brown & Root Services (BRS) is one of the dominant companies in field of military support services. The name Brown & Root has become synonymous with the contingency (or emergency) operations that have consumed the U.S. military's energies since the end of the Cold War. Since 1992, the firm has deployed employees to Afghanistan, Albania, Bosnia, Croatia, Greece, Haiti, Hungary Italy, Kosovo, Kuwait, Macedonia, Saudi Arabia, Somalia, Turkey, Uzbekistan, and Zaire. It is not an exaggeration to note that wherever the U.S. military goes, so goes Brown & Root. As Vice President Dick Cheney, its former CEO, said in an interview, "The first person to greet our soldiers as they arrive in the Balkans and the last one to wave good-bye is one of our employees."[1] U.S. Army peacekeepers in Kosovo even joke that they should have uniform patches that say "sponsored by Brown and Root."[2]

As with many other firms in the logistical support sector, Brown & Root moved into the business only after establishing itself in other areas, specifically engineering and energy services. As such, it is a civilian firm that entered into the military domain, rather than the reverse that has occurred with firms in the sectors. Being far more diversified, BRS's personnel size and gross revenue are far larger than comparable firms in the provider or consulting sectors. BRS's employees number roughly 20,000 and its overall gross revenues are close to $6 billion per year.

BRS, however, shares many critical aspects in common with Executive Outcomes and MPRI. It entered the market at roughly the same time, similarly sensing the business opportunities that became available from military downsizing and the concurrent expansion of interventions and other contingency operations. As with the rest of the industry, it directs a fair amount of its recruiting toward recently retired military officers. The corporate history of Brown & Root also evokes the recent changes in provider and consulting sectors toward mergers. It is just one part of a larger economic holding, in this case the Halliburton corporation, a global construction and energy services company with annual revenues of $16 billion and over 100,000 employees in 100 countries.

Support sector firms' forays into areas such as logistical outsourcing represent the opening of an enormous new market. Logistics is the aspect of military operations that deals with the procurement, maintenance, and transportation of military matériel, facilities, and personnel; in short, supporting the troops in the field. Their businesses also signify a profound shift in the manner that militaries operate. Although these functions may be often considered "back-end" or secondary, their fulfillment is critical to the military's ultimate success on the battlefield. History has shown that "logistics is the lifeblood of war at the operational and strategic level."[3]

In a sense, firms in the military support sector have become private "enablers" to public forces. Much like the provider sector firms that allow foreign investment into conflict zones, support sector firms such as Brown & Root make possible the deployment and operation of military forces. So essential is their assistance, that U.S. military planners no longer even envisage the possibility of a large-scale intervention taking place without Brown & Root or one of its business competitors providing the logistics.

ORGANIZATIONAL CHARACTERISTICS

The story of Brown & Root Services and the overall Halliburton company begins in 1919, a year pivotal in history for the Treaty of Versailles that redrew the map of Europe and laid the groundwork for another century of conflict. Back in the United States, Erle P. Halliburton established the New Method Oil Well Cementing Company in his one-room, home in Wilson, Oklahoma. One state over in Texas, brothers George and Herman Brown, with financial backing from their brother-in-law Dan Root, started the Brown & Root construction and engineering firm. The company soon had its first job, paving roads in San Marcos, Texas.[4]

Over the next fifty years, the two companies thrived, both reaching international prominence. Patenting the revolutionary Cement Jet Mixer, Erle Halliburton's company transformed the oil well construction and service industry. By the time its founder died in 1957, Halliburton had offices in nearly 20 countries.

Brown & Root, in turn, had also been able to weather the Great Depression. Its strategy for survival was to take on risky projects that many other firms would not consider, such as building some of the first offshore oil platforms and constructing the Mansfield Dam, located near Austin, Texas. World War II brought a bevy of business, including contracts for building the Corpus Christi Naval Air Station and several U.S. Navy warships. As the postwar economy boomed in the 1950s, the company experienced further growth in construction and engineering.

Following his brother Herman's death in 1963, George Brown approached Halliburton and sold Brown & Root for $36.7 million. The following decades saw the linked companies achieve stunning expansion, but also suffer dramatic losses. With the discovery of some of the world's richest oilfields under the North Sea and in the Middle East, Halliburton's drilling support operations went through a period of spectacular growth. Likewise, Brown & Root soon ranked as the largest engineering and construction firm in the United States. It also played a critical role in the NASA space program, including devising the ingenious makeshift carbon dioxide removal system that saved the lives of the Apollo 13 crew (featured in the film of the same name). By 1979, Brown & Root had expanded to 80,000 employees and Halliburton had another 100,000.

However, at the end of the 1970s, a lingering recession and the weakening of the oil market caused much trauma to both companies. Revenues plummeted and both trimmed their payrolls. During this period, the two companies consolidated into a more centralized business unit and brought their two decades-old merger to actual fruition. In 1986, as part of its diversification and niche marketing efforts, the company formed the Brown & Root Services subsidiary to focus on government operations and support work.

By 1990, the joint company was back on its feet and operated through over 100 subsidiaries around the world. As it had earlier in the firm's history, war played a role in rejuvenating revenue. Following the Persian Gulf conflict, Halliburton crews were hired to help bring 320 burning oil wells under control, and Brown & Root was selected to assess and repair all the damaged public buildings in Kuwait.

It was soon afterwards that Brown & Root Services made its critical expansion into the military services market. In 1992, it won a contract from the U.S. Army's LOGCAP (Logistics Civil Augmentation Program) to work with the military in planning the logistical side of contingency operations. It was the first time the U.S. military had ever contracted such global planning to a private organization.

Over the next decade, Halliburton expanded operations and also reorganized the entire company, merging all its administrative structures. In 1995, former U.S. Secretary of Defense Dick Cheney joined Halliburton as its President and Chief Executive Officer (CEO). In 1996, despite the weak oil market, the firm experienced its best financial performance in more than a decade. In part, this success was owed to BRS's lucrative military contracts, which brought in almost a billion dollars in added revenue.

By the end of 2001, Halliburton had a market capitalization of almost $21 billion, with almost 80 percent owned by institutional holders.[5] The Engineering and Construction Group (also known as Kellog, Brown, & Root, or KBR), under which the military support operations of BRS fall, comprised roughly 40 percent of this total revenue. In addition to government work, this group offers a wide variety of services to several markets, including the refining, chemicals, and manufacturing industries. The traditional internal management structure of BRS contrasts with the more military-style chain of command in other PMF sectors.

BRS's corporate report does not reveal exactly how much of its annual work is military-related, but, by subtracting out the amounts given for oil and gas industry customers, one can assume that it is roughly $1.7 billion in yearly revenue (1/3 of the $5 billion). Of significance, this segment grew at the same time that oil services contracts were in decline due to weakened oil prices, and the rest of the firm's competitors were suffering. In the three years after Brown & Root began its large-scale support operations in the Balkans, its stock grew at a 20 percent greater rate than an index of comparable companies in the oil service industry.[6] The company directly credited the increase in military support contracts with partially offsetting these lower revenues. By the end of the decade, the growing logistics support business had made Halliburton the nation's fifth-largest military contractor.[7]

The variety of operations undertaken by BRS is quite astounding. In addition to the military support operations, it has done everything from performing the security surveys and upgrades of 150 U.S. embassies after the Kenya and Tanzania bombings to building a Formula One car racing stadium in Melbourne that was named the world's best racetrack. BRS was also project manager for a number of facilities at the Sydney 2000 Olympics, including the athletes' village and Stadium Australia.

In sum, Brown & Root evolved from a small road paving firm into one of the world's largest service providers for facilities, infrastructure, communities, and installations. BRS's market niche is in offering government and private sector clients the lure of better, faster, and more cost-efficient capabilities in secondary support areas, which then allow the customer to focus on their own distinctive competencies.

Business and Politics: The Candidates from Brown & Root

A constant in Brown & Root's success has been strong links to the political world. In fact, it was one of the firm's earliest contracts that saved both it and the career of future President Lyndon Johnson. The firm began work on the Mansfield Dam in 1937 at the height of the Great Depression. A major problem was that Congress had not yet approved the $10 million project and the government did not yet actually own the land on which the dam was being built. However, the firm began work, banking on the gamble that it could influence the new Texas representative to get the dam project appropriations approved. Johnson was paid off (much of it, by his own later admission, in cash) and he was able to deliver federal approval and funding for the project. The Mansfield bet succeeded and secured the future of the company. It also connected the junior congressman to corporate donors who would prove critical to his own political future. The firm's support for the young congressman was an essential element to his advance through the political ranks, next bankrolling his Senate run.[8] As LBJ biographer Ronnie Dugger states, "Brown & Root got rich, and Johnson got power and riches."[9]

Brown & Root's political ties came under public scrutiny more recently, after former U.S. Secretary of Defense Dick Cheney was named Halliburton's CEO in 1995. Cheney made a deliberate effort not to participate in its subsidiary BRS's growing contracts with the U.S. military, to diminish the appearance of any undue influence because of his prior position. This included refusing several invitations from the U.S. Army to visit the Balkans contract zones.[10] However, Cheney's history certainly benefited the firm. At the very least, it provided government officials a greater measure of confidence in the company than would have been otherwise. In the five years before Cheney joined the firm, it received $100 million in government credit guarantees. During Cheney's term, this figure jumped to $1.5 billion. As Bob Peebler, Halliburton's vice president, notes, "Clearly Dick gave Halliburton some advantages. There's a lot of respect for Dick Cheney, both in the U.S. and around the world. From that perspective, doors would open."[11]

In summer 2000, Cheney resigned from the firm, when he was named to the George W. Bush presidential ticket. Many took note of the fact that the company's board of directors voted him a lucrative retirement package worth more than $33.7 million.[12] While on the campaign trail, he criticized the Clinton administration for overcommitting U.S. troops in the Balkans. The irony is that it was this very same surge in U.S. troop deployments, and the Pentagon's growing reliance on private companies such as Halliburton to support them, that led to the company's strong financial position for which he was duly rewarded.

Contingency Contracting: Unknown Costs, Known Profits

A particularly interesting aspect of Brown & Root's military support operations has been the contractual set-up devised to enable them. Technically, the type of contract is termed a "cost-reimbursement, indefinite-delivery/indefinite-quantity contract."[13] Essentially, in a cost-type contract the firm is guaranteed the remittance of the costs that it sustains in its operations. On top of this, an incentive fee is then awarded, which determines its profit level. Usually, 1 percent profit is guaranteed, but the amount could go up to 9 percent, based on performance evaluations. This type of contract is used when uncertainty exists over the size, length, and location of a potential military operation. Because of this, the government client cannot specify in advance the exact quantity of services that the firm will need to provide. To lock in the firm's future services, the client makes prior guarantees of minimal payment levels.[14]

The rationale in choosing a cost-type contract for buying military logistical support is that it provides the flexibility necessary to support operations where mission requirements may change frequently. For example, the Pentagon's original estimate of the number of troops that BRS would need to support in Bosnia was off by over 5,000. In addition, contracts are typically structured so that they can be used to support other operations in the region that may later be necessary. This aspect turned out to be quite useful in 1999. Brown & Root's services in Bosnia had to be rapidly expanded to support the new military operations related to the war in Kosovo.

One limitation of a cost-type contract, however, is that it requires a self-sufficient company with a global presence. The firm must be able to respond immediately to an undefined requirement, with minimal assistance from the client government in executing the contractual provisions. The firm must also be able to develop its own line of communications and supply, in that the military's lift capacities will be consumed in moving its own forces. Finally, the firm must have the financial capacity to operate on this large scale for up to 60 days without reimbursement, given the time required to set up complex financial systems to pay for the services. For each of these aspects, BRS's links to a larger corporate holding proved critical. For example, in supporting U.S. forces in Afghanistan, Halliburton's prior business in Central Asia helped BRS quickly solve difficult logistical situations and dealings with local officials.[15]

The Downside

In general, Brown & Root Services has been able to fulfill these contracts successfully. As Joan Kibler, spokesperson for the Army Corps of Engineers unit overseeing the firm's Balkans support contract, noted, "Their ratings generally have been very good to excellent."[16] American troops interviewed also have a generally positive reaction to the firm's performance in the field.[17]

However, not everything has gone smoothly for the firm in recent years. As explored further in chapter 11, problems occurred with escalating costs in the Balkans contact, which prompted a review by the General Accounting Office, the investigative arm of Congress. Perhaps as a function of the type of contract, the firm was accused of overstaffing and overcharging the U.S. Army on the costs; this predicament was exacerbated because the Army expanded its operations rapidly and at the outset did not monitor the company properly.[18] In addition, former employees have reported the firm to the U.S. Equal Employment Opportunity Commission, claiming discrimination and sexual harassment. A particular accusation was that the firm maltreated foreign employees. This including having segregated restrooms in the offices that staffed the Balkans support contract and posting security guards to keep foreign employees out of "American"-only restrooms.[19] Such alleged treatment of foreign employees even culminated with one ex-employee (who had been fired one month before he would have reached his retirement benefits) launching a computer virus on the firm and causing almost $200,000 worth of damage.[20] Another BRS whistleblower alleged that the firm fraudulently inflated costs on over 224 projects, and these allegations that resulted in a U.S. Justice Department lawsuit.[21] Outside the military support sector, Halliburton, also at the center of the asbestos industry, has been sued by over 237,300 separate claimants.[22] In the wake of the corporate financial scandals of the firms Enron and Worldcom, Halliburton has also come under investigation by the Securities and Exchange Commission for potential accounting fraud during Cheney's tenure.[23]

Considering its close political ties, a surprising issue with Halliburton and its Brown & Root holding has been concerns with contravention of U.S. foreign policy goals. A number of the firm's subsidiaries are based outside the United States and operate in countries that have not always been American allies, including Angola, Libya, and Algeria, in some cases, in violation of U.S. government sanctions. For example, in 1995, Brown & Root was fined $3.8 million for re-exporting U.S. goods through a foreign subsidiary to Mu'ammar Gadhafi's "rogue regime" in Libya.[24] In Angola, the firm played a role in bankrolling the government's war efforts and may have been linked to illicit arms sales.[25]

The conclusion that can be drawn from these episodes is that although the firm's mission is certainly not to oppose the goals of American foreign policy, sometimes concerns for the corporate bottom-line have led to make business decisions that are not always so clear-cut in a political sense.

HISTORY OF MAJOR OPERATIONS

Brown & Root's first military outsourcing contract came in 1992, when the DoD paid the firm $3.9 million to produce a classified report detailing how private companies—such as itself—could help provide logistics for U.S. troops deployed into potential war zones around the world. The initial contract called for a firm to produce a worldwide management plan for commercially provided logistical support of military operations. Thirty-seven total companies solicited for the initial contract, but BRS beat them out.[26] In order to plan for such a major undertaking, Brown & Root's history and unique expertise proved critical. Specifically, the company drew on its experience supporting large, remote oil field operations to win the contract.

The original worldwide concept required BRS to outline how a private company could provide immediate support to troops deployed in areas without either host support or preexisting U.S. bases (that is, transitional situations unlike what U.S. forces had enjoyed in basing during the Cold War). The initial requirement was that a firm be prepared to enable the deployment of 20,000 troops deployed in five base camps over 180 days, with the troop numbers expanding up to 50,000 beyond that.

Later in 1992, the Pentagon gave the BRS an additional $5 million to update its report for more specific contingencies.[27] That same year, the company won a five-year contract from the U.S. Army Corps of Engineers to implement the plans it had devised. Just a few months later, in December 1992, firm executives were surprised when they were called so soon to implement their plans. With the humanitarian crisis brewing in Somalia, they were asked to support the upcoming Operation Restore Hope. Brown & Root employees arrived in Mogadishu just 24 hours after the first U.S. troops and stayed until the final withdrawal in March 1995, when its employees left with the last U.S. Marines.[28] While in Somalia, the firm provided a variety of services to the deployed forces, from maintaining force transportation and supply lines to feeding the troops. The firm even hired local women to hand clean U.S. Army laundry (because it was cheaper than bringing in washing machines) and imported a mortician to clean up the bodies of killed UN peacekeepers, before shipping them out of the country.[29] For an extended period, BRS was the largest employer in Somalia, with some 2,500 local employees.

The firm followed the Somali operation in 1994 with small-scale deployments in support of U.S. troops in Rwanda (Operation Support Hope, aiding Rwandan refugees), Haiti (Operation Uphold Democracy, to pressure Haiti's transition to a civilian government) and Kuwait (Operation Vigilant Warrior, in response to Iraqi buildup along the Kuwaiti border). In each case, BRS provided increasing amounts of logistics support. These grew in scale over the operations' duration, particularly as greater numbers of U.S. troops withdrew and the firm took on more operational functions.

The Balkans Business Bonanza

Similar to the experience of MPRI, a major boost to BRS came from the crisis in former Yugoslavia. Brown and Root's initial business exposure to the Balkans war came in early 1995, when it deployed in support of Operation Deny Flight, under which U.S. planes patrolled the no-fly zone over Bosnia. BRS provided support services to the U.S. troops operating out of Aviano air base in Italy, with the contract amount running to $6.3 million.[30]

The biggest contract in the sector's history came later in 1995, when over 20,000 U.S. soldiers deployed to the region as part of the NATO IFOR peacekeeping mission. The U.S. Army paid Brown & Root $546 million to provide logistical support for the mission. Although the contract was originally designed just for U.S. troops, shortfalls among the allied militaries that deployed into the United States-led sector meant that BRS often provided similar support to other IFOR nations' forces. BRS's operations took place in Bosnia, as well as Croatia and Hungary, where other U.S. forces were deployed.[31]

Although the original Balkans Support Contract was held under the LOGCAP program, in 1997, BRS lost the general contract renewal competition to Dyncorp. However, to allow smooth continuation of operations, the Balkans region was cut out from LOGCAP and Brown & Root received a sole-source contract worth $405 million to continue providing military support services in Bosnia. In 1999, the firm beat out one other bidder for a five-year renewal of this contract, originally estimated to bring the company $180 million a year.[32]

However, yet again, the winds of war would benefit BRS's bottom line. Just a few months later, war in Kosovo broke out and the company's services were once more necessary. As the NATO air operations began, BRS employees operated right outside Kosovo's borders, providing logistics support to U.S. troops that deployed to Albania and Macedonia and also building and operating camps for the hundreds of thousands of Kosovar Albanian refugees that had been driven out of province.

Traditional aid groups, such as the Red Cross and other nongovernment organizations, were completely unprepared for the mass exodus that occurred in Kosovo and the potential humanitarian disaster that loomed if these refugees could not be fed and housed immediately. Lacking the quick deployment, construction, and supply capabilities to do it themselves, the aid community turned to NATO for assistance to build and maintain the massive camps needed to support the refugee population. The military, in turn, contracted the job out to BRS. Interestingly, NATO spokesmen would

Table 9.1

Military Logistics Roles Taken by BRS in Kosovo
- Engineering
- Construction
- Base camp operations and maintenance
- Structure maintenance
- Transportation services
- Road repair and vehicle maintenance
- Equipment maintenance
- Cargo handling and railhead operation
- Water production and distribution
- Food services
- Laundry operations
- Power generation
- Refueling
- Hazardous materials and environmental services
- Staging and onward-movement operations
- Fire fighting
- Mail delivery

---

take credit for the good publicity that this last aspect of the operation generated, but it was actually the private company that was central to these humanitarian efforts.

After the war ended in June 1999, U.S. troops deployed into Kosovo, as part of the NATO's KFOR peacekeeping force. The U.S. units made up roughly a fifth of the overall force and came to depend on BRS engineering and logistics support. The original contract ballooned from the $180 million a year estimated for just the Bosnia operation. In fact, the costs for 1999 alone reached almost $1 billion, and ate up the entire original five-year estimated contract amount. Much of the expense went for the intense build-up of support operations in Kosovo and its neighbors, with the remainder toward the continued sustainment of U.S. troops elsewhere in the region.[33]

The scope of and size of the ongoing BRS operation in Kosovo is staggering. In essence, the firm has built and now manages two large military bases, each roughly the size of a small town. Adding to the difficulty, these two bases were constructed from scratch, in the span of a few months, in the middle of open wheat fields. As an example of the difficulties, the larger of the two, Camp Bondsteel, accommodates 5,000 troops and required the creation of an infrastructure of roads, sewage, and power, both housing and work buildings, helicopter airfields, a detention center, and a variety of force protection measures, from guard towers to perimeter defenses.

In the first three months of BRS's deployment inside Kosovo, the firm built 192 barracks, which housed over 7,000 troops, thirteen helipads, two aviation-maintenance facilities, twelve mess-kitchen dining facilities, two large base dining facilities, and 37 temporary bathing facilities. At the same time as this intensive construction effort, the firm also supplied U.S. forces with the whole range of necessary logistics services, including delivering 1,134,182 high-quality meals, 55,544,000 gallons of water, and 383,071 gallons of diesel fuel. The contractor also serviced 671 latrines a total of 31,037 times, collected 89,228 cubic meters of trash, and loaded and offloaded 4,229 containers.[34]

These numbers represent a snapshot of some of the services provided by Brown & Root, but the list by no means captures the full extent of the firm's support to the military. In effect, the firm was the U.S. force's supply and engineering corps wrapped into one corporate element. BRS provided U.S. forces in the Balkans with 100 percent of their food, 100 percent of the maintenance for tactical and nontactical vehicles, 100 percent of hazardous material handling, 90 percent of water provision, 80 percent of fuel provision, and 75 percent of the construction and heavy equipment transfers.[35]

Although BRS did not perform right on the battlefield as is typical of a military provider firm, or advise the force as is typical of an advisory firm, it is not an exaggeration to say that its services were critical to the U.S. Army's mission in Kosovo. The entire lifecycle of the operation, from the troops being able to eat and sleep, to the smooth operation of their weapons systems and vehicles, were all guaranteed through private provision.

The accomplishment of Brown & Root in providing superior, rapid logistics and engineering services has clearly established a template for future military interventions. A critical aspect of privatizing these support functions is that aside from the potential financial cost benefits, it also has other added benefits. The firm's hire reduced the size of U.S. troop commitments by an estimated 8,900 troops and thus made the Balkan deployments more politically palatable.[36] The firm's support tasks also freed military personnel already on the ground for other duties more central to the mission's mandate.

THE FUTURE OF BRS: PLANNING FOR ALL CONTINGENCIES

Despite its successes in the Balkans, Brown & Root's future role in the military support sector took a heavy hit in 1997, when, as noted previously, it lost its valuable monopoly on the U.S. military contingency contracting business. Until this point, BRS had enjoyed a near monopoly, but Reston, Virginia-based rival DynCorp was able to beat it out and won the new five-year LOG-CAP global logistics support contract for the Army. The exact reason for BRS's loss is not public, but rumor is that in attempting to add profits, BRS had not provided as competitive bid as it could and Dyncorp was able to underbid through extensive use of subcontractors.[37]

However, as noted earlier, the Balkans support contract was cut out of the overall LOGCAP, allowing BRS to retain the most valuable segment of the program on a sole-source basis. The stated rationale for keeping BRS was because the firm already knew how to operate within these areas, had demonstrated past ability to support the operations, and that changing contractors in mid-mission would not only have been disruptive, but also generated additional costs, such as personnel duplication during the transfer.[38] With the Balkins contract in place until May 2004, current estimates of its value are roughly $1.2 billion.

In 2001, however, BRS recovered and won back the LOGCAP franchise in the next contract round, re-bolstering the firm's revenue flow. In the wake of the September 11 terrorist attacks, this proved lucrative once more. The firm was in place to handle much of U.S. logistics and base construction in Central Asia during the ongoing Operation Enduring Freedom. They also helped build the detention camp in Cuba.[39] The likely contract value of these operations is in the hundreds of millions. As *Newsday* writes, "The company and its parent, Halliburton, rack in the big bucks . . . in Afghanistan, Uzbekistan, Guantanamo, and just about everywhere else the war on terrorism is being waged."[40]

However, although a great deal of money has been made in providing support to these contingency operations, their overall future is not certain.

Two tensions are at play that will determine BRS's future growth. On one hand, the U.S. military is arguably overextended and under resourced.[41] Thus, whenever the U.S. military operationally deploys, previous cutback in logistics and engineering branches dictate that the force will require the support of military support firms such as Brown & Root.

On the other hand, these same factors make the business itself dependent on political winds. As a spokesman for the Army noted of BRS, "The [Clinton] administration helped set the course for them to build the business. Five years ago there was no Bosnia or Kosovo."[42] However, the new Bush-Cheney administration has argued against the over commitment of U.S. forces and cited the need to reduce U.S. forces levels in the Balkans. This could decline the value of the current contract the firm has for the region. The firm is also less likely to see that first flush of the nineties again, particularly with the entrance of new global competitors in the field, such as Dyncorp and Canada's AT Frontec.

Profiting through Diversification

Brown & Root appears to be quite aware of the pitfalls in relying on contingency contracting. It has responded to market uncertainties by following a basic precept of good business—diversification.

In the next few years, the firm plans to spread its market presence both laterally and vertically. Although it began by having the U.S. Army as its only military logistics client, BRS has begun to expand the range of contracts it provides to the U.S. government. In June 2000, the company won a worldwide support contract for the U.S. Navy that will bring in at least $300 million. It has also has begun targeting non-Defense Department agencies, winning a $100 million contract to improve security at U.S. embassies and a $40 million contract to maintain labs at the National Institutes of Health.[43] The firm's assessment is that the support sector will continue to accelerate in growth, with U.S. government outsourcing expenditures in its sector expected to reach up to tens of billions of dollars over the next decade.[44]

At the same time, BRS sees opportunities for diversifying and expanding its customer base beyond the United States. It has begun by providing similar military support services for NATO states and other close U.S. allies. A recent example is a contract to operate the Valley base for the Royal Air Force (RAF) in North Wales, where the British train RAF fighter pilots. BRS handles aircraft maintenance, armament support, avionics support, and overall facilities management. Other international contracts include running military dockyards for the Royal Navy and providing communications support to Australian defense forces. The experience in building and operating the refugee camps in Kosovo illustrates that humanitarian groups may yet be another client base to tap. There is also a further possibility of logistical contracting for multilateral peacekeeping operations. Its competitor

Dyncorp has already provided such support services to a number of UN missions.

This international diversification means, however, that the firm has begun to work for some surprising clients. In October 2000, the Russian Navy contracted a subsidiary of the firm for retrieval operations on the lost Kursk nuclear submarine. The contract amount was estimated to be in the range of $9 million and is one of the first examples of the Russians turning to the privatized military industry to bolster their severe force shortfalls.[45] In November 2000, the firm also joined a $283 million project with the U.S. Defense Threat Reduction Agency to assist the Russian government with the dismantling of intercontinental ballistic missiles (ICBMs) under the provisions of the Strategic Arms Reduction Treaty (START). Although obviously focused on arms controls, it still was notable for being one of the first forays of the industry into the nuclear weapons field.

The final results of this diversification program will not be known for some time, but the prospects look solid. Although volatility of oil prices may challenge energy services revenue on occasion, the development of the military logistical support business by BRS provides a steady, and thus highly valuable, growth factor to Halliburton. This synergy between the military and nonmilitary sectors allows the overall company to remain profitable, even in an environment that is suboptimal for some aspects of their business.

III. IMPLICATIONS

TEN

Contractual Dilemmas

> If you try to combine a Soldier and a Merchant in one person, you will labour in vain.
>
> —Admiral Cornelius Metelieff, 1608

Whenever we contract out a service, whether to a plumber or a lawyer, we typically have all sorts of concerns: Will the job be done properly and to our specifications? How can we monitor it to even tell? Are we being overbilled?

With PMFs, several intriguing predicaments compound this basic contractual process. The private military industry involves an unusual synthesis of economic motivations and political and military exigencies. One difficulty for PMF clients, that is, those contracting for services, is that the services they are contracting for not only are important, but often are crucial to their security. At the same time, they need to preserve a competitive market whose efficiency led them to outsource in the first place. Another genuine concern of all clients, even the most powerful state, is whether a private agent that fails in its contracting obligations can be readily replaced.

The result is that the privatized military industry introduces very real contractual dilemmas into the realm of international security. The overall issues of these contractual dilemmas come down to divided loyalties and goals. In any type of contracting, a "principal" (the actor paying for the service) commissions an "agent" (the one doing the job) to act on its behalf. But these two parties interests will never exactly coincide. Moreover, neither has complete information about the other's exact goals or behavior.

Thus, the complexities of the agency relationship consist of the principal's reliance on an agent with its own agenda.[1] With PMFs, clear tensions always exist between the security goals of clients and the firms' desire for profit maximization. For governments, the public good and the good of the private companies are not identical. Firms may claim that they only act in their client's best interest and that their staff, (in some cases primarily retired military officials), are highly trustworthy. But the locus of judgments about military action has changed, as well has the underlying motives. Here the agent enacts decisions critical to the security of the principal. Moreover, this agent is driven neither by goodwill nor honor, but rather by profit. Finally, all business takes place in the context of war or incipient war. That is, the PMF contracts are written for the most complex environment possible. War is a realm which military thinkers such as Carl von Clausewitz could only describe as a series of unique situations limited by numerous ambiguities.[2]

INCOMPLETE INFORMATION AND MONITORING DIFFICULTIES

When a principal contracts for services to an agent, the challenge of what is known as "incomplete information" always exists. Now being one step disconnected, the principal (or client) is longer exactly sure what is going on and often has to rely on information from the agent. In fact, one of the key lessons from general privatization is the importance of sophisticated mechanisms of monitoring and oversight to get around this problem. Independent mechanisms have been found necessary to protect the principal/client's interests and ability to make informed decisions on its own, without the agent's influence.[3] Other important requirements include clear and verifiable standards of performance; appropriate payment provisions with safeguards; an escape clause with unambiguous terms and conditions; and, where appropriate, performance incentives that both reinforce a job well done and penalize poor execution.[4]

The reality, however, is that contracts with the private military industry rarely meet these standards.

Monitoring Challenges

Impediments to successful monitoring of PMF contracts are many. It begins with the structure of the market. Contracts with PMFs do not have the usual control mechanism of the free marketplace (as envisioned by classical economists)—that of instant supply and demand. Instead, contracting in the privatized military industry is similar to contracting with what are known as "concentrated" or "entrenched" industries.[5] Not only is the competition fragmented, but the sanctions that a principal can apply to an errant agent are also limited. Given the current specialization in the market and self-imposed limits on the principals they may contract with (for example, security considerations normally require that U.S. military contracts be awarded to U.S.-based firms), clients may find a lack of suitable firms to maintain a truly competitive market.[6] This limited competition is also exacerbated when contract bids are "wired," that is, the contract winner has been predetermined. This has reputedly happened with certain politically connected firms, such as with MPRI's gain of the "Train and Equip" contract or Dyncorp's frequent U.S. State Department contracts. Such arrangements forget that the efficiency of privatization comes from greater competition, rather than simply that it is private.[7]

As a response, industry opponents and proponents alike cite the need for proper monitoring by public authorities.[8] However, full-time contract monitors not only raise contract costs, but also blur the chain of command and diffuse responsibility. Not only does this strip away the original advantages of going private, it is also inconsistent. For proponents of PMFs to lack trust in public institutions's ability to perform the missions, but then put faith in these same institutions's ability to oversee them is paradoxical, to say the least.[9]

Many instances of PMF contracts involve minimal oversight and/or clear requirements. The basic problem is that even in the best militaries, little to no doctrine is available on how to manage contractor resources and effectively integrate them. For example, the U.S. Army's logistics outsourcing in the Balkans had no focal point in its command structure either to review contractor performance or to access options for alternatives. Nor were established methods of systematic evaluation available, rather, reviews and oversight were accomplished on the fly.[10] As a result of this lack of planning, follow-up analysis found that local military commanders often did not think in terms of the cost ramifications of their decisions, driving up the price overruns.[11] These problems continued in later operations in Central Asia.

Likewise, contract terms with PMFs are often unspecific, lacking outside standards of achievement and established measures of effectiveness. This leaves the principal/client at the mercy of the agent to tell him how well the contract is going and what should be done next. In the case of the "Train and Equip" program in Bosnia, it is believed that the military consultant firm used its position of trusted expertise continuously to identify additional contract needs for the client. In effect, it pushed the goalposts back as the game progressed, to help it gain more contracts.[12]

Beyond these structural issues, the monitoring of PMF contracts is particularly difficult. They take place in the fog of war—a highly complex and uncertain environment. Moreover, the firms are not open to public scrutiny, and are often based elsewhere. An added complication is that in many cases, the actual consumer of PMF services may be different than the principal/employer. One example is the practice whereby states subcontract PMFs to supply military personnel and services to international organizations on their behalf. As a result, the usual relationship between buyer and seller, with mutually dependent interactions, no longer holds; the party actually paying for the service is not the recipient and does not see the actual delivery. Thus, the service agent/supplier may give less to the actual consumers than what was paid for.[13] PMFs, for instance, often lower their own staffing formulas whenever the opportunity allows. An example is when DynCorp's reportedly shortchanged the U.S. government by supplying unsuitable (overage and overweight) police on its behalf to UN peacekeeping operations in Kosovo.[14]

Another monitoring challenge involves the personnel typically managing contracts. A government or business client rarely provides training on how to monitor and, given the low priority of the positions, rarely assigns its best people to monitor contracts.[15] For example, the General Accounting Office (GAO) reported that effective oversight of the U.S. military's Balkans logistics contract, which ran over the original costs by hundreds of millions of dollars, was hindered by the fact that oversight personnel had not been trained sufficiently. In fact, the original lead contracting officer was an artillery officer with no contracting background.[16] Moreover, frequent personnel rotations on the client's military side mean that, even if monitoring officers built up experience and knowledge of working with PMFs, they soon leave, precluding any continuity except on the firm's side.

This "revolving door" syndrome also risks strict, unbiased supervision. In a number of instances, officials in agencies that monitor the industry have ended up working for the very companies they dealt with in their public capacity. As noted earlier, many PMF executives also maintain intimate relations with former colleagues still inside the military, including those they once commanded.[17] In addition, the reputations that retired officers built while in public service may cause government officials, as well as members of the legislature, to give undue credence to their lobbying efforts.[18] This is not to cast doubt on the general patriotism of PMF industry personnel, but to recognize the new responsibilities that they encounter in the private sector. The potential for conflicts of interest is inherent, particularly when making recommendations or influencing policy that may result in additional contracts from which their firm will benefit.

Many PMF executives honestly feel that they are free from such influence of profit concerns and that even in their private capacity they are acting in national interest. But as one analyst writes, "the danger in this lies in the increasingly complex nature of defining what is a country's national interest."[19] Many firms operate in gray areas where the national interest is not clear and thus more easily contorted to private advantage, even unconsciously. Private employees have distinctly different motivations, responsibilities, and loyalties than those in the public military. No matter their background, while in a private company, employees are directly responsible to the corporation and its executives; they are hired, fired, promoted, demoted, rewarded, and disciplined by the management of their private company, not by government officials or the public.[20]

The result is that blind trust is no substitute for proper monitoring mechanisms. The dilemma with PMFs is that good oversight is quite difficult to arrange, even in the best of circumstances.

Propensity Toward Profit

Although difficult to arrange, good monitoring is still necessary. The fundamental goal of corporations is the maximization of profit. Given their interest in this bottom line, firms will be tempted by any leeway to increase profits at their client's expense. Although they often claim that they only seek "satisfactory" profit levels, the definition of that still lies in the hands of the PMF's management.

The profit-seeking of PMFs affects the final output of military services from PMFs, in a way quite different than with public forces. The financial limitations of the contract will shape the nature of their activities, with costs dictating methods and techniques more directly than with a traditional public force military. For example, firms might limit expenditure on the more effective solution to ensure their profit margins, whereas public military bureaucrats tend to choose the bigger solution, no matter the cost.

A central concern is cheating or intentional overcharging. Any type of organizational slack leads to random inefficiency, but the privatization of services leads to direct incentives to distort actual costs.[21] That these services lie in the realm of national security is no protection. Private businesses have cheated public agents during war extending back to the Philadelphia merchants who swindled the Revolutionary Army while it starved at Valley Forge. The privatized military industry simply represents a new manifestation. Now, the cheating is also an opportunity on the services side, instead of overcharging for goods. The difference with privatized services is that client losses recur over the life of a contract, as opposed to one-time losses that occur in the purchase of an overpriced good—you pay for a $500 hammer once, you pay for superfluous employees every salary period.

Businesses often make their estimates of how much to charge public agents not by their estimate of intrinsic costs, but by how much they believe they can get away with. This is particularly true for the fixed-cost or rate of return contracts that prevail in the defense services world. Traditionally, companies succeed in the marketplace by lowering costs and improving performance. These efficiency gains are passed on to consumers as lower prices. In the fixed-costs scenario, however, companies typically have the opposite incentive: the firms' overall profits increase whenever their costs increase.[22]

Less than perfect competition in the market for military services makes this problem even more severe. Moreover, many contracts are relatively long-term, including lifetime support contracts for certain highly technical weapons systems. These contracts create an essential monopoly once signed, even if competitively bid. This can distort the original bidding, as firms have an incentive to low-ball initial bids, knowing they can negotiate add-ons later. Once a project is underway, many pressures for costs to increase mount, with few counter-pressures to lower costs.[23] Similarly, firms use previous contracts to stake a claim of unique expertise. This then lays the groundwork for follow-up, "sole-source" contracts that other firms are unable to bid for.

In economic terms, the result is what is known by economists as "ex-post rent extraction."[24] Once they have the contract in hand, an array of incentives exist for firms to overbill their clients. When the payment amount is determined by length of time, then it is likely the firm will bill up to the maximum allowable period. Likewise, if the billing amount is set by number of personnel required, the firm will likely hire as many billable employees as possible or pad their numbers with 'shadow' employees.

Typically, a PMF sets the level of services and the number of employees required on the basis of its own business practices. Clients tend to accept the firm's judgment, trusting the expert. When the level of services provided is actually questioned in depth, however, significant cost overruns often become apparent. For example, in 1999, the U.S. Army attempted to privatize certain military base services in Bosnia to BRS. Without even consulting the local base commander, the firm determined that it would bill 116 personnel for the contract; on examination, however, the Army determined that just 66 personnel were actually needed. Similarly, in May 2000, the commander of the U.S. Army brigade in Bosnia surveyed private operations in his area of responsibility. His findings were that 85 percent of BRS work crews had excessive crew size and 40 percent were not engaged in work at all.[25]

In trying to reach these higher personnel numbers, the firms are often also alleged to provide employees who do not meet the contract specifications, focusing on what can be billed for rather the actual skills required. For example, the employee responsible for teaching one firm's military command and general staff course had never graduated from a command and general staff college himself. Other industry interviewees cited instructors with no combat experience, including one who listed four years of ROTC education as military experience.[26] In other cases, managers in two different firms reputedly used their positions to hire their (unqualified) love interests as office staff, all at the client's cost.[27]

DynCorp's contract with the U.S. military for aviation support is an egregious example of such cutting corners with staffing. Among the personnel that the firm reportedly assigned to the maintenance of U.S. combat aircraft were employees whose only previous work experience was as waitresses, security guards, cooks, and cashiers. As one DynCorp mechanic working on the contract writes, "We have people who are working on aircraft with absolutely no aviation experience nor ground-equipment skills. Would you rather fly in a helicopter maintained by a waitress or an experienced aviation technician? . . . The management here is looking at the bottom line, and they surely do not seem to care what kind of person works on the helicopters. I guess that makes good business sense, but to me not at the cost of our servicemen and women."[28] DynCorp employees report that the number of aircraft that have crashed as a result of faulty maintenance and not enemy action, may be traced back to the fact that they were worked on by such unqualified, private firm personnel.[29]

These problems have parallels with normal contracting situations and, likewise, no principal/client's raw power can shield it from the risks associated with outsourcing. Both strong and weak states alike have experienced problems with firms taking advantage of their positions. In the course of the Balkans Support Contract, BRS is alleged to have failed to deliver or severely overcharged the U.S. Army on four of its seven original functional responsibilities. On the other end of client strength, Sandline is reputed to have charged above market rates to the tiny country of Papua New Guinea.[30]

The simple fact is that it is not clear that outsourcing always saves money, either in general industry or specific to military services. In a Deloitte & Touche survey of 1500 chief executives who had outsourced their own corporate services, only 31 percent believed that outsourcing had generated significant savings and 69 percent were disappointed in the overall outsourcing results.[31] Similarly, a RAND report on the private provision of professional military education programs in the U.S. found no cost savings.[32]

In fact, although the U.S. Defense Science Board, an advisory panel that has promoted military privatizing (not surprising in that it included industry executives), believed that over $6 billion in DoD savings would result from the first wave military outsourcing in the early 1990s, the claimed results are as yet unaccounted for. The GAO later reported the figure was overstated by at least 75 percent. Even lower savings figures are still unsubstantiated because of both poor accounting and contract cost growth.[33] The recurring pattern is that the military has set a policy of becoming more businesslike. It has not, however, fully examined whether doing so saves money or improves operations.[34]

Why Fight Hard?

Another contractual danger is the risk that firms may not perform their missions to the fullest. The principal cannot be present at all times and places (otherwise why contract at all?) and must rely on its agent's good faith execution of the contract. Agent incentives sometimes exist, however, both to prolong contracts and also not take undue risks, in order to protect their corporate assets.[35]

Given the nature of the work, the measures of PMF output are often imprecise, as military success depends on the opponent as well. Failure may be due to either enemy action or because of an agent's inability or unwillingness to perform. Even the establishment of clear proxies for measuring both contract effort and success provide an incomplete picture. An agent may be motivated to direct its efforts toward those representative goals rather than toward true success.[36] For example, a common complaint with PMF land mine clearance operations is that they often clear only major roads (both easier to clear and also more common measures of contract success), and the risky, but still necessary operations, such as clearing rural footpaths or the areas around schools are generally ignored.[37]

This scenario is most pernicious for a client's security with firms in the provider sector. A PMF that takes advantage of a client in a combat situation could end up amplifying or prolonging the conflict, or present other security risks. This certainly happened with hired forces in the Biafra conflict in the 1970s and many suspect it of the Ethiopia-Eritrea conflict in 1997–1999.[38] The Ethiopians essentially hired a small but complete air force from the Russian firm Sukhoi. Some contend, however, that the hired force failed to prosecute the war fully. It was willing to bomb civilian targets but rarely engaged Eritrea's air force (that was rumored to have hired Russian and Ukrainian pilots).[39] Concerns about the willingness of hired guns to fire on fellow nationals working for the other side have also surfaced in Yemen, Congo Brazzaville, and the Democratic Republic of the Congo (Zaire).[40] Similarly, in the Chechen conflict, the Russian army has had severe problem with its contracted units; 30 percent of contract soldiers have left before fulfilling their contractual obligations. Chechen rebel forces, who should know their effectiveness best, as they daily face them in the field of battle, cite contract forces as least likely to fight back when attacked and most easily bribed.[41]

An additional worry specific to the PMF industry is that links to other commercial entities may influence a firm to undertake actions that may not be in their client's best interest. Such connections mean that war may be fought not to end a conflict, but rather to help other private companies. EO's operations in Sierra Leone indicate this problem. A former soldier with EO notes, "when Freetown was secured, we were sent to recapture the Kono-district so DiamondWorks could start their mining. The right military decision would have been to follow the rebels into the jungle. The commercial interest negatively influenced the military decisions."[42]

One of the most damning claims is that certain firms have worked with both sides of a conflict to secure their own commercial position. Lifeguard allegedly supplied weaponry to the rebels in Sierra Leone. At the time, the firm was employed by several mining companies to safeguard their business sites from rebel attacks. The claim was that the firm arranged a quid pro quo to allow mining to continue unhindered in the war-torn region. Concurrently, Lifeguard was an associate of the firm of Sandline, which had been employed by the government to rid the country of the rebels.[43] Similarly, it has been reported that Sky Air Cargo, which provided aerial supply to the Sierra Leone government as part of the Sandline contract, also supplied the rebel side with weaponry.[44]

MILITARY OUTSOURCING AND THE LOSS OF CONTROL

The second danger with outsourcing is that the principal/client may become too dependent on the private military agent, risking what is known in economics as "ex-post holdup." That is, reliance on a private firm puts an integral part of one's strategic plans at the mercy of a private agent. This agent, however, is also affected by potential changes in market costs and incentives.

Moreover, a genuine concern is whether the government can quickly replace an outsourced service if the company fails in its provision. Often the services that clients risk losing from failed military outsourcing are neither peripheral, nor so easily withstood. In fact, this concern can result in two potential risks to the very safety and security of the principal or client itself: 1) the agent or firm might abandon the client when it is most needed, or 2) the agent might gain dominance over the principal. The former applies to all manners of clients contracting with firms in the provider and support sectors, whereas the latter is most likely limited to provider firms and their weaker clients. Industry advocates dismiss these risks, noting that firms doing so would sully their reputation for future contracts. But one can envisage instances where short-term costs or payoffs could trump considerations of reputation.

The Abandoned Principal: Broken Contracts and Over-reliance on Agents

The first scenario of an abandoned principal is driven by the fact that a firm may have no predilections against suspending a contract if the situation turns too risky, in either financial or real terms. Typically based elsewhere, PMFs risk no real punishment if they defect from contractual arrangements. It is true that their reputations may suffer, but in a number of situations they might choose to take a more rewarding single shot payoff or think that they can get away with it.[45] In game-theory terms, each interaction with a private actor in the international security market is sui generis, that is unique, or constituting a class alone. Exchanges take the form of 1-shot games, rather than guaranteed repeated plays.

The same potential for untimely exit holds true for an agent or firm's employees, over whom the client has even less control. Even if a PMF stays true to a contract, some of its employees may leave. The resultant loss is the same from the principal or client's perspective. The employees might be replaced, but a lag-time in services may not be anticipated by the PMF. In a dire situation, the results could be fatal.

One essential difference between exit by private employees and by those in public institutions is that leaving a PMF post is not desertion—punishable by prosecution and even death, but merely the breaking of a contract with limited enforceability. The simple matter is that no equivalent enforcement exists for PMFs to prevent desertion by their employees.

Thus, obligations and commitments of hired forces are less than those of public forces. Contracted employees are often easily discouraged by setbacks and casualties, and less apt to obey their officers when situations go sour.[46] Throughout history, this eventuality of breakdown and defection was the biggest risk from a hired army. As compared to a conscript army, when they return home, contract employees likely face no sanctions for defection as do conscripted soldiers.[47]

Another fear is that government functions may become hostage to the vicissitudes of the marketplace.[48] At the very least, a firm may choose the client's time of greatest weakness as the perfect situation to renegotiate contract terms. A pattern in the general outsourcing industry is that the outsourcer bids low, gets exclusive rights to control an entire department, and then reams the client with cost overruns. The client cannot refuse, as it is unable to replace the firm immediately for fear of disrupting its own operations. In many other industries, this outsourcing "siren song" has run entire companies aground.[49]

If the principal loses in-house capability, it is then at the mercy of its agent's compliance. An episode from recent Canadian military experience illustrates how unexpected problems can always arise whenever control is given over to private agents. In July 2000, the GTS Katie, a contracted military transport ship was carrying back from Bosnia a unit of Canadian Army soldiers, more than 550 vehicles, including tanks and armored personnel carriers, and 350 containers of ammunition and other sensitive military gear. Due to a financial dispute between two subcontracting agents, the ship began sailing in circles outside Canadian waters. Until the matter was resolved, the ship refused to make the delivery, essentially holding about one-third of the Canadian army's entire equipment and soldiers hostage. The standoff lasted for almost two weeks, during which time this sizable chunk of the Canadian military's inventory was unavailable, solely because its leadership had privatized transportation to save a minimal amount. As a defense analyst commented, "It's so embarrassing, it almost has a comedic flavour to it. But what would have happened if this had taken place when we were sending troops and equipment overseas instead of returning them to Canada? We would have a very significant problem to say the least."[50]

The essential point is that in outsourcing personnel and services, the client always risks becoming too dependent on the private agent. This danger is obviously more dire for weak clients, that are wholly reliant on firms in the provider sector, using them as a proxy for their own force capabilities. One of the reasons Sierra Leone's government was in such grim straits in 1995, before EO rescued it, was that a provider firm, GSG, had broken its contract and pulled out prematurely. GSG decided that the risks of serving the Sierra Leone government were no longer worth the benefits.[51] However, the threat extends across power differentials. For U.S. military planners, a worry of current outsourcing trends is that their forces are more reliant than ever on the surge capacity of private support sector firms. Despite this, few operational plans (or contracts) consider the risks, and field commanders, unaccustomed to these vulnerabilities, often operate unaware.

The particular dilemma is that if PMFs in United States service decide to pull out or resign, the firms and their employees legally cannot be forced to stay at their posts.[52] Civilians, even those fulfilling militarily essential roles, expressly do not fall under the Uniform Code of Military Justice (UCMJ) unless Congress declares war. However, such formal declarations have become increasingly rare, even in cases of full-scale hostilities, such as in Vietnam or the first Gulf War. In fact, any attempt to force civilian personnel to be held under UCMJ without this declaration would not only be "an egregious suspension of the supremacy of civilian constitutional authority," but also "tantamount to an admission by the political leadership that it has reduced the military to a point which requires the creation of a true, contracted 'Shadow Military.'"[53] As a result, military commanders cannot assume that PMF personnel will stay on the battlefield, or even in the theatre, simply because of military necessity or personnel shortages. Private employees may know the risks beforehand, but this fact makes no difference under the law.[54]

How might the dilemmas presented by a lack of control over agents play out for U.S. forces? Consider the increasing fear that weapons of mass destruction—including chemical or biological warfare—might be used in future confrontations, not by superpowers, but rather by any number of nation states, or anyone able to pay. Despite the growing risks of their use, one study has found that only 1 of 67 emergency essential contracts (for example, those covering mission critical areas) contained provisions to protect hired civilians against chemical or biological warfare. As a result, it is fairly likely that if such warfare was an imminent threat, military support firms and/or a significant number of their employees would decide the risks are not worth it and abandon their posts.[55]

The situation does not have to be so extreme for concerns with the loss of agent control to arise. The heaviest losses sustained by the U.S. military during the 1991 Gulf War were caused by a random Scud missile, equipped only with light explosives, that hit a military barracks at night, where it decimated an entire Army Reserve unit. Since that time, the unit's function—water purification, an innocuous, but essential job—has been privatized to a military support firm, as have tens of thousands of other military positions in critical areas.

If a similar scenario occurred in the future, a private firm might decide that its contract no longer makes sense, leaving the force without the technical capacity to supply itself. Or, its surviving employees might decide to get out of harm's way, with the same result. The essential fact is that the high level of reliance on outsourced support has not been tested in a real war situation.[56] The simple intuition suggests that, if hired personnel feel unsafe, some may decide that they simply aren't being "paid enough for this #%&"

and quit.[57] Even without a threat of violence, the risks of contractor walkout remain. For example, the Canadian Army contracted out its logistics support in the Balkans to AT Frontec and was plagued by high worker attrition rates (i.e., the employees simply quit too often), and the British Royal Navy plans for contracting out military repair yards have been threatened by labor strikes.[58]

Historical precedents of contractor walkout certainly exist, where private support units bailed out on forces that depended on them, with disastrous consequences. In World War I, for example, naval mine sweeping was originally handled by civilian-manned trawlers, since the task was seen as outside of the navy's mission—viewed as an overly technical task rather than 'real' warfare. However, in 1915, at the first naval action off the coast of Gallipoli, Turkey, the civilian manned trawlers working for the Allies pulled back when they came under fire. This left the way uncleared of mines, and as a result, 3 Allied battleships were sunk by mines and 3 more were severely damaged. Over 700 Allied sailors were killed.[59]

Essential or Non-Essential? No Longer the Question

The concern with military privatization, even in seemingly innocuous support areas, is that the entire military machine could quickly breakdown from their loss. Today, military personnel may no longer have the basic skills or equipment to perform the tasks that have been privatized.[60] Unfortunately, in the rush to privatize, this danger has been ignored.

As an example, under its own doctrine, the U.S. military is supposed to privatize only those services that are not "emergency-essential support" functions; that is, those functions which, if not immediately available, would not impair the military's mobilization and wartime operations.[61]

The reality is quite different. At the start of the 1990s, the U.S. Department of Defense Inspector General warned that a number of emergency essential services were beginning to be performed by civilian firms and that the U.S. military could not ensure that their service would continue during crisis or hostile situations.[62] However, in the years since, little evidence exists that concerns of lost control have been addressed. Rather, more than a million personnel have left the U.S. armed services and far more of such functions have been privatized. One illustration is the reversal of long-standing weapons purchasing requirements. The mandate once held that the military had to be able to achieve self-sufficiency in maintaining and operating new weapons systems within 12 months of their introduction. The new norm, however, is that instead of the military planning to do the job itself, weapons systems' contracts generally include service elements, detailing civilian-provided lifetime technical support.

This example illustrates the hazard of using business efficiency as a basis for military restructuring. If a military structure is to be capable of coping with the uncertainty that results from war and enemy action, a certain amount of redundancy must be deliberately built in.[63] Now, however, military personnel lack the training and skills to fill potential privatized voids.[64] If the military keeps privatizing key jobs, in times of crisis it may find that companies are unwilling to comply with its exact needs.

Another control aspect is the inability of private forces to switch between essential and nonessential functions. Certain combat limitations apply to civilian personnel serving in military support functions. As rear area forces are privatized to support sector firms, a commander will no longer have the option of using them to augment line units if the situation turns dire. For example, one of the classic stories of World War II is how, during critical stages of the 1944 Battle of the Bulge, U.S. Army support personnel (such as cooks, truck drivers, mechanics, and secretaries), were armed and sent to the front line to bolster weakened infantry units. Their relief helped turn the battle's tide.[65] Such times and potential needs are not past. Veterans of the 1993 Ranger operation in Mogadishu, Somalia, cite how support troops similarly had to help save surrounded U.S. troops. One of the veterans of that fight stressed that, even today, "Just as an infantryman needs to be ready to deal with change on the battlefield, so do our support troops. They need to be ready to grab their weapons and go out and fight."[66]

As support positions are privatized and eliminated, a beleaguered commander no longer has such insurance. Not only are support sector firms's employees often specialists either untrained or ill-equipped to shift to infantry roles, but their private status also carries legal uncertainties. Under international law, they risk being identified as illegal belligerents and potentially forfeit their rights and privileges of prisoner of war (P.O.W.) status.[67]

Finally, the concern remains about hired firms' standards of security. Typically, security at private firms, even when doing sensitive work, is lower than within military bureaucracies, which have long-established mechanisms for security assurance.[68] The recent travails of contracted Department of Energy labs provide an example of the security risks of privatizing.[69] Another is linked to the growth of information warfare. The nodes of connection electronic security, firewalls, access to information, encryption, core data between the military and its private agents are often particularly vulnerable. Hostile infiltration into a firm's lesser-protected systems not only risks the firm's failure to provide the client with necessary support, but also risks contamination of the client's systems.[70]

In fact, infiltration may not even have to occur, simple private cost cutting may suffice. When Airscan was contracted by the U.S. military to act as its "spies-in-the-skies" over the Balkans, the company used cheaper, unencrypted commercial television relays for the formerly secret broadcasts. Throughout Europe, anyone with a home satellite television receiver could watch live broadcasts of NATO peacekeeping and antiterrorist operations, meaning that it was easier to tune into a live video of U.S. intelligence activity than to get Disney cartoons (which were encrypted).[71]

Empowered Agents: The Real Danger of Lost Control

In addition to abandonment, some control risks raise even greater concern—specifically, the threat of the truly empowered agent of the provider sector category. This particular concern with private militaries goes well back in history. Machiavelli put it thus: "Mercenary commanders are either skilled in warfare or they are not. If they are, you cannot trust them because they are anxious to advance their own greatness by coercing you, their employer. If, however, the commander is lacking in prowess, as often as not, he brings about your ruin."[72] Hired guns may serve a client's wishes today, but force the client to honor their wishes tomorrow.[73]

PMFs argue that as they are companies, this risk is limited, claiming that the "fundamental law of a successful business is that the supplier is only as good as his last contract."[74] Firms that exploit the trust placed in them by a client would find their future sales growth threatened, and so arguably would be self-directed away from doing this in the first place.

In weak or failed states, however, military provider firms are typically the most effective local force, even with their small numbers. Moreover, friction between employer and employee is built into such a relationship and both parties have to look ahead to a time when their contractual relationship comes to an end. Thus, solidarity between hired troops and those who pay them has traditionally been not that strong.[75]

As a result, the risks of PMFs or their individual employees turning on their clients must be acknowledged. An unpleasant contract termination or any sort of dissatisfaction with the client's payment or orders could certainly have nasty repercussions. Those who fight for cash may fight with professionalism, but their loyalty will always be suspect, especially when more cash is on the table. "Hostile takeover" thus could take on new ramifications in military privatizing, with the agent moving to enforce its own interests by acting against its principal.

Traditionally, three situations indicate the potential for revolt by hired troops: 1) when the employer decides that he no longer needs the troops's services, and makes no guarantees about his future behavior toward them, 2) when the hired troops calculate that they can profit more by being taken onto the payroll of their employer's rival, or 3) when hired troops or their leaders decide that an opportunity to seize power exists and they can take over the employer's place.[76]

The precedent for hired troops to turn against their principals does exist. Historically, as explored in chapter 2, the "free companies," with which provider firms have certain parallels, had a fairly spotty record of loyalty. Examples from the 1300s include the Grand Catalan company that turned on its employer to set up its own Duchy in Athens, and the Norman army that Pope Gregory VII hired to break a siege of Rome by Holy Roman Emperor Henry IV. The Pope's force, mostly Muslims subcontracted by the Normans, managed to break the siege, but they then turned around and sacked the city themselves, massacring thousands and taking thousands more as slaves. Likewise, the common problem with privateers in the 1700s was that they often preyed on their patron's own shipping

Hired troops appear to be no more reliable in recent periods. The 1967 "Mercenary Revolt" in Zaire and the 1975 and 1990 coups in the Comoros illustrate. The 1961 French Foreign Legion revolt at the end of the Algerian War also indicates a clear example of willingness among foreign troops to fight against local nationals, even when they are brought under national military control.[77]

In fact, hired troops turning on their employers is not so shocking when one factors in the long history of employers turning on or betraying the trust of their troops. Even recently, over 150 Russian contract soldiers in Chechnya were allegedly killed by accompanying Russian military units, because of friction between the two forces.[78] Thus, hired troops might turn on clients in a pre-emptive attempt at self-preservation.

The evidence connected to the privatized military industry is obviously limited. But indications exist that in certain situations firms might decide to turn on their clients. In 1996, EO played a determining position in the internal politics of Sierra Leone. The firm is believed to have had a role in the overthrow of the Strasser regime, which had originally hired it, in favor of General Bio, whom the firm's executives considered a more effective leader and better partner.[79] The full extent of the firm's involvement is not known to outsiders, but it is believed that EO knew of the impending coup and neither reported nor opposed it, despite its contractual obligation to defend the government from all threats.[80]

Even if the firm itself remains loyal to its client, the reliability of its employees is by no means certain. Regular national soldiers are deterred from treason and revolt by a combination of patriotism, unit loyalty, and a fear of punishment. Even with these added pressures, some are treasonous anyway.

In contrast, for most soldiers within the PMF industry, these controls are lacking. There is little to no patriotic element, particularly when working for a foreign client. Some may feel loyalty to their firm, but it certainly cannot be as strong an emotional pull. Moreover, unit loyalty may also be limited, especially if personnel are distributed across a force or placed in bifurcated elements, such as air crews of one nationality flying support for infantry of another (e.g., EO's had Ukrainian pilots, but South African ground troops). The two may never even see each other in person, let alone build bonds of friendship that would lead them to eschew temptation. The fear of sanction may also be lessened with PMF employees. An employee who turned on the client could only be prosecuted in the client's state for treason and only if the attempt failed.

Not only must the client be concerned about contract employee loyalties, but firms themselves should also factor in counterintelligence, to establish and be certain of loyalty among their employees. However, none are known to have any such formal internal monitoring.

NOVEL INCENTIVE MEASURES

Agents are hard to monitor and the risks of military outsourcing entail that the agent's motivations to fight are not always what the principal would desire. A particular problem faces clients who contract military provider firms. Such clients are often the ones in the most need, but least able to pay. As a result, PMFs worry whether they will get paid. The outcome in a number of cases has been the creation of some curious structures that attempt to align principal and agent incentives.

Faustian Bargains
The first such incentive arrangement of profit sharing has been termed a "Faustian bargain" of sorts; that is, made for present gain without regard for future costs or consequences. The essential structure is that the firm is made a residual claimant of its client, akin to the corporate practice of paying a CEO only in stock to ensure high, unwavering motivation. Some PMFs' loyalties have been similarly locked in, by mortgaging valuable public assets to the firm or its business associates, often through veiled privatization programs.[81] To be paid, the firm has incentive to protect its new at-risk assets, thus binding its own fortunes with that of those client.[82]

The result often is a triangular system of profit sharing. The PMF, linked through shareholding or personal relationships to a broader corporate entity, simultaneously provides security to the government principal and its business ally's commercial operations. The government, in turn, provides the legitimacy, while the corporate entity provides the cash that indirectly pays the firm. As a consequence, the problem of securing destabilized regions becomes a viable business activity to the benefit of all parties.[83]

Cash-poor clients in Sierra Leone, Angola, and Papua New Guinea all allegedly paid for the agency of military provider firms in this way, by selling off mineral and oil rights either directly or indirectly to related companies. It is rumored that the rebel groups in Sierra Leone and Angola also had similar arrangements with rival corporations.[84] Key here are the linkages to multinational corporations and complex investment networks that the corporatization provides. The 'genius' from the firms's perspective is that corporate webs not only allow the bartering of security services for valuable concessions, contracts, and licenses, but also create exclusive business opportunities for other partners inside the same corporate structure.[85] Thus, firms that are weaker players in more competitive regions of the world economy gain an advantage in more dangerous zones through their partnerships with the PMF industry.[86]

As the Faustian name indicates, however, these arrangements create long-term losses for the principal that it may not have foreseen. The structure mandates that a potential valuable resource for the nation as a whole is sold off to satisfy short-term exigencies. The firm uses the hard circumstances of the client to induce it to give away possessions that it, or a succeeding regime, will later come to see as much more valuable. By mortgaging public assets today a government ensures less revenue for state coffers in the future, potentially creating generations of debt burdens for the populace as a whole.[87] In Sierre Leone in 1997, the government traded roughly $200 million worth of long-term diamond concessions, in exchange for a military bailout from the Sandline firm that was valued at $10 million.

This approach also threatens to reinforce approaches to natural resource development that are incompatible with sustainable economic and social development. The local state government remains integrated into the international economy only by means of an outside-owned corporation extracting raw materials, with extremely limited revenue distribution to the overall society locally.[88] In fact, little PMF contract money even goes through the local financial system, as the transfer, or "profit sharing," is typically untaxed and usually handled through offshore accounts.[89]

Strategic Privatization

"Strategic privatization" is another variation of this incentive structuring.[90] Even if a regime is not in military control of public assets (for example, a lucrative mine now held by rebel forces), as the globally recognized sovereign, it can still legally privatize and sell them off to a PMF or its corporate allies. In the previous scenario, the firm only had to defend assets under attack. With strategic privatization, the military firm must actively seek out and attack the government's opponent for payment. If successful, the rebels both suffer defeat and lose a valuable funding source, which the government did not control in the first place.

In corporate terms, this is a "debt equity swap." The PMF (or its corporate sponsor) takes a calculated business risk on the superiority of the military firm versus local adversaries, akin to swapping debt for stock shares as in the regular business world. Politically, it is a modern parallel to Michael Doyle's idea of "imperialism by invitation," where those who control ties to the international market acquire greater power over their local rivals.[91]

The Angolan government has made effective use of this strategy. In 1996, it developed a policy that all MNCs must provide their own protection, rather than depend on the state army to protect them. Not only did this policy lighten the load for the local Angolan army, but the government was also strategic enough in its thinking to sell concessions that placed mining companies astride its opposition's lines of communication.[92] The firms—and their combat protection—then battled with rebels to keep them out of their zones. This strategy is partly credited with the government's gains against UNITA.

The firms themselves deny that such arrangements occur, but their close ties with multinational corporations and the proliferation of associated firms that follow military firms into the region are hard to ignore (such as the linkages of Branch-Heritage with the most notable EO and Sandline operations as discussed in Chapter 8).[93] Even if these corporate links are not formalized, at the very least, the military firms provide associated companies that are potentially interested in investing in conflict zones with greater confidence in the prospect of a stable environment. They also might give a competitive advantage to associated firms, due to the ties that their PMF partners have already built up within the country. The local state government is more likely to trust such multifaceted corporations, as now they have a greater local stake to protect. These firms are less likely to disinvest at any future signs of instability, but instead actively help the government to quell it or at least be as supportive as possible depending on the sector.

It must be added, however, that many PMFs counter the concern that clients are mortgaging their futures by noting that clients are under no obligation to either hire them or to privatize their assets. Rather, they believe that their position is comparable to shareholders of a company bringing in new capital. The local agent's level of ownership may decline as a result, but they claim that the overall gain, in this case helping a government establish a secure environment that attracts an inflow of other business, is well worth it.

CONCLUSIONS AND COMPLICATIONS

The contractual dilemmas discussed in this chapter are only a beginning of the myriad of complications to consider. When contracting out military services, a host of questions arise: How do bankruptcies or mergers affect the continuation of services provided to a client? What happens in the case of a foreign takeover of the parent company, specifically if the new owners oppose the operations? Would an optimum strategy for a losing opponent be to attempt such a takeover in the boardroom, financially, rather than on the battlefield? All of these considerations lead to empirical expectations and questions quite different from those that arise when using one's own military.

ELEVEN

Market Dynamism and Global Security Disruptions

> The disjunction between the seriousness of international politics and the triviality of international relations theory is quite startling.
> —Professor R. B. J. Walker

One of the most standard conceptions of international security is that states are the central, and, in fact, only truly relevant actors in world politics. Indeed, for almost anyone who has taken an introductory international relations course in college, one of the first things he or she remembers is the typical opening lecture that compares global politics to a game of billiards: the table is the global political environment and the balls represent the sovereign power and relative position of states. The "game" of international politics thus is made up of the interactions among states, fueled by balances of power among them. In assessing both political calculations and the final outcomes of conflict, other actors are generally discounted.[1]

The burgeoning development of a privatized military industry implicitly challenges these assumptions. PMFs are private actors participating in warfare, a clear alternative to the supposed monopoly of states. What is more, the dominant theories of world politics originally drew their underlying theoretic foundations from microeconomic models. These political theories, however, certainly did not anticipate what would happen if the security system became linked with a very real market, with all its dynamic shifts and uncertainties.[2]

THEORY AND THE MILITARY MARKET

All markets do not operate perfectly, but instead often experience market friction, interference, and externalities, particularly when their structures are still emerging. With PMFs, the marketization of military services means that international security is complicated by potential market dynamism and disruptions. The "powers" are no longer exclusively sovereign states, but also include "interdependent players caught in a network of transnational transactions."[3]

In short, the privatized military industry represents alternative patterns of power and authority linked to the global market, rather than limited by the territorial state. This affects the dynamics of both interstate and intrastate security relations. Some might argue that the new industry represents no great change to international security, as it is merely another resource that states can use to enhance their power. Although this last aspect is true, in that many states have both used and benefited from PMFs, the total industry is also an independent, globalized supplier of services that are critical to security. It operates outside any one state's exclusive control or domain. In fact, the industry's general prosperity is a direct result of the weakening of state controls, not only in certain geographic zones of the world, but also over certain functional military areas. The demand for its services cannot be explained away by a worldview of pure state dominance.[4]

The new privatized military industry also means that state and nonstate actors alike now can access military capabilities formerly exclusive to strong states. Where state structures are weak, the result is a direct challenge to the local basis of sovereign authority, its ability to overwhelm all other challengers when it comes to violent force. But PMFs may provide a challenge to interests of regional powers or even great powers as well. They can aid forces, whom the leading states would rather not see succeed.[5] Some examples discussed later include PMFs that have worked for the governments of rogue states, such as Libya and Sudan, Colombian and Mexican drug cartels, and even radical Muslim jihadist groups.

The most important aspect, however, comes from the business structure of this new military actor. Even when PMFs are directly in the pay of a state (including even a superpower), the locus of judgment on how the military operations are carried out in the field is now outside state control. Through privatization, the state's agent of action is now no longer its national military, but instead a profit-motivated actor. The motivations are changed, and, some would argue, warped. As discussed in chapter 10, certain principal-agent dilemmas arise. These lead to a transformed relationship and, often, a much different outcome than with the standard use of public resources of power. The results also run counter to a number of key tenets of traditional security studies, such as the assertion that states seek to maximize their power by aiming for self-sufficiency, in order to minimize their reliance on others.[6] At the very least, the better paying PMFs are new competitors for the best military talent in their home state.[7]

The PMF industry also presents certain complications to conceptions of state sovereignty. For Max Weber, the most noted theorist about the modern state, one of the essential characteristics of a state is that it "successfully upholds a claim to the monopoly of the legitimate use of physical force in enforcement of its order."[8] Thus, the ultimate symbol of sovereignty is control over the means of internal and external violence; that is, the raising, maintenance, and use of military forces.[9]

Sovereignty defined under this standard is a general assumption of all the strands of international relations theory that presently dominate the field—realism, liberalism, and constructivism. Although they differ in what happens afterward, each presupposes systems made up of just sovereign states.[10] The entrance of a new private actor into the equation, however, illustrates that "sovereignty is not an absolute, timeless, and invariable attribute of the state."[11]

In short, whether we like it or not, change does happen in international politics; new actors materialize and old actors evolve. The emergence of the privatized military industry is just one aspect of this continual transformation. Unfortunately, the field of security studies gives us few analytical tools with which to understand this newest development and its impact. Our present theories of global balancing, bandwagoning, coercive diplomacy, deterrence, offense-defense dominance, or war termination all assume that the state is the sole provider of organized violence in the international system. With the introduction of capable PMFs, this supposition no longer holds so firm.

THE PRIVATE MILITARY MARKET AND FUNGIBLE POWER

The persistent focus of international relations theory has been on the distribution of coercive power across actors, especially military capabilities. In short, force is the 'ultima ratio' of international relations; no nation can reliably secure its own existence and well-being unless it can fend off the coercive capabilities of its neighbors, if not by itself, then with the help of allies.[12]

The ability to achieve these capabilities is a source of contention. Some claim that it is not that easy to transform economic assets and strength into military capabilities.[13] Financial capital does not directly equal military power. Rather, any dependence upon capital flows tend to suppress conflict among states.[14] In fact, they argue that the growing codependence among states in the economic realm is not a sign of vulnerability, but rather both raises the costs of aggression and lowers the incentives for war. In this theoretic liberal economic order, wealth is divorced from the coercive capabilities necessary for the control over territory, as are the rewards of this control This removes one of the main reasons for war.[15]

However, the military privatization phenomenon means that military resources are now available on the open market, often at better prices and efficiencies than could be provided by individual clients. So, contrary to predictions about the divorce of military and economic power, power is more fungible than ever.[16] Coercive capabilities are accessible to all with the money and wherewithal to seek them and former barriers to military strength are lowered. Put another way, PMFs mean that plowshares are more easily beaten into swords.

Although the creation of military force once required lengthy investments in terms of dedicated resources and time, now the whole spectrum of forces, from commando specialists to air forces, can rapidly be obtained by a client in a manner of weeks, if not days. Hence, economically rich, but population poor states, such as those in the Persian Gulf, are able to reach power levels above what they would be able to do otherwise. The same holds true for new states (Croatia) or even nonstate groups (CARE), which used to lack the institutional support and expertise to build or sustain a capable military force.

In addition, the new market means that actors are now able to add new specialized capacities, such as information warfare, or are even able to skip a generation of war skills (using consulting sector military expertise) that they would not be able to otherwise. Sudan, for example, has been able to field a squadron of Mig-29 fighter jets (considered by many the best in the world), flown by Russian contract pilots. The hired squadron gives the underdeveloped African nation the ability to detect and shoot down the most sophisticated weapons in the U.S. air arsenal, including the Tomahawk cruise missile and the F-117 and B-2 Stealth bombers.[17]

The orthodox state response to internal and external threats has been to boost military capability over the long-term or to seek alliances with other states. Now, states and other actors can build up their own security simply by hiring these capabilities off the international marketplace. However, in doing so, they maximize reliance on others.[18] Saudi Arabia, for example, has hired a slew of PMFs that do everything from planning and training to the maintenance and repair of weaponry. This contracting allows the kingdom to field a highly mechanized army, that is one of the most advanced in the Middle East, and certainly more capable than its population base would seem to support. In privatizing these duties, however, the Saudi units have become completely dependent on the contracted assistance; for even simple military exercises the Saudi military require the PMFs to undertake the planning and organization.[19]

With power made more fungible, the outcome might be a range of possible military leasing structures. One is a system akin to the hired units that proliferated in Europe from 1200–1850.

> As nations seeks ways to attain a surge capacity without the expense of sustaining a large peacetime military, and as they face difficulties recruiting from their own populations, contracting will be an attractive option for filling the ranks. Corporate armies, navies, air forces, and intelligence services may be major actors in 21st century armed conflict. This will open up new realms of strategy and policy.[20]

Another possibility is akin to the early medieval period, when highly expert military tasks, such as artillery and siege engineering, were often handled by hired specialists, rather than by regular soldiers. As military analyst Steven Metz notes, "Today, as warfighting becomes ever more complex and the costs of training and retaining technical specialists escalates, the same process is occurring."[21]

The final route might be a more postmodern outcome. Warfare would be carried out by loose, heterogeneous networks of state and nonstate military organizations. Some political or ideological in orientation, others profit seeking, but all operating in a constant flux of cooperation and conflict.[22]

Examples of all these abound. In the late 1990s, Ethiopia adopted a mix of the leased force and hired specialist scenarios, as it prepared to fight its neighbor, Eritrea. By common measures, a war between the two states was assumed unlikely, as neither had the force capacity or allies to translate into threatening capabilities. After experiencing early defeats, Ethiopia, like the Sierra Leoneans and the Croatians, decided that it too could seek out help from an alternative arena, the private sector.[23] The government hired Russian military experts, serving in a private capacity, to help run its air defense, multibarrel gun artillery, radar and electronic warfare. In addition, the firm Sukhoi sold Ethiopia a wing of Russian Su-27 fighter jets (equivalents to the U.S. F-15). More important, the firm also included in the contract the services of over 250 pilots, mechanics, and ground personnel, who would fly and maintain the planes. In effect, the firm leased out a small, but complete air force.[24] Ethiopia also hired its own set of private Russian ex-generals, who played a strategic planning role.[25] Intelligence reports assert that not a single meeting of the Ethiopian General Staff proceeded without the participation of the private Russian advisors, who guided the operation's planning and execution.[26]

Ultimately, this semiprivatized and totally revamped force would crush the Eritrean army in a lightning strike called "Operation Sunset." Similar to the Croatian experience, the war ended just weeks later. Having seen the effect such private military assistance had in turning Ethiopia into the leading regional power, analysts concluded that other states having similar border disputes may also turn to private help at the first sign of conflict.[27]

Indeed, this leasing model may well become a new model of quickly solving small wars. In 2001, Macedonia faced a separatist rebellion from an Albanian nationalist group. So, the government leased from Ukrainian sources a force of combat helicopters with crew, for use in its counterguerrilla operations. In fact, they modeled the plan after the governments of Equatorial Guinea and Sierra Leone in West Africa, that had earlier done the same.[28] Finally, the continuing war in Colombia offers a glimpse of the postmodern network scenario, where all sides in the conflict have linked up with privatized military help. While the government and multinational corporations have hired PMFs, the opposition as well has contracted out much of its intelligence and military functions. Flush with resources, Colombian political insurgents, drug cartels, international mafias, hired advisors, and other af-filiates have also made their own alliances. Thus, they are able to limit the exposure of their core, while making use of the latest technology.[29]

The ramifications of this new fungibility of power are obviously signifi-cant. By leasing military forces off a global market, the economic costs of maintaining a military force are externalized to outside the actor, as are the risks of political blowback from its deployment and losses. However, it also might mean a return to earlier periods of history, where private wealth and military capability went hand in hand, leading to more wars. Or as the an-cient Romans put it, *pecunia nevus belli*.[30] The ability to transform money rapidly into force returns the international system to the dangers of lowered costs of war.[31] A new international market of private military services means that economic power is now more threatening.

In sum, we often assume only the positive side of global markets and the profit motive. Globalism and the spread of capitalism are often viewed as di-minishing the incentives for violent conflict, so that the rise of global mar-kets, global civil society, and new transnational nonstate actors are viewed as immutable good things.[32] However, the emergence of a new form of transnational firms counters this liberalist assumption. PMFs are a different type of company that, instead, relies on the very existence of conflict for profit.

A DYNAMIC MARKET AND THE BALANCE OF POWER

The new privatized military industry not only eases the transformation of power into threat, but it also lies outside the state. It thus raises possibilities not contemplated by theories that exclusively focus on state behavior.

With PMFs, market uncertainties and dynamics are layered on top of the already difficult questions involved in the balance of power. The industry's potential to provide military capabilities rapidly not only makes threats to internal and external security more likely, but also more intricate to deal with. One area complicated by the existence of a private market of military services is the assessment of relative power.

Traditionally, the most reliable guide to who will prevail in a war is which side can marshal the most military power.[33] This rubric, however, is not that easy to make use of. Actors certainly have a motivation either to hide or over-state their strength. Moreover, raw counts of weapons might not be the best proxy for real power, as quality may matter more.

Hence, it was already difficult to access a rival's capabilities or force pos-tures. Now with PMFs, the combination of an openly accessible military ser-vices market and the new heterogeneity of military actors makes this appraisal even more difficult. When externalized onto an ever-changing market, a rival's potential capabilities or force postures are highly variable and able to transform rapidly. Thus, seemingly predictable power balances and deterrence relationships are now made unstable.

This increased dynamism in the balance of power could play out a number of ways. By hiring firms in the military provider sector, which could possibly be done in secret, an actor could quickly gain military capabilities that it did not have before, and rapidly gain either in force size or expertise. Or, clients could gain completely new proficiencies. One example is that agents without an information warfare potential could hire it off the open market and then attack unsuspecting or unprepared foes in a completely unexpected realm.[34] Even support sector firms could allow the deployment of military forces in ways that would otherwise not be expected.

With comprehensive military consulting services, clients can augment their military capabilities in a different, but just as effective, way. PMFs can aid in training and organizing clients' armed forces into a far more effective combat force and a thus more potent instrument of power. The end result is that a client might be able to enact what is known in the military intelligence community as a "training surprise." This is where rapid military restructuring takes place and completely new strategies and doctrines are adapted unbeknownst to a foe.[35] The possibility is increased that a state could be caught unaware at the new capability of their rival, as the Serbs (whose opponents had hired MPRI) learned in the aftermath of "Operation Storm."[36]

This shift in capabilities can affect assessments of power, and the balancing that results, in numerous manifestations, including the potential increase in miscalculation. Possibly engendered by a firm overselling its services, a client could develop a misplaced belief in the dominance of their reinvigorated offense and initiate war when they are actually not at an advantage.[37] This was a concern with contracts of military consultant firms in the unstable Balkans.

Likewise, this complication of security might move arms races onto the open market. That is, with PMFs involved, such competitions might begin to resemble instant bidding wars, rather than traditional military buildup over time. Arms races, in effect, become hiring races. For example, in the Ethiopia-Eritrea context, a twist on the traditional arms race emerged as the two sides competed first on the global military leasing market, racing to hire military skills (primarily from ex-Soviet sources), prior to taking the field of battle. The result is that the pace of an arms race is accelerated and "first-mover" advantages is heightened. These both impact on the likelihood of war initiation, as the sides might see shrinking windows of opportunity.[38]

Linked with the impact of military marketization on arms races are its resultant effects on arms control efforts. The monitoring and maintenance of agreements (particularly on conventional weapons), are equally made more difficult with the presence of PMFs. The privatization of military services means that military capability must no longer be closely held or kept in place. Thus, actual force capacities can be lowered without affecting the overall threat potential. For example, a state could make military cutbacks to stay in compliance with an arms control treaty, and thus reassure its neighbors. However, by hiring PMFs, yet it could then rapidly increase its armed force (by privatizing) in the very areas it cut back, and return to previous or even greater threat levels. In fact, it is questionable whether such an action would be in contravention of any standing arms control agreements, in that no current regime has treaty mechanisms designed to deal with private military leasing.

Although the previous examples explore how this new dynamism might make war more likely, in certain situations, the industry's presence and its disruptions could also act to lower the tendencies toward conflict. By making the balance of power harder to assess, greater uncertainty may deter some actors from engaging in conflict.[39] There is also the possibility that the announcement of a firm's hire may make a client's adversaries think twice about initiating war or more apt to settle, by changing the expected costs of victory.[40] Thus, one can envisage a scenario whereby effective corporate branding might have a deterrent effect, adding an entirely new layer of sophistication to the balance of power.[41] Likewise, hiring races in one region might muffle potential races elsewhere, by pulling slack out of the PMF market and raising the price for services. External markets shocks or failures could have a similar effect. Likewise, although they may make it more difficult in some aspects, private firms might also be able to bolster arms control efforts, by providing more efficient monitoring or by offering third-party verification activities.[42]

The end sum is that military market dynamics hold the capacity to make the balance of power more complex than ever. PMFs raise potential new structures and dynamics, certainly not anticipated by approaches not yet attuned to their presence.

THE PRIVATE MILITARY MARKET AND ALLIANCE BEHAVIOR

A particularly important area where private military firms might make international security more complex is in their unanticipated impact on alliances. The potential of the market might weaken patron-client controls, make burden sharing less necessary, and create new forms of alliance.

A critical structure in the global security environment has long been that between strong state powers ("patrons") and their controls over weaker, security-dependent states ("clients"), often located in the developing world.[43] Exemplified by state behavior during the Cold War, a bargain may be struck, where the patron provides aid and assistance necessary to the client's security. This support comes at a price, however. Military aid and protection is "used as a lever to promote objectives set by donor, which the recipient government would not have otherwise agreed to."[44] Objectives might include loyal behavior in foreign policy activity and support given in international forums. Patrons may also make internal requirements of the client; they may request that the military assistance provided only be used in certain ways or they may demand institutional or policy change. Thus, for a weak state, external aid often also brings costly concessions, risks of entrapment, and fears of abandonment.[45]

The private military market throws this relationship out of balance. In essence, weaker parties can exit the normal patron-client relationship among states, by becoming clients of a different sort. To gain military skills, training, and capabilities, they no longer have to accede to their patron's demands or limitations, but can contract for these on their own, often for better terms and packages.[46] Thus, the market gives small states a new degree of independence from large state support.[47] As a result, the traditional lever of military aid is less effectual for the patron.

The case of Papua New Guinea (PNG) and its patron Australia illustrates this point. From the 1970s to the present, Australia was the principal military aid donor to PNG. The main objective of the aid was to maintain Australian dominance in the South Pacific. However, Australia placed a number of limitations on the weapons and training that it would provide its client. When PNG requested help in training for counterguerrilla warfare against separatists on its Bougainville island, Australia refused, in particular motivated by human rights concerns about the local military. It also refused PNG's requests for assistance in developing capabilities in electronic warfare and logistics.[48] Thus, the PNG leadership always felt that Australia was intentionally keeping its forces weakened.[49]

The emergence of the privatized military industry however, offered the chance for PNG to evade Australian strong-arming in ways it did not have before. Rather than being dictated by its patron, it could develop military capabilities along the lines it saw fit. Faced with a rebellion in 1997, the government hired combat air support and commandos from the British firm Sandline. As explained by Prime Minister Julius Chan, "[W]e have requested the Australians support us in providing the necessary specialist training and equipment . . . They have consistently declined and therefore I had no choice but to go to the private sector."[50]

The episode illustrates that the availability of alternative private military options creates a new variable in patron-client relations. Of greater importance, under current conditions in the market, it is a change that works to the advantage of weaker states.[51]

PMFs might affect alliances in other ways as well. Studies of alliance behavior point to functional differentiation as a method to institutionalize an alliance.[52] States divvy up military tasks and so, by default, become more dependent on one another. However, PMFs now provide an alternative means of filling military specialty gaps. This means that alliance partners are potentially less reliant on one another than earlier conceived, with resultant weakening of their ties.

The consequences are potentially significant. For example, cases where an ally defects or does not support its partner's intervention or war decisions might no longer act as a restraint or veto. Almost any gaps from the withdrawal of the ally's forces can be replaced by military provider sector specialists. In the mid 1990s, for example, both the Angolan government and UNITA were faced with the withdrawal of their allies' military forces (the Soviets, Cuba, and the SADF). Both sides responded by filling out specialty areas with hired outsiders, who ran everything from command and control facilities to air defense.[53] Similarly, many of the competencies that the European NATO partners rely on the United States to supply for external deployment, such as lift capacity, logistics, and intelligence gathering and analysis, now can be supplied to an extent by support sector firms (including even by those that already provide these functions to the U.S. military). The result is that they are actually less bound by a potential veto on their out-of-area operations than conventionally thought.[54]

The implication is that future wars and interventions may well see a modularization of forces. In this setup, coalitions may be built from a multiplicity of military actors, potentially both public and private.[55] This means, however, that alliances might form and dissolve more quickly, and be more unpredictable in their makeup. The constant flux would also present a real challenge for those looking for the politically-correct side to join in a war. With such diversity, it becomes more difficult to figure who exactly are the "good guys."[56]

The market also opens up new forms of aid and alliance. Provision of military assistance has long been the option of choice for building and reinforcing political ties with allies. When a powerful state wants to establish close links with a weaker state, weapons are delivered and military advisors sent to train the weaker state's forces in their use and tactics. These personnel often even end up assisting an ally's force in their operations. Moving in the other direction, client officers are also often brought back to attend domestic military schools.[57] The general aim of these activities is to create tight linkages and shared outlooks between allies' military services.

However, as the market allows the easy transformation of financial resources into military might, the policy mechanisms of aiding an ally have begun to develop new modes. Military aid now can come in the simple form of cash infusions. In 1995, for example, moderate Arab states (including Saudi Arabia, Bahrain, and Kuwait) sought to aid the Bosnian government, while at the same time counter the radicalizing influence of Iranian military aid. They did so not by sending any of their own personnel but rather through funding the "Train and Equip" program, paying for military training provided by MPRI.

A rationale for this new form of aid is that it may be less likely to embroil a donor in an ally's fighting. It also means that donors of military assistance no longer must be states. Nonstate actors, including even a single rich individual, can become valuable potential allies, able to bolster a force or tilt local military balances indirectly, even from a great distance. Rakesh Saxena, for example, was a Thai businessman who financed the Sandline operation in Sierra Leone.[58] The implication is that the "Soros Effect," whereby private individuals have become critical players in international finance, can thus also move into international security.[59]

The significance for the United States is that although private market relations have long shaped American alliance politics, rarely have they become a direct alliance tool. In recent years, however, many of the military aid programs to new U.S. allies, such as to Macedonia and Nigeria, have been outsourced. In short, military-to-military contacts are increasingly being replaced by corporate-to-military contacts.

The concern with this is that the very nature of security aid's role in alliance politics might thus escape traditional, time-tested constraints. Unregulated privatized military assistance represents a significant departure from the government-sponsored security assistance programs as the U.S.'s Foreign Military Sales (FMS) and the International Military Education and Training (IMET) programs. The worry is that these military to military contacts are, in the view of U.S. senior officers, "a vital ingredient in the building of strong alliances."[60] However, in a new privatized military paradigm, this important binding mechanism is jeopardized.[61] Perhaps most important, the clear, upfront alliance commitment that official military aid embodies is replaced by a nonbinding trading relationship. Not only is it harder to use official military aid to help shape the international environment (the prime component of U.S. engagement strategy), but the ability to conduct coalition operations based on past mutual training experience would also be lowered.

A counterargument is that PMFs, in particular consulting sector firms, might dovetail with official military aid, by teaching doctrines similar to that of their home states, or encouraging professionalism. However, in comparison to official aid, PMF contracts are single-shot business transactions. Hired military aid comes with no political strings attached and thus, unlike formal aid, the client can use and dispose of these services readily, without concern for any favors that may require repayment.[62] Also, even if the training is similar to that provided by a state military, it is not the exact equivalent. It is now one step removed, more controlled by the local client's desires, altered by financial limitations, potentially outdated, and certainly does not build useful personal ties between the two allies' forces.

THE MARKET AND THE EMPOWERMENT OF NONSTATE ACTORS

Leading from the previous discussion on new forms of alliance, a critical aspect of the private military industry's rise is that it is essentially open to all customers. The result is that nonstate groups that were previously at a severe disadvantage in a state-dominated system, now have new force mobilization options and new paths to power.

In the typical picture of world politics, individuals and organizations must rely exclusively on the power and authority of the national government in whose jurisdiction they reside to secure their basic needs and amenities. Now, there are new power alternatives available from the international market. At the very least, these new privatized capabilities will allow nonstate agents to decrease the qualitative edge held by advanced militaries.[63] Although they may never rival the U.S. Army, one should not underestimate PMFs' capabilities. A number of U.S. military observers feel that PMFs could field units as, or even more, effective than any military in all of Africa, including the advanced South African forces.[64]

Some PMF executives argue that their firms only work for states, and only reputable states at that.[65] Their rationale is that they would be driven away from such potential customers by a longer-term perspective, aiming for more future contracts with state clients. However, both the structure of the market and the record so far argue against this. Much like the situation of a prisoner's dilemma game with a known ending point, in certain situations, high single-shot payoffs might trump.

The current global market for PMFs is essentially unregulated, lacking both formal controls and limits. So, the firms make the choice of whom to work for. Some have chosen to assist dangerous groups in the past when it was in their interests, and, provided the money is good and barring any great changes in international regulation, will likely continue to do so in the future.[66] Chapter 14 explores this point in further detail, but, suffice it to say, the worry with this present market sector is that such rogue firms,

> could fuse their power with that of arms traffickers, drug dealers, and terrorist groups, thereby creating an unholy alliance of non-state agents with the economic, military, and political power to overwhelm states and the state system in general. They could also assist rogue states unable to receive military aid through the international state system.[67]

The only situations where firms are even mildly limited restricted from working for antistate groups have been where the home state of the firm prevents this with strict domestic regulation.[68] However, if PMFs do not like such controls over their contracts, they have the easy option of pulling up stakes and reopening shop elsewhere in a more amenable situation. This is what many believed Executive Outcomes did in 1999. The firm dissolved when South African legislation became too difficult for contracting, but a number of successor firms with new names have opened up in other states without strong regulation.

Instances of military firms working for violent nonstate groups will more be the case with the lower-end, more itinerate provider sector firms, especially those having a tougher time succeeding in a competitive market. As noted in chapter 1, rebel groups in Angola, Sierra Leone, and DRC are all reputed to have received military help from private companies that provided specialized military skills and support. Likewise, less transparent firms such as Stabilco, Niemoller-Group, and GMR, have been accused of engaging in illicit arms and diamond dealings, aiding rebel groups, sometimes on multiple sides of conflicts.[69]

Indeed, there has also been a link with terrorist networks. In the late 1990s, a number of firms targeted the lucrative market of training young Muslims who were being recruited globally to join radical groups engaged in jihads, or "holy wars" in places such as Chechnya and Afghanistan. For example, Sakina Security Ltd. was a British firm that offered military training and weapons instruction to these recruits, as part of its "Jihad Challenge" package. The teaching included hand-to-hand combat techniques and how to "improvise explosive devices," both of which had obvious utility in terrorist actions.[70] Sakina was reported to have been affiliated with TransGlobal Security International. This was another British firm, which also reportedly ran military training camps (including teaching the use of machine guns) for radical Muslims.[71] Similarly, Kelvin Smith, an American government employee, ran a side business (based in Western Pennsylvania) that provided military training to groups purporting to be headed to the fighting in Bosnia and Chechnya. The training even involved mock terrorist-type attacks on utilities plants. Smith also purchased assault rifles and thousands of rounds of ammunition on behalf of the clients. Six members of the group trained by Smith later turned out to be members of al Qaeda, who were convicted in 1993 of planning a series of attacks around New York City. Smith, in turn, was sentenced to just two years for violating U.S. gun laws.[72]

Likewise, certain international criminal organizations, including Colombian and Mexican drug cartels, are reported to have received assistance in counterintelligence, electronic warfare, and sophisticated weaponry from what one might consider "rogue firms," such as Spearhead Ltd.[73] They provided their clients with capabilities that not only rivaled but were often superior to those of public security forces, doing "immeasurable damage to the war on drugs."[74]

The example of the many PMF spin-offs that worked for the various sides in the DRC war also reveals another new market twist. Even if their firms decide not to work for nonstate groups, there is also an opportunity for employees to work in more established PMFs and gain experience in private military operations and business management. Then, they can break off in search of higher returns at the head of their own companies. In a typical supply and demand market, they will be drawn to providing services to these other parties.

PMFS AND INTERVENTIONS: A PROFIT FROM PEACE?

Perhaps less perniciously, the market also opens up military options for more reputable nonstate actors, such as international and regional organizations.

One example is driven by the rise of private intelligence firms. The possibility now exists for entities that previously lacked their own intelligence capability to buy such services off the open market. One likely client type is international institutions, such as the UN, or regional organizations such as the South African Defence Community (SADC) or Western European Union (WEU), that have been increasingly active in operational scope and thus have growing intelligence requirements. Unfortunately for them, national sensitivities among member states about sources and methods have hampered their previous efforts at intelligence collaboration. Today, these organizations can instead purchase such capabilities off the global market, no longer dependent on what their state constituents are willing to share. The United Nations has already taken advantage of this option, recently hiring one firm to provide intelligence on the UNITA rebels' guns-for-gems trade in Angola, while it paid another for its satellite observation of Iraqi arms sites.[75] The International Monetary Fund (IMF) has also begun to contract with private firms for its own intelligence capacity.[76]

However, it is in the area of peacekeeping interventions that the industry truly alters the possibilities of these organizations. The intervention choices of both the UN and regional groups are normally limited by the weaknesses of their member states, in terms of both material capabilities and willingness to deploy forces. Now, the hire of private firms of both the military provider and support sectors can fill in client and institutional shortfalls and allow these organizations to undertake operations that they would not be able to otherwise.

For instance, the Economic Community of West African States (ECOWAS) is an organization of relatively poor West African states. Its militaries are severely limited in certain specializations critical for effective external intervention, particularly lacking air support and logistics. In both Liberia and Sierra Leone, ECOWAS forces were, nonetheless, able to deploy, primarily due to the facilitation of PMFs, such as ICI Oregon and PAE. Likewise, current UN operations increasingly make use of military support sector firms for logistics, air transport, demining, and security consultation. In the East Timor operation, the UN contingent includes forces from two South African firms, KZN Security and Empower Loss Control Services, who provide local intelligence, while Dyncorp supplies the UN's logistics, transport, and communications.

More controversial, however, have been recent discussions of using military provider sector firms in privatizing the peacekeeping role.[77] As noted in chapter 4, severe flaws remain in the current UN peacekeeping system, most importantly that forces are often unavailable due to member-state unwillingness. Even when forces are provided, the donated national units are often slow and cumbersome to deploy, poorly trained, underequipped, and ineffective when challenged, due to either lack of motivation or a flawed mandate. Local parties are thus often unimpressed by UN forces and their actions show their contempt. In 2000, for example, lightly armed, underaged RUF forces in Sierra Leone held hostage hundreds of UN troops with impunity.[78] In sum, "UN peacekeeping efforts all too often turn into multilateral, multi-billion dollar failures, bedeviled by confusion of lines of command and rules of engagement."[79]

Accordingly, certain analysts, with the enthusiastic backing of PMF executives, have proposed military provider firms as a new type of peacekeeping forces. Their essential belief is that "Private companies . . . can do it faster, better, and much cheaper than the United Nations."[80] With the overall dissatisfaction over the current state of peacekeeping, proponents of studying this idea have expanded to include many traditional supporters of the United Nations, including past commanders of UN peacekeeping operations, a number of humanitarian advocates, and even Sir Brian Urquart, who is considered the founding father of UN peacekeeping.[81] There remains, however, great institutional opposition to the concept inside both the United Nations and the overall humanitarian community, so that it is far from certain.[82]

The advocates' proposal is that by privatizing aspects of peacekeeping, the effectiveness and efficiency of operations might be increased. PMFs, lacking the procedural hang-ups that hamper international organizations, can specifically target their recruiting at more capable personnel, are less threatened by the internal national tensions that plague multinational forces, are likely to be better equipped, and can take quicker and more decisive action.[83]

The contrasting examples of the experiences in Sierra Leone of EO and the multilateral operations is the most often cited case for this proposal. The private EO operation was about 4 percent of the UN's operation in size and cost. More important, it is also generally considered to have been far more successful. It defeated the rebel force in a matter of weeks and restored enough stability for the country to hold elections, something that the UN required years to accomplish.[84]

There are three primary scenarios for privatizing peacekeeping, listed here in order of those most likely to least likely to occur over the next decade. In the first, firms would provide active protection to humanitarian workers and their operational assets, such as convoys or warehouses. "The business of providing humanitarian aid has become increasingly dangerous. In virtually every part of the world, those providing aid to distressed populations have been robbed, beaten, raped, abducted and murdered."[85] In fact, more Red Cross workers were killed in action in the 1990s than U.S. Army personnel.[86]

Where they once kept PMFs at an arm's distance, humanitarian groups may soon become a vital part of the industry's customer base. In a recent project sponsored by the aid group CARE and the UN Department of Humanitarian Affairs, Janice Stein writes,

> NGOs should consider the privatization of security for humanitarian purposes . . . Since the core dilemma humanitarians face is the ability of predators to prey on civilians and NGO staff at will, and since nations and the UN are increasingly hesitant to furnish the necessary means to provide that security, it is worth exploring whether in the face of the privatization of assistance, the privatization of security is also appropriate.[87]

Although the ability of the humanitarian actors to create a consensual environment themselves is severely limited, military provider firms would be able to provide site and convoy protection that would allow much more effective aid actions in nonconsensual environments.[88] In addition to the direct benefit, guarding humanitarian groups and their assets might also lessen pressure on outside governments to do something and also prevent local insurgents from gaining control of supplies, potentially helping to avoid the type of rationales that led to the United States/United Nations intervention into Somalia.[89] The extension of this scenario to a broad practice is not all that unlikely. Already, there are isolated instances. At least seven UN bodies already use firms such as Armorgroup in security roles.[90] Likewise, the aid group Worldvision received escort from the Sandline/Lifeguard operations in Sierra Leone.[91] Indeed, since humanitarian organizations operating in places such as Somalia have been forced to contract with local warlords, the more formal business alternative might be preferable.

The second scenario for international organization's bolstering themselves by the PMF market is where a firm would act as a "Rapid Reaction Force" within an overall peacekeeping operation. In this case, the PMF would be hired to provide the much needed "teeth" for peace operations. Although smaller in number than the rest of the operation, they would offer often underequipped and poorly motivated peacekeeping forces the backing of their sophisticated military talent.[92]

Whenever recalcitrant local parties break their agreements or threaten the operation (such as in Sierra Leone where UN forces were blockaded by the RUF rebels), the firms would be the ones that provide the 'muscle' role that the U.N. blue helmets are currently unable to fill. Used judiciously as part of longer-term conflict management efforts, they might provide the short-term force necessary to stabilize situations at critical junctures in the operation.[93] The British military demonstration off Sierra Leone in Fall 2000, when the UN operation was threatened, provides the precedent for how a small force can be critical in both deterring local adversaries and stiffening the back of the overall operation.[94] In fact, it is privately contracted helicopter gunships (which had been hired by EO and then Sandline), flying for Sierra Leone's government, who are credited with rescuing embattled UN peacekeepers there on numerous occasions.[95]

The third, and most controversial scenario involves privatizing the entirety of an operation. The proposal is that, when states choose not to undertake humanitarian interventions and UN forces are neither ready nor willing, the operations would be turned over to private firms.[96] On their hire, the PMFs would deploy to a new area, defeat any local opposition, set up infrastructures, and then, only once the situation was stabilized, potentially hand over to regular UN peacekeepers.

Although it may sound quite extreme to some, in fact, this very scenario was a live option during the Rwandan refugee crisis in 1996. It was discussed both inside the UN and at a U.S. National Security Council session that, in lieu of UN peacekeepers whom no states were willing to supply, the EO firm be used to create a secure humanitarian corridor. The plan was dismissed when the question of who would actually pay the bill was raised.[97] At the same time, a separate 'business pitch' on behalf of Sandline was made to the U.S. Secretary of the Army by his former business associates, now working on behalf of the firm; it was also turned down after being forwarded to higher levels of decision.[98]

EO, in fact, had already performed a business exploration of whether it had the capacity of intervening into Rwanda, doing so internally at the time of the original genocide in 1994, which killed well over 500,000 people. Internal firm plans claim that EO could have had armed troops on the ground in 14 days and fully deployed 1500 personnel, supported by its own air and fire support, in six weeks. The concept of the operation would have been the creation of "security islands" that would be used to provide safe havens for refugees and disaster relief. Figure 11.1 illustrates the structure of the proposed force.

The estimated costs for a 6-month operation would have been $600,000 per day ($150 million total) and possibly hundred of thousands of people might have been saved.[99] This private option compares quite favorably with

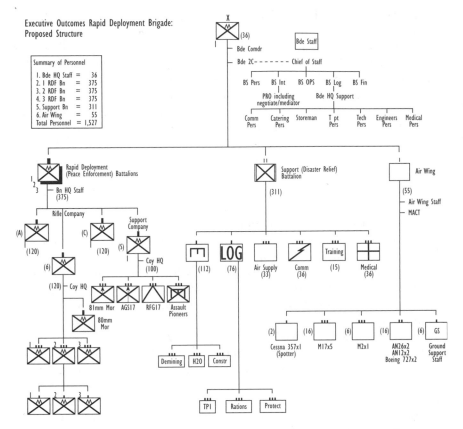

Figure 11.1. The Proposed Executive Outcomes Rwanda Peacekeeping Force

the eventual UN operation that deployed belatedly after the killing, and primarily in a humanitarian role. The UN operation also ended up costing approximately $3 million per day, more than five times the cost of the proposed privatized intervention.

The concept of the private sector profiting from peace operations has the potential to radically transform the very nature of UN peacekeeping, opening up all sorts of new options. For example, firm executives have even proposed the use of PMFs to retake foreign cities, such as Mogadishu, Somalia, that have been lost to warlords and lawlessness. The firms would stabilize them and turn them over to local or UN administration after the level of conflict is reduced, thus allowing failed states to rejoin the international system.[100]

The critical question, however, is that even if the firms might be more efficient than UN operations, do they provide a long-term solution to conflict resolution? The key to any durable peace is the restoration of legitimacy, in particular the reconstitution of control of organized violence to public authorities.[101] Unfortunately, if peacekeeping is privatized, the "companies become a temporary means of propping up the existing order, but do nothing to address underlying causes of unrest and violence."[102]

In the end, privatizing peacekeeping could provide huge potential and certainly greater flexibility to the UN, but it is important to realize that these potential gains come at the risk of all the dilemmas raised in the rest of this work, particularly those in chapters 10 and 14. The firms may be hired to act on behalf of the international community, but, being profit motivated, will potentially operate quite differently. Moreover, military provider firm employees are often untrained in the culture of peacekeeping, tending to come from elite forces fundamentally about combat, rather than peacekeeping.[103] The difficulties of integrating a better-paid private force within a larger UN force also have been unexplored by the proponents of the plans. There would likely be high resentment among the peacekeepers towards the PMFs, which could risk suboptimal outcomes on the ground. Finally, many of the arguments made against the United Nations having its own standing army would also apply as well to it having a private army (including issues of Security Council dominance by a small number of states, UN command and control, and risks of the force getting stuck in potential quagmires).

If the United Nations does forge ahead with privatizing peacekeeping, a particular worry would be if it primarily relied on contractual limitations to bind the firms. This would risk premature withdrawal by the forces, without consideration for the political costs and risks to those depending on their protection or, even worse, the firm acting to extend a contract by prolonging the conflict.[104] It is important that clear mechanisms of accountability, control, and transparency of the firms be in place. In particular, there must also be assurances of corporate independence (i.e., only using firms expressly unlinked to other business networks that might warp their motivations); the maintenance of competition to ensure quality and replacement; clear standards to ensure a quality product; outside vetting of personnel; the attachment of independent observer teams; and, the requirement that firm personnel place themselves under the jurisdiction of international tribunals for any violations of the laws of war.

THE EMPOWERMENT OF PRIVATE INDUSTRY

In each of these previous situations, private companies are active in the realm of international security and their employees are taking larger roles within the military environment. This risks the potential overempowerment of private industry, where greater military effectiveness may be distributed across the international system to harmful ends.

One implication may be particularly relevant with military provider sector firms operating within weak states. If linked with broader corporate allies or clients, it could manifest itself as corporate imperialism. One has to remember that, even in the United States, big industries were dominions apart until the end of the 19th century. They had their own armed forces and enforced their own laws, often with great abuses. Indeed, the eventual preponderance of public law is only a 20th century achievement.[105]

The one aspect that formerly limited the power of multinational corporations was their physical weakness, which kept them dependent on the local state and only able to operate in zones of relative stability. This security was provided by the state, meaning that their operations and even survival as a viable business were conditional on the local state carrying out its responsibilities.[106]

Today, this limit no longer necessarily holds true. PMFs possess a capacity for armed force that rivals and even surpasses local state functions. They can transfer this to their multinational corporation clients. Thus, multinational corporations and their allied private military firms now have the capability to engage in what they term "security-led investment," in which the physical weakness of the local state is irrelevant to their business operations.

A number of multinational corporations have already created bastions within weak states or situations of internal conflict, protected by their own armed forces hired from military provider sector firms. Unfortunately, the interests of such empowered corporations are often not in line with those of the local society or government. PMFs could thus act as leaders in a new corporate dominance, or as the UN special rapporteur put it, "the multinational neocolonialism of the twenty first century."[107] At the very least, as explored in chapter 14, such protected corporate bastions provide security only to rich outsiders and act to deflect threats onto poorer, and thus less protected, portions of local society.

Private firms reject this thesis of a new type of corporate imperialism, noting that generally they have been invited in by legitimate governments.[108] Such a response, however, misses the parallel to 19th-century imperialism, which also usually began when a weak ruler requested the original intervention.[109] In a manner, PMFs and their corporate sponsors can be viewed as exploiting power struggles for financial gain, the hallmark of an imperial past. Their frequent integration into large financial holdings and intricate contractual bonds makes the linkage even more telling.[110]

That powerful outside business interests often have a certain measure of control over the actions of the weak local state is generally accepted; private military firms, however, continue the potential reach of their control to the military realm. Already, a number of transnational corporations have been linked to violent conflicts, including providing equipment and support to local military forces that do their bidding, in order to expand their own business interests.[111] PMFs represent the next logical step in the services side, and, as such, become simply a more direct extension of the power of outside corporations. Although such scenarios may sound preposterous to those residing in secure, established states, it is important to remember that a number of PMFs possess skills and forces on call that are often greater, or equal to, those of many military forces in weaker states. Many consider the firms to be "powerful enough to dislodge any government in Africa" and thus a real concern for any local authorities that dare to challenge them.[112]

With this expansion of corporate interests and power, an increased danger also arises that PMFs and their corporate allies will come into conflict, not just in a business sense, but also through means of violence. The frequent warfare that occurred between the various mercantile companies in the 1600s and 1700s provides a worrisome historic precedent.[113] With new capabilities, widely divergent interests, and great sums of money at stake, corporate forces might again enter battle, further expanding the privatization of war. In fact, this scenario may already have occurred. EO is rumored to have engaged forces of Omega Support Ltd. in Angola. Violence among firms has also been reported in the DRC and Sierra Leone, often over competing mining claims.[114]

Likewise, it is easy to envisage situations where military provider forces might engage forces managed by advisory firms or even target the backing given to an adversary by a support sector firm. Even the possible privatized UN operations (for instance, if they were to be sent to the DRC) could find themselves facing private soldiers on the other side, in effect the complete proxyization of war. For the United States, the implications of such a system raise an array of foreign policy questions that seem almost too fantastic to consider.

> In a system where corporations or cartels have their own power that transcends the strictly economic, the United States will have to decide what sort of relationship to have with transnational corporations or multinational cartels. Should, for instance, the United States consider signing treaties, perhaps even non-aggression pacts with powerful corporations? And, if the corporations do appear to pose an actual challenge to the power of the state, should the U.S. Government pursue a strategy designed specifically to prevent the accumulation of non-economic power by corporations? And, what should U.S. policy be toward transnational security companies such as the highly successful Executive Outcomes composed of former South African soldiers. Clearly if power continues to accrue to transnational corporations, the United States will have to re-think some of the basic tenets of its approach to security and world politics.[115]

As this alludes to, an added danger of greater private power is the risk that empowered corporate actors themselves will become competitive not only with weak local states, but also to the national interests of other powers, including even their own home states. Transnational corporations often possess interests that diverge from those states where they were originally based (such as which partners are appropriate to trade with, or which local leader should be in power). Even when their home is a powerful state, some have chosen to act against the home-base interests. Examples of American-based arms manufacturers and technology firms that sold their goods to foreign enemies of the United States abound; nothing would seem to make PMFs, who have even less oversight on their services, any different.

Obviously, the likelihood of a corporate-military nexus challenging powerful states is a distant scenario, but historic precedent certainly exists for private business enterprises to become direct military competitors of states, even those from their own homelands. For example, in a dispute over territory their joint forces had seized in India, the East India Company blockaded British troops, while the Hudson's Bay Company once fired on a Royal Navy squadron to drive it away from its harbors. Likewise, the Dutch East India Company claimed its own sovereign right to sell territories to the enemies of the United Provinces.[116]

PMFs argue that they have been proven to act responsibly within national interest. But, as explored in greater depth in chapter 14, they are also responsible to their clients. Thus, the possibility always exists that profit interests and national interests may come into conflict, with little guarantee that the firm will not follow its paying client, at the expense of its former homeland. Moreover, responsible choices in the past provide no certainty that corporate policy will not change in the future (perhaps in an economic downturn or if the client pool shrinks). These firms possess skills and capabilities that bring them onto the level of state functions; there is no assurance that they will not attempt to rival them for the right price.

CONCLUSIONS: THE NEW POWER OF THE MARKET

In sum, although a near explosion in the extent and range of privatized military activity has occurred around the globe, analysis has not kept pace. The theorized system of hard "billiard ball" states may gradually be replaced by a multilayered international order resembling that of previous eras.[117] Conceptions of the international security environment exclusively based on the sole power of states miss out on some of the important changes that the privatized military industry portends. The result is that states in the current global system may be like dinosaurs toward the end of the Cretaceous period: powerful but cumbersome, certainly not superceded, but no longer the unchallenged masters of their environment.[118]

The marketplace of violence presents a number of potential changes upon international security, effecting both the possible means and outcomes of conflict. And, the PMF phenomenon is only just emerging. The evidence so far indicates that the industry will grow in size, scope, activity, and resultant influence within the international security sphere. Thus, it is important to be attuned to both PMFs' presence and possibilities.

TWELVE

Private Firms and the
Civil-Military Balance

All members of society have an interest in its security . . . but the officer
corps alone is responsible for military security to the exclusion of all
other ends.

—Samuel Huntington, *The Soldier and the State: The Theory
and the Politics of Civil-Military Relations, 1957*

T he balance of soldier and state has traditionally been delicate. On
one hand, a government requires an effective, functioning military
for its survival. Civilian leaders must give trained military officers
both the leeway to make proper decisions and the resources to accomplish
their tasks. To do otherwise is to risk domestic stability or provoke external
aggression. However, just as a strong military apparatus can be the bulwark
of state security, it can also become a risk to the regime itself. Maintaining
proper control of the military is a key priority of governance, one that is particularly difficult in weak or developing states, where power often comes
from the barrel of a gun.

The introduction of a third party into the mix, specifically private military firms, only further complicates the situation. Even in stable countries,
where the risk of military coups or mutiny is relatively unthinkable, the rise
of the privatized military industry raises concerns about the relations among
public authorities and the military apparatus. PMFs not only reshape the institutional balance of regime and military, but can also have an almost shocking impact on civil-military relations.

"OPERATION CONTRAVENE": ALTERING THE CIVIL MILITARY BALANCE

The case of "Operation Contravene" in Papua New Guinea (PNG) illustrates
just how deeply PMFs can alter the traditional balance between civilian policymakers and their military leaders. PNG is an island nation located in the
Southwest Pacific near Australia. During World War II, these islands were
the site of some of the fiercest battles between the Allies and the Japanese.
PNG is a relatively poor nation, highly dependent on foreign aid and with a

population of around 4 million people speaking some 715 different languages, one of the world's most ethnically fragmented countries.[1]

The vast majority of political power in PNG is centered on the namesake island of New Guinea and the capital city of Port Moresby. However, for most of PNG's short state history, the primary export was copper mined on the island of Bougainville over 800 miles away. Almost 45 percent of the net export for the entire nation came from Bougainville's massive Panguna copper mine.

In the late 1980s the relationship among the islands began to fall apart. A secessionist movement led by the Bougainville Revolutionary Army (BRA) began; the central issue was local displeasure over the environmental impact of the mine and generous financial packages given to outside mining groups. The dispute quickly became violent. Although the armed rebels never numbered more than 1000 fighters, the combination of their local support, the difficult jungle and mountainous terrain—perfect for an insurgency, and the weakness of the Papua New Guinea Defense Force (PNGDF) meant that the central government was unable to re-establish control over Bougainville. In the fighting that ensued over the next decade, more than 10,000 people died and 35,000 were displaced, quite high numbers considering the relatively small population on the island.

The PNGDF was usually short of pay and ill-equipped for the war. For heavy weaponry, the whole army had only a small number of armored Landrover trucks and some mortars. It also had some old Vietnam-era Huey transport helicopters, given by the Australians, but the PNGDF was expressly forbidden to arm them.[2] Despite entreaties to outside powers for assistance, none was forthcoming. Australia, its former colonial ruler, vacillated in its foreign policy toward PNG. It provided limited military and general aid, but denied the PNGDF any specialist training or sophisticated weaponry. It also worked diplomatically to block any other equipment transfers from other Western states.[3]

By late 1996, the PNG government headed by Prime Minister Julius Chan began to grow desperate. A recent offensive designed to end the war had instead been a massive failure and a number of PNGDF troops were taken hostage. National elections were impending and Chan's government was under great pressure either to end the war, or at least show progress. The result was "Operation Contravene."

With no hope of outside aid from allies, the government began to test the privatized military market. The PNG government hired Sandline International, a London-based military provider firm, to bring order to Bougainville. Interestingly, the initial meeting between the client and firm included not only PNG government officials and executives of Sandline but also representatives of the mining firm Branch Energy Ltd, who reportedly discussed linked investments in the mining sector.[4]

In January 1997, a deal was struck. Sandline was contracted to train the

PNGDF's Special Forces and gather intelligence on the BRA. Once these were completed, the firm would conduct offensive operations to render the BRA ineffective, retake the Panguna mine, and provide any necessary follow-up operational support (the text of the contract is available in Appendix II).[5] The contract was approved by the PNG National Security Council, an executive branch body, but importantly without either public discussion or parliamentary notice.

After a $1.3 million "discount" was negotiated, the overall contract amount came to $36 million dollars, half "up front" and half to be paid within 30 days of the firm's deployment. The contract amount was equivalent to roughly 150 percent of the PNGDF's yearly budget.[6] This massive expenditure contrasted with the lack of support the PNGDF received from its own civilian leadership and, as a result, enraged its troops when it became public.

The sources of the contract monies were twofold: the use of unauthorized budgetary cuts, and the nationalization and sale of the Panguna mine. Given the fact that the mine was in rebel territory at the time and similar arrangements had been made in other PMF operations in Africa, many theorize that a broader arrangement had been reached. They surmise that Sandline or, more likely, connected financial holdings (the Branch Heritage Group) would receive a share of the mine's ownership (either directly or through a 'sweetheart deal') and thereby have a financial stake in its security.[7] Adding fuel to the suspicions is a later revelation that the former Papuan minister of defence had $500,000 paid into his bank account five days after the contract.[8] It is believed he may have acted as a conduit for bribes to other ministers. Significantly, the PNGDF force commander, General Jerry Singirok, had also been receiving bribes in roughly the same period (whereas, in his case from a competitive arms supply company, JS Franklin, which did not want Sandline to win the contract).[9]

The contract entailed that Sandline would provide a 16-man training unit that would later be rolled into a larger company-sized force. This "strike force" would combine a special forces ground unit, with its own air and fire support, including two Soviet-made Mi-24 attack helicopters, two Mi-17 assault helicopters, six rocket launchers, and several grenade launch systems. It would also have its own electronic warfare, intelligence, and medical capabilities.

The increase in firepower and tactics envisioned by Sandline would have entailed a massive escalation of the conflict. They included a plan to decapitate the BRA by targeting its individual commanders and then next "mopping up the enemy" (in the words of the firm's operational plan).[10] Indications are that the Sandline personnel expected to engage in heavy fighting, with large amounts of ammunition being brought in and company representatives inquiring to hospitals in the region about their facilities for handling casualties.[11]

In an interesting attempt at avoiding any possible external prosecution for mercenary activities, the contract stipulated that Sandline personnel be deputized "special constables," sworn in as PNG police officers, but given military rank. This provision meant that although they were not Papua New Guinea citizens, they would nevertheless have the legal authority to carry weapons, arrest local citizens, and act forcibly in "self defense" (to be interpreted by the firm itself).

Excepting its overall commander, Colonel Timothy Spicer, retired, and founder of the firm, the majority of the actual troops Sandline delivered to PNG were later discovered to be employees of EO. Spicer claims that Sandline subcontracted out to the South African firm because his new firm lacked immediate manpower. He also cited a need for black soldiers, so it would not look like white soldiers were running the entire show.[12] When the linked financial holdings between the two firm's principals are taken into account, along with the fact that Nic Van Den Bergh, EO's president and later tactical commander of the PNG operation, signed the original contract, the subcontract with EO may instead have been a case of intra-firm trade.

It was not until the Sandline troops arrived on the ground that the civil-military balance in PNG teetered out of control. The local military's concerns with the contract and the privatization of their war were manifold. Its leaders felt:

- the money would have been better spent on itself than on the outside firm,
- the hire of Sandline was not only insulting to their professionalism, but also an infringement on national sovereignty,
- the close ties that Sandline's executives established with the civilian leadership had supplanted local military commanders' positions,
- any potential backlash against the firm's operation would instead remain with the local military, who had to deal with the conflict in the long term, and,
- the firm might become a palace guard and be used to dominate the local military.[13]

In March 1997, the situation crossed the brink. The overall PNGDF commander, General Jerry Singirok, publicly condemned the regime's contract with Sandline as corrupt and a wrongful devolution of proper public authority. He also cited the escalation of bloodshed and civilian casualties that the PMF's operation's likely would entail.[14] He called on President Chan, his civilian commander in chief, to resign. Chan responded by firing Singirok and announced that the general would be charged with sedition. At this point, Singirok ensconced himself in his barracks, surrounded by loyal military forces. The two began to engage in a public war of words, with the majority of the army siding with its longtime commander.

Details of the Sandline contract were then leaked to the public. Although demonstrating that Singirok actually had known about the contract beforehand, the level of force anticipated in the forthcoming operations shocked the Papua New Guinea public. Facilitated by the military, demonstrations broke out in the capital city. They quickly escalated into violent riots in support of the military that the civilian regime sought to put down. There were raised tensions between the military and other security forces, that stayed loyal to Chan, including armed face-offs between the two that took place within the context of the public demonstrations. The usual civil-military and society-state relations had completely fallen apart.[15] Fortunately, a full-scale civil war was averted. Chan's civilian regime soon backed down and resigned in favor of an interim government.

During this period, Sandline personnel, whose heavy weapons were still in transit, stayed outside of the fray. Once President Chan resigned, Sandline personnel were quickly flown out of the country (except Spicer, who was detained on a minor weapons charge, to ensure his testimony in the following judicial inquiry).[16] The termination of operations was so abrupt that the helicopters and other heavy arms bought for Sandline to use on Bougainville were stranded in transit. As the national budget had already been tapped for the equipment, the PNGDF was then left with the problem of what to do with the stranded shipment of weapons, which it had neither the money nor skills to operate, let alone maintain. Ultimately, the bulk of the weaponry and ammunition was either sold off or dumped at sea.

Sandline never completed its mission and the original contract had questionable legality, since it was signed without parliamentary approval. So, the new regime that had replaced Chan's balked at paying the second half of the $36 million. However, the firm retaliated by suing the PNG government and put a lien on the state's assets, including securing court orders for the seizure of the Papua New Guinea's diplomatic missions in the United States, the Philippines, Germany, and Luxembourg. It also put a claim on the bank account into which European Union trade payments to the country were deposited. The two parties went to an international arbitration panel, set up under a clause in the contract. The panel agreed with the firm's position that a change of regime did not relieve the new PNG government from the previous government's commitments. Eventually, PNG paid the full amount, as the lawsuit was threatening investor confidence and risked a much needed $250 million international bond that it was set to issue.[17]

The paradoxical impact of "Operation Contravene" and the ensuing mutiny is that, ultimately, the crisis gave room for moderates on both sides of the Bougainville conflict to negotiate. Given the military's demonstrated lack of capability to defeat BRA, its action against Sandline foreclosed the military option to end the civil war. The mutiny by the PNGDF, which likely prevented a bloodbath on Bougainville, also demonstrated to the BRA that all parties on the government side were not inherently set on its destruction.[18] A negotiated power sharing solution was achieved, implemented by international observers. In the inquest after the revolt, three of the military officers involved were found guilty of mutiny, and Singirok, its leader, was barred from future office for accepting bribes from the competing arms supplier.

INSTITUTIONAL BALANCE AND THE PRIVATIZED MILITARY FIRM

Although democracy appears to have survived in Papua New Guinea, this episode offers important insight. PMFs can impact traditional paradigms of civil-military relations in ways unexpected by both policymakers and theoreticians.

From its very beginning, the underlying basis of current civil-military relations theory has been fairly simple. Essentially it is a story of balancing proper civilian control with the military professionals' need for autonomy to do their jobs properly.[19] Although ongoing debates over where exactly these lines of control should be drawn, the whole of civil-military relations theory, regardless of its viewpoint, sticks to this general assumption of a dualistic balance between soldiers and state. Presently, civil-military relations theory does not fully account for any potential role of external, third-party influences on this two-sided structure.

Very little exploration of the impact of outside actors on civil-military relations or regime survival has occurred, and certainly no studies have been performed on corporate military actors in this role.[20] This general absence of study has been somewhat justified, in that the role of outsiders has often been muted in modern civil-military relations. Only 4 percent of the mutinies and coups that have occurred involved foreign military intervention, and these were primarily by superpower or colonial patrons, who are even less likely to do so in the present context.[21]

However, civil-military relations and questions of what conditions stabilize or destabilize internal relations remain of marked importance to strategic affairs, particularly with the continuing pervasiveness of coups as a means of power transfer in developing regions. Although the rate of violent government overthrow hit its high point in the 1960s, it still remains a real risk in the 21st century.[22] Among others, the military coups in Pakistan, Fiji, and Cote d'Ivoire in 2000 all serve as reminders that political succession by extraconstitutional means is as likely as ever. Considering the relative decline in interstate wars, the real danger for many regimes still lies within.

Coups may remain important, but does a need exist to explore any possible link to PMFs? Although they possess great skills, few military firms are able to muster forces above the size of a battalion-level task force. An argument can thus be made that the small personnel size of PMFs (relative to the thousands of soldiers in the local military) should limit their impact. If so, their discussion in the context of civil-military relations would be unnecessary.

Experience thus far proves otherwise. Despite the relatively low numbers of employees involved, PMF operations helped turn around entire conflicts in Angola, Croatia, Ethiopia, and Sierra Leone. As "Contravene" evidenced in Papua New Guinea, they also can greatly affect the balance of soldier and state. The reason is that the introduction of even a small group of highly skilled outsiders "can be a significant factor in many developing countries, given that coups have often been effected with just a few scores or hundreds of combatants."[23] As examples, successful coups in Gabon, Seychelles, Ghana, and Benin all involved forces numbering in the low hundreds or even less. Similarly, large, advanced states such as South Korea have experienced successful military coups that involved less that 1 percent of their total military forces.[24] In essence, the use of force in coups operates as a tipping balance. Given the right combination of disposition and opportunity, a successful coup requires only minimal numbers of supporters, as long as they are located in the right places. PMFs certainly can have something to say about any of these.

PMFS AND THE THREAT TO CIVIL BALANCE

PMFs' influence on civil-military relations is primarily dependent on the type of firm and the circumstances of its deployment. As a result, two primary amendments of civil-military theory are required in order to incorporate private military firms.

The potential for private firms to disrupt civil-military relations is most contingent on the type of firm and the context of its contracting. In a stable relationship between regime and military, the introduction of firms in the provider and consultant sectors threatens the institutional balance, in a number of ways, summarized in Amendment 1 (Table 12.1). For the most part, the possibility of negative PMF influence depends on whether the private firm supplants core public military positions or roles.

The hire of a PMF can have a potential negative influence on the status of the local military and thus a potential disruption to civil military relations. When private firms are contracted for military roles, usually at the decision of the civil government, it is often taken as proof of the failure of the local military to carry out its own responsibilities properly in the first place. It is thus frequently perceived as a vote of "no confidence" by the regime. Military leaders often see it, as in the words of one PNGDF officer, "a defeat to get someone else to come and fight for you."[25] Equally, the inadequacies of local armies can be thrown into sharper relief by an outside military firm's hire. Their prestige, political leverage, and access to resources all might be sharply reduced by their evident inability to perform the functions that justify their existence.[26]

Accordingly, by negatively impacting on the status of the local military,

Table 12.1

Amendment 1: Provider and Consultant PMFs Will Be Destabilizing to Civil-Military Relations if:

A) They impinge on the local military's prestige,

B) Their line employees receive higher pay than local soldiers for similar tasks,

C) They are kept separate and distinct from the local force rather than being integrated,

D) Their officers are placed in command positions or stand in the way of normal promotion tracks,

E) And/or if they enact programs that threaten the local force with obsolescence or demobilization

---

PMFs can be interpreted as a threat to the local military's position in society. This can create a disposition on the part of the local military, or some disaffected group within it, to act. Hire of a PMF is not only read as an erosion of state sovereignty, but also taken as an erosion of the military's place as the institution designed to maintain it. This aspect is critical to coup risks. A military's "corporate spirit," its self-considered autonomy and prestige, is extremely important to morale; if threatened, it can be an impetus for action against its own regime.[27]

The firm's entrance as a third party tied to the civilian leadership may also leave military leadership feeling isolated or excluded from the inner circle of power, causing further resentment.[28] Military bitterness at exclusion and lost prestige, resulting from the introduction of new parallel forces, has been the driving force behind many coups throughout history.[29] Specific to PMFs, the options taken by local armies opposed to their hire have been pre-emptive action, as what happened in Papua New Guinea in 1997, or strategic acquiescence, a tactic taken by the Sierra Leone Army, also in 1997. In the latter case, the military leadership chose to bide its time after the government hired EO. Then, once the private firm was out of the country and the regime lacked its private protection, the army toppled the government. In fact, the army leadership worked in connivance with the rebel forces that it was supposed to be fighting.

Military coups are also often initiated to protect parochial interests or because of the personal complaints of military leaders.[30] In fact, historical studies reveal that individual, monetary-related grievances, such as reductions in pay or business access, are the catalyst of roughly 33 percent of all military coups.[31] Thus, if the firms are perceived to receive better financial benefits or threaten military personnel's future standing, the hire of PMFs may also foment bitterness within the national army, and perhaps revolt.[32]

Although their personnel numbers may be small in comparison to the local militaries, the relative economic costs related to contracts with PMF hiring are often quite high. In order to afford them, funds must often be diverted and military budgets cut, causing further antagonism. For example, months after the suspension of the Sandline operation, the PNGDF's chief of staff complained that the expenditure on the PMF had left his force so short of funds that it was having trouble feeding its troops.[33]

The pay that PMFs offer also usually far surpasses the pay that personnel receive in comparative positions in official state militaries. For example, the salary for employees of the EO firm was as much as 5 times that of those in the South African military, where it was based, and 10 times that of the client militaries it worked alongside. PMF personnel also tend to arrive with vaunted military backgrounds and superior military equipment compared to what the more modest local force had access to. Such advantages are often the reason firms were hired in the first place, but also can also exacerbate local military bitterness.[34]

The combination of these tensions and resentment certainly might lead the local military to action. However, even if no formal revolt or coup is planned, hostility can still boil over into violence on a smaller scale. In a contract during the Angolan civil war, for example, reported confrontations occurred between EO personnel and Angolan government forces, in particular with the paramilitary "Ninja" unit, although both parties were supposed to be fighting on the same side. These not only hampered EO's movements, but also are rumored to have resulted in at least one shootout between elements of the two forces. Similar incidents occurred during a contract that the firm had in the civil war in the Democratic Republic of the Congo (Zaire). The historical cases of placing better-paid, hired forces alongside lesser-paid, local public forces also do not bode well. For example, Swiss regiments serving in the French army after the Napoleonic wars were paid 200–300 percent more than the ranks in regular French regiments received. Several times they got into full-scale battles with French units based nearby. Ultimately, the tensions boiled over into a catalyst for the 1830 revolt that toppled Bourbon rule.[35]

In addition to disparities in pay scales, outside hired officers might also be interpreted as standing in the way of advancement of local officers, effectively nullifying future career goals. This is a concern more applicable to employees of firms in the military provider sector who take over tactical leadership roles, but also may include those from consulting sector firms that provide strategic leadership. The historic precedent of officer revolts centering on this cause range from Egypt in the 1840s to Congo in the 1960s. This was also a complaint in the Papua New Guinea case with Sandline as well.[36]

Firms in the consulting sector may also incite resistance from the local military by recommending or implementing reform or restructuring programs. These programs often threaten sections of the local military with obsolescence and ensuing demobilization. Consultants' hire also might portend the disruption of what traditional soldiery see as the proper ordering of their institution and society. Privatized military reform can thus be understood as an attack on very real vested interests and/or local military leaders' professional identity and role in the social order. Historically, a number of military reform efforts led by outsiders, from the Ottoman Empire and Russia to Japan and Egypt, resulted in violent internal confrontations.[37] Similarly, the hire of MPRI in Nigeria in 1999 led to heightened tensions among the general staff and reports of thwarted coup attempts.[38]

Other tensions might result from potential organizational incompatibilities in training, doctrinal disagreements, unclear chains of command, and cultural mores. At the center of all of these are likely to be differing expectations of the respective roles of private and public forces that can create misperceptions, mutual negative stereotypes, distrust, status differentials, and competition. An exacerbating factor is that foreigners in general, and foreign military personnel in particular, often exhibit ignorance of or insensitivity toward local customs and institutions; employees of PMFs are no exception.[39]

In conclusion, the introduction of PMFs can cause harmful consequences to the civil-military balance under the conditions outlined in Amendment 1. If their hire is handled in a way that threatens the prestige, the autonomy, or the corporate interests of the local military, the public force as a whole may respond by challenging the firm or the government behind the hire. Likewise, personal grievances, prompted by jealousy, blocked careers, or reform threats, may prompt action by individuals within the local military. In either case, the introduction of an outside private military agent can have massive consequences for relations between the local government and its public force. Even the very rumor that a private firm is to be hired can prompt violent action, as it did in the Solomon Islands in 2000.[40]

REINFORCING THE REGIME: THE COUNTERWEIGHT OF PRIVATE FIRMS

At the same time that they create certain new risks to civil-military relations, PMFs also possess the ability to be stabilizing to the overall balance, again linked to certain industry sectors, in certain conditions. These are summarized in Amendment 2. Much like Amendment 1, the intent is that qualifying conditions can be made, without abandoning the core of civil-military theory. In fact, these amendments leverage useful lessons from the findings of the standard literature.

A basic dilemma for governments in weak states is how to balance the need for capable military forces and maintain these forces' loyalty. Considering that almost 100 successful coups have happened in Africa alone since the 1960s, leaders' fear of their own militaries is understandable.[41] In some cases, leaders try to prevent military coups by ethnicizing their militaries, that is, by filling them with ethnic or tribal kin groups. Others try to defeat the risk by intentionally weakening their own militaries' capabilities. For many, however, a tried solution has been to create a counterweight, in the form of a private army or rival paramilitary organization that is used to check and balance the threat from the local military. In fact, the current literature on civil-military relations within developing states indicates that such counterweights are one of more successful means of maintaining weak regime rule.[42]

Units of foreigners often serve as these counterweights.[43] In particular, autocratic rulers have long surrounded themselves with palace guards made up of foreigners, including such notable historic examples as Byzantine Varangian guard made up of Vikings, the French kings' Scottish and Swiss palace guards, the Spanish dictator Francisco Franco's Moors, and Congolese ruler Mobutu's Moroccans.

It is in this role that military provider firms are attractive to beleaguered regimes. Much like the dogs of the character "Napoleon" in George Orwell's book *Animal Farm,* they can be used to intimidate and deter any attempts at domestic challenge, even by the local military. Contracting with private firms allows vulnerable leaders to rid themselves of perceived unreliable officers and marginalize units that have become a rogue militia of rivals.[44]

The record of PMFs thus far indicates that they provide an effective means for regimes in immediate danger to stay in power. For example, EO is generally credited with stopping at least two coup attempts against the government regimes that it supported in Sierra Leone (see chapter 7). The actions following these coup preventions provide further evidence of the impact a capable PMF can have, and what occurs when this counterweight is lost. In late 1996, the newly elected Kabbah regime in Sierra Leone decided that it no longer needed the firm's military assistance. The firm, in turn, warned their client that without its support the civilian government could not expect to last longer than 100 days. Nevertheless, the regime chose to terminate the contract. Disgruntled army officers toppled the regime on the 95th day. Only after the regime hired Sandline (another military provider firm) was it able to re-seize power. Similar circumstances are reported to have occurred in Congo-Brazzaville, where the hire of the Israeli firm Levdan in 1994 allowed a new president to create a new force loyal to him and replace military units, loyal to the former leader, that he did not trust.[45]

It is also possible that the hiring of firms in the consulting sector might mute the risk of coups, specifically in conditions where they can safely restructure civil-military relations. Samuel Huntington, one of the founders of civil-military theory, argues that two things establish long-term civil-military stability: enhancing the capacity and professionalism of militaries (that is, focusing military attention on functional specialization and the strategic and technical demands of warfare, rather than on local political concerns) and strengthening the institutions that exercise oversight of the military.[46] Military consulting firms can help accomplish both of these, through contracts that provide military training and restructuring assistance to military bureaucracies.

As evidence of their potential good works, consultant firms often make pointed reference to contracts they administer that train military officers how to exist within a civilian-run democratic system. MPRI, for example, often extols its present contract in Nigeria, where the firm has been hired to help "reprofessionalize" Nigeria's military after decades of failed military rule and corruption. As part of this contract, MPRI produced 62 specific recommendations on ways to restore the professional stature that the Nigerian military enjoyed in the past and create a civilian oversight structure. These recommendations include plans for establishing an office, with functions similar that of the Pentagon's Office of the Secretary of Defense, which would construct a budget, establish regular pay, and formulate a national strategy.[47]

This dual contract illustrates an important proviso, however. PMF-led professionalization programs will likely not guarantee the aimed for results unless balanced with efforts to bolster oversight mechanisms. Without oversight, evidence demonstrates that professionalization programs in transitional or developing states tend to backfire and might even promote a tendency to launch more coups.[48]

A few conclusions can be drawn from the limited evidence available. Acceptance of outside training is more likely in newly formed militaries or in those forces held under subjective controls (that is, infused with the particular values of the regime, either as the result of past struggle or as a result of its place as the political party's army) than those with longstanding military traditions.[49] Local militaries also appear more amenable to PMF consultant assistance if they have faced defeat in war, or some other shock has shaken their worldview and caused them to realize their need to change. For example, the militaries of Bosnia and Croatia were quick to accept hired consultants' advice, whereas Nigeria and Colombia, who felt they still had the situation well in hand, were not. Another mitigating factor may be the firms' instruction in new military technologies, used as a kind of carrot to win over professional military opposition, by appealing to their functional desires.[50]

Although having less effect than the other forms, firms in the military support also can act to reinforce the civil-military balance. Their role in outsourcing can pull the local military out of secondary functions which have commercial equivalents and often result in corruption. As was seen in dur-

Table 12.2

Amendment 2:
PMFs Will Be Stabilizing to Civil-Military Relations If:
A) Provider firms are able to counterweight immediate local threats,
B) Consultant firms can act to professionalize the local force under civilian controls,
C) Consultant firms' hire enhances the local military's status,
D) Support firms help move local militaries out of commercial functions,
E) And/or they help release demobilization pressures.

---

ing Mobutu's rule in Zaire, rampant corruption can result in the formation of independent power bases and broad military disaffection with the system. Lower-level leaders often refuse to perform roles without pay-offs and the regime's power remains in constant crisis. By taking over these functions, military support firms thus lower the internal military competition for self-enrichment. However, much like with the contracts in the consulting sector, there are certain limitations. Rather than wholesale privatizing, a gradual turnover is more likely to ensure stability. This way, the introduction of the firm is not seen as an immediate and overwhelming material threat to local leaders.

Finally, an added way that the general presence of the industry might act to stabilize civil-military relations is not linked to any one private military sector, but actually results from the industry's effect as a pressure release valve. By providing a new professional outlet for disgruntled military forces, PMFs can indirectly weaken the risk of domestic opposition. In short, a number of nations are quietly happy about the emergence of the new privatized military industry, as it is an alternative way to keep demobilized or recently retired soldiers busy. Although regular unemployment is always a concern to governments, unemployed former soldiers possess skills that, if they become disaffected, can make them uniquely dangerous and disruptive.

South Africa is a prime example of this factor. Given the checkered history of the soldiers who had served in the elite units of the apartheid-era South African military, the new African National Congress (ANC) government in South Africa led by Nelson Mandela had a particular incentive to see that these soldiers stayed out of domestic trouble, especially during the first multiracial elections in 1994. This may in part explain the lack of sanction when EO first fought in the Angolan civil war. In public, the Mandela government was decidedly against the firm's activities, as EO was acting in contravention of the "new" South Africa's attempt to become a responsible regional power.[51] However, in private, it quietly tolerated and even facilitated early EO recruitment of these forces. The rationale was the government's belief that "it would remove from South Africa a number of person-nel who might have had a destabilising effect on the forthcoming multi-racial elections."[52] The ultimate outcome was that the South African elections went off without a hitch, while hundreds of potential agitators, with high levels of military skills, were kept busy making money abroad.

CIVIL-MILITARY RELATIONS IN STABLE STATES

The focus of this discussion so far has been on the potential impact of PMFs on civil military relations in their most dire circumstances, where the risks of internal violence are real and tensions between the local government and its military agent often bubble over into coups. However, the privatized mil-itary industry also has a potential influence on civil-military relations in es-tablished, stable states, such as the United States or Britain, where the risks of civil-military violence are negligible.

Mainstream civil-military theory and practice dictate a clear divergence among the military institution, the political arena, and the economy. How-ever, even in states such as the United States, this has begun to erode. As se-curity analyst Chris Dietrich writes, "The traditional ethos of the military as 'more than just a job' has been partially replaced by a corporate outlook, forcing the military in countries such as the United States to market the ex-tent to which military service was ideal training for later corporate employ-ment."[53]

There is a growing belief that old-fashioned military virtues are particu-larly threatened by increasing military contracting with the PMF industry and the overwhelming presence of ex-soldiers in its employment rolls. The argument of these opponents, who often include officers presently serving in public forces, is that the armed forces' professionalism must not to be as-sociated with or compromised by commercial enterprise. To do so poten-tially endangers the fabric of communal loyalty.[54] This is particularly so when a firm that primarily draws its employees from the home-state military goes to work for other states. As U.S. Army Colonel Bruce Grant states, "When former officers sell their skills on the international market for profit, the entire profession loses its moral high ground with the American peo-ple."[55]

In the United States, the military is the most respected government in-stitution in the American public's judgment, consistently ranking among the highest esteemed professions.[56] This stems from the perceived integrity and values of the soldiers within it and the spirit of selfless service embod-ied in their duty on behalf of the country. As Huntington wrote, the military professional's "relation to society is guided by an awareness that his skill can only be utilized for purposes approved by society through its political agent, the state."[57]

PMFs, however, alter this exclusivity. In essence, the firms market the unique expertise that their employees gained from service in the publicly funded military; the codes, rules, and regulations that once made these military services uniquely society-orientated no longer bind them. The public's respect is thus potentially jeopardized by military personnel leaving public service while still remaining in the military sphere. As Grant continues, his fear is that, "ultimately, the privatization of US military services under direct foreign contract corrupts our military both in the eyes of society and from within the ranks."[58]

The ultimate effect of this remains to be seen. It is clear, however, that private military activity does indeed associate the military profession with the profit motive, in opposition to the very values that incur public esteem. By seeing ex-military officers cashing in on the expertise and training that public monies paid for, many now in the military worry that the public's faith in the good motives of its military leadership and respect for the institution will then be diminished. Those in service also fear that the military pension system might be called into question; profit is being incurred from the very same service for which the public is paying retired personnel back.

CONCLUSION: PRIVATELY TILTING THE BALANCE

PMFs are hired because they possess skills and capabilities that provide them greater effectiveness than reliance on traditional state security institutions. But these same assets, which make them so attractive to governments under threat, also can infringe on the relations between the local military and its civilian leaders.

In the end, the introduction of an outside, corporate party into the civil-military paradigm can seriously impact the domestic distribution of status, roles, and resources. Therefore, PMFs must be a new consideration in civil-military relations.

THIRTEEN

Public Ends, Private Military Means?

> The history of these black ops doesn't inspire confidence. If overtly
> they're shooting down civilian planes, it makes you wonder what's being
> done covertly.
>
> —Andrew Miller, Amnesty International

When one looks to execute policy, it is presumed that it has to be done through a government agency. The rise of the private military industry, however, shows that this is no longer the case. Perhaps most important, they offer an often politically expedient policy privatization. This can be both a good and a bad development.

PRIVATIZING "PLAN COLOMBIA"

The current PMF operations in Colombia illustrate how public policy can by privatized through PMFs. They may also well demonstrate the dangers of running foreign policy through private business proxies.

Colombia ranks increasingly higher in U.S. foreign policy not only because of its economic importance (more than 400 of the *Fortune*-500 companies do business in Colombia and 25,000 U.S. citizens work there), but also its location at the center of the international drug trade.[1] After almost four decades of warfare, the Colombian government has been unable to control large swaths of its territory taken over by rebel forces. It has also has failed to stem the flow of drugs from within its borders to the booming market inside the United States.

Thus, by the late 1990s, the United States found it in its interests to help the Colombian state regain control of its territory, not only to help regional stability, but also as part of its long-term "War on Drugs." The result was "Plan Colombia," a U.S.-funded $7.5 billion strategy to eradicate the cocaine trade in Colombia. The aid package involves using military force to combat drug traffickers and other programs to encourage crop substitution, to wean peasant farmers from the income derived from growing coca and poppies.

The problem for the strategy is that the U.S. Congress has placed strong limitations on exactly what the U.S. military can do to support it. These are primarily due to concerns about the risks to U.S. soldiers and also worries about supporting a local military with an egregious human rights record, particularly its countenance of paramilitary death squads. Consequently, although Colombia is the 3rd largest recipient of U.S. military assistance, U.S. troops are legally restricted in which Colombian units they can train (only those proven free of human rights violators) and in which type of operations they can assist. U.S. troops can aid the Colombians in their counternarcotics operations, but are proscribed from aiding in counterinsurgency efforts. However, the two operations are often indistinguishable. As explored in chapter 4, Colombian rebel groups (in particular, the FARC) have found it profitable to join in the lucrative international narcotics business, so that their bases serve both military and drug trade functions. The result is that for the guerillas, the "War on Drugs" is also a war on them.[2]

PMFs have begun to be utilized as an alternative way to circumvent these policy restrictions. Privatized military assistance can bypass Congressional oversight and provide political cover to the White House if something goes wrong.[3] Beginning in the second term of the Clinton administration, the United States quietly arranged the hire of a slew of PMFs, whose operations in Colombia range far beyond the narrow restrictions placed on U.S. soldiers fighting the drug war. Rather, the firms' operations are intended to help the Colombian military finally end the decades-old insurgency.

The full entirety of the firms' operations are not known, as the State Department has not released the list of contracts given to private companies in connection with Plan Colombia, but certain elements have entered the public record. Congressional investigators estimate the figure being spent on these firms at between $770 million and $1.3 billion.[4]

At the strategic advisory level, MPRI is known to have drafted the top-to-bottom review of the Colombian Defense Ministry, which laid the groundwork for the 3 phases of "Plan Colombia." The contract in Colombia was headed by a former U.S. Army Major General and involved roughly 20 personnel.[5] Congress received no updates about MPRI's mission and both the firm and the Pentagon refused any public requests to review the contract.[6] Northrop Services is also known to have provided military support services to Colombian forces, including operating radar sites.[7]

More important, however, is what has been occurring at the operational level. Linked to multinational corporation contracts, a number of firms in the military provider sector have been active in Colombia, including Armorgroup and Silver Shadows. There have also been unconfirmed reports of ex-U.S. Navy Seals working for Virginia Electronics, a firm operating on the Colombian-Peruvian border. They are said to be running the U.S.-backed "Riverine" program that uses gunboats to interdict rebel supply lines.[8]

However, most integral to "Plan Colombia" has been the Virginia-based

DynCorp firm, which, at the time of writing, had between 300–600 contracted employees in Colombia, as part of a contract to man the U.S. State Department's air wing. The firm officially provides pilot training and technical support to the Colombian National Police units performing drug crop eradication (using aerial defoliants, as in Vietnam). Reportedly, however, DynCorp is also engaged in aerial reconnaissance and combat advisory roles for the Colombian military. In fact, several reports indicate that the firm's personnel (most are ex-U.S. military) are engaged in combatant roles, fighting in counter-insurgency operations against the Colombian rebel groups.[9] Indeed, the DynCorp personnel have a local reputation for being both arrogant and far too willing to willing to get "wet," that is, to go out on frequent combat missions and engage in firefights.[10] In anonymous interviews, firm pilots acknowledge that their operations are high risk, as they are a high-priority target for the guerrillas. But, they find the pay of $90,000 per year (tax free) rewarding as well.[11]

The equipment DynCorp and its subcontractors brought into Colombia are an added indication that the firms are going well beyond that which the U.S. Congress would have approved. For its contract with State Department's national anti-narcotics section, the firm uses OV-10s, a military plane originally designed for reconnaissance and light attack in counterinsurgency wars.[12]

Although U.S. military personnel are under strict legal restrictions from engaging in counterinsurgency operations, it is clear that the firms are not bound by the same rules. DynCorp's operations in Colombia entail more than just crop dusting, but also engage in combat with the local FARC rebels. In February 2001, when the rebels downed a Colombian military helicopter, a DynCorp search and rescue team, made up of ex-U.S. special forces personnel armed with machine guns, landed and rescued the crew, while DynCorp Huey helicopter gunships provided covering fire. It was the first public revelation that not only did the firm have four of its own helicopter gunships, but that they had fired at rebel forces in retaliation, and may covertly play more offensive roles.[13] This was no mere crop dusting; instead, as one Congressional staff member noted, "This is what we call outsourcing a war."[14]

The firm's spokesperson declined to comment on the incidents, citing contractual obligations (a much different response than U.S. government personnel would give after a military engagement), and DynCorp's employees are under strict orders from firm executives to avoid contact with journalists. It is known, however, that three Dyncorp pilots have died since the operations began. The firm claims that the pilots died from accidents rather than military engagements, however, no public outcry nor crash investigations ensued, unlike what would have happened in an incident involving U.S. military personnel. Likewise, when a former U.S. military special forces medic employed by DynCorp died of a reported heart attack in October 2000, the U.S. embassy did not have to release the background or next-of-kin information that it would have had it been a U.S. soldier.[15]

Besides the potential violations of U.S. law if the firms are being used to supersede congressional legislation, the use of a proxy to perform U.S. military action in Colombia could also have serious consequences for the war. The firms' involvement threatens to radicalize hardliners both in the Colombian military and on the rebel side. These privatized operations also threaten to escalate the war, both in intensity and in geographic scope. PMFs have operated across regional borders and concerns remain that any escalation will lead refugees to flee the higher scale of fighting and flood neighboring states.[16]

From the United States's perspective, the firms' operations also bring U.S. military personnel in the region (or even inside the United States, where the rebels do have the capability to reach) under an increased threat of retaliation. Although the distinction between Dyncorp personnel and U.S. military personnel might be clear to some, the Colombian rebels do not see it that way. They see the "Yankees" as one and the same, whether they work for Dyncorp or for the U.S. military. The perceived benefits of disinvolvement through policy privatization thus might seriously backfire on U.S. soldiers, who are not the ones profiting from the operations.[17] As Robert White, former U.S. ambassador to El Salvador and current head of the Center for International Policy, notes, "Once this juggernaut starts rolling, it's extremely difficult to put a stopping point on it. Once there are a few Americans killed, it seems to me that things begin to unravel. And then you find yourself, indeed, fully involved."[18]

THE FIRM AS AN ALTERNATIVE MEANS OF POLICY

The Colombian episode illustrates how PMFs give policymakers new latitude in when, how, and where military force is introduced. The extensive PMF involvement in the war in Colombia and its neighboring states by U.S.-based firms has been entirely without Congressional notification, oversight, or approval. PMF activities provide a new option for outside parties to reset a local environment, while officially staying uninvolved and not bearing risks. A similar rationale appears to have been used in Sierra Leone in 1997, where both the United States and Britain originally supported Sandline's activities to overthrow the Koroma regime, but then claimed no association once it was publicized as being in violation of UN arms embargos.

Hiring private military firms as a substitute for official action gives a cover of plausible deniability that official forces now lack. Unlike front companies, the personnel involved are outside of government and maintain no direct tie with government budgets. So, even the limited legislative oversight over covert operations (such as that embodied in the Senate Select Committee on Intelligence) is restricted. In fact, under current U.S. law, as long as the contract is under $50 million, any U.S. military firm can work abroad with without notification being given to Congress.[19] Many contracts naturally fall under this amount, while larger ones are easily broken up to do so. In addition, Congress tends to focus its attention on official aid programs (rather than "unofficial" programs) and, even if looked at, PMFs offer extra layers of protection from scrutiny by shrouding activities within an unfamiliar, often foreign business network. "Consequently, a private firm can train another nation's army without congressional notification, much less congressional approval. Thus, significant foreign policy actions related to foreign security assistance do not receive the benefit of the checks and balances system inherent in our system of government."[20]

Hence, the activities of PMFs often coincide with borderline situations in which official policy involvement is politically difficult. An added advantage of externalization is that it offers the ability to deflect criticism. If something goes awry in an operation, the activities of a firm are easier for governments to deny and the blame simpler to shift.[21] For example, if lives are lost or the mission fails, the political ramifications are muted when the policy agent is private, rather than public forces.

There are also times when an outside government must maintain the appearance of evenhandedness, despite having an interest in aiding one side in a conflict. PMFs allow new way to resolve these dilemmas.

This is a particular trait of advisory sector firms and was the thinking behind the U.S. government arranging the hire of MPRI in 1995 to administer the Train and Equip program for Bosnia. Both U.S. foreign policy goals and domestic political considerations mandated that the Bosnian military had to be built up into an effective force. Importantly for the Clinton administration, the Republican-controlled Congress supported rearming the Bosnian side, such that it threatened to prevent approval for the IFOR deployment and even become a presidential campaign issue. At the same time, the United States needed to maintain an air of evenhandedness as it was the primary implementer of the Dayton Peace Plan and the biggest troop contributor to IFOR. So, the United States settled on the privatized solution, which allowed its policy to accomplish these contradictory goals.[22] The Bosnian Army received its training and buildup, while the U.S. military could claim to both regional and domestic critics that it was not directly involved; rather that the training was simply 'the work of a private firm.'

Military consulting firms also offer the possibility of providing military assistance to allies with negative images, which would otherwise unable to garner Congressional approval. For example, both Angola and Equatorial Guinea are nondemocratic states with poor human rights records, that by law are ineligible for U.S. military assistance. However, with the emergence of PMFs, the United States has been able to offer to arrange the privatized equivalent for both. Similar discreet moves were made to aid the Nigerian military in Liberia with support sector assistance in 1996–97, again against the law (in this case sanctions against the Abacha dictatorship), but in line with U.S. policy goals.

Although their domestic hire appears linked to efficiency rationales, much of the push behind the use of support sector firms by the U.S. military in recent external contingency operations also appears to stem from PMFs acting as a means to get around public policy restrictions. For example, the hire of BRS in the Balkans was not driven solely by how much money that the outsourcing could save. Equally important, by privatizing logistics, Congressional troop caps would be avoided and the administration would avoid the domestic political uproar of calling up National Guard and Reserves troops.[23]

In sum, the possible advantage of a shift toward privatized policy means is that by avoiding public debate or legislative controls, the government executive body may be able to undertake a much more "rational" foreign policy.[24] It can fulfill geopolitical interests without risk to public forces. From this perspective, the sometimes inefficient limits of a democratic system on governing are lessened. "When budget constraints and political sensitivities make it imprudent to overtly commit the power, prestige, and tax dollars of the United States directly, an administration can still implement foreign policy through private contracting."[25]

NEGATIVE EXTERNALITIES OF FOREIGN POLICY PRIVATIZATION

Using private firms as a means around policy controls, though, is not without its potential problems. Rather, such outsourcing usually works better in theory than how it turns out in reality. The outcome often includes the negative consequences that result from privatization, felt both in the immediate result and in such policies' long-term effect on democratic governance.

Despite attempts to stay officially and publicly aloof, plausible deniability does not always ensure that states will not be implicated in the work of PMFs based in their country or employing their ex-soldiers. In fact, the use of some private firms may even raise more suspicions, as their histories often give the operations an air of secret dealings and covert operations. Thus, the potential impact of this on regional relations may even be riskier than the use of an official military assistance program.

Part of the first problem is due to the difficulties involved in distinguishing the policy agent. There is obviously no guarantee that opponents on local battlefields will recognize that the forces they fight are private firms and not official forces. Military provider firms in particular, often have an incentive to keep their operations as secretive as any official covert action and moreover, often make use of the same tactics and equipment as the official forces in which they trained. Thus, when a local guerilla force is hit by U.S.-made gunships, piloted by U.S. citizens, and using U.S. tactics, it is completely logical for them to assume that the attack involved official United States forces. Even if official denials are issued and disclaimers that the actions were that of private firm employees rather than U.S. soldiers, they are likely to be unconvinced. They might thus seek to retaliate against U.S. forces, rather than just the firm's employees. As noted earlier, Colombian rebels have made threats to U.S. military forces after incursions with PMFs.[26]

Even with consulting sector firms the concurrent interests and close connections between privatized military firms and their home governments usually causes a sort of "guilt by association." For example, the flaw of the United States government's claim that it was completely disassociated from the MPRI contracts with Croatia and Bosnia, was that few in the region believed it. As the Chief of Staff of the UN mission in Bosnia, put it, "It's a pretty thin facade."[27] The European nations also participating in the IFOR operation all opposed the training program and protested against it to the U.S. government, which they saw as the true source behind it. Similarly, the Bosnian Serbs cited MPRI's activity as official U.S. policy and evidence of U.S. bias against them in the implementation of the peace agreement. As a result, the use of a PMF did little to disinvolve the United States in regional eyes. Rather, it just made the situation all the more murky, raising further regional suspicions. The typical perception of MPRI's contract was the one expressed by an official Croatian news report headlined, "U.S. Military to Train Federation Troops."[28]

Similar problems have hampered other states' external foreign policy aims. After the assistance that private Russian firms gave to Ethiopia in its recent war, Russian political analysts worried that the situation would permanently endanger the government's relations with Eritrea, and potentially damage relations with other states in the region.[29] Likewise, given its previous history of intervening into the states around it, the post-apartheid South African government has cultivated the image of a reformed, fair regional power. However, at numerous times, the government has come under criticism for the activities of former South African military personnel outside its borders, including those fighting for PMFs in Angola and Congo. As a result, "South Africa's Foreign Affairs Department has gone on record slamming Executive Outcomes as "mercenaries," saying it wants them out of Angola as they tarnish South Africa's image as an impartial regional power."[30]

Aside from the problem of distinguishing between public and private action, there are other problems of using private firms as public policy implementers that arise. The use of privatized policy agents circumvents time-tested congressional and public reviews that are integral to the democratic system of checks and balances in government. Such limitations are in place for a valid reason. Going around them may often prove embarrassing or have negative associations. For example, the 1997 use of Sandline in Sierra Leone to circumvent UN arms embargoes and public troop limitations became a true debacle for the British government and nearly resulted in the forced resignation of Foreign Minister Robin Cook. The supposedly covert Foreign Ministry operation was actually uncovered by an investigation by the British Customs Agency, which had been notified by a member of the House of Lords. The *London Times* described it as "a classic example of Whitehall at its undercover worst."[31] Likewise, prior assistance from MPRI became linked with occurrences of ethnic cleansing in Krajina by the Croat Army. This tied both the firm and its proponents in the U.S. government to accusations of war crimes that certainly benefited neither.[32]

Perhaps the most well-known example of the unforeseen pitfalls of privatizing such operations happened in spring 2001, when a CIA surveillance plane was conducting counternarcotics operations in Peru. The plane was actually staffed by employees of Aviation Development Corporation, a company based in Montgomery, Alabama. In a tragic turn of events, it mistakenly directed the shoot-down of a private passenger plane that, rather than carrying drug runners, turned out to be carrying a family of missionaries. An American mother and her seven-month-old daughter were killed.[33] As one U.S. government official noted of the firm, "They [the PMF employees] have a higher impression of their tactical and technical proficiency than they should. Not one person on that aircraft had a commission from the U.S. government to do what they were doing. No one took an oath to the Constitution. They were just businessmen."[34]

Similarly, support sector firms may permit operations to occur that maybe should not. If an operation cannot deploy without privatized assistance because it lacks both public and congressional support for the proper troop numbers, then perhaps the original rationale deserves further debate. The end mission goals may well be unsustainable without the citizenry's backing. The halfhearted support of U.S. forces in the Balkans perhaps illustrates this.

THE IMPLICATIONS FOR DEMOCRACY

A larger issue, however, is that military service privatization represents a unique step in the process of outsourcing public institutions to the private market. The ideas of garbage collection, prison administration, and even public schools being run by for-profit firms have all become generally accepted as ways to make public services more competitive. The use of a privatized military actor as a foreign policy tool, however, is not just about achieving greater cost competitiveness. In the end, it is the outsourcing of the affairs of state to a private corporation because its lies beyond public controls. The potential dangers of this are extensive.

Lost oversight is the first issue of concern. When governments engage in official military and foreign policy endeavors, the policy is held accountable by a wide range of supervision, both from within their own agencies and in the competitive branches of government, such as the legislative and the judiciary. The result is a balance that keeps each branch within the law and holds their relative power in check. This division of responsibility is at the crux of a successful democracy.

However, PMFs allow leaders to short-circuit democracy by turning over important foreign policy tasks to outside, unaccountable companies. As one journalist described it, when policymakers have the option of "hiring consultant mercenaries to do a messy job, it is easier for Washington [or any other capital] to ignore the consequences and fudge the responsibility."[35]

Private firms offer an alternative mechanism for the executive body to conduct secret operations without other branches being involved. Congress only has authority over official policy, not over private entities. It is also often possible to arrange for a PMF to be paid by other parties or use off-budget funds. Thus, there is frequently no opportunity for legislative oversight.

For those firms based in the United States, often the only bureaucratic requirement is for a simple export license from the State Department's Office of Defense Transitions Assistance. This is usually easy to obtain and also comes from a process outside public view. In fact, the State Department office cannot provide information on PMF contracts to the public, due to the claimed need to protect proprietary information. The firms, in turn, claim that they cannot provide information without government approval, creating what some call "a wall of silence."[36] Hence, even the Freedom of Information Act is useless as a way to discover the truth behind many PMF policies. Moreover, as previously discussed, Congress is only notified if the contract is for more than $50 million.[37] Often, even this relatively weak restriction is not available as many of the firms are intentionally chartered in extraterritorial accounts not subject to such national approval.

Even when the government directly hires PMFs, their existence outside of normal governmental structures makes proper oversight more difficult. Whereas the Defense Department is required by law to answer Congressional and press queries when U.S. forces are deployed abroad, private firms are not. Thus, they easily evade questions from Congress or the press. In sum, "By adding a new layer of secrecy and unaccountability, the use of private contractors offers the government even greater opportunities to conduct covert foreign policy."[38]

As Arthur S. Miller once wrote, "Democratic government is *responsible* government—which means *accountable* government—and the essential problem in contracting out is that responsibility and accountability are greatly diminished." Thus, the use of private firms by the government has placed "the influence over, and sometimes even control of, important decisions one step further away from the public and their elected representatives."[39] Such marginalization of the legislature is a contravention of the role the Founding Fathers intended for Congress in the Constitution. The legislature was intended to be equal to the other branches and to provide the democratic voice of the citizenry in shaping policy.

As a consequence, this particular form of privatization removes military expertise from the realm of public accountability. In doing so, it potentially upsets both the balance of powers within government and also the delicate Clausewitzian trinity among the government, the military, and the people.[40] It blurs the lines between a military that directly works for the state and one that works for profit, not dependent on the local populace's membership and support.

In the end, PMFs may present great advantages, enabling an executive branch to carry out what it sees as rational, unimpeded foreign policy. However, if an operation cannot gain the backing of the public to send in uniformed forces, then maybe it is not as much in the state's geopolitical interests as the leadership originally perceived.

FOURTEEN

Morality and the Privatized
Military Firm

Friars (giving their usual greeting to wayfarers):	God give you peace!
Sir John Hawkwood:	God take you from your alms!
Friars:	We meant no offence, sir.
Sir John Hawkwood:	How, when you pass by me and pray that God would make me die of hunger? Do you not know that I live by war and that peace would ruin me?

From Froissart's *Chronicles*

Private military firms provoke an amazing range of responses. On one hand, their very corporate existence rests on their capability to solve peoples' and states' problems of security. Thus, they have numerous supporters who point out the positive functions they have performed. The areas in which many PMFs operate, particularly those in the provider sector, are often the scenes of the worst violence in the world today. Rarely is their hiring the first choice of states or other clients. More often, it is the result of frustration at the failure of other, more traditional options. If a state cannot provide security and protection for its citizens, and no other public party is willing to help, then it seems hypocritical to say that private options must be forsworn absolutely.

PMF successes have also meant that in areas that need them most they can achieve an immense amount of support from the local public. Outside observers typically expect the firms to be treated as scorned mercenaries and are often shocked to see the honor afforded to the firms and their employees. As one journalist in Sierra Leone put it, "Rarely, if ever, have 'dogs of war' enjoyed such respect."[1]

At the same time, PMFs rest on a confused and precarious moral position. They are private entities paid to provide what the government traditionally is supposed to be doing. Moreover, they directly benefit from the existence of war and suffering; it is a precursor to their hire. An uneasiness also exists with ex-soldiers selling military training that the public paid for, on the private market. As they are little understood, people often use mercenary terms to describe them by default. As such, the firms often provoke a quite hostile reaction and have been viciously attacked in the public arena.

The reality behind these divergent views is far more complex. To simply paint all PMFs as purely good or purely evil is plain wrong. They are private actors operating in the public realm of warfare. As such, tensions exist between their potential positive and negative human rights impacts.

THE MORAL HAZARDS OF MILITARY PRIVATIZATION

Members of PMFs bristle at almost any negative characterizations of their business, in particular allegations that they are the equivalent of mercenaries or are more susceptible to commit war crimes. They argue that, in fact, they deserve an opposite normative status. They claim that the laws of the market work to limit any such tendency, as their ultimate long-term profit is dependent on a good public image.

By privatizing military services, certain motivations for good behavior appear to be increased. In specific, military firms do not simply kill for no good reason. Thus, blanket accusations of the industry as a whole as being an enterprise of evil, violent greed, generally ring false on deeper examination. Rather, PMFs are businesses with certain goals. Military provider firms do use violence, but their general goal is not violence for its own sake, but rather to achieve the task for which they were hired. Considering the increasingly messy wars of the twenty-first century, the firms' personnel also operate with far greater military professionalism than most actors in local conflicts. Their standards of discipline are usually higher than the underpaid local militaries or rebels, which often degenerate into looting forces. Unlike local troops, as outsiders they are also less likely to hold specific grudges against any one local ethnic group or faction and have less reason to commit atrocities as payback for historic grievances.[2]

Consulting sector firms likewise can play a positive role in professionalizing clients' security forces. They can teach local forces standards of military behavior and pass on advice that brutality is not an essential element of strategy. The firms frequently also offer instruction in international laws of warfare as a part of their training packages, if the clients so desire.

However, these propensities are balanced by opposite moral hazards that can lead to negative consequences from a human rights standpoint. One of the fundamental issues from a normative standpoint is that the public good and the private firm's good are not always identical. The organizing intent of a private company is to generate internal profit, whereas public agencies are constructed with wider demands. That is, private companies as a rule are more interested in doing well than good.[3]

Although the claim that they are outsiders to a conflict is true, once the ink on the contract has dried the PMF does become an interested actor, with a stake in the final outcome of a conflict. That they are outside interlopers is also no guarantee against taking part in revenge actions. Historically, foreign troops often were brought in to take actions against local populations that domestic troops could not be relied on to do.[4]

Similarly, corporate responsibility and a nice public image have their limits. As profit-driven actors, they will make operational decisions also influenced by their bottom lines. So, although it is wrong to assume that military provider firms just kill for money, there may be some situations where transgressing human rights may be in their corporate interests. For example, Executive Outcomes may have benefited in a public relations sense by running medical dispensaries, but it became a leader in its sector by helping clients to win wars. The result were tactical choices towards that goal, at certain other costs. Some aid workers charged EO personnel with using indiscriminate and excessive force in its campaigns in Sierra Leone and Angola.[5] Similarly, when EO helicopter gunship pilots flying over the thick jungle canopy reported that they were having trouble distinguishing between guerrillas and civilians, they were reportedly told, "Kill everybody." Reports claim they followed the orders, just they as they were hired to do.[6] This may also influence the choice of weaponry. The firm is known to have used Fuel Air Explosives (FAE) in its Angola operations.[7] Also known as "vacuum bombs," the use of FAEs is regarded by some international bodies as a transgression of human rights in that they are particularly toresome and prone to indiscriminate use.[8]

Likewise, for military consulting sector firms, the normative record from professionalization programs is not particularly encouraging. The firms maintain an interest in making sure that the client is satisfied. The problem is that this does not always mesh with other normative goals, such as human rights protection. For example, MPRI employees report that their teaching on the military code of conduct and the laws of land warfare in the Bosnian program was kept minimal, as the clients/students were uncomfortable with the subject.[9]

Moreover, once a client has left a military instruction program, no controls exist over what they may do with the training and advancement opportunities provided. They may choose to disregard certain teachings or pick and choose what they follow. One has only to think of Idi Amin in Uganda and the "Emperor" Jean-Bedel Bokassa in the Central African Republic (both Western-trained soldiers, who later became the worst of despots) to see how this may play out negatively.[10] Even professionalization programs that include instruction on the laws of warfare can fail to work out as expected. The number of foreign graduates from the U.S. military's School of the Americas (SOA), who were later involved in atrocities in their home states illustrates this quite graphically.[11]

Military training provided to those outside of controls can result in both unintended consequences and even deliberate misuse by the client. The crux is that with privatized offerings, even the most minimal of public controls are lost.

> Providing training without strings to organize and wage war is much like letting the genie out of the bottle. We cannot predict how, when, or why it will be used. The unintended consequences of widespread privatized military assistance around the globe could be disastrous. A better-trained army may just be enough to trigger a regional war or power struggle, not to mention the possibilities of internal repression.[12]

For example, MPRI has claimed that as part of its advisory services, it only trains the Bosnian Army for defensive operations. This may be true, but the end result is a strengthening of capabilities and confidence that may spill over into aggressive Bosnian action if the NATO peacekeeping force were to leave. Similarly, MPRI's training of the Croatian army may have unintentionally spilled over into the Kosovo conflict. A number of Croat military officers, who earlier had trained at the MPRI-run program, later resigned and joined the rebel KLA organization in Kosovo, including even the overall commander of KLA, General Agim Ceku. During the years leading up to the Kosovo operation, the KLA was labeled as a terrorist-like entity by U.S. policymakers and at times operated in opposition to U.S. foreign policy goals in the region. The KLA's activities certainly fell outside what the firm had intended in its original instruction. There were also rumors that KLA members received tactical training at MPRI programs in Bosnia, potentially without the firm even knowing that the personnel it was training were not Bosnian troops.[13] As the KLA has become dissatisfied with NATO's implementation of peace in the region, the organization has increasingly come into conflict with both U.S. troops and the Macedonian military, to whom MPRI is also currently providing military training and consulting.[14] This duality has further complicated the United States's relations in the region and with its NATO partners.[15]

Perhaps even more worrisome than unintended consequences, is the possibility that direct market incentives may encourage a firm to go "rogue." When faced with stiff competition, firms often seek ways to differentiate themselves. Although one option is to build up a positive brand name, other firms may do the opposite and focus on what has been called the "low rent district" in the industry.[16]

Rather than working only for respectable governments or selling their professionalism, such rogue PMFs might instead stress another comparative advantage, their willingness to perform any task or work for any party willing to pay the right price. These clients include rebel movements challenging local state governments or transnational groups such as drug cartels or terrorists. Weaker, impoverished countries that lack the means to hire reputable firms may also be drawn toward hiring those operating at the cheaper end of the market.[17] The simple fact is that there are no guarantees over where or for whom the firms will work. Much like what has a happened with rogue currency traders in international financial markets, PMFs can easily find a hospitable business environment either where regulation is weak due to a lack of governance or where the host state sees them as useful tools for its own foreign policy goals.[18]

In addition to the firms discussed previously that provided training to jihadist groups, another striking example of this phenomenon is Spearhead Limited, an Israeli PMF that reportedly has specialized in working with rebel groups and drug cartels. Run by a former Lt. Colonel in the Israeli Army, the firm is reputed to have provided military assistance to the forces of Colombian drug lords Pablo Escobar and Jose Gonzalo Rodriguez Gacha, two of the Medellín cartel's most violent bosses. Later, the firm was reputed to have provided training to the Cali cartel and to right-wing paramilitary death squads. These groups were linked to the assassinations of two Colombian presidential candidates and an airline bombing that left 111 people dead.[19] In the aftermath of the bombing, the firm's president was convicted by an Israeli court for illegally exporting military arms and information to a Colombian paramilitary group. He was fined $13,400, hardly a deterrent to other PMFs considering this path.

THE PRIVATIZED DIFFUSION OF RESPONSIBILITY AND ACCOUNTABILITY

The next areas of concern from a normative standpoint are the domains of responsibility and accountability. Public military forces have all manner of traditional controls over their activities, ranging from internal checks and balances, domestic laws regulating the activities of the military force and its personnel, parliamentary scrutiny, public opinion, and numerous aspects of international law.[20] PMFs, however are only subject to the laws of the market. Current international law only speaks to the role of individual mercenaries of the traditional sort and has been found inapplicable to the actions of the industry.[21] Consequently, the possibility of legal recourse against these firms is very slim.[22] There is also no agency or legislative oversight in the way there might be on traditional militaries. Other than its shareholders, there are no real checks and balances on a PMF.

As a result, an additional outcome of privatizing elements of military services is that the responsibility for a public end—security—is diffused across a number of actors, public and private. As such, accountability also becomes diffused and more difficult to track. The question of who monitors, regulates, or punishes a company or its employees that go astray does not lend itself to a clear answer, particularly when many firms are chartered in offshore accounts. In traditional business, the local state security institutions are responsible for enforcing the laws within its sovereign area. With PMFs, usually it is the very weakness of the public institutions that has resulted in the hire of the firm.

The normative uncertainty then becomes who exactly ought to be held responsible if something does go wrong when a PMF is hired. One example is a contract in 1997 that the DSL firm had with British Petroleum (BP) to ensure the protection of its pipelines in Colombia. Employees of DSL allegedly trained a local Colombian military unit (the Colombian 14th Army Brigade, which has been linked to past atrocities, including the massacre of civilians) in counterinsurgency techniques using ex-SAS personnel as its military trainers. Employees of the firm also reportedly fed the 14th Brigade with intelligence on local citizens (including environmentalists and community leaders) who opposed BP's project. Provided with this information from private sources, the Colombian military would then deal with the local leaders directly, that is by kidnappings, torture, and murder, or indirectly through associated paramilitary groups.[23] In another case in Colombia, the Airscan firm was contracted by Occidental Petroleum and Ecopetrol to provide aerial security and reconnaissance to help protect their pipelines from rebel attack. In performing this contract, its pilots coordinated an air strike carried out by Colombian air force pilots. The strikes mistakenly targeted the wrong village and killed 18 unarmed civilians, including nine children.[24] In neither case were PMF employees held accountable or punished for their actions.

The dilemma these cases present is the difficulty of assessing the exact lines of responsibility. Who can and should be punished for these crimes? The soldiers who did the actual deeds? Their government? The individual employees of the PMFs? The overall military companies? Their clients? The clients' owners (stockholders)? Or even their customers, who bought their gas that helped pay for the firm that directed the killings? Obviously, although it is murky exactly where the lines of responsibility stop, it is very clear that privatizing security actions only complicates the issue.

ADVERSE SELECTION, PMF-STYLE

The next moral area of concern is that of adverse selection. Although certain military firms may strive toward respectability, the very nature of provider sector activity also means that there may be a mechanism that draws in disreputable players looking for the cover of legitimacy. Specifically, the privatized military industry provides an employment opportunity for those previously drawn toward mercenary work or who have been forced out of public military activities for past misdeeds.[25]

On the executive side, it should not be reassuring that many of the major actors in the Iran-Contra and BCCI scandals are now associated with the industry.[26] On the employee side, firms are not always looking for the most congenial workforce, but instead recruit those operators known for their effectiveness. For example, many former members of the most notorious and ruthless units of the Soviet and apartheid-era South Africa regimes have found employment in the industry. In the past, these individuals acted without concern for human rights and certainly could do so again. Doug Brooks, a leading industry proponent who heads a PMF lobby group, puts it even more bluntly. The firm's best employees are often ". . . not nice guys. You wouldn't want them to marry your sister."[27]

This issue of adverse selection becomes particularly worrisome when placed in the context of the industry, with its layers of moral hazard and diffused responsibilities. Thus, even if PMFs are scrupulous in screening out their hires for human rights violations (which is difficult for a firm to accomplish, given that most of its prospective employee's resumes do not have an "atrocities committed" section), it is still difficult for them to monitor their troops in the field completely. Moreover, if employees do commit violations, little incentive exists for a firm to report its own employees to any legal authorities; to do so risks scaring off both clients and other prospective employees, whereas a successful cover-up or quiet release of the perpetrators carries less risk. These employees who have committed violations, then, may be hired by another firm unaware of their crimes. If external legal action were attempted, it is also doubtful that a firm would even allow its employees to be tried in a weak client state's judicial system.

In the Balkans operations, for example, a number of DynCorp employees were implicated in sex crimes (including "owning" girls as young as 12 years old), prostitution rackets, and the illegal arms trade. DynCorp's Bosnia site supervisor even videotaped himself raping two young women. None were ever prosecuted, but instead were spirited out of country, away from local authorities. Moreover, the company then fired the employees who had "blown the whistle" on the criminal activity, for which it was later sued under the Racketeer Influenced Corrupt Organization Act (RICO).[28]

WHOM TO SELL TO? THE LACK OF LIMITATIONS IN CLIENTELE

Another concern with PMFs is to whom exactly the firms can and do sell their services. Some industry proponents say that although their accountability is not formalized as with a public agency, the firms in the industry answer for their actions in two ways: through home government informal oversight mechanisms, and the law of the market. These are claimed to mitigate risks of misbehavior from a normative perspective.

The evidence so far, though, suggests that neither mechanism has worked as well as industry proponents often claim. For example, some PMFs claim that by maintaining close ties with their home governments, they will inherently know what the government's goals are and not go astray. However, on numerous occasions, firms have made plans to support regimes or non-state groups about whom the home state government or public had normative concerns. For example, Sandline planned to work with the KLA (the Kosovar rebel group) in 1998 and had to be prevented from doing so by British Foreign Office intervention. Likewise, MPRI requested a license to assist the corrupt and failing Mobutu regime in 1997, but was denied by the State Department. If informal ties had performed their suggested function, these applications would not have happened in the first place.[29] Similarly, other reports have linked a number of firms with less savory clients, Airscan and Ronco with supplying military aid to the rebel forces of the Sudanese People's Liberation Army and the Rwanda Patriotic Front (RPF) in Rwanda, in contravention of strict U.S. laws against giving these groups aid. The firm NFD is rumored to have worked for both the governments of Libya and Sudan, neither of which are regimes that South Africa (nor the United States) would like to see prosper.[30] Spearhead worked with drug cartels, certainly not in the interest of Israeli policy aims, even though its president was still in the Israeli Army reserves.[31]

In fact, sometimes the firm's influence is enough to wear down its home government's objections over time and overcome the original normative concerns. Chapter 8 discussed one example, MPRI's two-year lobbying effort to work with the military dictatorship of Equatorial Guinea. Ultimately the fear of an American PMF losing a contract to a foreign firm overcame the relevant policy desks' concerns over aiding a repressive dictatorship allied with foes of the United States. Another way a firm might escape such controls is by setting up subsidiaries in the client state; this technically isolates the process from the home government.

When the only form of accountability and oversight is an informal connection between the firm and its home state, the difficulties become even more pronounced with a government that is somewhat weaker or has a problematic relationship with the firm.[32] For example, Executive Outcomes certainly had tense relations with the post-apartheid government in South Africa—it was the very impetus for the firm's formation. In turn, the government openly expressed its concern over the allegiance of companies in the EO network.[33] Informal ties between the two could hardly be relied on, given this situation. Likewise, Sakina and Transglobal (the two firms discussed in Chapter 11 that reportedly ran jehadi training courses) had no known contact with their home governments.

Another way that accountability allegedly is maintained is through self-regulating market mechanisms. The firms frequently "dismiss accusations that they would work for 'rogue' governments, prolong conflicts for financial gain, work for two warring parties simultaneously, or commit heinous human rights abuses, by referring to the constraints of the market."[34] Their argument is that any firm that acts in an unaccountable or reckless manner would hurt its long-term financial interests and thus would automatically choose against such an action.[35] The firm Control Risks, for example, reputedly turned down a lucrative contract with the Burmese military government, directly because of such public relations concerns.[36]

Yet, the industry's operations in Zaire/Congo illustrate how market mechanisms do not always provide full assurance or accountability in clientele. In 1997, the director of EO stated explicitly that the firm would not work for the Mobutu government, since Zaire was supporting hostile acts against Angola, its employer at the time, and that the Mobutu regime of Zaire was, in his words, "politically suspect." However, despite his public stance, the firm is, in fact, reported to have contacted President Mobutu for work.[37] By the time the Mobutu regime fell, several military firms found themselves working for both sides of the conflict, including EO, Stabilco, and Omega Support Ltd. Thus, in that PMFs worked for all sides, the hope that market forces would shape the industry in any one normative direction appears misplaced. Sudan and Angola are other wars where PMFs have fought on both sides.

The problem is that, as any stockholder of Enron or Worldcom could explicate, market constraints are a weak reed. They rely only on firms' good normative judgment, which may often be influenced by countervailing profit motivations. In fact, some firms may indeed decide that going for the "quick score" is worth the risks of long-term market costs. Provided the money is good (and many rebel, criminal, and terrorist organizations own assets measured in the hundreds of millions and even billions of dollars), it is not impossible that a massive short-term payoff will trump long-term goals. Or, they may think that they may be able to avoid market punishment by keeping their operation secret.

The ultimate issue of accountability in clientele selection is that the decision remains in the firm's hands. A standard industry claim is that legitimate firms "only work for legitimate governments."[38] The problems with this circular statement, though, are manifold.

To begin, there is no standard metric for deciding what is a "legitimate" government. The contestation over the government's legitimacy is often the reason for the PMF's hire in the first place.[39] The main criterion for determining state legitimacy is often simply whichever regime happened to be in power at the time. The problem is that by limiting themselves to state regimes, PMFs would be agents of the status quo, aiding only those regimes with the money to retain power, while potentially suppressing more legitimate resistance movements or preventing the chances for a conflict to reach a negotiated solution. For example, the Nelson Mandela-led African National Congress and even the Founding Fathers of the United States were groups once classified as rebels or terrorists before they overturned unpopular regimes and became internationally recognized, democratic governments.

On the other hand, even when a government is formally recognized by the international community, it still may not be seen as legitimate by a large proportion of its society. Or, it may not be undertaking fully lawful actions. As an illustration, there is evidence that EO explored a contract fighting for the Rwandan Hutu government in 1994, to help it against the rebel pro-Tutsi RPF.[40] Using this measure of putting sovereignty first, the firm was certainly in the right, in that it would have been working for an established government. The problem is that elements of this very same established government were in the midst of planning one of the worst genocides of the twentieth century.

If firms do try to determine what governments to work for based on a deeper, moral form of legitimacy, the issue is still not clearly evidenced. The CEO of Sandline and then SCI, Tim Spicer, broached this problem in an interview in 1999. He admitted that, if asked, he was not quite sure whether his firm would work for either the current military regime in Pakistan or the civilian government that it had topped. "Both have tics and both have crosses."[41] States skirt such issues in their foreign aid and alliance programs, often choosing to see as legitimate that which is in their own interest. PMFs likely have the propensity to do so as well, just supplanting the political and national elements that make up state interests with profit interests.

Moreover, the idea that the firms would always use moral grounds as the basis of their choice of client has been disproven. For example, Spicer has claimed that his firm's "strict, self-imposed code of conduct" prevented it from working with pariah governments and that the firm turned down working for President Mobutu of Zaire on these grounds.[42] However, his own autobiography notes that Sandline seriously considered a deal with Mobutu and even visited Zaire to explore it, despite the regime's obvious profound corruption. Ultimately, the firm decided against the contract because it appeared clear that Mobutu was going to lose the war, certainly not a decision made on the basis of purely ethical judgment.[43]

Even the alleged rule that the firms would only work for governments is not so hard and fast. Sandline claims to work only for clients whom it sees as the "good guys," meaning that in certain circumstances, it in fact will work for nonstate organizations fighting against states.[44] The firm attempted to work with the KLA and has said it would also be willing to work for the Iraqi resistance.[45] The important fact, again, is that it is the firm—responsible only to its owners—that decides who is the "good guy." As previously noted, other firms have not been so choosy and have consciously chosen to work for nonstate groups such as drug cartels that certainly have no claim to normative status.

Indeed, even if the firm makes a good faith attempt to make a moral choice in whom it works for, there are no guarantees on what may follow. History reveals that the perceived "good guys" of today often turn out to have dark designs and that the most righteous and noble causes can backfire or seem oddly immoral later. This has plagued states and may also apply to PMFs. For example, many of the Afghan "freedom fighters" that the United States trained in the 1980s either became part of radical Islamic terrorist organizations or joined the medieval Taliban militia. Similarly, Bechtel worked for Kabilia's rebel group in Zaire, which, once in power, became as corrupt and oppressive as the regime it replaced.[46]

IS SECURITY A PUBLIC OR PRIVATE GOOD?

One of the most traditionally accepted functions of government is, as the U.S. Constitution put it, "to provide for the common defense." The essential belief is that security is "a fundamental public service" that requires a "special public trust."[47] Thus, a general feeling is that those who carry out its core missions should be responsible to the public and not to other entities.

Accordingly, a particular troublesome aspect of security granted by means of a PMF is its effect on the public good. When the government delegates out part of its role in national security through the recruitment and maintenance of armed forces, it is abdicating an essential responsibility. When the forms of public protection are hired through private means, the citizens of society do not enjoy security by right of their membership in a state. Rather, it results from the coincidence between the firm's contract parameters, its profitability, and the specific contracting members' interests. Thus, when marketized, security is often not about collective good, but about private means and ends.

In fact, the concerns over outsourcing functions central to a society's protection and stability is that reliance on outside firms might undermine the social contract. When government is no longer responsible for aspects of security, the rationale for citizen loyalty is thus weakened. Indeed, to the extent that it fails to impose its own monopoly of force, a regime's very legitimacy is contested.[48] Politics are now directly and openly linked with economic interests (in normative terms, a return to a tymocratic or money-based system of governance), which can lead to breakdown of respect for governmental authority, and also delegitimizes its right to rule.[49] Or, as one analyst described the industry in more strident terms, "These khaki and Brooks Brothers clad mercenaries endorse the idea that power belongs to those who can afford it."[50]

Any loss of government legitimacy is a reason for concern, as when this happens regimes and their agents often become more reliant on coercion if they want to stay in power.[51] When linked to commerce, this tendency may even be heightened. Historically, private commercial ventures in governing colonial zones (ranging from the experiences in the Belgian Congo Free State, the Portuguese Mozambique and Nyassa companies, the British Royal Niger Company and South Africa Company) resulted in massive abuses of power against local populations. They also demonstrate the travesties that result from treating government responsibilities as an adjunct to commercial operations.[52]

The privatization of security also risks strengthening divisions inside countries. A particular illustration of this is the risk of privatizing space through the creation of "commercial enclaves." In weak or conflicted states, many multinational corporations see security as just another function that they have to provide themselves, comparable to providing their own electricity or building their own infrastructure. So, in the search for the best protection, the firms, particularly those operating in the midst of civil wars, often hire provider sector military services to protect their investments.[53] But when security is turned into a commodity that can be bought or sold, society is, in effect, polarized.[54]

As an example of how this process works, during the Mozambique war the investment conglomerate Lonrho provided its own protection through a $15 million contract signed with the British firm DSL (later Armorgroup). It later replaced the more expensive ex-British special forces DSL teams with Nepalese Gurkhas from Gurkha Security Guards. The hired protection included a 1,400-strong militia, watchtowers, and tanks. Although Lonrho profited greatly from the operation, the rest of Mozambiquan society suffered greatly from rebel attacks that shifted against less protected villages.[55] The same dynamic, where foreign commercial enclaves received higher protection than local citizenry, has held true in a number of other wars in the last decade, from Algeria and Angola to Sierra Leone and Sudan.

In other words, the problem when security is a profit-driven exercise is that the wealthy are inherently favored. Those portions of society who can afford it will employ the best protection, such as that offered by provider sector firms. Those who cannot afford the protection are often left behind. Not only are the worst threats deflected from the privately protected areas, but also those portions of society that cannot afford protection have to rely on declining, unstable, or nonexistent public means (whose top personnel often shift to the better-paying private side).[56]

The result is that privatizing security potentially hurts the poor disproportionately, worsening already deep social cleavages. Moreover, determining who garners protection and who does not, is not just an economic move but carries an underlying political action. Creating closed-off 'enclaves' involves the setting of internal boundaries. Such privatized enclaves are in a sense an abandonment of the public realm in security. They represent a "secession of the successful" from the rest of society.[57]

CONCLUSIONS: THE GRAYNESS OF THE PRIVATIZED RESPONSE

At the heart of matter is whether private, for-profit companies and their employees should be involved in protecting the most precious assets of states and their citizens. As has been seen, the main concern with privatizing security is that the military market is far from perfect. PMF activities create all sorts of externalities, not all of which are guaranteed positive.

On one hand, private firms point to their relative discipline and the market incentives to good behavior. At face value, these would seem to limit them from engaging in grossly inappropriate behavior as their ultimate long-term profit line is dependent on their public image. They also point to the positive impact they might have in helping to professionalize a local force or supplant ineffective forces that cannot end conflicts. A number of people in war-torn states such as Sierra Leone are alive today due to the rise of the PMF industry. Thus, in the context in which the firms operate, they often can accomplish worthy ends. When their private commercial aspirations are aligned with the public interest, they hold the capacity for better moral outcomes than what would occur otherwise.

The issue is not so simple, however. The firms are not altruistic by any measure. When the means of security are privatized, certain mechanisms of moral hazard and adverse selection might lead firms astray. Just as in the rest of commerce, war is business where nice firms do not always finish first. Aspirations of corporate responsibility and a positive public image may be overridden by the need to fulfill a contract or be seen as an effective firm 'that gets things done.' Even if they try to act only in the purest moral sense (which is unlikely, given their structure), there are also the risks of unintended consequences over the services they provide. Moreover, a diffusion of responsibilities and lack of accountability exists in their operations, particularly in the present unregulated, globalized market. The combination of these factors holds the possibility of heightened rogue behavior by certain firms or their employees, a negative impact on human rights, and increased societal challenges from the devolution of governmental responsibilities. In other words, considerations of the commonweal are matters of morality, whereas the bottom line is fundamentally amoral.

The result is that PMFs have an ambiguous status when it comes to morality and ethics. Although it may not be satisfying to those who see the world in stark terms, to make a blanket, normative judgment about the entire privatized military industry is analytically incorrect and ethically unfair. The phenomenon should be considered on its own terms and placed in the proper context. As former UN adviser David Shearer writes, "Private military forces cannot be defined in absolute terms: they occupy a gray area that challenges the liberal conscience. Moral judgments on the use of mercenaries are usually passed at a distance from the situations in which these forces are involved. Those facing conflict and defeat have fewer moral com-punctions."[58]

At their best, PMFs may be able to equal public institutions in their po-tential for protecting society. However, privatizing military services can also result in added incentives and potentials for far more negative conse-quences than their proponents would like to admit. Their market lacks any measure of regulation and has certain propensities for moral harms. Therein lies the ambiguity. Just as the public institutions of the state have served both good and evil ends, so too can the privatized military industry.

FIFTEEN

Conclusions

Frankly, I'd like to see the government get out of war altogether and leave the whole feud to private industry.

—Major Milo Minderbinder, *Catch-22*

In 1999, when Executive Outcomes, a pioneer firm in the privatized military industry closed, some analysts read this to be a death knell for the entire industry. Their belief was that the privatized military industry was a passing post–Cold War phenomenon, which would disappear because of an overall lack of legitimacy and steady contracts.[1] Others argued that the privatized military industry was here to stay, albeit limited to a minor market niche. The firms, they reasoned, would only operate in isolated, failed states, meeting very specific supply and demand criteria. In particular, the activity of such firms would be restricted to the mineral-rich, but essentially lawless, areas of sub-Saharan Africa.[2]

It would appear, however, that these analysts spoke too soon. Or, rather, in focusing on one individual firm's closure, within one sector, within one region of the world, they overlooked wider global trends of a broader industry. Such dour predictions failed to take into account the breadth of privatized military industry, the variation of its business sectors, the wide scope of its activity, and its growing and broadened client base.

THE FUTURE OF THE PRIVATIZED MILITARY INDUSTRY

As long as war exists, so will a demand for military expertise. PMFs will resultantly benefit from any slack given by traditional sources of security. The overall history of public versus private military actors indicates that the privatized military industry will continue to play a significant and increasing role in international security in the next decades. Moreover, it will likely do so for all measures of clients. The simple reason is that the very same structural conditions that led to the industry's original growth still appear to be in place. Few dampening forces loom, while pressures for further expansion remain on the rise. As one recent conference report noted, "The supply of private security forces and the demand for them are growing by leaps and bounds."[3]

The gap in the market of security that lead to PMFs in the first place re-mains. The open military market is still flooded with weaponry, military ca-pabilities outside the state continue to expand, and the demand from internal and external conflicts is not waning. Developing states' capacities appear ever weaker and little evidence suggests that the leading powers will militarily re-engage in regions unless they have strategic importance. The world community institutions, such as the United Nations or regional peace-keeping, also appear quite distant from any real capability of dealing with in-stability. "Indeed, thirty years from now, the period from the early 1960s to the early 1990s may appear as little more than an aberration because the su-perpowers and the great powers were briefly willing to exert a military pres-ence in many states that obviated the market for private security forces."[4]

Continued changes in the nature of war and the realm of privatization will also play a role in sustaining the industry's health. The growing effects of technology in the revolution in military affairs only reinforce private firms' critical importance to high-level military functions and expose states' inability to supply such activities on their own.[5] Likewise, continued reduc-tions and restrictions in force structure "make using a logistics-support con-tractor like Brown & Root almost mandatory."[6] Thus, not only has an opening been created for PMFs to operate within this former state sphere, but the continuing "trend towards worldwide privatization seems to indicate that the marketing of military services will continue to be a growth industry for the foreseeable future."[7]

Moreover, states and other international agents tend to emulate the most successful military formats and practices in the system.[8] So, for every suc-cessful use of a private military firm, the market will likely expand. In effect, the phenomenon that economists call "Say's Law" might be at work in the security market: the mere existence of a supply of firms will call forth added demand for their services.[9]

A similar effect may also be felt in the normative arena, in that every suc-cessful military privatization sets a new precedent and expands the realm of the possible. The interest of nonstate actors (including multinational cor-porations and humanitarian groups) in working closer with PMFs is likely to grow, as they face increasingly messy operational environments.[10] Each ex-pansion thus gives other such actors greater leeway to follow suit in hiring PMFs. "At the same time, rebel movements and other non-state actors might also see the advantages of hiring military assistance to bolster their forces, and there is little to stop private security companies working for them."[11]

Even the tragic events of September 11, which were read by many as al-tering the entire dynamic of global security, have not diminished the in-dustry's prospects. Rather, the attacks only further illustrated that, contrary to prevailing assumptions of international relations theory, warfare is no longer an exclusive affair of men in uniform, fighting for their state's political causes. Rather, warfare, as it was often in the past, has become a multi-faceted affair, involving men and women, inside and outside the public military, fighting for a variety of causes—political, economic, religious, social, and cultural—that often have little to do with the state.

In fact, the PMF industry was one of the few for which the economic outlook was improved, rather than harmed by the September 11 attacks. Although the rest of the U.S. economy and then the global economy sunk into doldrums from the shock, the prices of those in the private military industry listed on stock exchanges jumped roughly 50 percent in value, with L-3 (MPRI's parent firm) even doubling. This increase reflected a belief that the attacks had levied the equivalent of a "security tax" on the global economy.[12] The attacks created a heightened sensitivity to security and an increased demand for spending on military-style protection, from which PMFs were seen to benefit. A number of new firms were even launched in the aftermath of the attacks, hoping to tap the broadened market. One example is Janusian, a British venture that seeks to provide protection and intelligence against terrorist attacks. "It is perhaps an awkward but unsettling truth that the events of September 11, which brought such pain and tragedy to so many people, has given the corporate security world a new lease on life."[13]

The policy responses to the terrorist attacks also helped solidify the industry's health. Indeed, one Defense Department official's comments on impact of September 11 for PMFs were telling, "The war on terrorism is the full employment act for these guys . . . A lot of people have said 'Ding, ding, ding, gravy train.'"[14]

The U.S. military operations in Afghanistan, as well as the UN relief efforts, all involved a large degree of contracted logistics, including having BRS build and operate military bases all over Central Asia and Dyncorp working on related jobs in the Philippines.[15] Likewise, "Phase II" of the U.S. plan to defeat terrorism involves increasing levels of military assistance around the globe. Military consultant firms are expected to be a major beneficiary of these new programs, including leading the effort in building a new Afghan force, similar to contracts in the Balkans.[16] Finally, the multi-million-dollar bounty on Osama bin Laden has led to reports of private operations being started up in Pakistan by some military provider sector firms, many of which have experience operating in the region.[17] Of interest, a recent poll taken found that only 11 percent of Americans opposed the idea of contracting private soldiers to hunt down terrorist leaders, and one congressman even submitted a bill reauthorizing the old practice of privateering toward that aim, indicating a shift in outlook toward private soldiers.[18]

The PMF industry also stands to benefit from the shift in focus and resources created by the attacks. Efforts against terrorism mean that the United States and its coalition allies may become engaged in regions of new strategic relevance, which had previously fallen out of the scope of policy, such as U.S. forces' deployment to Afghanistan, Yemen, and the Philippines. However, this comes at a cost. Their attention and force levels in other areas will drop, creating a gap that PMFs will fill. For example, when U.S. military air reconnaissance assets were shifted out of the Balkans to more active operations in Southwest Asia, a PMF (Airscan) was contracted to replace this function for the NATO force. Similarly, the likelihood of Western military forces deploying in humanitarian operations with no link to an antiterrorism campaign are even lower, creating a further push for PMFs taking on this role.

In sum, the privatized military services phenomenon appears likely not only to endure, but also to thrive in the coming years. Indeed, some groups have described the further proliferation of PMFs as almost "inevitable."[19] Thus, as shocking as private firms supplying military services might have been a few years back, it is no exaggeration to say that are "the wave of the future in terms of defense and security."[20]

FUTURE AVENUES FOR THEORY AND RESEARCH

The emergence of this industry will affect international security in a number of critical ways. As a result, security analysts must face the very real existence of corporate actors with a direct role in the military field. Most fundamentally, PMFs challenge one of the basic premises of the study of international security: that states possess a monopoly over the use of force, and thus the study of security can be based on the premise that states constitute the sole unit of analysis. As explored in previous chapters, outdated assumptions about the exclusive and permanent role of the state in the security sphere certainly require re-examination and amendment to account for recent developments, including the rise of PMFs.

The broadening of civil-military relations theory to allow for private, third-party impacts is an example of how this can be done in a way that adds to, rather than devalues, the core of existing theories. Similarly, building in the impact of the broader military outsourcing market would strengthen theories of arms races and conflict formation. The Ethiopia-Eritrea example illustrates how a prediction based on present theory fails without these changes. Thus, further, more specific empirical tests on the impact of PMFs in such areas as the likelihood of interventions, their effect on arms races, regional conflicts, level of human rights, and evolving changes in international law and norms are all future avenues for research and study.

Viewed in this light, the findings of this book also suggest that if bound by parochialism we will miss out on understanding. Wherever useful, scholars should being willing to integrate tools and findings from other fields. Insofar as military services are now provided in markets, students of international security might well take counsel from the study of related arenas, including: business strategy, the politics of international markets, the new economics of organizations, and research on business sectors marked by contract competition and agency issues.[21] For example, the study of alliance and coalitions must now allow for the potential of PMFs, with new possibilities of state-firm and inter-firm networks. Learning about how such networks might form and operate is thus useful. Likewise, the impact of "branding" might become relevant in certain conflict situations, including the possible effect of PMFs' reputations deterring or provoking war. Evidence also suggests that, with the entrance of PMFs, strategic decisions taken in wars might be motivated not by their local effect, but rather by their greater impact as marketing tools in dealings with future clients.[22]

PMF POLICY RECOMMENDATIONS

A fundamental premise of this book is that the study of international relations and indeed of political science generally should be concerned not just with theory and research, but with real world relevance as well. The new private military industry poses issues and challenges that must be addressed by governments, militaries, humanitarian advocates, and beyond.

The critical first step toward any successful policy is to broaden the understanding of the issue at hand. Heightened appreciation is required of the privatized military industry's potential and its underlying dynamics and challenges. In short, any policy toward PMFs that is born of ignorance is unlikely to yield the best results.

Just as militaries recently have had to develop a system for working with NGOs and aid groups, so too they should begin to consider how they will deal with PMFs during operations, as they will increasingly encounter them in the field. These range from establishing specified rules of engagement, attuned methods of targeting, and developing regulations for the status and treatment of private military personnel when captured as prisoners of war.

Multilateral and nonstate organizations, in turn, must develop their own policies toward PMFs. Nongovernment organizations and multilateral institutions, including the United Nations, the World Bank, and the International Monetary Fund, must become more aware of their own direct and indirect interfaces with PMFs. Some international agencies have hired the firms, while other branches of the same organizations concurrently have excoriated the practice. The United Nations in particular is guilty of this hypocritic duality. Equally, many international financial bodies provide loans that ultimately end up paying for PMF contracts in weakened states. Such organizations should immediately establish their own official policies toward the industry and actually implement them. At a minimum, they should establish checklists to use in vetting PMFs, before they even consider hiring them.

Chapter 11 explored how PMFs alter traditional expectations of international security. As a result, intelligence organizations must become attuned to firms' presence. In particular, they must pay heed to the firms' abilities to shift local force levels and threat potentials. Likewise, the impact of corporate branding and marketing, and the potential of state-firm and inter-firm networks are not just academic matters, but might very well become relevant in certain conflict situations.

Many foreign policy pundits and policy activists, particularly those working in the humanitarian community, have begun to comment and act on the privatized military industry. Some condemn the firms wholesale, while others extol them at every opportunity, despite the fact they usually have minimal expertise on the topic. Their search for headlines may well backfire with negative results in the field. A key is to recognize the tensions that exist between economic efficiency and military effectiveness on the one hand, and private motivation and political accountability on the other. Informed citizens, in turn, must also be sure to distinguish between sincere policy advocates and paid lobbyists. The media has a responsibility in aiding this effort to explore the industry with more depth and forthrightness.

A pressing policy concern is the lax and haphazard way in which governments have privatized their own military services over the last decade. The simple fact that one can outsource does not always mean one should. Rather, each contract decision should be given due consideration and not be taken before a fully informed, risk-based assessment.[23] At the higher decision-making levels, the general practice of military service privatizing should be re-examined. Specifically, senior officials should critically evaluate the purported costs savings and overall implications of turning over essential military services to the private market.

Given the control problems discussed in chapter 10, wherever possible private contracting should be kept out of critical battlefield areas. These are sectors over which the commanders must have 100 percent assurance that their orders will be carried out. When the military requires a service, it should be sure to examine first the possibilities offered within the force, across other service branches, and then to trusted allied forces. Even in situations with marginal economic cost, these military options provide the insurance of established military structures. Otherwise, the combination of business agency issues, along with the normal fog and friction of war, present real dangers of potential losses of control that could be decisive in battle.[24]

If an informed decision is taken to outsource military activity, then it must be done in a clear and well-thought-out manner. There must be a dedicated focus on managing the relationship to protect the public interest. Trust only goes so far in the business environment that governments are now entering. The cost-saving advantages of competition must be maintained, for that was the very reason private sphere services were sought in the first place. For this reason, the present practice of sole-source contracts should be ended wherever possible, since it combines the dangers of a monopoly with the inefficiencies of a government bureaucracy. Contracts, instead, should be broken down in order to mitigate the risks and increase savings.[25] At the same time, clients should remain aware of reducing potential redundancies in privatizing. For example, the U.S. military might not be served by separate and parallel logistics support sector agents for each of the four services (as is the likely outcome with the LOGCAP program), but rather choose an integrated but subcontracted system.

The contract-making process is also quite important. The current norm of hiring firms to perform exploratory analyses and then paying the very same companies to enact their own recommendations is rife with risk. As a first step, potential clients should establish independently what they feel is a reasonable cost (i.e., what expenses a prudent firm would incur in the course of conducting a competitive business), before consulting with a firm on this basis. They should then seek out other competitive offers.

A key realization of contracting is that a firm becomes an extension of government policy and, when operating in foreign lands, its diplomat on the ground. As such, the firm's reputation can precede it and implicate the government as well. Thus when selecting the bids, the government should also keep in mind firms' public reputations. As an illustration, the sex crimes committed by DynCorp employees in the Balkans have stuck to the firm's international brand recognition (a search of the Internet reveals over 800 citations of "DynCorp" with "sex trade"), such that when governments sign even mundane military base support contracts with the firm, the contracts end up being described by the press in such terms as "American Firm in Bosnia Sex Trade Row Poised to Win MoD contract.[26]

A business-savvy government would also do well to establish prior acceptable and sound business practices for the contract, in order to determine a metric for weighing the bids, rather than just relying on what obviously self-motivated firms bring to the table. Likewise, "hard-wired" bidding processes where a pre-set winner has already been determined rarely work to clients' benefit; they should be avoided. If possible, contract terms should also be negotiated with motivating structures in mind. Incentives should be built in to maximize performance, while punishment for cost overruns should be established.

No matter the level of perfection in the original contract agreement, proper supervision and administration of the contract is critical to head off the negative side effects of a private agent's profit motive. This is doubly important in the military sphere. Managing a complex, ongoing relationship without a clear concept of how the results will be measured is impossible. A prior "scorecard" of firm and client responsibilities and desired results must be clearly defined in advance. Preferably, a mechanism for multiple performance evaluation periods should also be established.[27]

A definitive way to enforce responsible contracts must also be set up in advance, so that if fraud or defection by the firm is discovered, the process and regulations that were broken are not revisited, but rather the perpetrator is immediately punished. The sanctions should also be heavy enough to deter others in the future.[28] Most important, privatizing services does not mean turning over oversight. Links with the PMF must be established at the tactical, operational, and strategic level, to ensure that client interests are maintained.

Such requirements of properly managing military outsourcing may require new skills for public service jobs. If the decision is made that military service privatization is the preferred option for future operational savings, public organizations must then invest in developing the new leadership competencies that will be demanded of them. For example, proficiency in communications, negotiation, strategic planning, project management, and even marketing will be critical for those working on military privatization issues, often more so than traditional command or bureaucratic skills. One option is to ensure that those personnel who oversee PMF contracts have business experience themselves. This could be accomplished by providing fellowships for military officers at cutting-edge businesses, whose success also hinges on outsourcing (analogous to the present fellowship program that places officers into academic institutions). This would provide the military a better institutional expertise in privatization.[29] Given their increasing role in the successful execution of military operations, there must also be an adequate number of these public eyes and ears. Currently, there are just two such contracting oversight officers per division in the U.S. military. As experienced in the Balkans and Central Asia, this is certainly not enough at the present level of outsourcing in contingency operations, let alone at potential future levels.[30]

There is also little evidence that the strategic and doctrinal implications of privatizing critical military services on the battlefield are being addressed.[31] For example, the exact points of interface between public forces and contracted forces may be places of particular vulnerability that an adversary might exploit in either the physical or electronic realm. Likewise, force commanders must be aware of the risks and take efforts to mitigate the contractual dilemmas outlined in chapter 10 that could hamstring a force.

Successful use of privatized military support begins with key unit leaders facing the issues at their home station, rather than being introduced to them in the midst of a crisis. As one U.S. Army colonel writes, "With any military operation, the 'five Ps' prevail: Prior planning prevents poor performance. The contractor must be integrated into the planning process, or major disconnects will occur during the military operation when it's time."[32]

Pilot studies and joint training exercises of various sizes and scope should be implemented to identify shortfalls and failures when contracting with PMFs. Careful analysis will identify changes required to optimize outsourcing results and establish clear tenets and objectives.[33] Specific areas to explore include how to diminish the risks of dependence and defection and how to establish regulations and standards that take into account the new reality of civilians deployed on the battlefield. These include the exact rules of engagement, identification requirements, and where they fall under military command. If privatized military support firm employees do not bear arms because of legal concerns, then additional force protection requirements must also be thought out, to ensure that those providing critical support are not a source of vulnerability. Although PMFs should obviously be consulted in these reviews, it seems intuitive that the actual writing of them should not be privatized, as has happened with prior field manuals.

Legal Maneuvers

If this industry is to be around for the coming decades, then how to regulate it is an important concern. Unfortunately, the applicable international legal definitions and regimes relating to private military actors focus on individual mercenaries, and have been found inapplicable to PMFs. Moreover, the very definitions that international law uses to identify mercenaries (the combination of Article 47 of the 1977 Additional Protocols to the Geneva Conventions and the 1989 International Convention against the Recruitment, Use, Financing and Training of Mercenaries) include a series of vague, yet restrictive requirements. The result is that it is near impossible to find anyone, anywhere who fits all the criteria.[34] In fact, one commentator within the PMF industry has noted that anyone who manages actually to get prosecuted under the existing anti-mercenary laws actually deserves to "be shot and their lawyer beside them."[35] Even if these legal definitions were not vague, few credible mechanisms are available to implement or enforce them at the international level.

National-level legal approaches mirror the weaknesses of international law. The vast majority of domestic laws and ordinances across the globe either ignore the phenomenon of private military actors altogether, deferring to the issue back to the flawed international level, or fall well short of being able to define or regulate the industry.[36] Only a small number of nations have regulations that even apply to the PMF industry and none is considered effective or even fully fleshed out at this time. For example, in cases where their contracts also involve arms transfers, U.S.-based PMFs must seek licenses under the International Traffic in Arms Regulations. But the actual licensing process itself is idiosyncratic.[37] "The Defense and State Department offices that have input into the process vary from contract to contract, and neither the companies nor independent observers are exactly clear about how the process works."[38] In addition, under current United States law as long as the contract is under $50 million any U.S. military firm can work abroad with no congressional notification requirement.[39]

Finally, once a PMF receives a license, no specific oversight requirements are in place to monitor how the contract is actually carried out. U.S. embassy officials in the contracting country are charged with general oversight, but no official actually has a dedicated responsibility to monitor the firms or their activities. Instead, many see this as contrary to their job requirements. When asked whether his office would pursue the employees of Airscan who had coordinated air strikes in Colombia that killed civilians, including nine children, one State Department official responded, "Our job is to protect Americans, not investigate Americans."[40]

Even if more states had better laws, the reality is that many PMFs operate as global businesses, with their contract activities occurring elsewhere. Many PMFs also operate in institutionally weak areas, such as failed state zones, where the local government is either unwilling or unable to enforce its own laws. This means that any observation of and enforcement against them defers back to their home state. Extraterritorial observation and enforcement, however, is almost impossible to carry out effectively. In addition, the organizational form of most PMFs also allows them to circumvent legislation. Being service-orientated businesses, operating on the global level, and often having small infrastructures, PMFs have the ability to move across borders or transform themselves, whenever and wherever they choose.

The overall result of these various factors is a general vacuum in law. At present, PMFs are relatively free of any form of legal control to prevent or punish abuses by the firms or their employees. As a result, a number of regulatory schemes have been offered by various interested actors. Many, in fact, have been proposed by the firms themselves, who recognize regulation as the means to increase their respectability and or even market dominance (by squeezing out firms that do not meet their proposed standards).[41] However, on closer analysis, other than providing voluntary guiding principles, these proposals remain far too self-biased or underdeveloped for implementation.

Given that PMFs are offering services of concern to society as a whole, it would appear that ordinary business privacy norms do not apply in full. The firms must realize that they have to be open to a higher degree of scrutiny, including full disclosure of equity partners and client lists. Their current lack of full transparency has backfired, as it feeds concerns about firms' ulterior motives and certainly bars any realization of full legitimacy.[42]

As a first step, industry-wide standards of transparency, human rights, and best practices, should be developed, akin to the Health, Safety, and Environment practices that the oil industry established in the late 1980s.[43] However, as the same example illustrates, although industry self-regulation is certainly welcome, it is not the final answer to assuage public concerns. Voluntary codes provide a baseline for excoriating firms that break rules they have signed, but often are simply a weak mechanism for shaming the shameless. In short, they give the cover of prior untested compliance without any real commitment. External regulation carried out by public bodies is the only way that any real protection can be established.

If governments want better control over the impact of the industry, then stronger and clearer regulation is necessary of both the firms that are based in their territory and those with whom they contract. Essential requirements include more transparent licensing processes, government oversight over local PMF contracts, and the establishment of financial and operational reporting requirements of the firms.[44] The business services provided by PMFs are military in orientation, but also impact the realm of foreign policy. Oversight should thus be multi-agency, involving the Commerce, State, and Defense Departments, or their local equivalents, in order to ensure full coverage of the nuances of the issues.

Such improvements in regulation are needed even in the few states that already have laws on the books that deal with PMFs. For example, the U.S. Congress should establish a more consistent and transparent licensing process that specifies oversight of U.S.-based PMFs and sets strict and public reporting requirements. The concern over the activities of certain PMFs in Colombia could be used as a basis for building the political will behind this. The current overly high monetary threshold for notification to Congress of pending contracts should also be lowered to make it more difficult for sizable military services to escape public monitoring.[45] Likewise, the Military Extraterritorial Jurisdiction Act could be expanded to include the activities of U.S.-based PMFs and/or PMF employees who are U.S. citizens working abroad, regardless of their client. Presently the Act only applies to civilian contractors working directly for the U.S. Department of Defense on U.S. military facilities; it does not apply to contractors working outside U.S. facilities, those working for another U.S. agency (such as the CIA), nor to U.S. nationals working overseas for a foreign government or organization.[46]

As these developing national standards become better suited to deal with the legal complexities of the PMF industry, leading states would do well to assist the process of international harmonization.[47] For example, the British government is presently pondering its own licensing approach toward PMFs, and laid out a set of potential options in a "Green Paper."[48] However, this paper took two full years to craft and immediately came under fire from Parliament.[49] Thus, at the time of publication, it appears that the British plan has been kicked further down the road. Eventually, some sort of regulatory scheme must be enacted by the government, in which the greater the observation and transparency, the better. Whatever the outcome, however, the British government's interests would be best suited by making sure its regulatory scheme is widely disseminated and explained to its allies and other interested states, including perhaps linking up with a wider European Union policy that could be harmonized with the United States's policies.

Such national-level responses only provide a stopgap, however. Unless each and every state develops sufficient legal controls—an unlikely development—rogue PMFs will still be able to slip through the seams of the law. A globalized industry demands a globalized response.

The substance of such an international regulatory system is a source of great potential debate and thus requires careful consideration of the process by which it is to be achieved. One compromise that guards representative public interests is the convening of a special task force on the industry under the auspices of the UN Secretary General and his Special Rapporteur on Mercenarism.[50] A body of international experts, with input from all stakeholders (governments, the academy, nongovernment organizations, and the firms themselves), could establish the parameters of the issues, build an internationally recognized database of the firms in the industry, and lay out potential forms of regulation, evaluation tools, and codes of conduct that public decision-makers could then weigh and decide upon. This task force could ultimately become the core of a permanent international office designated to handle such issues on a normal basis.

If so approved, this office could perform audits of PMFs that would make them sanctioned businesses, in a process akin to the present list of UN-approved contractors. This would include subjecting PMF personnel databases to appraisal for past violations of human rights. As a sanctioned business, not only could a firm work on behalf of the United Nations, but would also be in a better position to gain contracts from any other clients, ranging from humanitarian groups to large multinational companies, who are concerned about their image. PMFs, thus, will be motivated to support this system, in that it "clears" them for business with lucrative market sectors.

The same body could then review any contracts made with these cleared firms, with right of refusal. This would help control any propensity of PMFs to work for unsavory clients or engage in contracts that are contrary to the public good. If it approved of the contract, the body would then have the option to provide operational oversight where it sees a need. In certain cases, most likely provider firms carrying out combat activities, the international body could send teams, made up of neutral and independent military observers, to ensure that the firm not only followed the international laws of war, but also was not engaged in any breach of its operating obligations. These independent observer teams should have powers not only to monitor, but also certain powers to suspend payments, in order to establish their authority over the firm.

If the firm was found in violation of its contract terms or any laws of war, it would risk punishment. The exact nature of these sanctions, however, is another area in dispute and is generally unexplored in the various monitoring plans. PMFs would prefer that sanctions be solely market-based, with offending firms removed from the list of approved companies. Although this may be appropriate for instances where firms commit contract violations, it is insufficient for more egregious violations in the human rights sphere. In addition, market-based sanctions are also not a sufficient deterrent for controlling actions by individual PMF employees. One solution is to require that both firms and their employees agree in their original contract terms to face any legal sanction that the International Court of Justice or another international legal body determined to be commensurate with their violations.[51]

Development of such oversight processes will require time and political will. Hopefully, it will not first require the catalyst of a major abuse or crisis related to PMFs to jumpstart the process.

FINAL THOUGHTS

In the end, no policy toward the phenomenon of military privatization can be effective without an understanding of the industry, its dynamics, and its range of possibilities and challenges. Ideally, this work has provided the beginnings of that independently established base of knowledge.

Over the last half-century, the international environment has transformed. It has seen the rise of a host of new actors, from international organizations and multinational corporations to nongovernmental groups and transnational networks. In the realms of politics, business, science, law, trade, finance, communications, crime, and advocacy, these actors have each globalized new functions and capabilities. They now share the global system with sovereign states, that have often been equally transformed. Within each functional domain, some of these groups are weaker than states and some are stronger. They all interact, bargain, cooperate, and conflict.[52] Now, with privatized military firms, the ability to wage war has become a globalized function.

Just a decade ago, a book on private firms being players in the global security system would have been simple fiction. The private military industry is now a reality. Its emergence raises possibilities and dilemmas that are not only compelling and fascinating in a theoretical sense, but also driven by their real world relevance. It is thus paramount that our understanding of privatized military firms continues to be developed.

In conclusion, the old proverb used to be that 'War is far too important to be left to the generals.' For the 21st century, a new adage may be necessary: War is far too important to be left to private industry.

Postscript: The Lessons of Iraq

On March 19, 2003, U.S. forces invaded Iraq. It was a defining moment for U.S. foreign policy, causing repercussions for America's standing in the world that will likely last for decades. The Iraq war was also a defining moment for the privatized military industry. In a sense, the war was a new testing ground, not only for the industry but also for whether the trend lines laid out and predicted in *Corporate Warriors* (which was written before the war, over the period 1999 to 2002) would hold up.

As the book discusses, the privatized military industry started in the early 1990s, driven by the end of the Cold War and associated political, economic, and ideological changes. It was growing in size and scope each year, but that growth exploded after the Iraq invasion. It was as if the industry of private military services, already thriving at the time *Corporate Warriors* was first published, was put on steroids. In turn, the dilemmas laid out in the book became even thornier.

WHY CORPORATE WARRIORS IN IRAQ?

Historians will debate many things about the Iraq war, its motivations and miscalculations. But consensus already has started to build that insufficient U.S. forces were sent for the mission expected of them because of a failure of leadership, or pure hubris on the part of civilian leadership in the United States, especially President Bush, Vice President Cheney, and Secretary of Defense Rumsfeld and their so-called neoconservative cheerleaders. Indeed, a few months before the invasion, Rumsfeld publicly excoriated one of his senior military advisors, Army General Eric Shinseki, for even suggesting that the operation might not be a "cakewalk," as some were predicting, and that additional U.S. troops would be needed after the initial fight. Like Cassandra's in the tales of the Trojan War, Shinseki's warnings were first ignored and then, too late, proved true.

Even worse, the planning for the Iraq operation focused only on the invasion itself, and there were no realistic plans or structures in place for what would come after it. This was the height of folly. It ignored a most basic lesson of Carl von Clausewitz, one of the thinkers most cited at military academies; Clausewitz wrote that in war one should ensure "not to take the first step without considering the last."

As the military and the Bush Administration wrestled with the policy dilemmas caused by this lack of planning, private military contractors seemed to provide an attractive answer to many of their problems. The key difference from prior wars in the modern era is that previously this alternative had not existed.

It is sometimes easier to understand how the use of private military contractors came about by looking at the issue in reverse. A core problem that U.S. forces faced was insufficient troops, and there were several potential answers—but each of them was considered politically unpalatable. The first possibility would have been not to invade the country and instead to focus on the actual group that had attacked the U.S. on 9/11, al Qaida, which had been based in Afghanistan not Iraq.[1] Indeed, if most Americans had been informed that the operation would require hundreds of thousands of troops, leave thousands of them dead, cost hundreds of billions of dollars, and last for years, all the while targeting a foe that was not linked to 9/11, they likely would have demurred. But that was not the way the public debate went in 2003. Driven by calculated misuse of intelligence reports, the debate focused more on Iraqi weapons of mass destruction that turned out to be nonexistent.

With the decision made to invade Iraq, one answer to the problem of insufficient forces would have been for the Bush Administration to send more regular forces, beyond the original 135,000 planned. However, this would have necessitated publicly admitting that the administration, and most particularly Secretary Rumsfeld, was wrong in its planning. Plus, such an expanded force would have been incredibly onerous for a regular force already stretched thin by the war in Afghanistan, as well as by broader global commitments.

Another option would have been a full-scale call-up of the National Guard and Reserves, as originally envisioned for such major wars in what was called the "Abrams Doctrine." To do so, however, would have prompted widespread outcry among the public (as now the war's effect would have been felt more deeply at home), the last thing the Administration wanted as it headed into what was a tight 2004 Presidential campaign.

Some proposed persuading other allies to send their troops in, much as NATO allies and other interested members of the UN had sent troops to Bosnia and Kosovo, to help spread the burden. This would have involved tough compromises, however, such as granting UN or NATO command of the forces in Iraq, in which the Bush Administration simply had no interest. Plus, much of the world vehemently opposed the invasion, in which the Bush Administration often seemed to delight in the run up to the war (recall the whole "Old Europe" and "freedom fries" silliness). So, the likelihood of NATO's or the UN's sending troops was always minimal.

By comparison, the private military industry was an answer to these problems and, importantly, an answer that had not existed for policymakers in the past. It offered the potential backstop of additional forces but at no political cost. That is, there was no outcry when contractors were called up and deployed. As well, if the gradual death toll among American troops threatened to slowly wear down the President's approval ratings, contractor casualties were not counted in official death tolls and had no impact on these ratings. Hence, they were looked at by policymakers as almost a "positive externality," to use an economic term. That is, the public usually didn't even hear about them, and, when they did, they had far less blowback on the government. Notice the irony that for all the focus on contractors as a private solution, the costs savings were political in nature.

From what we can see from tracing the contracts, the decision to employ contractors in Iraq did not come in one single, grand conspiratorial meeting (as many detractors of Vice President Cheney often assume), but rather through an ever expanding series of decisions at multiple levels. Time and again a need cropped up (be it truck drivers for fuel convoys or guards for civilian leaders) that the military either did not want to divert limited forces to satisfy or could not meet with the troops on hand. Private military contractors then were hired, and, as the discussion in the book of Say's Law foretold, once one service had been carried out in one sector, it soon expanded to other sectors and across the system.

Today, because of a lack of sufficient management and oversight, neither the U.S. Congress nor the Pentagon knows exactly how many contractors are working for the United States in Iraq, exactly how much has been spent on them, or even how many have been killed or wounded. In 2005, I was even contacted by the Pentagon to help them determine these numbers. Imagine running a business where you don't even know the number of employees you are paying; Enron had better accounting than this, yet that is the problem in Iraq still today.

Estimates of the number of contract personnel in Iraq vary widely. In 2006, the United States Central Command estimated the number to be around 100,000 (such a perfectly round figure raises some questions). The same year the Director of the Private Security Company Association of Iraq estimated that 181 private security companies were working in Iraq with "just over 48,000 employees." In 2007 an internal Department of Defense census of the industry found that almost 180,000 private contractors were employed in Iraq (compared with 160,000 total U.S. troops at the time). Even this figure was thought by officials to be low, because a number of the biggest companies, as well as any firms employed by the Department of State or other agencies or NGOs, were not included in the census.[2]

So, almost five years in, no one has an exact head count of contractors in Iraq. Part of the confusion lies in the various ways that different observers categorize the industry. For example, the lower estimates tend to count only armed military provider types (or, as they sought to be called in Iraq, "private security"), whereas the higher counts tend to include the entire industry of companies providing military services and sometimes lump in contractors carrying out non-military functions, such as reconstruction.

We may not know the exact number, but we do know that even the lowest estimates place the number of contractors at a significant percentage of the U.S. presence, perhaps even greater than 100 percent. We thus know that the number is far larger than the size of any U.S. Army division and, even more, greater than the sum of all the troops that other nations have sent to Iraq combined (today at roughly 12,000 and in steep decline due to withdrawal plans). So, for all President Bush's talk of building a "Coalition of the Willing," the reality is that the Iraq war has seen the creation of something new: a "Coalition of the Billing."

With these greater numbers come greater costs. By one count, as of July 2007, more than 1,000 contractors have been killed in Iraq and another 13,000 wounded (again the data are patchy, with the only reliable source being insurance claims made by contractor employers and then reported to the U.S. Department of Labor).[3] Since the "Surge" started in January 2007 (this was the second wave of increased troop deployments, focused on the civil war), these numbers have accelerated; contractors have been killed at a rate of nine a week. These figures mean that, again, the private military industry has suffered more losses in Iraq than the rest of the coalition of allied nations combined. The losses are also far greater than any single U.S. Army division has experienced.

It is important to note that the contractors paid for by the U.S. taxpayer (either directly via the U.S. government or indirectly via companies employed by the U.S. government to do things like reconstruction that in turn hire PMFs) come from all over the world. In addition to Iraqi and U.S. citizens, contractors working in Iraq also include citizens from at least thirty other countries, some of whom were hired in violation of their home state laws. Indeed, a special investigation by the *Chicago Tribune*, in an article that won the Polk Award for best international reporting, revealed how some subcontractors used deception and coercion to recruit such "third party nationals" to work at U.S. bases in Iraq.[4]

These numbers in personnel translate into immense financial figures as well. The Senate Armed Services Committee estimated that reliance on contract employees has "grown dramatically" during the last few years, reaching $151 billion in 2006 (again, this figure likely uses a wide definition of contractor services and includes overall Pentagon operations, not just Iraq).[5] For example, the largest contract in the war has been with Halliburton-KBR, one of the case studies in *Corporate Warriors*. Continuing its work with the LOGCAP program, it provided the Iraq mission's logistics, as well as the efforts to restore the Iraqi oil system, which was originally folded under Pentagon contracting (many claim without proper competition). By summer 2007, the contract value for just this one company's work in Iraq was reported to be worth as much as $20.1 billion.[6]

To put this into context, the amount paid to Halliburton-KBR for just that period is roughly three times what the U.S. government paid to fight the entire 1991 Persian Gulf War. When putting other wars into current dollar amounts, the U.S. government paid Halliburton about $7 billion *more* than it cost the United States to fight the American Revolution, the War of 1812, the Mexican-American War, and the Spanish American War *combined* (interestingly, the $2.2 billion that the U.S. Army has claimed Halliburton overcharged is almost double the amount in current dollars that it cost the United States to fight the Mexican-American War, a war that won the United States Arizona, New Mexico, and California).[7] Having made $2.7 billion in profits in 2006, the firm announced in 2007 that it would be relocating to the United Arab Emirates, where it won't have to pay taxes or worry about an extradition treaty with the United States.

While many people focus on the booming numbers, even more important to the discussion of the industry are the roles that private soldiers performed, each critical to the success or failure of the operation.

Before the invasion of Iraq, private contractors helped with such roles as war-gaming and field training exercises in Kuwait. Their most important role, though, was handling the logistics and support during the war's buildup (For the armchair generals that sometimes downgrade the military importance of logistics, General Omar Bradley perhaps put it best, "Amateurs talk about strategy. Professionals talk about logistics."). For example, the massive U.S. complex at Camp Doha in Kuwait, which served as the launchpad for the invasion, was built, operated, and even guarded by an armed private contractor force.

During the invasion of Iraq, private military employees served these and a variety of critical roles, from handling the logistics and support for troops as they advanced into Iraq to maintaining, fueling, and arming many of the most sophisticated weapons systems like the F-117 stealth fighter, Apache attack helicopter, F-15 fighter, and U-2 reconnaissance aircraft. They even helped operate highly technical combat systems like the Global Hawk UAV and the air defense systems in both the Patriot missile batteries and on board numerous U.S. Navy ships.

But it was in the ensuing occupation period where the firms' roles expanded even further. While President Bush declared "Mission Accomplished" at his infamous May 1, 2003 aircraft carrier landing press event, violence in Iraq escalated over the next years. As the mission grew more difficult, private military firms began to be used as a stopgap, in lieu of sending more U.S. troops to fill the lack of significant allied support.

Private military personnel from all three business sectors discussed in the book played key roles. Military support firms provided logistics and other forms of technical support and assistance; military consulting firms provided the training of the post-Saddam police, paramilitary, and army, as well as other analytic roles, including in the military intelligence realm that would later prove so controversial; and military provider firms multiplied on the ground. They provided convoy escort and protection of key bases, offices, and facilities from rebel attack. Even the top U.S. official in Iraq, Coalition Provisional Authority head Paul Bremer, was guarded by a private military contingent from the Blackwater firm, replete with three privately-crewed armed helicopters that were the same model that U.S. special operations forces used. In short, the Iraq operation could not have been carried out without private military support.

At same time, the darkest episodes of the Iraq war all involved privatized military firms. These included the allegations of over-billing and other forms of war profiteering that have swirled around Vice President Cheney's old Halliburton-KBR firm, the tragedy of four employees of the Blackwater military provider firm being killed and mutilated on video at Fallujah and the subsequent battles that engulfed the area, and the Abu Ghraib prison abuse scandal, where private military employees were reported by U.S. Army investigators to have been an integral part of the pattern of abuse.

Simply put, when the histories of the Iraq war are written, by necessity, the private military industry will fill the pages. The somewhat hidden industry that *Corporate Warriors* introduced to the world has truly come into its own.

If the book raised the importance of an industry early on, how does the book's analysis of the trends look in retrospect? Did *Corporate Warriors* stand up to the changes that played out over the next few years after it was published? Did it prove useful to people working in the field or politics and policy?

THE REACTION TO *CORPORATE WARRIORS*

Looking back on the book almost five years after *Corporate Warriors* was published, my admittedly biased eyes believe that it has held up to the ultimate test case of Iraq.

It has sold beyond the academic audience for which it was originally intended and has been translated into languages ranging from Japanese to Urdu. It was named a co-winner by the American Political Science Association of the Gladys M. Kammerer award, among the finalists in international affairs books of the year by the Gelber Prize, and a "top ten summer read" by *Businessweek*. The work was featured in the History Channel documentary

Soldiers for Hire and provided background for plotlines in the TV drama *The West Wing* and the movie *Blood Diamonds*. Even more exciting for an academic like me was the positive response from the folks working in the field, from being invited to lecture on the topic at military bases to being emailed by a contractor I had originally interviewed for the book that he had just picked up a copy at Bagdad International Airport (BIAP, one of the early hubs for the industry in Iraq).

I should be clear, though, that not everyone was happy with the book and the subsequent articles that flowed from its research. Since it came out, I have received two death threats, three assault threats, and two threats of lawsuits from companies that didn't like their dirty laundry being aired. Fortunately, none came to fruition; they were meant for intimidation, and when that didn't work they backed off.

I must confess, though, that what made me angriest was not the threats but that the firms behind them were doing so with my money. That is, they were using funds that originated in significant part from U.S. taxpayers not only to try to influence public policy to their own advantage but also to try to chill public discussion on a matter of public policy.

This is not even to discuss the industry's hiring of various lobbyists, who spread their presence and wealth around congressional and executive branch offices. I even gathered what I called my own posse, lobbyists who made a point to show up at talks I gave whenever they could. They stood in the back of the room and asked questions that ended with something along the lines of "and don't you agree that my company is the best company in the world?" (Sadly, we lost a real player, whom I called C-B 1, when his company lost most of its contracts after it got caught submitting false claims to the U.S. government).

It is not that firms shouldn't have a voice, but we must recognize that this voice represents only a private interest and, again, is also indirectly paid for by U.S. taxpayers.

So oddly enough, the emergence of the private military industry often brings me to some deep questions over the health and vitality of our democracy. Thinking about private military firms doing jobs once held by soldiers evokes the memory of former President Dwight Eisenhower, who is likely spinning in his grave at this embodiment of his worst fears of a "military industrial complex."

Yet, I actually think that the guidance of the very first American conservatives is more helpful. The authors of the *Federalist Papers,* John Jay, Alexander Hamilton, and James Madison, who helped guide our Constitution, warned about the role of any private interests not responsive to the general interests of a broadly defined citizenry. The Founding Fathers' plan for government in the United States sought to make officials responsive to the general interests of this citizenry. In turn, they also set up internal controls designed to check the ambitions of those holding power within government. Their worry was that, when private interests move into the public realm and the airing of public views on public policy are stifled, governments tend to make policies that do not match the public interest. I wonder how they would look at the situation today.

Regardless of the fans and foes, the book has found a diverse audience. It has been an assigned text at venues ranging from Yale Law School to the U.S. Army War College. I was also asked to serve as a resource on the private military issue to the U.S. Congress, U.S. Department of Defense, the CIA, and the European Union. It struck a particular chord in the military law community, and I've given talks to the Air Force, Army, and National Guard and Reserves JAG communities. Perhaps I am proudest that stemming from the book's research, I was able to help in the various efforts to bring to light the role of private contractors in the Abu Ghraib prison abuse scandal and the Halliburton contract controversies in Iraq.

THE FINDINGS OF *CORPORATE WARRIORS* AND IRAQ

The reason for the continued utility of *Corporate Warriors* seems to be that the arguments made in the book still hold true. My main conclusions were (1) that a new industry had entered global politics, (2) that it was important, and (3) that our policies and understanding were not yet ready for it.

When I first started the research, a senior professor informed me that I would do well to quit graduate school and instead "Go become a screenwriter in Hollywood," for thinking to waste his time on such a fiction as private companies operating in war. If anything, a flaw of the book is not that I had too much imagination but rather that I didn't have enough. As I look now at the numbers serving in Iraq, as well as the deployment of such firms as Blackwater to New Orleans after Hurricane Katrina, the rapid expansion of the industry boggles even my mind.

Maybe it comes from being a little older and more jaundiced (rather than wiser), but I think I had too much faith in the public sector's ability to manage and control the industry's rise. The book laid out the positives and negatives of the industry but made a point that the negatives could be avoided only by careful oversight, management, and debate about the proper parameters of outsourcing. Instead, many of the trends and implications that the book warned about presented themselves not merely in full form but in manners even worse than I had projected. The simple reason is that while the privatized military industry has developed at a breakneck business pace, government has been slow to respond.

Current international law is still written primarily to deal with individual mercenaries and has almost no bearing on the industry. Regulation and oversight at the national level also are still minimal. The result is that military firms and their employees continue to exist within a gray area of the law, with an uncertain legal status and minimal accountability. A number of incidents in Iraq illustrate this. For example, a reported 100 percent of the translators and up to 50 percent of the interrogators at the Abu Ghraib prison were private contractors from the Titan and CACI firms respectively. The U.S. Army found that contractors were involved in 36 percent of the abuse incidents that it identified happened at the prison. It also cited six particular employees as being potentially culpable in the abuses.[8] Whereas the enlisted U.S. Army soldiers who were named in the Abu Ghraib abuse reports were properly court martialed for their crimes, not one of the private contractors named in the U.S. Army investigation reports has yet been charged, prosecuted, or punished, with the U.S. Army believing that it does not have jurisdiction.

In another incident, armed contractors from the Zapata firm were detained by U.S. forces, who claimed that they saw the private soldiers indiscriminately firing not only at Iraqi civilians but also at U.S. Marines. Again, they were not charged, as the legal issues could not be squared. Private military firms may be part of the military operation, but they and their employees are not part of the military—nor its chain of command or code of justice.[9]

Other cases included the Aegis "trophy video," in which contractors set video of themselves shooting at civilians to Elvis's song "Runaway Train" and put it on the Internet, the alleged joyride shootings of Iraqi civilians by a Triple Canopy supervisor (which became the subject of a lawsuit after the two employees, who claim to have witnessed the shootings, lost their jobs), and a reported shooting on Christmas Eve 2006, when a Blackwater employee allegedly got drunk while inside the Green Zone in Bagdad, got into an argument with a guard of the Iraqi Vice President, and then shot him dead with ten bullets.[10]

In none of these cases was anyone charged, prosecuted, or punished.

·   Indeed, more than 100,000 private military contractors have been deployed in Iraq for almost five years, and not one has been prosecuted or punished for any crime of conduct on the battlefield. While this is in huge contrast to the many U.S. and allied soldiers who have been prosecuted for crimes large and small in Iraq (as every force has its bad apples), perhaps a more illustrative point of comparison is with civilian life. The town of Westport, Connecticut, for example, has roughly the same per capita income (over $70,000 a year) as the PMF population in Iraq, but even this comfortable suburb has a crime rate above 28 per 1000 citizens, as compared to the 0 per 1000 crime rate of PMFs in Iraq. Thus, the private military industry has an astonishing comparison with either military or civilian equivalents. We can only then conclude that with PMFs, we have stumbled upon the perfect "Stepford" village in Iraq, where human nature has been overcome in the midst of a war zone, or we must admit that we have a clear combination of an absence of law and political will.[11]

Corporate Warriors also laid out how the mix of the profit motive with the fog of war raises difficult implications. Each of the types described in the book played out in Iraq. First, when it comes to military responsibilities, the incentives of the private companies to turn a profit may not always be in line with the client's interests or those of the public good. While in an ideal world there would be good competition, management, and oversight, producing cost and qualitative efficiencies, government contracting is not always set up to ensure this. Thus, the general concerns with any contracting handover (overcharging, overbilling hours, providing insufficiently trained personnel, quality assurance issues, etc.) cross over into the military realm.

This has been at the center of the war-profiteering allegations made at such firms as Halliburton-KBR and Custer-Battles. These firms were operating under "cost-plus" contracts ripe for abuse, with the examples in Iraq ranging from selling overpriced gasoline to charging for services not actually rendered (such as billing for meals that were not cooked for the troops or convoys shipping "sailboat fuel," as Halliburton truck drivers laughingly termed charging the government for moving empty pallets from site to site).[12] According to testimony before the House Committee on Oversight and Government and Reform, the Defense Contract Audit Agency has identified more than *$10 billion* in unsupported or questionable costs from battlefield contractors—and it has barely scratched the surface.

Such corruption doesn't just represent lost funds, it represents lost opportunities for what those funds could have been used on to actually support the mission. The situation got so bad that the Special Inspector General for Iraq Reconstruction (SIGIR) dubbed corruption as the "second insurgency" in Iraq.[13]

As the military continued to award PMF contract after contract with little examination, including to some of the same questionable characters who made their appearance in the book (such as Tim Spicer, who won a $293 million contract with his new firm Aegis), it became clear that it was learning little from past mistakes. One of the great challenges is that while the amount of contracting has boomed, the number of government contract officers (the "eyes and ears" of the government, who do monitoring and oversight) has shrunk. By one count, the number of Pentagon defense services contracts is up by 78 percent since the late 1990s, while the number of officials responsible for overseeing them is *down* by over 40 percent.[14]

Equally, the Pentagon seems not to be using its buying power to sanction and shape the market. For example, in 2007, it awarded the new Logistics Civilian Augmentation Program (LOGCAP), potentially worth up to $150 billion, to Halliburton-KBR, DynCorp, and Fluor Corp. Yet, the government has also reported that it has cited those three companies for twenty-nine cases of serious misconduct in the last decade of contracting (the category includes "false claims against the government, violations of the Anti-Kickback Act, fraud, conspiracy to launder money . . .").[15]

Even more important, PMFs lie outside national military controls and structures, so clients must also worry about how they can replace such services if things go awry or the firm or its employees refuse to carry out orders in the midst of a crisis. During the summer of 2003, the upsurge of violence in April 2004, and a wave of contractor kidnappings of July 2004, U.S. forces in Iraq faced a subsequent surge of firms delaying, suspending, or ending operations. Their concern for their private personnel and assets was valued as more important than the public mission, with resultant stresses on supplies such as fuel and ammunition, and troops' welfare, even forcing troops onto food rations. Retired Army Major General Barry McCaffery testified to Congress in 2007 about his worries that these were just warning signs of the problems that will result from turning over so much of the system to private firms. "Under conditions of great danger such as open warfare . . . they will discontinue operations. Our logistics system is a house of cards."[16]

This issue came to the fore again in September 2007. A convoy guarded by Blackwater contractors was reportedly attacked in Baghdad, and a raging gunfight ensued. At least eight civilians were killed in the crossfire and another thirteen wounded. The firm members described their actions as self defense, while the Iraqi government described their actions as a "crime" and claimed that the firm had "opened fire randomly." The Iraqi government, which was already quite angry with the firm after a series of earlier incidents, including the aforementioned Christmas Eve 2006 shooting and several armed standoffs between Iraqi police and Blackwater contractors, then announced that the firm's license to operate in Iraq was revoked and that it would be banned from the country. There were two problems: Blackwater, which was one of the biggest firms operating in Iraq at the time, actually had no license with the Iraqi Interior Ministry for them to revoke (illustrating the complete lack of controls and mismanagement within this space), and kicking out the company would leave the U.S. State Department in Iraq without security in the middle of a war zone. It was a classic case of over-outsourcing. The U.S. government's diplomatic security force had been hollowed out at the same time that the need for it had expanded (Note: a consortium of companies led by Blackwater received a $1 billion contract to do the global State Department diplomatic security job the year before, so it was never a lack of money that was the cause of the hollowing). The embassy was so reliant on the company that it had no back-up plan for what to do without them. Within hours of the Iraqis' announcement, Secretary of State Condoleezza Rice had to call the Iraqi Prime Minister to ask him to allow the firm to stay, hampering other U.S. efforts to pressure the very same government for action on political reform.

In addition to corporate priorities, PMFs have also introduced a new level of decision at the soldier/individual employee level. Whereas soldiers have no legal discretion once they enlist or are drafted, an individual employee decides who he or she wants to work for, where, when, and for what price. Even when deployed, employees have the choice of when to stay or leave (whether they get a better job offer from a competing firm, think the mission or their superiors are not worth it, or simply grow tired of the job or want to see their families). We even saw several companies shut down because they had employee strikes in Iraq (usually angry third world nationals, striking because their wages were lower than those of Western citizens working for the same companies), something that a soldier cannot do.

As in all industries there are mixed results in performance. Many PMF employees have endured greater risks and dangers than their military equivalents, including battles in Iraq during which PMFs rescued coalition forces, rather than the other way around. A particular 2004 battle in Najaf was widely reported. Blackwater employees helped protect a CPA headquarters and rescue a wounded marine, while fighting off hundreds of attackers, using company helicopters for supply and support.

At the same time, though, turnover within many firms was quite high and air flights home were often full of PMF employees, who had decided it was time to leave with their bank accounts full and their heads still on their shoulders. An added complication is that unlike the experience with Executive Outcomes, many firms hired employees that had never worked together or brought in a mix of third party nationals (in Iraq, the PMF nationalities range from American and British to lower-paid Salvadorans, Fijians, and Serbs). Thus, cost savings can come at the price of lesser bonds of group loyalty or patriotism, showing how gains in one area can harm another.

We also saw a growing tension between private contractors and American military units and how they coordinate their activities (or not). This was heightened by the fact that contractors often made twice as much or more as U.S. soldiers, despite the fact that the same taxpayers are the source of the money for both. In June 2006, the Government Accountability Office reported that "private security providers continue to enter the battle space without coordinating with the U.S. military, putting both the military and security providers at a greater risk for injury."[17]

As a result, U.S. military officers frequently expressed their frustrations with sharing the battlefield with private forces operating under their own rules and agendas and worried about the consequences for their own operations. For example, Brigadier General Karl Horst, deputy commander of the U.S. Third Infantry Division (responsible for the Baghdad area) tellingly put it, "These guys run loose in this country and do stupid stuff. There's no authority over them, so you can't come down on them hard when they escalate force. They shoot people, and someone else has to deal with the aftermath."[18]

At times, the issue reached the theater of the absurd. In July 2007, contractors were reported to have set up their own adult "escort service" inside the heavily fortified U.S.-controlled Green Zone in Bagdad. The on-line advertisements for the contractors' "hooker-in-residence" (which even showed a registration logo of the industry's trade group) stressed that "the members of PMC community has [sic] an exclusive arrangement" and U.S. soldiers were banned from the compound. As a newspaper article about the episode jokingly described, "The divide between uniformed soldiers and private military contractors is about to get wider."[19]

Corporate Warriors also foretold how the private military market has grown in global size and operations but remains effectively unregulated. This means that a broader set of military capabilities are available outside state control, with the decision of who gains such skills and expertise mainly left to the firms themselves.

To put it another way, there are insufficient controls over who can work for these firms and who these firms can work for. PMF employees have ranged from distinguished and decorated veterans to those we would rather not see represent the government. For example, there are now working privately in Iraq more ex-elite British SAS troops than currently serve in the entire active-duty SAS. Darker examples in Iraq range from one firm's hiring an ex-British Army soldier who had just been released from jail for having worked with Irish terrorists to another firm's bringing in a contingent of ex-Apartheid South African soldiers, including one who had admitted to firebombing the houses of more than sixty political activists back home. The skill sets also varied widely. Many firms had incredibly stringent recruitment and training standards and others reportedly did not. Indeed, U.S. Army investigators of Abu Ghraib prison abuse found that "approximately 35 percent of the contract interrogators [author's note: hired by the CACI firm] lacked formal military training as interrogators."[20]

The problem of clientele mirrors that of the employee equation, with corporate best practices at great variance and often in contradiction. For example, as more complex emergencies overwhelm the collective international capacity to respond effectively, the emerging private military marketplace has stepped forward to offer humanitarian organizations a new means to enhance their capacities without turning to traditional state military assistance. This is the option being quietly chosen by many humanitarian clients.

A limited study I carried out after *Corporate Warriors* found that humanitarians have contracted PMFs in war zones such as Afghanistan, Bosnia, the DRC, East Timor, Haiti, Iraq, Kosovo, Mozambique, Sierra Leone, Somalia, and Sudan. In total our study found more than forty contracts between PMFs and humanitarian actors (and it was by no means a comprehensive survey).[21] The firms have gone to work for the full gamut of humanitarian actor types, including privately funded NGOs (both secular and religious), state agencies, and international agencies. The extent of how things have changed is illustrated by one non-governmental humanitarian organization that hired a PMF in Iraq to protect its facilities and staff; the humanitarian group even had its own sniper teams, who killed several insurgents.

The problem is that, although the privatized military industry may open up possibilities, its use in such a way also poses fundamental questions about the future of the humanitarian ethic of neutrality. Its also raises simple problems of execution. Despite the huge amount of hiring, the research found only three humanitarian agencies that had formal documents on how their workers should relate to PMFs and their staff and only one organization that had detailed oversight guidance for its PMF employees, such as instructions on rules of engagement. However, even that organization had difficulty implementing the guidelines, given the lack of expertise within its country teams.

These sorts of challenges are tough enough when companies are working for what most would describe as "the good guys." But, as the book discusses, it is an even more difficult issue to decide who are the good guys, especially when private interests become part of the equation. The 2005 "rent a coup" episode in Equatorial Guinea, involving the Logo Logistics firm, illustrates the problem of teasing out exactly what is the right or moral thing to do in the absence of external guidance or rules. On one hand, the firm and its private funders (including, allegedly, Sir Mark Thatcher, the son of the former Prime Minister) were convicted for plotting the violent toppling of a government, for reasons of profit.[22] On the other hand, the would-be victim, President Teodoro Obiang, was a corrupt dictator, who took power by killing his uncle and runs one of the most despicable regimes on the continent. Raising more questions about equity is that today many of the PMFers who took part in the planned coup are in jail, while the alleged funders of it are not.

Corporate Warriors also discusses the question of how the extensive use of private contractors in public military roles raises a series of long-term questions for the military itself.

The military has long seen itself as a unique profession, set apart from civilian society as it is held accountable for the safety and security of that society. The introduction of PMFs and their recruiting from within the military, to take on military roles, brings a new dynamic into this realm. PMFs represent the metamorphosis of this once unique professional identity into the regular civilian marketplace; at the same time many of the public roles that the regular military had once monopolized have been lost.

Thus, as the Iraq war has brought this issue to light, soldiers tend to have a mixed attitude about PMFs. They feel overstretched and overburdened in today's incredibly challenging security environment. PMFs are thus filling a gap in the force structure that soldiers both recognize and worry about. Additionally, PMFs offer the potential for many soldiers to have a second career that keeps them in an occupation they know and love.

There are, however, also brewing concerns within the military about what this industry will mean for the long-term health of the profession, as well as general resentment of firms and individuals using the training and human investment, which the public military provided, for private profit. Soldiers also look at many of the roles taken over by firms—from training to technical support—and worry whether the loss of these professional skills and functions will hamstring the military in the future.

A particular problem area that Iraq has brought to the fore is how an expanding PMF marketplace has the potential to hurt the military's retention of talented soldiers. Soldiers in the PMF industry can make anywhere from two to ten times what they make in the regular military. In Iraq, the rates have grown astronomically, with some former Special Forces troops being paid as much as $1000 a day.

While soldiers have always had competing job options in the civilian marketplace, such as Air Force pilots leaving to fly airliners, the PMF industry is significantly different. PMFs keep the individual within the military and, thus, public sphere. More important, the private military industry is directly competitive with the public military. It not only draws its employees from the military, it does so to fill military roles, thus shrinking the military's purview. The overall process is brilliant from a private business standpoint and self-defeating from the public military's perspective. PMFs use public funds to recruit on the basis of higher pay and then charge back the military at a higher rate, all for the human capital investment that the military originally paid for.

The issue has become pointed for elite Special Operations units, as they have the most skills (from the longest human capital training investment) and, in turn, are the most marketable for the PMFs. Elite forces commanders in Australia, New Zealand, United Kingdom, and the United States all have expressed deep concern. One U.S. special forces officer described the issue of retention among his most experienced (ten plus years) troops, so integral to unit cohesion, as "at a tipping point."

The policy responses to this problem have so far been insufficient. Some militaries, like Australia, now quietly allow their troopers to take a year's leave of absence, in the hope that they will make their quick money and return, rather than be lost to the market forever. The U.S. military response is to bid against itself. With private firms offering attractive salaries in the six figures (again funded by the taxpayer), it is offering re-enlistment bonuses of up to $100,000 to troops in the special operations forces, to try to persuade its elite troops not to leave.

Finally, *Corporate Warriors* laid out how the private military industry provides the new possibility of seeking public policy ends through private military means. This allows governments to carry out actions that generally would not meet with legislative or public approval. This can be an advantage in meeting unrecognized or unsupported strategic needs but can disconnect the public from its own foreign policies. As the stark public division over the Iraq war illustrates, this can be dangerous for public policy. If an operation can drum up support only if the costs are shielded from the public, then maybe it shouldn't take place.

In sum, the Iraq war has confirmed and extended the findings laid out in *Corporate Warriors*. The growth of the privatized military industry has been phenomenal and almost Internet-like in the scale of numbers and profits.

Indeed, while Iraq may eventually be looked at as a bubble in the private military industry (in that many of the PMFs that started up solely for Iraq business may have made a lot of quick money but will likely go out of business when the conflict cools down), the overall industry shows no signs of weakening in the present security environment. The supply and demand forces that shaped the rise of PMFs are still in place. The results are both new possibilities for military efficiency and new military capabilities. However, the absence of regulation and oversight raises a series of worrisome dilemmas, particularly given the especially public nature of this new private industry.

EFFORTS TO CATCH UP TO CORPORATE WARRIORS

As I write this postscript, various efforts are underway that might shape and reform the future environment in which private militaries operate.

First, we are now starting to see a debate within the U.S. military as to whether some roles and functions should not have been outsourced in the first place and whether a roll back is needed. I give regular lectures at U.S. military advanced training schools, and I have been struck by how the tenor toward such firms has changed over just the last few years. It started with very few officers being aware of the industry, evolved to a general awareness but no firm views, and grew to a brewing debate and discord over whether contracting has gone too far and is ultimately harming mission goals.

This will continue as more of the Iraq-generation field officers advance in the ranks. For example, U.S. Army Colonel Peter Mansoor is one of the most influential military thinkers on counter-insurgency. In 2007, he told *Jane's Defense Weekly* that the U.S. military needs to take ". . . a real hard look at security contractors on future battlefields and figure out a way to get a handle on them so that they can be better integrated—if we're going to allow them to be used in the first place. . . . If they push traffic off the roads or if they shoot up a car that looks suspicious, whatever it may be, they may be operating within their contract—to the detriment of the mission, which is to bring the people over to your side. I would much rather see basically all armed entities in a counter-insurgency operation fall under a military chain of command."[23]

Likewise, after not dealing with the issue for a full decade, the U.S. Congress has started to wake from its slumber.

In Fall 2006 Senator Lindsay Graham slipped into the 2007 Defense Bill a clause that could potentially place contractors and others who accompany the U.S. military in the field under the U.S. military's Uniform Code of Military Justice (UCMJ). That is, he changed the law defining UCMJ to cover civilians not just in times of declared war but also contingency operations. Graham has stated in the press that he believes it will "give military commanders a more fair and efficient means of discipline on the battlefield" by placing "civilian contractors accompanying the Armed Forces in the field under court-martial jurisdiction during contingency operations as well as in times of declared war."[24]

The reaction from contractors in press reports to this potential massive change for those who operate in U.S. war zones has been mixed. Many have worried about how it might be applied in practice (military law is vastly different from civilian law), and many feel that is unnecessary. There are also questions as to the circumstances under which it might be applied and to which contracts or even nationalities. Graham's change wasn't noticed when it first came out (the news of the legal change was first broken in a blog I did a few weeks later), so many contractors were annoyed that they had to find out about this major change from the Internet, rather than from their own firm or from trade groups paid to stay on top of these things.[25] Others, usually ex-military personnel, took the attitude that they lived under military law for years while in service, so "it's not a big deal."

The reaction from the U.S. military has been positive. One officer even tracked me down at my office in Washington, D.C. to say that he thought the news was "awesome" and was emailing his fellow officers back in Iraq to let them know about it. For foreign militaries, there seems to be an attitude of wait and see what happens next, before they explore similar measures for contractors they employ.

At this time the Pentagon has yet to issue to its officers a guide to how to make Graham's legal change workable. Until it does, the law remains inactive; we have no way of knowing how and if it will be used.

More broadly, there have been several efforts to bring some transparency and oversight to the U.S. side of the industry. Key players have been Representatives Jan Schakowsky and David Price and Senators Barack Obama and James Webb.

Obama, who is running for President at this time (illustrating how far the issue of private militaries has risen in interest), sponsored the Transparency and Accountability in Military and Security Contracting Act of 2007, which brings together the reforms sought by Schakowsky and Price on the House side. The bill aims to end the mystery that surrounds this trade and create the reporting requirements needed for good governance: how many contractors the United States has hired, their roles and functions, the amounts being spent, and how many have been killed or wounded, none of which are tracked now. It also calls for a strategy for figuring out when contracting makes sense and when it doesn't, rather than continually handing off clearly governmental jobs to connected companies. The bill orders the Pentagon to re-evaluate its use of contractors and determine what roles are appropriate or not for private firms and what must be kept in the control of those in uniform. For those times when contracting is appropriate, the bill creates standards and requirements that contractors must meet, as well as a central contracting office in theater, to better manage spending and oversight, and a linkup to the FBI to investigate any suspected criminal actions. Finally, the bill begins the process of setting clear legal status of contractor personnel with respect to investigations and prosecution of abuses by private military contractors.

Webb, a veteran himself, has sought to create a Commission on Wartime Contracting, which would investigate how the contracts in support of military operations in Iraq and Afghanistan were carried out and seek out waste and fraud. It is modeled after a similar commission famously led by Harry Truman before he was named Vice President. But, again illustrating the vast changes in the defense industry, Truman's commission looked at military manufacturing during World War II, while its twenty-first century version would focus on private military services.

As with much of the industry, it remains to be seen what will happen with this legislation. It also remains to be seen how other nations will respond, as these potential reforms touch only one part of what is a truly global industry. My hope is that such reforms are just one step within a larger set of defense initiatives that are needed to put our soldiers and our taxpayers before our CEOs.

Iraq has taught us a great deal about the private military industry. We need to update and clarify the laws on both national and international levels. We clearly need to question when PMF contracting is appropriate and when it is not and to examine the practice of no-bid and cost-plus contracts. We need to launch a program of oversight, reform, and management. We must restore the government's ability to manage such contracts, rebuilding our contract officer corps. Finally, we need to start working the market, rather than being worked by it. That is, we must develop a new level of punishment for any waste and theft that undermines security.

My goal for the book when it came out in 2003 was that it would provide the guideposts to better understanding the industry. I hope that *Corporate Warriors* will remain a useful resource in the years ahead, as these issues are debated by policymakers, the military, the industry, and the public.

In conclusion, *Corporate Warriors* started out with stories of private companies fighting in war, something that would have been fiction in most of the twentieth century. As we learned in the book and now see in Iraq and elsewhere, the privatized military industry is a reality of the twenty-first century. This entrance of the profit motive onto the battlefield opens up vast, new possibilities and raises a series of troubling questions—for democracy, for ethics, for management, for law, for human rights, and for national and international security. It is time for us to begin answering them.

P. W. SINGER

August 1, 2007

PMFs on the Web

Note: This is a partial listing of the PMFs with a presence on the web at the time of publication. It is intended more for illustrative purpose than as a complete survey of the industry.

AKE Limited	http://www.akegroup.com
Airscan	www.airscan.com
Alpha	www.alfa-m1.ru/about/about-eng.html
AMTI	www.amti.net
AOgroup-USA	www.aogroup-usa.net/who.htm
Archangel	http://www.antiterrorconsultants.org/
Armorgroup	www.armorgroup.com
ATCO Frontec	www.atcofrontec.com
Aviation Development Corp.	www.aviationdevelopment.com
Beni Tal	www.beni-tal.co.il
Betac	www.betac.com
Blackwater USA	http://www.blackwaterusa.com/
Blue Sky	www.blueskysc.com
BRS (Halliburton)	www.halliburton.com/brs/brs.asp
CACI Systems	www.caci.com
DFI International	www.dfi-intl.com
Chilport Ltd.	www.chilport.co.uk
Combat Support Associates	http://csakuwait.com/
Control Risks Group	www.crg.com
Cubic	www.cai.cubic.com
Custer Battles	www.custerbattles.com
Drum Cussac	www.drum-cussac.com
Dyncorp	www.dyncorp.com
Eagle Group International	http://www.eaglegroupint.com/index.asp
EFFACT	http://www.effact.i110.de/home.htm
E.G. & G. Services	www.egginc.com
Erinys	http://www.erinysinternational.com/
Evergreen Helicopters	www.evergreenaviation.com
Executive Outcomes (archive)	http://web.archive.org/web/19980703122204/http://www.eo.com/

Global Impact	www.closeprotection.ws
Global Univision	www.globalunivision.com
Gormly	www.gormlyintl.com
Gray Security	www.graysecurity.com
The Golan Group	www.grupogolan.com
Groupe Earthwind	http://www.groupe-ehc.com/
Hart Group	www.hartgrouplimited.com
HSS International	www.hikestalkshoot.com
I-Defense	www.idefense.com
International Charter Inc.	www.icioregon.com
International Security Solutions	http://iss-internationalsecurity solutions.com
International SOS	www.internationalsos.com/company/
L-3Communications	www.l-3com.com
Logicon	www.logicon.com
Marine Risk Management	www.marinerisk.com
Mideast Security	www.globalic.net/security.htm
MPRI	www.mpri.com
NFD	www.nfddesigns.com
Northbridge	www.northbridgeservices.com
Olive Security	http://www.olivesecurity.com
Pacific Architects and Engineers	www.paechl.com
Pistris	www.pistris.com
Ronco	www.roncoconsulting.com/ index.html
Rubicon	www.rubicon-international.com/ cases/sierra.htm
SAIC	www.saic.com
Sandline	www.sandline.com
Seven Pillars	www.7pillars.com
SCS	www.southerncross-security.com
SOA	www.specialopsassociates.com
Strategic Communications	www.behavioural.com
Strategic Consulting International	www.sci2000.ws
Sukhoi	www.sukhoi.org/eng/home.htm
TASK International	www.task-int.com
THULE Global Security	www.brainstemdowry.com/work/ thule/intro.html
Trident	www.trident3.com
Trojan Security International	www.trojansecurities.com
TRW	www.trw.com/systems_it/defense.html
UPES	www.yomari.net/upes/gurkha.html
Vector Aerospace	www.vectoraerospace.ca
Vigilante	www.vigilante.com
Vinnell	www.vinnell.com

APPENDIX 2

PMF Contract

The following is a copy of the contract Sandline signed with the government of Papua New Guinea, representative of the agreements that provider sector firms make. It became available after the two parties went to international arbitration in a dispute over payment. The contract was obtained through the Project on Papua New Guinea at Australian National University (http://coombs.anu.edu.au/SpecialProj/PNG/htmls/Sandline.html).

AGREEMENT FOR THE PROVISION OF MILITARY ASSISTANCE DATED THIS 31 DAY OF JANUARY 1997 BETWEEN THE INDEPENDENT STATE OF PAPUA NEW GUINEA AND SANDLINE INTERNATIONAL

THIS Agreement is made this day of January 1997 between the Independent State of Papua New Guinea (the State) of the one part and Sandline International (Sandline), whose UK representative office is 535 Kings Road, London SW10 OS2, of the other part.

WHEREAS

Sandline is a company specialising in rendering military and security services of an operational, training and support nature, particularly in situations of internal conflict and only for and on behalf of recognised Governments, in accord with international doctrines and in conformance with the Geneva Convention.

The State, engulfed in a state of conflict with the illegal and unrecognised Bougainville Revolutionary Army (BRA), requires such external military expertise to support its Armed Forces in the protection of its Sovereign territory and regain control over important national assets, specifically the Panguna mine. In particular, Sandline is contracted to provide personnel and related services and equipment to:

Train the State's Special Forces Unit (SFU) in tactical skills specific to the objective;

gather intelligence to support effective deployment and operations;

conduct offensive operations in Bougainville in conjunction with PNG defence forces to render the BRA military ineffective and repossess the Panguna mine; and

provide follow-up operational support, to be further specified and agreed between the parties and is subject to separate

service provision levels and fee negotiations.

IT IS THEREFORE AGREED AS FOLLOWS:

The State hereby agrees to contract and utilise and employ the services of Sandline to provide all required and necessary services as are more particularly described hereafter.

Duration and Continuation

The duration of this contract shall be effective from the date of receipt of the initial payment, as defined in paragraph 5.2 below, for a maximum initial period of three calendar months (the initial contract period) or achievement of the primary objective, being the rendering of the BRA militarily ineffective, whichever is the earlier. The State shall have the option of renewing this agreement either in part or in whole for further periods as may be required.

Notice of renewal, termination or proposed variation of this agreement is to be served on Sandline in writing by the State at least 45 days before the expiry of the current period. Non-communication by the State shall be regarded by Sandline as automatic renewal of the relevant parts of this agreement for a further three months period on the same terms and this precedent shall continue to apply thereafter.

Service Provision

Sandline shall provide the following manpower, equipment and services:

(a) A 16 man Command, Admin and Training Team (CATT), to deploy in PNG and establish home bases at Jackson Airport and the Jungle Training Centre at Wewac within one week of commencement of this agreement, which is deemed to be the date on which the initial payment relating thereto in accordance with paragraph 5.2 below is deposited free and clear in Sandline's nominated bank account. The role of the CATT is to (i) establish links with PNG defence forces, (ii) develop the requisite logistics and communications infrastructure, (iii) secure and prepare facilities for the arrival of the contracted equipment, including air assets, (iv) initiate intelligence gathering operations, and (v) commence SFU training.

(b) Further Special Forces personnel which will deploy to PNG within 10 days of the arrival of the CATT, together with helicopter and fixed wing aircrew and engineers, intelligence and equipment operatives, mission operators, ground tech and medical support personnel. This force will absorb the CATT as part of its number, therefore bringing the total Strike Force head-count to 70. This Strike Force shall be responsible for achieving the primary objective as specified in paragraph 1.1 of this agreement and the full com-plement will remain in country for the initial contract period as defined in the said paragraph.

Note: at no time will Sandline personnel cater the sovereign territory of an-other nation nor will they breach the laws and rules of engagement relating to armed conflict. Once the operation has been successfully concluded, Sand-line personnel will be available to assist with the ongoing training, skills en-hancement and equipping of the PNG defence forces.

(c) Weapons, ammunition and equipment, including helicopters and aircraft (serviceable for up to 50 hours flying time per machine per month), and elec-tronic warfare equipment and communications systems, all as specified or equivalent to the items listed in Schedule 1. Upon termination of a contrac-tual relationship between the State and Sandline and once all payments have been received and Sandline has withdrawn from theatre any remaining stock of equipment shall be handed over and become the property of the State. Se-lected Sandline personnel will remain in country to maintain and supple-ment such equipment subject to a separate agreement relating thereto.

Note: delivery into theatre of the contracted equipment shall be via air into Jackson Airport or such other facility as may be considered appropriate. The equipment will be delivered in full working order in accordance with man-ufacturers' specifications. After its delivery, any equipment lost, damaged or destroyed during Sandline's deployment shall be immediately replaced at the cost of the State.

(d) personal kit, including US pattern jungle fatigues, boots and webbing, for Sandline personnel.

(e) All international Transport arrangements for the shipment in/out of equipment and deployment in country of Sandline personnel but not for the movement of such equipment and personnel within the country if this needs to be achieved by way of commercial service providers.

(f) The provision of medical personnel to treat any Sandline casualties and their evacuation if necessary.

(g) A Project Co-ordinator who, together with the Strike Force Commander and his Senior Intelligence offer, shall maintain liaison with and provide strategie and operational briefings and advice to the Prime Minister, De-fence Minister, NEC, NSC, the commander of the PNG defence forces and his delegated officers as may from time-to-time be required or requested.

Sandline shall ensure the enrolment of all personnel involved in this contract as Special Constables and that they carry appropriate ID cards in order to legally undertake their assigned roles.

Responsibilities of Sandline

Sandline will train the SFU in tactical skills specific to the objective, such as live fire contact, ambush techniques and raiding drills, gather intelligence to support effective deployment and plan, direct, participate in and conduct such ground, air and sea operations which are required to achieve the primary objective.

Both parties hereto recognise and agree that the force capability to respond to all emergency and hostile situations will be constrained by the manpower and equipment level provided within the terms of this agreement. The achievement of the primary objective cannot be deemed to be a performance measure for the sake of this agreement if it can be demonstrated that for valid reasons it cannot be achieved within the given timescale and with the level of contracted resources provided.

Sandline shall supply all the personnel and maintain all services and equipment as specified in paragraph 2.1 above to the appropriate standards of proficiency and operational levels as is generally expected from a high calibre, professional armed force.

Sandline shall further provide a project co-ordinator to act as the liaison officer between the company's management and the nominated representatives of the State. This individual will convene and attend regular meetings at such venues as he may be so directed.

Sandline shall be responsible for any expense resulting from the loss or injury of any of its personnel for the duration of the agreement unless same is caused by the negligence of the State, its personnel or agents in which case all such costs will be fairly claimed against the State by Sandline and promptly paid for the benefit of the persons involved.

Sandline will ensure that the contents of this agreement shall remain strictly confidential and will not be disclosed to any third party. Sandline will not acknowledge the existence of this contract prior to the State issuing notifications in accordance with paragraph 4.11 below and will not take credit for any successful action unless this is mutually agreed by the parties. Furthermore, Sandline and its personnel are well versed in the requirement to maintain absolute secrecy with regard to all aspects of its activities in order to guard against compromising operations and will apply the necessary safeguards.

Responsibilities of the State

Immediately on signing this agreement the State automatically grants to Sandline and its personnel all approvals, permissions, authorisations, licences and permits to carry arms, conduct its operations and meet its contractual obligations without hindrance, including issuing instructions to PNG defence forces personnel to co-operate fully with Sandline commanders and their nominated representatives. All officers and personnel of Sandline assigned to this contract shall be enrolled as Special Constables, but hold military ranks commensurate with those they hold within the Sandline command structure and shall be entitled to give orders to junior ranks as may be necessary for the execution of their duties and responsibilities.

The State will ensure that full co-operation is provided from within its organisation and that of the PNG defence forces. The Commanders of the PNG defence forces and Sandline shall form a joint liaison and planning team for the duration of this agreement. The operational deployment of Sandline personnel and equipment is to be jointly determined by the Commander, PNG defence forces and Sandline's commander, taking account of their assessment of the risk and value thereof.

The State recognises that Sandline's commanders will have such powers as are required to efficiently and effectively undertaken their given roles, including but not limited to the powers to engage and fight hostile forces, repel attacks therefrom, arrest any persons suspected of undertaking or conspiring to undertake a harmful act, secure Sovereign assets and territory, defend the general population from any threat, and proactively protect their own and State Forces from any form of aggression or threat. The State agrees to indemnify Sandline for the legitimate actions of the company's and its associates' personnel as specified herein and to assume any claims brought against the company arising out of this agreement.

The State shall pay or shall cause to be paid the fees and expenses relating to this agreement as set out in paragraph 5.1 below. Such fees and expenses to be paid as further specified in paragraph 5.2, without deduction of any taxes, charges or fees, and eligible to be freely exported from PNG. All payments to be made in US Dollars.

The State shall cause all importation of equipment and the provision of services to be free to Sandline (and any of its sister or associated companies as notified to the authorities) of any local, regional or national taxes, withholding taxes, duties, fees, surcharges, storage charges and clearance expenses howsoever levied and shall allow such equipment to be processed through Customs without delay. Further, all Sandline personnel will be furnished with the necessary multiple entry visas without passport stamps and authorisation to enter and leave the country free from hindrance at any time and shall be exempt from tax of any form on their remuneration from Sandline.

The State will promptly supply at no cost to Sandline and its sister and associated companies all End User Certificates and related documentation to facilitate the legitimate procurement and export of the specified equipment from countries of origin.

[4.7] The State will provide suitable accommodation for all Sandline personnel together with all related amenities, support staff to undertake role such as messengers and household duties, secure hangerage and storage facilities for equipment, qualified tradesmen and workmen to clear and prepare operating sites, all aviation and ground equipment fuel and lubricant needs, such vehicles and personnel carriers as reasonably specified for the field and for staff use, foodstuffs and combat rations, fresh drinking water, and sanitary and other relevant services and ancillary equipment as Sandline may specify from time-to-time to undertake its activities without hindrance.

If any service, resource or equipment to be supplied by the State in accordance with paragraph 4.7 above is not forthcoming then Sandline will have the right to submit an additional invoice for the procurement and supply thereof and may curtail or reduce operations affected by its non-availability until payment has been made and the said equipment is in position.

The State agrees and undertakes that, during the period of this agreement and for a period of 12 months following the date of its expiration, it will not directly or indirectly offer employment to or employ any of the personnel provided hereunder or otherwise in the employ of Sandline and its associates. Any such employment will be constructed as a continuation of the contract for the employees concerned and Sandline shall be entitled to be paid accordingly on a pro-rata basis.

The State and the PNG defence forces will ensure that information relating to planned operations, deployments and associated activities is restricted to only those personnel who have an essential need to be briefed in. Appropriate steps will be taken to prevent press reporting, both nationally and internationally, or any form of security breach or passage of information which may potentially threaten operational effectiveness and/or risk the lives of the persons involved. Sandline's commanders have the right to curtail any or all planned operations which they determine are compromised as a result of failure in security.

If deemed necessary due to external interest, the State shall be responsible for notifying and updating the International Community, including the

United Nations and representatives of other Governments, at the appropriate time of the nature of this contract and the underlying intent to protect and keep safe from harm Papua New Guinea's Sovereign territory, its population, mineral assets and investing community. The content and timing of all such formal communications will be discussed and agreed with Sandline before release.

Fees and Payments

Sandline's inclusive free for the provision of the personnel and services as specified in paragraph 2.1 above and also in Schedule 1 attached for the initial contract period is USD36,000,000 (thirty six million US Dollars).

Payment terms are as follows. All payments to be by way of cash funds, either in the form of electronic bank transfers or certified banker's cheques.

On contract signing 50 percent of the overall fee, totaling USD18,000,000 is immediately due and is deemed the "initial payment".

Within 30 days of deploying the CATT, the balance of USD18,000,000.

This contract is deemed to be enacted once the initial payment is received in full with value into such bank account as Sandline may nominate therefor. Payments are recognised as being received when they are credited as cleared funds in our account and payment receipt relies on this definition.

All fees for services rendered shall be paid in advance of the period to which they relate. Sandline reserves the right to withdraw from theatre in the event of non-payment of fees for any renewal to the original contract period.

The financial impact of variations, additions or charges to the personnel provision and equipment supply specified herein will be agreed between the parties and any incremental payment will be made to Sandline before such change is deemed to take effect. There is no facility for rebate or refund in the event of a required reduction or early termination of service delivery within a given contract period.

Applicable Law

In the event of any dispute or difference arising out of or in relation to this agreement the parties shall in the first instance make an effort to resolve it amicably, taking account of the sensitive nature of this arrangement.

The aggrieved party shall notify the other by sending a notice of dispute in writing and, where amicable settlement is not possible within 30 days thereafter, refer the matter to arbitration in conformity with the UNCITRAL rules applying thereto.

This agreement shall be construed and governed in accordance with the Laws of England and the language of communication between the parties shall be English.

Amendments and Supplements

This agreement may only be altered, modified or amended by the parties hereto provided that such alteration, modification or amendment is in writing and signed by both parties.

Schedule 1 ("Oyster" Costings) forms part of this agreement.

IN WITNESS WHEREOF the parties hereto have set their hands on the day and year first written above.

For the Independent State of Papua New Guinea:

Name: Chris S Haiveta
Witness: (indecipherable)

Name: Vele Iamo
Occupation: A/Deputy Secretary

For Sandline International:

Name: Tim Spicer OBE.
Witness: (indecipherable)

Name: J.N. Van Den Bergh
Occupation: Consultant

Table A.1
Sandline-PNG 1997 Contract: Operation Contravene's Equipment

Item	Quantity	Cost (U.S. Dollars)
Special Forces Team:		(Subtotal: 7,100,000)
Manpower	40, plus 2 doctors	4,500,000
Positioning		100,000
Equipment:		2,500,000
AK-47 Assault Rifle	100	
PKM Light Machine Gun	10	
RPG-7 Grenade Launcher	10	
60mm Mortar	10	
82mm Mortar	6	
AGS-17 30mm Automatic		
Grenade Launcher	4	
Makarov Pistol	20	
7.62x39 (for AK-47)	500,000	
AK-47 magazines	1,000	
7.62x54 (for PKM)	250,000	
12.7mm ball	100,000	
12.7mm tracer	25,000	
Ammo links	250,000	
PG-7 rocket grenades	1,000	
30mm Grenades (AGS-17)	2,000	
60mm HE mortar rounds	2,500	
82mm HE mortar rounds	2,500	
Illumination grenades	200	
Smoke/Frag Grenades	800	
Personal kit and uniforms	100	
Mission Support:		(Subtotal: 29,170,000)
Mi-24 Hind Attack Helicopter	2	8,200,000
Ordnance:		2,500,000
57mm rocket launcher pods	6	
57mm high explosive rocket	1,000	
23mm ball	20,000	
23mm tracer	5,000	
23mm links	125,000	
Mi-24 Aircrew	6	680,000
Mi-17 Assault Helicopter	2	3,000,000
Mi-17 Aircrew	6	860,000
Spares-Helicopters		1,500,000
Surveillance Platform-CASA-12	1	2,400,000
"On board Systems"	1	4,850,000
SP Aircrew	4	280,000
SP Trainers	included	120,000
SP Spares		600,000

continued

Table A.1
Continued

Item	Quantity	Cost (U.S. Dollars)
Ground System	1	600,000
Mission Operators	5	480,000
Ground Staff	5	270,000
Electronic Warfare Trainers	included	120,000
Project Coordinator	1	Included
Personnel Equipment	30	250,000
Personnel Movement		250,000
Insurances		Included
Logistics Support		Client Responsibility
Communications Equipment:		(Subtotal 1,100,000)
HF Radio System	1 + 15	400,000
Hardened Tactical Radio System	1 + 16	500,000
Satellite Comms Units	15	200,000
Contract Total		37,370,000
Minus Package Price Reduction		−1,370,000
FEE TO CLIENT:		36,000,000

Notes

1. ABC, BBC, CNN, Fox News, Australian Broadcasting Company, Voice of America, International Herald Tribune, New York Times, National Post, Wall Street Journal, Washington Times, Sunday Times, Sunday Telegraph, Guardian, Independent, Johannesburg Star, and CNSNews, are a smattering of media voices that have talked about privatized military firms.

2. From liberal pundit Michael Kinsley and columnist William Pfaff, to Ivan Eland, the director of defense policy studies at the conservative Cato Institute.

3. Jonathon Broder, "Mercenaries: The Future of U.N. Peacekeeping? *Fox News* (June 26, 2000). Transcript available at http://www.foxnews.com/world. See also HR 1591 http://thomas.loc.gov/cgi-bin/bdquery/D?d107:3:./temp/~bdQ8UA::|/bss/d107query. html|

4. Global Coalition for Africa, *African Social and Economic Trends,* Annual Report 1999/2000. Available at: www.gca-cma.org; "Sierra Leone—Soldiers of Fortune," Australian Broadcasting Corporation Documentary, Producer Mark Corcoran (August 2000). Transcript at: www.abc.net/foreign

5. Australian Broadcasting Corporation, "Dogs of War," Lateline, Broadcast May 18, 2000. http://www.abc.net.au/lateline/archives/s128621.htm

6. More information on the IPOA is available at www.ipoaonline.org.

7. Examples include David Isenberg, *Soldiers of Fortune Ltd.: A Profile of Today's Private Sector Corporate Mercenary Firms,* Center For Defense Information Monograph (November 1997); David Shearer, *Private Armies and Military Intervention* (London: International Institute for Strategic Studies, Adelphi Paper no. 316, February 1998); Peter Lock, "Military Downsizing and Growth in the Security Industry in Sub-Saharan Africa," *Strategic Analysis* 22, no. 9 (December 1998). Thomas Adams, "The New Mercenaries and the Privatization of Conflict," *Parameters* (Summer 1999): 103–116. Available online at: http://carlisle-www.army.mil/ usawc/ Parameters/99summer/adams.htm

8. "Numerous articles on the new private security forces begin by noting how their corporate veneer and military professionalism differentiate them from the old dogs of war. However, little has been done to follow-up these observations by understanding the nature of private security forces as firms and analyzing the particular market they confront." Jeffrey Herbst, "The Regulation of Private Security Forces" *The Privatisation of Security in Africa,* ed. Greg Mills and John Stremlau (Pretoria: South Africa Institute of International Affairs, 1999), p. 117.

9. Jackkie Cilliers, "Book review: Sean Dorney, *The Sandline Affair—Politics and Mercenaries and the Bourgainville crisis. African Security Review* 9, no. 1 (February 2000).

10. Doug Brooks and Hussein Solomon, "From the Editor's Desk," *Conflict Trends* 6 (July 2000). http://www.accord.org.za/ publications/ct6/issue6.htm

11. Indeed, one author even compares the firms to "Messiahs." Doug Brooks, "Messiahs or Mercenaries?" *International Peacekeeping* 7, no. 4 (2000): 129–144. Other examples include Doug Brooks, "Write a Cheque, End a War Using Private Military Companies to End African Conflicts," *Conflict Trends* no, 6 (July 2000). http://www.accord.org.za/ publications/ct6/ issue6.htm; William Hartung, "Mercenaries, Inc.," discussion article, Committee Against Corruption in Saudi Arabia, 1996, available at: www.cdi.org; Ken Silverstein, "Privatizing War,"

Nation (July 7, 1998); Abdel-Fatau Musah and Kayode Fayemi, *Mercenaries: An African Security Dilemma* (London: Pluto Press, 2000).

12. Peter Fabricus, "Private Security Firms Can End Africa's Wars Cheaply," *Saturday Star* (*Johannesburg) (*September 23, 2000). Also see Sandline's website www.sandline.com

13. Consequently, as the former head of U.S. Drug Enforcement Agency operations in Colombia notes, "To get somebody out there to do those operations, you almost have to have that shady past." Ted Robberson, "U.S. Launches Covert Program to Aid Colombia," *Dallas Morning News* (August 19, 1998).

14. As the firms grow more corporate and realize that their operations depend on a positive pubic opinion they are acting to reverse a negative public image with increased openness. Sandline and MPRI stand out as two of the most savvy at this public relations task, as their websites, listed in Appendix 1, reveal.

I. AN ERA OF CORPORATE WARRIORS?

1. James Traub, "The Worst Place on Earth," New York Review of Books, June 29, 2000. http://www.nybooks.com/nyrev/WWWfeatdisplay.cgi?20000629061F; UN Development Programme, UN Human Development Index 2000. Available at http://www.undp.org/hdr2000/english/HDR2000.html

2. Laura Silber and Allan Little, *Yugoslavia: Death of a Nation* (New York: Penguin Books, 1997), 357; Samantha Knight et al., "The Croatian Army's Friends." *U.S. News & World Report,* August 21, 1995, p. 41.

3. Roger Cohen, "After Aiding Croatian Army, U.S. Now Seeks to Contain It," *New York Times,* October 28, 1995, p. 5.

4. Charlotte Eager, "Invisible U.S. Army Defeats Serbs," *Observer,* November 5, 1995.

5. Interviews with Croat Defense officials, Fall 1996; David Halberstam, *War in a Time of Peace* (New York: Scribners, 2001), pp. 335–336.

6. Interview with member of U.S. Government negotiating team, Fall 1996.

7. For more see Halberstam, *War in a Time of Peace;* Michael O'Hanlon and Ivo Daalder, *Winning Ugly: NATO's War to Save Kosovo* (Washington, D.C.: Brookings Press, 2000. "It's Off to War Again for Big U.S. Contractor," *Wall Street Journal,* April 14, 1999, A21.

8. As quoted on Halliburton website. http://www.halliburton.com/BRS/brsss/brsss_1199_balkansd.asp

9. Trevor Jones and Tim Newburn, *Private Security and Public Policing* (Oxford: Clarendon Press, 1998), 30; Elliott Sclar, *Selling the Brooklyn Bridge: The Economics of Public Service Privatization* (New York: Twentieth Century Fund, 1999).

10. Jones and Newburn, *Private Security and Public Policing,* p. 29.

11. Perhaps the best work on this was Coase's study of the history of lighthouses. Lighthouses used to be cited by economists as one of the few clear-cut examples, outside of national defense, of public goods that required the involvement of government. It turned out, however, that they were wrong and that even lighthouses were operated by private firms at one time. Ronald Coase, "The Lighthouse in Economics" *Journal of Law and Economics* 17 (October 1974): 357–376.

12. Paul Taibel, "Outsourcing & Privatization of Defense Infrastructure." A Business Executives for National Security Report, 1998. Available at http://www.bens.org/pubs/outsrce.html.

13. J. Michael Brower, "Outland: The Vogue of DOD Outsourcing and Privatization," *Acquisition Review Quarterly* 4 (Fall 1997): 383–392; Adam Smith, *The Wealth of Nations,* 1776. Available at http://www.socsci.mcmaster.ca/~econ/ugcm/3ll3/smith/wealth/wealbk05

14. Before the advent of the state in the 1600s, soldiers were privately equipped, being required to bring their own weapons and accoutrements to the battlefield. The universalizing effects of state bureaucracies quickly ended this practice, as uniform forces were mustered into the public service and states began to manufacture all their own weapons, from swords on up to battleships. Yet this was not to be a permanent arrangement. When it became obvious in the late nineteenth century that public arsenals could not keep up in cost and qual-

ity with private arms manufacturers (like Krupps and Vickers), this responsibility was transferred back outside of government control. William McNeill, *The Pursuit of Power* (Chicago: University of Chicago Press, 1982), p. 272.

15. Max Weber, *Theory of Social and Economic Organization* (New York: Free Press, 1964), 154. See also Martin Van Creveld, *The Rise and Decline of the State* (Cambridge: Cambridge University Press, 1999); John Hoffman, *Beyond the State* (Cambridge: Polity Press, 1995).

16. David Friedman, *The Machinery of Freedom: Guide to Radical Capitalism* (Lasalle, Ill.: Open Court Press, 1989), 143–159. Murray Rothbard, *For a New Liberty: The Libertarian Manifesto* (New York: Macmillan, 1978).

17. Bruce Grant, "U.S. Military Expertise for Sale: Private Military Consultants as a Tool of Foreign Policy." *National Defense University Institute for National Security Studies, Strategy Essay Competition.* 1998, available at http://www.ndu.edu/inss/books/essaysch4.html.

18. Samuel P. Huntington, *The Soldier and the State: The Theory and Politics of Civil-Military Relations* (New York: Random House, 1957) 37; see also Charles Moskos, and F. Wood, eds., *The Military: More Than Just a Job?* (Washington D.C.: Pergamon Brassey's, 1988).

19. Many refer to the firms as Private Military Companies or PMCs, but as explored in chapter 6, they are really only referring to just one sector within an overall industry. PMF captures the overall phenomenon of privatizing military services, not just those tactical ones. Tim Spicer, *An Unorthodox Soldier: Peace and War and the Sandline Affair* (Edinburgh: Mainstream, 1999), p. 15.

20. Doug Brooks, and Hussein Solomon. "From the Editor's Desk." *Conflict Trends,* no. 6, July 2000. http://www.accord.org.za/publications/ct6/issue6.htm

21. Al J. Venter, "Market Forces: How Hired Guns Succeeded Where the United Nations Failed," *Jane's International Defense Review,* March 1998.

22. Kevin O'Brien, "Military-Advisory Groups and African Security: Privatised Peacekeeping," *International Peacekeeping* 5, no. 3 (Autumn 1998): 78–105.

23. According to one anecdote, when Princess Diana toured Angola's minefields, she believed the British soldiers in her escort to be seconded SAS personnel. After the visit, she profusely thanked them for their efforts and happily posed for a picture with them. They too turned out to be employees of a PMF. Daniel McGrory and Nicholas Woods, "Soldiers for Sale," *London Times,* May 9, 1998. Available at www.the-times.co.uk/cgi-bin/Backissue.

24. Al Venter, "Out of State and Non-State Actors Keep Africa Down," *Jane's Intelligence Review* 11 (May 1, 1999).

25. But it was possibly a cover for French intelligence and perhaps not a truly private firm. O'Brien, "Military Advisory Groups and African Security."

26. Dena Montague and Frida Berrigan, "The Business of War in the Democratic Republic of Congo: Who Benefits?" *Dollars and Sense* (July/August 2001).

27. Khareen Pech, "South African Mercenaries in Congo," *Electronic Mail & Guardian,* August 28, 1998. Stabilco is notable in being run by a former EO employee, Mauritz le Roux.

28. In a key operation of the war the firm's commando units seized the Inga dam from Ugandan army troops fighting in support of the rebels. This was a crucial victory, as the area is one of the most strategic points in all of the DRC. The outcome, however, was different from that of the EO successes elsewhere on the continent. When Kabila failed to pay the firm and his forces left a number of its employees stranded in the field, the company withdrew from fighting on his behalf—this is part of the reason why the war has lingered on. Interview with PMF executive, June 2001.

29. United Nations Commission on Human Rights. "Report on the question of the use of mercenaries as a means of violating human rights and impeding the exercise of the right of peoples to self-determination," 57th Session, Item 7, Special Rapporteur, Jan. 2001; Andrew Parker and Francesco Guerrera, "Ex-Soldiers Find There Is Money to Be Made Out of Wars," *Financial Times.* April 17, 2001.

30. Charles Smith, "Wars and Rumors of Wars: Russian Mercenaries Flying for Ethiopia: Advisers, Pilots, Artillerymen Engaged in 'Large-scale Offensive' against Eritrea," *World Net*

Daily, July 18, 2000; Thomas Adams, "The New Mercenaries and the Privatization of Conflict," *Parameters* (Summer 1999): 103–116. Available online at: http://carlisle-www.army .mil/usawc/Parameters/99summer/adams.htm. "Russians Fly for Both Sides in Horn of Africa," *London Times*. February 19, 1999. Gennady Charodeev, "Foreign Wars: Russian Generals Involved in a War between Ethiopia and Eritrea," *Izvestia*, May 26, 2000, pp. 1, 4.

31. O'Brien, "Military Advisory Groups and African Security."

32. Venter, "Market Forces," and David Shearer, *Private Armies and Military Intervention*. London: International Institute for Strategic Studies, Adelphi Paper 316, February 1998, p. 36.

33. "SA Mercenaries Teach Ivorians How to Fly," *Sapa-AFP*, November 12, 2002.

34. Human Rights Watch, *Landmine Monitor: Africa Report*, 1999. http://www.hrw.org/ hrw/reports/1999/landmine/WEBAFR1.html

35. "Puntland Elders Oppose British Maritime Firm's Plans to Set Up Base," *BBC Summary of World Broadcasts*, July 29, 2000.

36. Deborah Avant, "The Market for Force: Exploring the Privatization of Military Services," prepared for discussion at the Council on Foreign Relations Study Group on *Arms Trade and the Transnationalization of the Defense Industry: Economic versus Security Drivers*.1999, p. 1.

37. Chris Stephen, "KLA trains refugees to recapture border territory," *Irish Times*, April 7, 1999; Christian Jennings, "Private U.S. Firm Training Both Sides in Balkans," *Scotsman*, March 3, 2001. http://www.thescotsman.co.uk/world.cfm?id=5134

38. "Canadian, Anglo-Italian Firms to Train UK Navy," *Reuters*, July 25, 2000. http://ca.dailynews.yahoo.com/ca/headlines/ts/story.html?s=v/ca/20000725/ts/canada _navy_ col_1.html

39. Simon Sheppard, "Soldiers for Hire," *Contemporary Review*, August 1999. "RAF Puts Refuel Job on Market," *London Times*, December 22, 2000.

40. "UK Outlines Revised Plans to Privatise Defence Research," *Jane's Defence Weekly*, March 26, 2000. http://www.janes.com/defence/editors/uk_plans.html

41. House of Commons, *Private Military Companies: Options for Regulation*, HC 577, February 12, 2002.

42. Shearer, *Private Armies and Military Intervention*, p. 24. Many, though, estimate the total number of personnel be closer to 1,000,000, given their ties to the Russian mafia.

43. "British-Russian Security Venture," *Intelligence Newsletter*, no. 304, January 30, 1997.

44. "Russian Contract Soldiers in Chechnya Poor Quality, Often Quit," *Russia Today*, October 2, 2000. http://www.russiatoday.com/news.php3?id=205234. Estimates are that contract soldiers make up 40 percent of the Russian force in Chechnya in 2000. About a third of these, however, tend to leave the force before their contracts are up, adding to the Russians' many difficulties in the conflict.

45. O'Brien, "Military Advisory Groups and African Security."

46. Ken Silverstein, "Mercenary, Inc.?" *Washington Business Forward*, April 26, 2001; Jonathan Wells, "U.S. Ties to Saudi Elite May Be Hurting War on Terrorism," *Boston Herald*, December 10, 2001.

47. Ken Silverstein, "Privatizing War," *The Nation*, July 7, 1998; Yves Goiulet, "Mixing Business with Bullets," *Jane's Intelligence Review*, September 1997.

48. Juan Tamayo, "U.S. Civilians Taking Risk in Drug War for Colombia," *Miami Herald*, February 26, 2001.

49. Kate Taylor and Terry J. Gander, "Mine Clearance in Cambodia," *International Defense Review*, February 1, 1996, p. 5.

50. Yves Goulet, "Mixing Business with Bullets," *Jane's Intelligence Review*, September 1997.

51. Michael Sheridan, "Briton Quits Indonesia over 'Psych War' Claims," *Sunday Times*, August 6, 2000. http://www.Sunday-times.co.uk/news/pages/sti/2000/08/06/stifgnasio2001 .html

52. Paul Daley, "Civilians May Form Special Reserve," *Age* (Melbourne), April 28, 2000. http://www.theage.com.au/.

53. Christopher Bowe, "Agency Aims to Swell the Ranks," *Financial Times,* August 10, 2000.

54. Marcia Triggs, "Army Contracts Out Recruiting." *Officer,* 78, no. 3, April 1, 2002; "Britain Uses Agency to Recruit for Military," *Reuters.* March 12, 2001.

55. "A Bill before the U.S. Congress Would Prohibit the Use of Private Firms in the Fight Against Drugs," *Bogota Semana,* May 7, 2001.

56. Ted Robberson, "U.S. Launches Covert Campaign to Aid Colombia," *Dallas Morning News,* August 19, 1998. Tod Robberson, "Contractors Playing Increasing Role in U.S. Drug War," *Dallas Morning News,* February 27, 2000.

57. Andre Linard, "Mercenaries SA," *Le Monde Diplomatique,* p. 31; Christopher Goodwin, "Mexican Drug Barons," *Sunday Times,* August 24, 1997; Patrick J. Cullen, "Keeping the New Dogs of War on a Tight Leash," *Conflict Trends,* no. 6 (July 2000); Stefaans Brummer, "SA Arms 'Stoke' the Burundi Fire," *Mail & Guardian,* December 5, 1997.

58. Juan Toro, "Colombia Militia Enjoys Support" AP, September 6, 2000; "Mercenaries and Arms Dealers in the Post-Cold War World: Interview with Ken Silverstein," *Connection,* August 11, 2000. Transcript available at http://www.theconnection.org/archive/2000/08/0811a.shtml

59. As one regional expert noted, "It's the privatization of the Colombian Army. Who do they owe allegiance to—BP or the Colombian State?" Eduardo Gamerra, a professor at Florida International University, as quoted in Diana Jean Schemo, "Oil Companies Buy an Army to Tame Colombia's Rebels" *New York Times,* August 22, 1996.

60. David Pugliese, "Canadians Turn to Private Firms for EW Training, Combat Support," *Defense News,* September 7, 2000. The air combat support service contract is expected to last an initial 10 years and is valued at $42 million Canadian annually.

61. Tamayo, "U.S. Civilians Taking Risks."

62. William Arkin, "The Underground Military," *Washington Post,* May 7, 2001. http://washingtonpost.com/wp-dyn/articles/A44024–2001May4.html

63. Douglas Farah, "Cartel Hires Mercenaries to Train Security Forces," *Washington Post,* November 4, 1997. Whether the specialists utilized are actually incorporated or linked to security firms is unclear, so the linkage to the companies is tenuous. But the fact that it is even possible speaks volumes.

64. Kevin Sullivan, "Tequila Shooters Take Aim at Cactus Rustlers," *Washington Post,* August 11, 2000, p. A01. http://washingtonpost.com/wp-dyn/articles/A5683–2000Aug10.html

65. International Consortium of Investigative Journalists, "Making a Killing: The Business of War," The Center for Public Integrity, October 28, 2002.

66. Gordon Lubold, "Privatization Means Fewer Corps Cooks," *Marine Corps Times,* January 8, 2001, p. 9.

67. "Improving the Combat Edge through Outsourcing," *Defense Viewpoint,* vol. 11, no. 30, March 1996.

68. Steven Myers, "U.S. Spy Sub Said to Record Torpedo Blast Aboard Kursk," *New York Times,* August 29, 2000. http://www.nytimes.com/library/world/europe/082900russia-sub.html. The ship was the *Loyal,* designated a Special Mission Support (SMS) ship.

69. Silverstein, "Privatizing War."

70. Steve Alvarez, "MPRI: A Private Military," *Stars and Stripes,* October 30, 2000. http://www.stripes.com/servlet/News/ViewArticle?articleId=100033570&buildId=100033587

71. Christian Lowe, "Navy, Marine Corps Consider Privatizing Some Aerial Refueling" *Defense Week* August 21, 2000, p. 1; Christian Lowe, "Services Look to Contractors to Fly 'Adversary' Aircraft," *Defense Week,* September 25, 2000, p. 1.

72. Steven Saint, "NORAD Outsources," *Colorado Springs Gazette,* September 1, 2000.

73. One in fifty Americans deployed to the Gulf in 1990 was a privately employed civilian. By the time of the Bosnia deployment in 1995–6, the ratio was down to 1 in 10. This ratio will continue to shrink, as more and more functions are turned over to the private sector through competitive sourcing, privatization, and changing logistics practices, such as lifetime

contractor logistics support. Stephen Zamparrelli, "Contractors on the Battlefield: What Have We Signed Up For?" Air War College Research Report, March 1999, p. 8; Department of the Army, *Contractors on the Battlefield*, FM 100–21. Washington: Headquarters. September 1999. p. iii, FM 100–21, p. v.

74. More significant, though, are the number of conflicts in the 1990s that didn't involve large-scale U.S. troop deployments but did see military firms acting in the interest of the western powers (Colombia, Sierra Leone, Angola, etc.), a private role that perhaps relieved the need for official intervention.

75. South African Institute of International Affairs, "Private Security: Phantom Menace or Evil Empire?" *Intelligence Update*, May 11, 2000.

76. Robert Wall, "Army Leases 'Eyes' To Watch Balkans," *Aviation Week & Space Technology*, October 30, 2000, p. 68.

77. Robert Little, "American Civilians Go Off to War, Too," *Baltimore Sun*, May 26, 2002.

78. "Dyncorp's Assignment: Protect Afghan Leader," *Washington Post*, December 2, 2002.

79. Interview with PMF employee, March 2002.

80. Carol Rosenberg, "Building of Prison at Guantanamo Begins," *Miami Herald*, February 28, 2002.

81. Venter, "Out of State and Nonstate Actors Keep Africa Down." EO declined and the offer was made superfluous by the death of Abacha that year.

82. Janice Thomson, *Mercenaries, Pirates, and Sovereigns: State Building and Extraterritorial Violence in Early Modern Europe* (Princeton, N.J.: Princeton University Press, 1994).

83. O'Brien, "Military Advisory Groups and African Security."

84. Weber, *Theory of Social and Economic Organization*, p. 154; Van Creveld, *The Rise and Decline of the State*, p. 408.

2. PRIVATIZED MILITARY HISTORY

1. From "The 10,000" of Xenophon in ancient Greek literature to the spate of mercenary films in the late 1960s to present-day television series. Examples include Xenophon, *Anabasis*, books I–VII, English translation by Carleton L. Brownson (Cambridge: Harvard University Press, 1922). Fictional book accounts include Frederick Forsythe, *The Dogs of War* (New York: Bantam, 1974). Movies include *Dark of the Sun* (MGM, 1968) and *The Wild Geese* (Fox, 1975). TV series include "Soldier of Fortune Inc." The best-selling CD-ROM computer game in 1999 was "Mercenaries (Mech Warrior 2)."

2. Janice Thomson, Mercenaries. *Pirates to Soverens: State Building and Extraterritorial Violence in Early Modern Europe* (Princeton: Princeton University Press, 1994).

3. Jeffrey Herbst, "The Regulation of Private Security Forces," in Greg Mills and John Stremlau, *The Privatization of Security in Africa* (Pretoria: South Africa Institute of International Affairs, 1997), p. 117.

4. Frederic C. Lane, *Profits from Power: Readings in Protection Rent and Violence Controlling Enterprises* (Albany: SUNY Press, 1979).

5. Larry Taulbee, "Reflections on the Mercenary Option," *Small Wars and Insurgencies* 9, no. 2 (Autumn 1998): 145–163.

6. Lane, *Profits from Power*, p. 83.

7. Martin Van Creveld, *The Rise and Decline of the State* (Cambridge: Cambridge University Press, 1999), pp. 29, 138.

8. Taulbee, "Reflections on the Mercenary Option," p. 145.

9. G. T. Griffith, *The Mercenaries of the Hellenistic World* (Groningen, The Netherlands: Boom's Boekhuis N.V., 1968), p. 4.

10. Xenophon, *Anabasis*, books I–VII.

11. Greg Yocherer, "Classic Battle Joined," *Military History* (February 2000). http://www .thehistorynet.com/MilitaryHistory/articles/2000/02002_cover.htm

12. Hans Delbruck, *History of the Art of War: Within the Framework of Political History* (Westport, Conn.: Greenwood Press, 1975), 2:250.

13. John Haldon, *Warfare, State, and Society in the Byzantine World, 565–1204* (London: UCL Press, 1999).

14. John Glubb, *Soldiers of Fortune: The Story of the Marmalukes* (London: Hodder and Stoughton, 1973).

15. Genoese crossbow units were among the most highly valued and were present at most major battles, until they were decimated by English longbows at Crecy (1346).

16. Genoa even gave all its Mediterranean possessions to a private company to protect. G. V. Scammell, *The English Trading Companies and the Sea* (London: Trustees of the National Maritime Museum, 1982), p. 5.

17. Philippe Contamine, *War in the Middle Ages* (New York: Basil Blackwell, 1984), p. 158.

18. William McNeill, *The Pursuit of Power* (Chicago: University of Chicago Press, 1982), p. 77.

19. By 1342, the Florentine army was composed of 2,000 mercenaries and only 40 citizen cavalry. C. C. Bayley, *War and Society in Renaissance Florence: The "De Militia" of Leonardo Bruni* (Toronto: University of Toronto Press, 1961), p. 15.

20. The bulk of feudal levees and city militia was infantry and was unable to withstand a heavy cavalry charge, unlike professional hired troops who developed the cohesiveness to withstand such a charge through long service together. "There was also increasing specialization in the military. The crossbow, for example, led to heavier plate armor which was costly and physically demanding to wear. Mercenaries were also likely to have kept up with technical progress in military matters." David A. Latzko, "The Market for Mercenaries," paper presented at the Eastern Economic Association Meetings, Crystal City, Virginia, April 4, 1997.

21. Van Creveld, *The Rise and Decline of the State*, p. 158.

22. David Ormrod, *The Reign of Edward II* (New Haven: Yale University Press, 1990), p. 103.

23. David Ralston, *Importing the European Army* (Chicago: University of Chicago Press, 1990), p. 6.

24. Contamine, *War in the Middle Ages*, p. 158.

25. Anthony Mockler, *The New Mercenaries* (London: Sidgewick & Jackson, 1985), p. 28.

26. Michael Howard, *War in European History* (London: Oxford University Press, 1976), p. 17.

27. Anthony Mockler, *Mercenaries* (London: Macdonald and Company, 1969) 1969, p. 39.

28. Contamine, *War in the Middle Ages*, p. 159.

29. Mockler, *Mercenaries*, 1969, p. 44.

30. Ibid., p. 42.

31. Howard, *War in European History*, p. 26.

32. Mockler, *Mercenaries*, p. 30–31.

33. Ibid., p. 65.

34. Ibid., p. 54.

35. Howard, *War in European History*, p. 26.

36. Ibid., pp. 18–19.

37. V. G. Kiernan, "Foreign Mercenaries and Absolute Monarchy," in *Crisis in Europe, 1560–1660*, ed. Trevor Aston (London: Routledge & Kegan Paul, 1965), p. 70.

38. Ralston, *Importing the European Army*, p. 5.

39. Howard, *War in European History*, p. 15.

40. Ibid., p. 28.

41. Ibid., p. 131

42. "Money nourishes war," or "No money, No Swiss." Van Creveld, *The Rise and Decline of the State*, p. 407. Howard, *War in European History*, p. 38. Van Creveld specifically compares the period to today and says the military entrepreneur business will return.

43. Howard, *War in European History, p.* 29. See also Fritz Redlich, *The German Military Enterpriser and His Work Force: A Study in European Economic and Social History* (Wiesbaden: Franz Steiner Verlag, 1964).

44. Kiernan, *Foreign Mercenaries and Absolute Monarchy*, p. 132.

45. Howard, *War in European History*, p. 29.

46. Martin Van Creveld, *Supplying War: Logistics from Wallenstein to Patton* (Cambridge: Cambridge University Press, 1977), p. 6.

47. Jeremy Black, *European Warfare: 1453–1815* (London: Macmillan, 1999), p. 61.

48. Ibid., p. 54.

49. Robert L. O'Connell, *Of Arms and Men: A History of War, Weapons, and Aggression* (New York: Oxford University Press, 1989), p. 111.

50. Latzko, *The Market for Mercenaries*. See also McNeill, *The Pursuit of Power*, p. 137.

51. Van Creveld, *The Rise and Decline of the State*, p. 149.

52. Mary Kaldor, *New and Old Wars* (Stanford: Stanford University Press, 1999), p. 16.

53. Deborah Avant, "From Mercenaries to Citizen Armies: Explaining Change in the Practice of War," *International Organization* 54, no. 1 (Winter 2000): 43.

54. Eliot Cohen, *Citizens and Soldiers: The Dilemmas of Military Service* (Ithaca: Cornell University Press, 1985); John Gooch, *Armies in Europe* (London: Routledge, 1980); Barry Posen, "Nationalism, the Mass Army, and Military Power," *International Security* 18, no. 2 (Summer 1993).

55. Avant, "From Mercenaries to Citizen Armies," p. 41.

56. Thomson, *Mercenaries, Pirates, and Sovereigns*, p. 19.

57. Examples of which include what Elizabeth I did by disclaiming the acts of her privateers versus the Spanish and what the Swiss did with their mercenary units. Avant, "From Mercenaries to Citizen Armies," pp. 44–45.

58. Van Creveld, *The Rise and Decline of the State*, p. 161.

59. Ibid.

60. Thomson, *Mercenaries, Pirates, and Sovereigns*, p. 38; C. C. Bayley, *Mercenaries for the Crimea: The German, Swiss, and Italian Legions in British Service, 1854–56* (Montreal: McGill-Queens University Press, 1977).

61. For more on the former, see Richard Smith, *Mercenaries and Mandarins: the Ever-Victorious Army in Nineteenth Century China* (Millwood, N.Y.: KTO Press, 1978).

62. All figures from Thomson, *Mercenaries, Pirates, and Sovereigns*, pp. 28–31.

63. Hector MacDonnell, *The Wild Geese of the Antrim MacDonnells* (Dublin: Irish Academic Press, 1999).

64. Mockler, *The New Mercenaries*, p. 14.

65. Mockler, *Mercenaries*, p. 127. The war also saw the Americans commission over 800 privateers.

66. The Declaration argued, "He is at the moment transporting large armies of foreign mercenaries to complete the works of death, desolations and tyranny, already begun."

67. Van Creveld, *The Rise and Decline of the State*, 1999, p. 288.

68. David Isenberg, *Soldiers of Fortune, LTD:* A profile of today's private sector corporate mercenary firms, Center for Defense Information monograph, November 1997.

69. There was also a French East India Company, as well as various West India companies, and even the Hudson's Bay Company in Canada.

70. Howard, *War in European History*, p. 41.

71. Thomson, *Mercenaries, Pirates, and Soereigns*, p. 32.

72. The *Universal Dictionary* as quoted in *The Rise of Merchant Empires*, ed. James Tracey (New York: Cambridge University Press, 1990), p. 39.

73. Tracy, *Rise of Merchant Empires*, p. 196.

74. Russell Miller, *The East Indiamen* (New York: Time-Incorporated, 1980), p. 101.

75. Thomson, *Mercenaries, Pirates, and Sovereigns*, p. 37.

76. Tracey, *Rise of Merchant Empires*, p. 87.

77. Howard, *War in European History*, p. 44.

78. Ibid., 43.

79. Charles Jenkinson, as quoted in *The East India Company in Eighteenth Century Politics*, by Lucy Sutherland (Oxford: Clarendon Press, 1979), p. 137.

80. Thomson, *Mercenaries, Pirates, and Sovereigns*, p. 39.

81. Tracey, *Rise of Merchant Empires*, 163. See also Adam Hochschild, *King Leopold's Ghost: A Story of Greed, Terror, and Heroism in Colonial Africa* (New York: Houghton Mifflin, 1999).

82. The reputation of this arch-mercenary, however, took a severe hit in the summer of 2000, when he was caught in a conspiracy to secretly take over a number of profitable nudist colonies. Henri Quetteville, "French Mercenary 'Is Behind Nudist Coup,'" *Electronic Telegraph* (UK), August 11, 2000. http://www.telegraph.co.uk/et?ac=003272189007435&rtmo=fqqlvrMs&atmo=gggggDVK&pg=/et/00/8/11/wnude11.html

83. United Nations General Assembly. "Report on the question of the use of mercenaries as a means of violating human rights and impeding the exercise of the right of peoples to self-determination, submitted by the Special Rapporteur of the Commission on Human Rights." 51st Session, Item 106, August 29, 1995.

84. Valery Yakov, "Russia's 'Wild Geese'—Or, An Evening with a Mercenary," *Current Digest of the Post-Soviet Press,* May 5, 1993.

85. P Douglas Porch, *The French Foreign Legion* (New York: Harper Collins, 1991); Adam Nathan and Michael Prescott, "Gurkhas Called Up to Fill Army Ranks," *Sunday Times,* (London), June 11, 2000.

86. The British Ministry of Defence even maintains a Loan Service Department, which seconds, or loans, British servicemen to foreign armies. Tim Spicer, *An Unorthodox Soldier: Peace, War and the Sawdune Affair,* (Edinburgh: Mainstream Publishing, 1999) p. 39; Thomson, *Mercenaries, Pirates, and Sovereigns,* p. 91.

87. Thompson, *Mercenaries, Pirates, and Sovereigns,* pp. 90–91.

88. Latzko, "The Market for Mercenaries."

89. Lock, "Military Downsizing."

90. H. W. Parke, *Greek Mercenary Soldiers: From the Earliest Times to the Battle of Ipsus* (Oxford: Oxford University Press, 1933), p. 18.

91. George Wilnius, *The Merchant Warrior Pacified* (New York: Oxford University Press, 1991), p. 11.

92. Lock, "Military Downsizing."

93. Mockler, *Mercenaries,* 1969, p. 279.

94. Lester Langley and Thomas Schoonover, *The Banana Men: American Mercenaries and Entrepreneurs in Central America, 1880–1930* (Lexington: University Press of Kentucky, 1995).

95. Thomson, *Mercenaries, Pirates, and Sovereigns,* p. 2.

3. THE PRIVATIZED MILITARY DISTINGUISHED

1. Others, such as Executive Outcomes, Sandline, and Ibis Air, are also suspected to be part of conglomerates but either deny them or reputedly have hidden the corporate associations through offshore accounts.

2. Peter Tickler, *The Modern Mercenary* (London: Thorsons, 1987), 15.

3. *Webster's Dictionary* (Springfield, Mass.: C. & G. Merriam Co., 1996) available at www.Dictionary.com.

4. 1977 Additional Protocols to the Geneva Conventions, Article 47.

5. Anthony Mockler, *The New Mercenaries* (London: Sidgewick and Jackson, 1969), p. xiii.

6. Contamine, *War in the Middle Ages,* 99.

7. Mockler, *The New Mercenaries,* p. 21.

8. Ibid.

9. One ad read, "Any fit young man looking for employment with a difference at a salary in excess of 100 (pounds) a month should telephone 838–5203 during business hours. Employment initially offered for six months. Immediate start." As quoted in Mockler, *The New Mercenaries,* p. 61.

10. Mockler, *The New Mercenaries,* p. 62. The pride of the Congo mercenaries in their unprofessionalism differs radically from how current PMFs would describe their own employees.

11. Kevin O'Brien, "PMCs, Myths, and Mercenaries: The Debate on Private Militaries Companies," *RUSI Journal* (February 2000).

12. Kevin O'Brien, "Military Advisory Groups and African Security: Privatized Peace-keeping," *International Peacekeeping* 5, no. 3 (Autumn 1998).

13. "Foreign Special Operations Forces," *Special Warfare: Professional Bulletin of the John F. Kennedy Special Warfare Center and School* 11, no. 2 (Spring 1998). The mass military downsizing, economic dislocation, and rapid criminalization seen in Ukraine in the 1990s seem to be driving this trend.

14. Information on the White Legion from Sean Boyne, "The White Legion: Mercenaries in Zaire," *Jane's Intelligence Review* 9, no. 6 (June 1997): 278–281; Alex Vines, "Mercenaries and the Privatisation of Security in Africa in the 1990s," in *The Privatisation of Security in Africa,* eds. Greg Mills and John Stremlau (Pretoria: South Africa Institute of International Affairs, 1999); O'Brien, "Military Advisory Groups and African Security"; "Serb Snatched by Rogue NATO Bounty Hunter," *Sunday Times, July 23, 2000.* See www.Sunday-times.co.uk

15. Abdel-Fatau Musah and Kayode Fayemi, *Mercenaries: An African Security Dilemma* (London: Pluto Press, 2000). Guy Arnold and Anna Leander are other critics of PMFs who see no inherent difference. Guy Arnold, *Mercenaries* (London: St. Martin's Press, 1999); Anna Leander, "Global Ungovernance," Copenhagen Peace Research Institute Working Paper, 2002.

16. United Nations Commission on Human Rights, "Report on the question of the use of mercenaries as a means of violating human rights and impeding the exercise of the right of peoples to self determination." 53rd Session, Item 7, Special Rapporteur, February 20, 1997.

17. Juan Carlos Zarate, "The Emergence of a New Dog of War: Private International Security Companies, International Law, and the New World Order," *Stanford Journal of International Law* 34 (Winter 1998): 75–156.

18. See Appendix 1.

19. As quoted in Andrew Gilligan, "Inside Lt. Col. Spicer's New Model Army," *Sunday Telegraph,* November 24, 1998.

20. Miller, *East Indiamen,* 1980, p. 63.

21. David Shearer, *Private Armies and Military Intervention* (London: International Institute for Strategic Studies), Adelphi Paper no. 316, February 1998, p. 21.

22. Xavier Renou, "Promoting Destabilization and Neoliberal Pillage: The Utilitization of Private Military Companies for Peacekeeping and Peace Enforcement Activities in Africa," paper presented at ISA/APSA International Security Conference, Denver, November 2000.

23. For more on front companies, see Christopher Robbins, *Air America: The Story of the CIA's Secret Airlines* (New York: G. P. Putnam's Sons, 1979).

24. Ken Silverstein, "Mercenary, Inc.?" *Washington Business Forward,* April 26, 2001.

25. This is not to say, however, that one should not be wary of the possibility that an ostensibly private firm might actually be a front. Several French firms, including Iris Service and ABAC, are thought not to be autonomous but rather might be institutionally related to French intelligence. Thus they are not included in considerations of the industry in this study. Renou, "Promoting Destabilization," and O'Brien, "Military Advisory Groups."

4. WHY SECURITY HAS BEEN PRIVATIZED

1. As noted in chapter 2, similar situations, both on the supply side and at the demand side, prevailed in earlier periods as well after the conclusion of climactic conflicts.

2. Colonel Tim Spicer, quoted in Andrew Gilligan, "Inside Lt. Col. Spicer's New Model Army," *Sunday Telegraph.* November 22, 1998.

3. The determination of what is a "war" or conflict zone is one of those odd political science disputes over something that should be quite simple. Many studies use raw statistical measures, such as whether 1,000 people have been killed or not, but this appears to be driven by arbitrary, and often inaccurate, figures and not connected to the context of the violence and its impact. For the purposes of this book, the NDCF count is used, which combines political, social, economic, and military measures, both qualitative and quantitative, to determine whether a state is at conflict or not. It has also been among the best predictors of fu-

ture violence. National Defense Council Foundation, *World Conflict List 2001* (December 2001). Other sources on this topic include Chris Gray, *Postmodern War: The New Politics of Conflict* (New York: Guilford Press, 1997), p. 49; Mark Duffield.

4. "Internal Conflict: Adaptation and Reaction to Globalisation," *Cornerhouse*, Briefing 12, 1999, http://cornerhouse.icaap.org/briefings/12.html; Ted Robert Gurr, Monty G. Marshall, and Deepa Khosla, *Peace and Conflict 2000: A Global Survey of Armed Conflicts, Self-Determination Movements, and Democracy* (College Park, Md.: Center for International Development and Conflict Management, University of Maryland, 2000), http://www.bsos.umd.edu/cidcm/peace.htm.; Taylor B. Seybolt, (in collaboration with the Uppsala Conflict Data project), "Major Armed Conflicts," *SIPRI Yearbook 2000* (Oxford: Oxford University Press, 2000), pp. 15–75; Peter Wallensteen and Margareta Sollenberg, "Armed Conflict 1989–99," *Journal of Peace Research* 37, no. 5 (May 2000): 649–635.

5. Crawford Young, "The African Colonial State Revisited" *Governance* 11, no. 1 (January 1998): 114.

6. Michael Brown, "The Cause of Internal Conflict," in *World Security: Challenges for a New Century*, ed. Michael Klare and Yogesh Chandrani (New York: St. Martin's Press, 1998), p. 181.

7. William Thom, "Africa's Security Issues through 2010," *Military Review* (Department of the Army Professional Bulletin 100–99–5/6, vol. 80, no. 4 (July–August 2000), http://www.cgsc.army.mil/milrev/English/JulAug00/thom.htm

8. William Reno, *Warlord Politics and African States* (Boulder, Colo.: Lynne Rienner, 1998), p. 1.

9. Jeremy M. Weinstein, "Africa's 'Scramble for Africa'": Lessons of a Continental War," *World Policy Journal* 17, no. 2 (Summer 2000).

10. Duffield, *Internal Conflict*.

11. Michael Renner, "The Global Divide: Socioeconomic Disparities and International Security," in *World Security: Challenges for a New Century*, ed. Michael Klare and Yogesh Chandrani (New York: St. Martin's Press, 1998), p. 275.

12. P. W. Singer, "Caution: Children at War," *Parameters* 31, no. 4 (Winter 2001).

13. Thomas Homer-Dixon. "Environmental Scarcities and Violent Conflict: Evidence from Cases," *International Security* 19, no. 1 (Summer 1994): 5–40.

14. Ian Lesser, *Countering the New Terrorism* (Santa Monica: RAND Corporation, 1999).

15. Ralph Peters, "The New Warrior Class," *Parameters* 24 (Summer 1994): 24; John Keegan, "Natural Warriors," *Wall Street Journal*, March 27, 1997, p. A20.

16. As General Barry MacCaffrey, the former U.S. drug czar, notes of the FARC, "They've got more automatic weapons in one of their battalions than the Colombian Army does." Philip Rees, "Colombia-Drug Wars," *BBC*, November 11, 2000. The cartels, in turn, have even acquired Russian-made submarines. Jan Mckirk, "Drug Sub in Andes Linked to Russians" *Independent*, September 10, 2000.

17. Andre Linard, "Mercenaries SA," *Le Monde Diplomatique*, August 1998, p. 31. www.monde-diplomatique.fr/1998/08/Linard/10806.html; Christopher Goodwin, "Mexican Drug Barons Sign Up Renegades from Green Berets," *Sunday Times*, august 24, 1997; Patrick J. Cullen, "Keeping the New Dog of War on a Tight Lease," *Conflict Trends*, no. 6 (July 2000). http://www.accord.org.za/publications/ct6/issue6.html; James Adams, *The Next World War* (New York: Simon & Schuster, 1998), p. 105.

18. Samia Aoul et al., "Towards a Spiral of Violence?—The Dangers of Privatizing Risk Management in Africa," Memorandum, Working Group on Human Rights in Congo, Development and Peace, Mining Watch Canada, February 2000.

19. Shearer, *Private Armies and Military Intervention*, p. 27.

20. C. J. Van Bergen Thirion, "The Privatisation of Security: A Blessing or a Menace?" South African Defence College Paper, May 1999.

21. Lock, "Military Downsizing" 1998. One firm, Centre for Counterintelligence and Security Studies, is even jointly run by ex-KGB spies and their old FBI trackers.

22. Stephen Zamparrelli, "Contractors on the Battlefield: What Have We Signed Up For?" Air War College Research report, March 1999.

23. In only last few years alone, there has been a 300 percent increase in U.S. military commitments, and these do not seem to be reducing. Donald T. Wynn, "Managing the Logistics-Support Contract in the Balkans Theater," *Engineer* (July 2000), http://call.army.mil/call/trngqtr/tq4–00/wynn.htm

24. Bonn International Center for Conversion (BICC), *An Army Surplus—The NVA's Heritage*, BICC Brief no. 3, 1997. Available at www.bicc.de/weapons/brief

25. BICC, *An Army Surplus*.

26. Greg Mills and John Stremlau, "The Privatisation of Security in Africa: An Introduction," in *The Privatisation of Security in Africa*, ed. Greg Mills and John Stremlau (Pretoria: South Africa Institute of International Affairs, 1999), p. 4.

27. Stephen Metz, *Refining American Strategy in Africa*, U.S. Army War College, Strategic Studies Institute, April 2000, p. 24. http://carlisle-www.army.mil/usassi/ssipubs/pubs2000.htm

28. Michael Ruppert, "When the Children of the Bull Market Begin to Die," *From the Wilderness* (October 2000).

29. Michael Klare, "The Kalashnikov Age," *Bulletin of the Atomic Scientists* 55, no. 1 (January/February 1999). http://www.bullatomsci.org/issues/1999/jf99/jf99klare.html

30. Robert Neild, "Expose the Unsavory Business behind Cruel Wars," *International Herald Tribune*, February 17, 2000.

31. Jasit Singh, *Light Weapons and International Security* (New Delhi: Institute for Defense Studies and Analysis, 1995).

32. United Nations, Report of the Expert of the Secretary-General, Graça Machel, "Impact of Armed Conflict on Children." Document A/51/306 & Add 1. August 26, 1996. The equivalents are about 5 USD.

33. David Kaiser, *Politics and War* (Cambridge, Mass.: Harvard University Press, 1990).

34. Lock, "Military Downsizing."

35. Van Creveld, *The Rise and Decline of the State*, p. vii.

36. Thomas Friedman, *The Lexus and the Olive Tree* (New York: Farrar, Straus and Giroux, 1999).

37. The fall was particularly acute for former superpower battleground countries such as Sudan, Somalia, and Zaire, where aid in the period went down in the range of 60 percent to 100 percent. Global Coalition for Africa, *African Social and Economic Trends*, Annual Report 1999/2000, www.gca-cma.org

38. Metz, *Refining American Strategy*, p. 8.

39. Van Creveld, *The Rise and Decline of the State*, p. 337.

40. Neild, "Expose the Unsavory Business behind Cruel Wars."

41. William Thom, "The African Military: Problems and Prospects," *Africa Digest* 18, no. 2 (September 1995): p. 8.

42. Herbert Howe, *Ambiguous Order: Military Forces in African States* (Boulder, Colo.: Lynne Rienner, 2001), pp. 40–61.

43. Anthony D. Marley, "Problems of Terminating Wars in Africa," *Small Wars and Insurgencies* 8, no. 3 (Winter 1997): 116.

44. Global Coalition for Africa, *African Social and Economic Trends*, Annual Report 1999/2000. www.gca-cma.org; Herbert Howe, *Ambiguous Order: Military Forces in African States* (Boulder, Colo.: Lynne Rienner Publishers, 2001).

45. Metz, *Refining American Strategy*, 10.

46. Herbert Howe, "To Stabilize Tottering African Governments," *Armed Forces Journal International* (November 1996).

47. For example, a DoD study found that only 7 of 46 African militaries could deploy just a single battalion for an external operation, while none could provide sustained transportation of personnel and equipment. Howe, *Ambiguous Order*.

48. Jason Sherman, "Arm's Length," *Armed Forces Journal International* (September 2000): 30.

49. "South Africa-Nigeria: Military relationship," *IRIN*, April 18, 2000.

50. Ivan Watson, "Aiming at African Peace," *San Francisco Chronicle,* January 26, 2001, p. 12.

51. "South Africa's Army 'Unfit,'" *BBC News,* July 15, 2002. http://news.bbc.co.uk/hi/english/world/africa/newsid_2129000/2129563.stm

52. P. W. Singer, "AIDS and International Security," *Survival* 44, no. 1 (Spring 2002): 145–158.

53. *U.S. International Response to HIV/AIDS,* Washington: Department of State, January 1999, http://www.state.gov/www/global/oes/health/1999_hivaids_rpt/contents.html

54. Claire Bisseker, "Africa's Military Time Bomb, *Johannesburg Financial Mail,* December 11, 1998.

55. Herbert Howe, "Global Order and Security Privatization" *Strategic Forum,* no. 140, May 1998, Institute for National Strategic Studies, National Defense University, http://www.ndu.edu/inss/strforum/forum140.html.

56. For example, in 2000, the *America's National Interest* report, which laid out the agreed bipartisan areas of U.S. priorities, did not even make a single mention of the entire continent of Africa. The Commission on America's National Interests, *America's National Interest,* July 2000.

57. Edward N. Luttwark, "Where Are the Great Powers? At Home with the Kids," *Foreign Affairs* (July/August 1994).

58. James Adams, *The Next World War,* p. 279.

59. Hohn Diamond, "Wary U.S. Offers Little Help in Sierra Leone Crisis," *Chicago Tribune,* May 18, 2000.

60. Maria Dowling and Vincent Feck. "Joint Logistics and Engineering Contract," *Contractors on the Battlefield,* Air Force Logistics Management Agency, December 1999.

61. Jeffrey Ulbrich, "French No Longer Africa Gendarmes," AP, May 23, 2001. Shearer, *Private Armies and Military Intervention,* p. 29.

62. General Jean-Paul Raffene. The French decision was driven by several factors, including a change in political leadership and France's decision to downsize its military and make it an all-volunteer force, which, as Raffenne put it, "lessens France's ability to intervene overseas." Jim Fisher-Thompson, "French General Details Renewed Commitment to Africa," *USIS,* June 3, 1999., http://www.eucom.mil/programs/acri/usis/99jun03.htm

63. Gilligan, "Inside Lt. Col. Spicer's New Model Army."

64. Dennis Jett, *Why Peacekeeping Fails* (New York: Palgrave, 1999), p. 18.

65. Margaret Karns and Karen Mingst, "The Evolution of United Nations Peacekeeping and Peacemaking: Lessons from the Past and Challenges for the Future," in *World Security: Challenges for a New Century,* ed. Michael Klare and Yogesh Chandrani (New York: St. Martin's Press, 1998).

66. Stephem Mbogo, "Mercenaries? No, PMCs." *West Africa Magazine,* September 18, 2000, pp. 10–13.

67. Mark Malan, "Lean Peacekeeping Turns Mean: Crisis and Response in Sierra Leone," paper presented to ISS security seminar, South Africa, May 18, 2000.

68. For example, the countries involved in the UN operation in Sierra Leone include Bangladesh, Bolivia, Canada, China, Croatia, Czech Republic, Denmark, Egypt, France, Gambia, Guinea, India, Indonesia, Jordan, Kenya, Kyrgystan, Malaysia, Mali, Nepal, New Zealand, Nigeria, Norway, Pakistan, Russian Federation, Slovakia, Sweden, Tanzania, Thailand, United Kingdom, Uruguay, and Zambia.

69. Chris Mcgreal, "Nigerian Peace Force Accused of Sabotage," *Guardian,* September 14, 2000, http://www.guardianunlimited.co.uk/international/story/0,3604,366353,00.html

70. Van Creveld, *The Rise and Decline of the State,* p. 384.

71. Christopher Piening, *Global Europe: The European Union in World Affairs* (Boulder, Colo.: Lynne Rienner, 1997); Kenichi Ohmae, *The End of the Nation State: The Rise of Regional Economies* (New York: Free Press, 1995).

72. For more on ACRI, see http://www.eucom.mil/programs/acri/ and http://www.usinfo.state.gov/regional/af/acri/

73. Charles Tilly, *The Formation of National States in Western Europe* (Princeton: Princeton University Press, 1975).

74. Jessica Matthews, as quoted in "It's Not Just Governments That Make War and Peace Now," *New York Times*, November 28, 1998.

75. Stephen Metz, *Armed Conflict in the Twenty-first Century: The Information Revolution and Postmodern Warfare* (Strategic Studies Institute, U.S. Army War College, 2000), p. 62, http://carlisle-www.army.mil/usassi/ssipubs/pubs2000/conflict/conflict.htm

76. Neild, "Expose the Unsavory Business behind Cruel Wars."

77. Metz, *Armed Conflict*, p. 54. For more on these groups' technical advantages over government agencies, see Paul Kaihla, "The Technology Secrets of Cocaine Inc." *Business 2.0* (July 2002). *www.business2.com*

78. William Broad, "Private Ventures Hope for Profits on Spy Satellites," *New York Times*, February 10, 1997, p. 1.

79. Chris Westwood, "Military Information Operations in a Conventional Warfare Environment," Air Power Studies Centre Paper, no. 47, 1995. www.defense.gov.au/apsc/publish/paper47.htm; Tom Regan, Wars of the Future . . . Today," *Christian Science Monitor,* June 24, 1999.

80. Metz, *Armed Conflict*, p. 14.

81. Michael Mandelbaum, "Is Major War Obsolete?" *Survival* 40 (Winter 1998) p. 35.

82. Martin Van Creveld, *Technology and War* (New York: Free Press, 1989), p. 1.

83. Ibid., p. 378.

84. "RMA Data Base," sponsored by the Project on Defense Alternatives. http://www.comw.org/rma/

85. The Pentagon already relies on a commercial telecommunications infrastructure, which, for economic reasons, tends to use the most cost-effective systems, rather than the most secure. Metz, *Armed Conflict*, xiii; "$2.4 Billion Needed for Pentagon Computer Security." UPI, September 13, 2000.

86. "NSA Head: Tech Weakness Makes U.S. Vulnerable," CNN.com, February 12, 2001.

87. The best example was "Eligible Receiver," which proved the power of private groups in this realm. A team of 36 privately hired hackers gained root access (the highest level of control) of 36 of the government's networks. They had the ability to create power outages in every major city, disrupt military communications, including taking out most of PACOM, and even gained access to computer systems on navy vessels at sea. The fact that NSA hired them off the street illustrates how such a team could work for anyone. Chris Westwood, "Military Information Operations in a Conventional Warfare Environment," Air Power Studies Centre Paper, no. 47, 1996. http://www.defence.gov.au/aeorspacecentre/publish/paper47.htm

88. Rathmell, 1998.

89. Metz, *Armed Conflict*, p. 76.

90. Carl Conetta and Charles Knight, *Defense Sufficiency and Cooperation: A U.S. Military Posture for the Post-Cold War Era*, Project on Defense Alternatives Briefing Report 9, March 1, 1998, p. 31.

91. A few numbers might illustrate this point. Of the 2.3 million full-time personnel employed by the U.S. Department of Defense only 200,000 are in combat positions. For every troop in the field, there are 4 civilians serving in some support function. Business Executives for National Security Tooth to Tail Commission, "Defense Department Headquarters—Too Many Chiefs, Not Enough Warriors," Update no. 7, November 14, 1997. Available at www.bens.org/pubs.

92. Westwood, *Military Information Operations*.

93. Thomas Adams, p. 115. Adams, however, defines firms under the old mercenary rubric, a position that is examined in chapter 3.

94. Eugene Smith, "The New Condottieri and U.S. Policy," *Parameters* (Winter 2002–2003): 116.

95. James Adams, *The Next World War*, p. 113.

96. Earle Eldridge, "Civilians Put Expertise on the Front Line," *USA Today*, December 8, 2001.

97. Loren Thompson, as quoted in Robert Little, "American Civilians Go Off to War, Too," *Baltimore Sun,* May 26, 2002.

98. Bryan Bender, "Defense Contracts Quickly Becoming Surrogate Warriors," *Defense Daily,* March 28, 1997, p. 490.

99. Michael Ignatieff, *The Warrior's Honor: Ethnic War and the Modern Conscience* (New York: Henry Holt, 1998).

100. Mats Berdal and David Malone, eds., *Greed and Grievance: Economic Agendas in Civil Wars* (Boulder, Colo.: Lynne Rienner, 2001).

101. Metz, *Armed Conflict,* p. 24.

102. Mary Kaldor, *New and Old Wars* (Stanford: Stanford University Press, 1999), p. 1.

103. Blaine Harden, "Africa's Gems: Warfare's Best Friend," *New York Times,* April 6, 2000.

104. Paul Collier and Anke Hoeffler, "Greed and Grievance in Civil War," *World Bank Policy Research Paper,* no. 2355, May 2000.

105. Kaldor, *New and Old Wars,* p. 102.

106. Duffield, "Internal Conflict."

107. A typical example is the FARC in Colombia, which started out as a Marxist revolutionary group and is now a prime player in the international cocaine trade. Michael Klare, "The Kalashnikov Age," *Bulletin of the Atomic Scientists* 55, no. 1 (January/February 1999). http://www.bullatomsci.org/issues/1999/jf99/jf99klare.html

108. Eric Berman, *Re-Armament in Sierra Leone,* Small Arms Survey Occasional Paper 1, December 2000.

109. "Sierra Leone: Briefing on the Civil War," *IRIN,* May 31, 2000.

110. Douglass C. North, *Institutions, Institutional Change, and Economic Performance* (Cambridge: Cambridge University Press, 1990); Geoffrey Garrett and Barry Weingast, "Ideas, Interests, and Institutions," in *Ideas and Foreign Policy,* ed. Judith Goldstein and Robert Keohane (Ithaca: Cornell University Press, 1993).

111. Harvey Feigenbaum and Jeffrey Henig, "Privatization and Political Theory," *Journal of International Affairs* 50 (Winter 1997): 338.

112. "The Thatcher Revolution," *Economist,* September 21, 1996, p. 8.

113. In Italy, for example, $5 billion in state assets were sold off from 1983 to 1989. In long-statist France $11.5 billion was privatized in 1987 alone. The number of state employees dropped by 800,000. Van Creveld, *The Rise and Decline of the State,* p. 370.

114. Duffield, "Internal Conflict."

115. Van Creveld *The Rise and Decline of the State,* p. 376.

116. *Privatization '98,* Reason Public Policy Institute, 12th Annual Report on Privatization and Government Reform, 1998.

117. *Privatization 1997: A Comprehensive Report on Contracting, Privatization, and Government Reform,* Reason Public Policy Institute, 11th Annual Report on Privatization, 1997.

118. Lock, "Military Downsizing."

119. William Reno, "Foreign Firms, Natural Resources, and Violent Political Economies," *Social Science Forum,* March 21, 2000.

120. Lock, "Military Downsizing."

121. *Privatization '98.*

122. For a discussion of this dynamic, see David Held, Anthony McGrew, David Goldblatt, and Jonathan Perraton, *Global Transformations: Politics, Economics, and Culture* (Stanford, Calif.: Stanford University Press, 1999), pp. 103–123.

123. Duffield, *Internal Conflict.*

124. "Outsourcing 2000," *Fortune,* May 29, 2000, pullout section.

125. Paul Taibel, "Outsourcing and Privatization of Defense Infrastructure," A Business Executives for National Security Report, 1998. Available at: http://www.bens.org/pubs/outsrce. html.

126. Business Executives for National Security Tooth to Tail Commission. "After Kosovo: Operation "Restore Balance." Update no. 33, May 25, 1999. Available at www.bens.org/pubs

127. "Outsourcing 2000."

128. Business Executives for National Security Tooth to Tail Commission, "Logistics Transformation: DoD's Opportunity to Partner with the Private Sector," Issue Brief, October 1999. Available at www.bens.org/pubs.

129. Taibel, *Outsourcing and Privatization of Defense Infrastructure*, 1999.

130. Business Executives for National Security Tooth to Tail Commission, "Logistics Transformation."

131. Van Creveld, *The Rise and Decline of the State*, p. 417.

132. Ibid., p. 406.

133. *Jenny Irish, Policing for Profit*, ISSS Monograph Series, no. 39, 1999, p. 6.

134. Edward Blakely and Mary Snyder, *Fortress America: Gated Communities in the United States* (Washington, D.C.: Brookings Institution Press, 1997), p. 126.

135. Ibid., p. 133.

136. As quoted in Elizabeth Rubin, "An Army of One's Own," *Harper's Magazine*, February 1997.

137. Jack Kelley, "Safety at a Price: Security Is a Booming, Sophisticated, Global Business," *Pittsburgh Post-Gazette*, February 13, 2000.

138. Martin Schoneich, "Fighting Crime with Private Muscle: The Private Sector and Crime Prevention" *African Security Review* 8, no. 5 (1998): 17.

139. Irish, *Policing for Profit*, p. 5.

140. Christopher Coker, "Outsourcing War," *Cambridge Review of International Affairs* 13, no. 1 (1998): 95–113.

141. Blakely is an example of the former.

142. Kenneth Binmore and Larry Samuelson, "An Economist's Perspective on the Evolution of Norms," *Journal of Institutional and Theoretical Politics* 150, no. 1 (1994); Geoffrey Garrett and Barry Weingast, "Ideas, Interests, and Institutions," in Judith Goldstein and Robert Keohane, *Ideas and Foreign Policy* (Ithaca: Cornell University Press, 1993).

143. Van Creveld, *The Rise and Decline of the State*, p. 409.

144. Richard Sennett, *The Fall of Public Man* (New York: Alfred A. Knopf, 1977).

145. Ruppert, "When the Children of the Bull Market Begin to Die."

146. Sinclair Dinnen, "Trading in Security: Private Security Contractors in Papua New Guinea," in *Challenging the State: The Sandline Affair in Papua New Guinea*, ed. Sinclair Dinnen (Canberra: National Centre for Development Studies, Research School of Pacific and Asian Studies, Australian National University, 1997), p. 11.

147. Juan Tamayo, "Colombian Guerrillas Fire on U.S. Rescuers," *Miami Herald*, February 22, 2001.

5. THE GLOBAL INDUSTRY OF MILITARY SERVICES

1. "Can Anybody Curb Africa's Dogs of War?" *Economist, January 16, 1999.*

2. Ibid.

3. David Isenberg, "The New Mercenaries," *Christian Science Monitor,* October 13, 1998, p. 19.

4. Jeffery Herbst, "The Regulation of Private Security Forces," in *The Privatisation of Security in Africa*, ed. Greg Mills and John Stremlau (Pretoria: South Africa Institute of International Affairs, 1999), p. 118.

5. Daniel McGrory and Nicholas Woods, "Soldiers for Sale," *London Times*, May 9, 1998.

6. Ibid. McGrory and Woods cite up to $450 per day for deployment in a combat zone, in this case for European Security Operatives, of Westgate, Kent. Others have cited up to $1,000 per day. These figures all depend on the nature of the work and the environment.

7. The all-volunteer SAS never before had to go out and recruit. Michael Evan, "SAS Struggles for Recruits as Who Pays Wins," *Times*, February 26, 2002.

8. Paul De La Garza and David Adams, "Military Know-How Finds Niche—And Some Critics," *St. Petersburg Times*, December 3, 2000.

9. Ibid.

10. Esther Schrader, "Companies Capitalize on War on Terror," *Los Angeles Times*, April 14, 2002; Lock, "Military Downsizing," 1998; Gumisai Mutume, "Private Military Companies Face Crisis in Africa," *Inter Press Service*, December 11, 1998; Correspondence with Frost & Sullivan Investments, Sept. 2000; We can also determine some subsector revenues, such as the $400 million mine countermeasures market or the $2 billion spent on privatized military training within the United States in 1999.

11. International Alert, *The Politicisation of Humanitarian Action and Staff Security*, Workshop Report (April 24, 2001).

12. Armorgroup's internal sales growth, for example, was a respectable 27 percent during one quarter, with overall revenue growing 35 percent. Armor Holdings, "Armor Holdings, Inc. Reports Record Third Quarter Operating Results Of $0.22 Per Diluted Share Before Merger & Integration Charges and Other Unusual Expenses," *PRNewswire*, November 14, 2000.

13. Jack Kelley, "Safety at a Price: Security Is a Booming, Sophisticated, Global Business," *Pittsburgh Post-Gazette*, February 13, 2000.

14. Data and figure from Armor Holdings. "Proxy Statement; Annual Meeting of Stockholders to be held on June 15, 2000." Company report June 2000, p. 12.

15. Gopal Ratman, "Defense News Top 100," *Defense News*. July 30, 2001, p. 49.

16. Ken Silverstein, "Mercenary, Inc.?" *Washington Business Forward*, April 26, 2001.

17. Cyril Zenda, "Mine Tech Earns World Honours," , *Financial Gazette* (Harare), May 3, 2002.

18. Justin Brown, "The Rise of the Private-Sector Military," *Christian Science Monitor*, July 5, 2000. http://www.csmonitor.com/durable/2000/07/05/f-p3s1.shtml

19. Correspondence with Frost & Sullivan, 2000.

20. David Isenberg, *Soldiers of Fortune Ltd.: A Profile of Today's Private Sector Corporate Mercenary Firms*. Center For Defense Information Monograph (November 1997).

21. C. J. Van Bergen Thirion, "The Privatisation of Security: A Blessing or a Menace?" South African Defence College paper, May 1999.

22. "Ex-SAS men in secret rescue," *New Zealand Herald*, March 9, 2000. http://www.nzherald .co.nz. The operation was run without approval from, and actually under the noses of, the New Zealand military forces deployed to the region, another example of how companies can act contrary to their own governments.

23. Kevin O'Brien, "PMCs, Myths and Mercenaries: The Debate on Private Military Companies," *RUSI Journal* (February 2000).

24. "Risky Returns: Doing Business in Chaotic and Violent Countries," *Economist*, May 20, 2000.

25. Alexi Barrionuevo, "Threat of Terror Abroad Isn't New for Oil Companies like Occidental," *Wall Street Journal*, February 7, 2002; Alfredo Rangel Suarez, "Parasites and Predators: Guerillas and the Insurrection Economy of Colombia," *Journal of International Affairs* 53, no. 2 (Spring 2000): 577–601; Nancy Dunne, "Dope Wars (Part II): Crackdown on Colombia," *Financial Times*, August 9, 2000.

26. Jimmy Burns, "Corporate Security: Anxiety Stirred by Anti-Western Sentiment," *Financial Times*, April 11, 2002.

27. "Corporate Security: Risk Returns," *Economist*, November 20, 1999.

28. "Risky Returns: Doing Business in Chaotic and Violent Countries," *The Economist*, November 20, 1999.

29. The new nature of warfare has meant that this presence of mining and lucrative returns will often be intimately connected with the potential for conflict, as noted in chapter 4.

30. As quoted in Kelley, "Safety at a Price." The firm specializes in executive protection and risk assessment.

31. William Reno, "Foreign Firms, Natural Resources, and Violent Political Economies," *Social Science Forum*, March 21, 2000. Available at http://www.social-science-forum.org/ new_page_27.htm. This contract, in turn, was guaranteed by loans from the U.S. government and the World Bank.

32. "Corporate Security: Risk Returns."

33. www.airpartner.com. Another competitor is International SOS, a firm that offers global medical assistance, www.internationalsos.com.

34. Herbst, "The Regulation of Private Security Forces," p. 125.

35. Correspondence with the firm Frost & Sullivan.

36. Anna Leander, "Global Ungovernance: Mercenaries, States and the Control over Violence," *Copenhagen Peace Research Institute Working Paper,* 2002.

37. Colum Lynch, "Private Firms Aid U.N. on Sanctions: Wider Intelligence Capability Sought," *Washington Post,* April 2001. http://www.washingtonpost.com/wp-dyn/articles/A44304-2001Apr20.html

38. Antony Barnett, "Anger at Kosovo Mines Contract: Firm Accused of Human Rights Abuses Wins Million-pound Government Deal," *Observer,* Sunday May 7, 2000. http://www.observer.co.uk/uk_news/0,6903,218247,00.html

39. Kelley, "Safety at a Price."

40. Juan Carlos Zarate, "The Emergence of a New Dog of War: Private International Security Companies, International Law, and the New World Order," *Stanford Journal of International Law* 34 (Winter 1998): 75–156.

41. Armor Holdings, "IBNet Announces Joint Marketing Agreement with Armorgroup," Armorgroup press release, April 7, 2000. Available at www.armorholdings.com; "Princes of Private U.S. Intelligence," *Intelligence Newsletter,* February 8, 2001.

42. It specifically trained in deep penetration and the targeting of NATO nuclear facilities, but also played an active role in Soviet interventions abroad, including Afghanistan. Interview with former U.S. Defense Attaché to Moscow, June 2000.

43. ArmorGroup—Company Brief. ArmorGroup Marketing Presentation received February 2000.

44. "America's 100 Fastest-Growing Companies," *Fortune,* September 6, 1999; "100 Fastest-Growing Companies" *Fortune,* September 2000. http://www.fortune.com/fortune/fastest/csnap/0,7130,45,00.html

45. ArmorGroup—Company Brief. ArmorGroup Marketing Presentation received Feb. 2000.

46. Brian Shepler, a Senior Equity Research Analyst for SunTrust Equitable Securities Corporation as quoted in ArmorGroup—Company Brief.

47. "Securicor to acquire Gray Security Services," *London Stock Exchange Regulatory News Service,* September 15, 2000.

48. "L-3 Communications Announces Acquisition of MPRI," *Business Wire,* July 18, 2000. Interestingly enough, L-3 also makes the "black box" flight recorders that make the news every time a plane crashes.

49. Silverstein, "Mercenary, Inc.?"

50. South African Institute of International Affairs, "Private Security: Phantom Menace or Evil Empire?" *Intelligence Update.* (May 11, 2000).

51. Vines, "Business of Peace," 2. This happened in Sierra Leone, where midway through the operation EO pulled personnel from its Angola operations for a final push on RUF strongholds.

52. Frederic C. Lane, *Profits from Power: Readings in Protection Rent and Violence Controlling Enterprises* (Albany: SUNY Press, 1979) pp. 41, 44, 46.

53. South African Institute of International Affairs, "Private Security."

6. THE PRIVATIZED MILITARY INDUSTRY CLASSIFIED

1. Aoul, 2000.

2. Zarate, *Emergence.*

3. Doug Brooks and Hussein Solomon, 2000.

4. Spicer, p. 41; O'Brien 2000; Doug Brooks, "Hope for the 'Hopeless Continent': Mercenaries," *Traders: Journal for the Southern African Region,* no. 3 (July–October 2000).

5. South African Institute of International Affairs, "Private Security: Phantom Menace or Evil Empire?" *Intelligence Update,* May 11, 2000.

6. Others have attempted to differentiate private military companies from private security companies by their client lists, which hardly makes sense, given the broad crossover in clientele. International Alert, *Private Military Companies and the Proliferation of Small Arms: Regulating the Actors* (January 2002).

7. Robert Mandel, "The Privatization of Security," *Armed Forces & Society* 28, no. 1 (Fall 2001): 129–152.

8. International Alert, *The Politicisation of Humanitarian Action and Staff Security,* Workshop Report, April 24, 2001; Sean M. Lynn-Jones, "Offense-Defense Theory and Its Critics," *Security Studies* 4, no. 4 (Summer 1995): 660–691; Stephen Van Evera, "Offense, Defense, and the Causes of War," *International Security* 22, no. 4. (Spring 1998): 5–43.

9. James W. Davis, Jr., "Correspondence: Taking Offense at Offense-Defense Theory," *International Security* 24, no. 3, (Winter 1998); Keir Lieber, "Grasping the Technological Peace: The Offense Defense Balance and International Security," *International Security* 25, no. 1 (Summer 2000): 179–206.

10. A web search brings up 2460 references in the context of the U.S. military.

11. Department of the Army, *Contracting Support on the Battlefield,* FM 100–10–2, April 15, 1999.

12. *Privatization 1997: A Comprehensive Report on Contracting, Privatization, and Government Reform,* Public Policy Institute, 11th Annual Report on Privatization, p. 17.

13. Spicer, *Unorthodox Soldier,* 43.

14. "Can Anybody Curb Africa's Dogs of War," *Economist,* January 16, 1999.

15. Jay M. Garner, "The Next Generation of Threat to U.S. Military Superiority . . . 'Asymmetric Niche Warfare,'" *Phalanx* 30, no. 1 (March 1997); Alvin Toffler and Heidi Toffler, *War and Anti-War: Survival at the Dawn of the 21st Century* (Boston: Little, Brown, 1993); Ralph Peters, "The New Warrior Class," *Parameters* 24 (Summer 1994).

16. Chris Gray, *Postmodern War: The New Politics of Conflict* (New York: Guilford Press, 1997), p. 126.

17. A historic example is the addition of Swiss pikemen to the French force in 1479. Already possessing what were considered the best native cavalry and artillery in Europe, the Swiss mercenary units gave the French clear superiority over all rivals in all arms, leading to their dominance for the following decades. McNeill, *The Pursuit of Power,* p. 119.

18. "Can Anybody Curb Africa's Dogs of War?"

19. Doug Brooks, "Write a Cheque, End a War Using Private Military Companies to End African Conflicts," *Conflict Trends,* no. 6 (July 2000). http://www.accord.org.za/publications/ct6/issue6.htm

20. Daniel McGrory and Nicholas Woods, "Soldiers for Sale," *London Times,* May 9, 1998.

21. Global Coalition for Africa, 1999/2000, *African Social and Economic Trends,* Annual Report 1999/2000. www.gca-cma.org

22. Justin Brown, "The Rise of the Private-Sector Military," *Christian Science Monitor,* July 5, 2000.

23. Interestingly, other firms, such as Booz-Allen & Hamilton, have both civilian management consulting and military consulting divisions.

24. Spicer, *Unorthodox Soldier,* p. 42.

25. Bill Burnham, "Traction Doesn't Lie," *Inter@ctive Investor,* February 1, 2000. http://www.zdnet.com/ebusiness/stories/0,5918,2431101–4,00.html

26. More on the firms' motivation in doing such in chapter 11.

27. "First and foremost, we are military consultants, particularly at the level of command, control, communications and intelligence." Spicer, *Unorthodox Soldier,* p. 21.

28. Peter Tickler, *The Modern Mercenary* (London: Thorsons, 1987), p. 126.

29. Esther Schrader, "U.S. Companies Hired to Train Foreign Armies," *Los Angeles Times,* April 14, 2002.

30. Tim Cross, "Logistic Support for UK Expeditionary Operations," *RUSI Journal* (February 2000).

31. Department of the Army, *Contractors on the Battlefield*, FM 100–21 (Washington: Headquarters, 1999):1–2; Vincent Transano, "History of the Seabees," Naval Historical Center, accessed Nov. 2000. http://www.history.navy.mil/faqs/faq67–1.htm; William Huie, *Can Do! The Story of the Seabees* (New York: E. P. Dutton, 1944); Zamparrelli, p. 5.

32. Mira Wilkins, ed., *The Free-Standing Company in the World Economy, 1830–1996* (Oxford: Oxford University Press, 1998), 3. In past historic contexts, such freestanding companies operated on the frontiers of the age and were closely associated with imperial ventures. Multinational corporations came later, building out through the creation of corporate branches or associated overseas companies.

33. Craig Copetas, "It's Off to War Again for Big U.S. Contractor," *Wall Street Journal*, April 4, 1999, A21.

34. Andrew Goodpaster, *When Diplomacy Is Not Enough*, Report to the Carnegie Commission on Preventing Deadly Conflict, July 1996, p. 26.

35. Thomas J. Milton, "The New Mercenaries —Corporate Armies for Hire," *Foreign Area Officers Association Journal* (1997).

36. Bob Gilmour, "St. Albert Officer to Lead Forces' First Private Contract on Overseas Mission," *Edmonton Journal*, July 6, 2000.

37. Ian McDougall, "The New Supply Motto for the Canadian Forces Could Be 'Welcome to Wal-Mart,'" *Toronto Sun*, March 13, 2002; "Military Outsourcing Plan Draws Fire from Unions," *CBC (Canadian Broadcasting Corporation)*, May 16, 2002.

38. General Omar Bradley put it thus, "Amateurs study strategy, professionals study logistics," *Air Force Field Manual 1–1: Basic Aerospace Doctrine of the United States Air Force* (Washington D.C.: U.S. Government Printing Office, 1992), 1:14.

39. Jack Kelley, "Safety at a Price: Security is a Booming, Sophisticated, Global Business." Also responsible for criminal policing, Pinkerton introduced such innovations as the mugshot and the rap sheet.

40. Justin Brown, "Internet Challenges Old Assumptions About Spying," *Christian Science Monitor*, April 6, 2000.

41. Andrew Rathmell, "The Privatisation of Intelligence: A Way Forward for European Intelligence Cooperation," *Cambridge Review of International Affairs* 11, no. 2 (Spring 1998): 199–211.

42. James Risen, "CIA Instructs Agencies to Use More Commercial Satellite Photos," *New York Times*, June 26, 2002.

43. Toffler, *War and Anti-War*, p. 161.

44. Martin Chulov, "Anger over Private Spies," *Australian*, July 5, 2001.

45. "I Could Tell You, But I'd Have to Kill You: The Cult of Classification in Intelligence," Stratfor.com, Weekly Global Intelligence Update (September 18, 2000) available at www.stratfor.com

46. Stan Correy, "The Business of Cybersecurity—The War Against Privacy?" *Australian Broadcasting Corporation*, August 20, 2000. http://www.abc.net.au/rn/talks/bbing/s167110.htm; "The World War Web?" *Industry Standard*, February 12, 1999.

47. Tom Regan, "Wars of the Future . . . Today," *Christian Science Monitor*, June 24, 1999.

48. Correy, "Business of Cybersecurity."

49. Carl Franklin, "SAS General Dares to Fight Cyber-Terrorists," *U.K. Sunday Business*, June 26, 1999. See also www.idefense.com

50. Itochu is a Japanese conglomerate with 1,027 subsidiaries and affiliates that ranks among the world's largest companies. For more information, http://www.itochu.co.jp.

7. THE MILITARY PROVIDER FIRM: EXECUTIVE OUTCOMES

1. United Nations Commission on Human Rights. "Report on the question of the use of mercenaries as a means of violating human rights and impeding the exercise of the right

of peoples to self determination." 53rd Session, Item 7, Special Rapporteur, February 20, 1997.

2. An unofficial unit history homepage is located at http://www.netcentral.co.uk/~cobus/32BAT/

3. Elizabeth Rubin, "An Army of One's Own," *Harper's Magazine,* February 1997.

4. Reportedly, some members of the old ANC military wing found employment alongside their former enemies in EO. But this is unconfirmed.

5. Andrew Donalson, "Like Nails from Rotting Wood," *Sunday Times* (Johannesburg) (October 1, 2000). http://www.suntimes.co.za/2000/10/01/insight/ino1.htm; Emsie Ferreira, "Koevoet: It Was a Luvverly War," *Dispatch,* September 28, 2000. http://www.dispatch.co.za/2000/09/28/features/KOEVOET.HTM

6. Shearer, p. 42; Isenberg, 1997; Howe, 2001.

7. Al J. Venter, "Market Forces: How Hired Guns Succeeded Where the United Nations Failed," *Jane's International Defense Review,* March 1998.

8. Rubin, "Army of One's Own."

9. Jim Hooper, "Diamonds Are a Guerilla's Best Friend," *Fielding Worldwide* (1998).

10. Rubin, "Army of One's Own."

11. Executive Outcomes (EO). Corporate Webpage: www.eo.com, accessed March 7, 1998. The site is no longer available, but maintained on archives listed in the Appendix.

12. The following information is compiled from Yves Goulet, "Mixing Business with Bullets," *Jane's Intelligence Review* (September 1997); Chris Gordon, "Mercenaries Grab Gems," *Weekly Mail & Guardian,* May 9, 1997; Shearer, *Private Armies,* 43; Isenberg, *Soldiers of Fortune.*

13. Tim Spicer, *An Unorthodox Soldier: Peace and War and the Sandline Affair* (Edinburgh: Mainstream Publishing, 1999), and Jonathon Carr-Brown, "Sandline 'Paid Bribe' to Win War Contract," *Sunday Times,* July 2, 2000. http://www.sundaytimes.co.uk/news/pages/sti/2000/07/02/stinwenwso1024.html

14. *The Impasse in Sierra Leone,* Center for Democracy and Development (London, U.K.), www.cdd.org.uk/pubs/sierraleone.htm accessed December 1999.

15. As quoted in Gordon, "Mercenaries Grab Gems."

16. *Impasse in Sierra Leone.*

17. Shearer, *Private Armies;* Venter, "Market Forces."

18. *Impasse in Sierra Leone.*

19. Spicer, "Unorthodox Soldier," p. 190.

20. Goulet, "Mixing Business"; Pech and Beresford, 1997; Al J. Venter, "Gunships for Hire," *Flight International* (August 21, 1996): 32; Al J. Venter, "Sierra Leone's Mercenary War," *Jane's International Defense Review* (November 1995).

21. Rubin, "Army of One's Own," p. 46.

22. EO webpage.

23. Ibid.

24. "Crude Awakening: The Role of the Oil and Banking Industries in Angola's Civil War and the Plunder of State Assets," A report by Global Witness (February 2000). Available at: http://www.oneworld.org/globalwitness/

25. Ibid.; UN Development Programme, *UN Human Development Index 2000.* Available at http://www.undp.org/hdr2000/english/HDR2000.html

26. Arnaldo Simoes, *Africa Portuguesa: A Colonizacao Construiu e a Descolonizacao?* (Torres Novas: Grafica Almondina, 1998). *Angola em chamas* (Queluz, Portugal: Edicao Literal, 1977); Blaine Harden, "Africa's Gems: Warfare's Best Friend," *New York Times,* April 6, 2000.

27. Spicer, *Unorthodox Soldier,* p. 144, O'Brien, "Military Advisory Groups," p. 98.

28. Spicer, *Unorthodox Soldier,* p. 144.

29. O'Brien, "Military-Advisory Groups," p. 98.

30. Stephaans Brummer, "Investing in the Bibles and Bullets Business," *Weekly Mail & Guardian,* September 16, 1994.

31. Spicer, *Unorthodox Soldier,* p. 46.

32. Shearer, *Private Armies*. Many in the firm felt that Clinton was actually shilling for MPRI. Interview with PMF executives, May 2000, June 2001.

33. Spicer, *Unorthodox Soldier,* p. 44

34. Philip van Niekerk as quoted in Shearer, *Private Armies,* 48.

35. Shearer, *Private Armies,* 48. Likewise, regional observers claimed "Beyond dispute is that the South Africans, who handle intelligence, logistics, communications, training, and planning, have made all the difference between a fighting force and an ill-disciplined band." Herbert Howe, "Global Order and Security Privatization," *Strategic Forum,* no. 140 (May 1998): 38.

36. Marina Jimenez, "Canadians Seek Fortune in Land of Anarchy, Violence," *The National Post* (Canada), August 23, 1999, available at http://www.nationalpost.com/news .asp?f=990823/61015.html.

37. International Crisis Group (ICG). *Sierra Leone: Time for a New Military and Political Strategy,* ICG Africa Report no. 28 (April 11, 2001).

38. United Nations Development Programme, UN Human Development Index 2000, available at http://undp.org/hdr2000/english/HDR2000.html.

39. Ryan Lizza, "Sierra Leone, the Last Clinton Betrayal," *The New Republic,* July 2000. http://www.tnr.com/072400/lizza072400.html.

40. For more on the doctrine behind this, see P. W. Singer, "Caution: Children at War," *Parameters* 31, no. 4 (Winter 2001).

41. The practice had its roots in attempts to scare the populace from voting in elections; the government's slogan had been, "The future is in your hands." ICG, April 2001, p. 10.

42. Al J. Venter, "Sierra Leone's Mercenary War," *Jane's International Defense Review,* November 1995.

43. Rubin, "Army of One's Own," 47.

44. Alex Vines, "Mercenaries and the Privatisation of Security in Africa in the 1990s," in *The Privatisation of Security in Africa,* ed. Greg Mills and John Stremlau (Pretoria: South Africa Institute of International Affairs, 1999), p. 70. This episode demonstrates two things: the significant variation in the effectiveness and impact of privatized military firms, and the dangers of reliance on a private firm that can exit a contractual relationship at any time (discussed further in Chapter 11). Negative publicity from this ensured that GSG was no longer able to get lucrative contacts. At last information, it remains little more than a letterhead company.

45. Vines, "Mercenaries," in *Privatisation,* ed. Mills and Stremlau, 53. Reportedly, the firm Branch, now Diamondworks, got the concessions in a deal that had them pay a base of $250,000 base rent a year ($50,000 to local chief) and give the government 5 percent of diamonds and 37 percent of the net profits It must be noted that the participants involved deny these linkages. The question still remains then, how and why the SL government got the money.

46. William Reno, "Foreign Firms, Natural Resources, and Violent Political Economies," *Social Science Forum,* March 21, 2000.

47. Peter Fabricus, "Private Security Firms Can End Africa's Wars Cheaply," *Saturday Star (Johannesburg),* September 23, 2000. This attitude stands in sharp contrast to the fear of the RUF, that the UN peacekeeping mission in Sierra Leone has displayed.

48. Stuart McGhie, "Private Military Companies: Soldiers of Fortune," *Jane's Defense Weekly,* May 22, 2002.

49. Glenn McKenzie, "Unruly Militia Defends Sierra Leone," *Associated Press,* July 5, 2000.

50. Shearer, *Private Armies,* p. 51.

51. Khareen Pech and David Beresford, "Africa's New Look"; Khareen Pech and Yusef Hassan, "Sierra Leone's Faustian Bargain," *Weekly Mail & Guardian,* May 20, 1997.

52. ICG, "Sierra Leone," April 2001.

53. Marina Jimenez, "Canadians Seek Fortune in Land of Anarchy, Violence," *National Post* (Canada), August 23, 1999. http://www.nationalpost.com/news.asp?f-990823/61015 .html

54. Allan Robinson et al. "Mercenaries Eye Sierra Leone," (Toronto) *Globe & Mail,* Au-

gust 1, 1997; Colum Lynch, "U.S., Britain Implicated in Africa Coup," *Boston Globe,* May 9, 1998.

55. The Kabila government failed to pay for its end of the contract and ultimately stranded part of the EO force in the field, leading the firm to end the contract and withdraw from the country.

56. Douglas Brooks, "The Business End of Military Intelligence: Private Military Companies," *Military Intelligence Professional Bulletin,* September 1999.

57. Alex Vines, "The Business of Peace: 'Tiny' Rowland, Financial Incentives and the Mozambican Settlement," *Accord: An International Review of Peace Initiatives.* http://www.c-r .org/acc_moz/contents_moz.htm.

58. Reno, "Foreign Firms," p. 47.

59. O'Brien, "Military-Advisory Groups," pp. 50–53.

60. Isenberg, *Soldiers of Fortune.*

61. Vines, "The Business of Peace," p. 2.

62. Chris Gordon, "Mercenaries Grab Gems," *Weekly Mail & Guardian,* May 9, 1997.

63. Herbert Howe, "To Stabilize Tottering African Governments," *Armed Forces Journal International* (November 1996).

64. Brummer, "Investing."

65. As quoted in Danicl Burton-Rose and Wayne Madsen, "Government of, by, and for the Corporations: Corporate Soldiers: The U.S. Government Privatizes the Use of Force," *Multinational Monitor* 20, no. 3 (March 1999). Available at: http://www.essential.org/monitor/ mm1999/mm9903.07.html#rose

66. Republic of South Africa, Foreign Military Assistance Bill No. 54 of 1997, Pretoria: Ministry of Defence, April 1997.

67. Interview with PMF executives, Feb. 2001, June 2001.

68. Kim Nossal, "Bulls to Bears: The Privatization of War in the 1990s," in *War, Money, and Survival,* ed. Gilles Carbonnier (Geneva: ICRC, February 2000); Christopher Clapham, "Africa Security Systems: Privatisation and the Scope for Mercenary Activity," in *Privatisation of Security in Africa,* ed. Mills and Stremlau, p. 40; Chris Dietrich, "The Commercialisation of Military Deployment in Africa," *African Security Review* 9, no. 1 (January 2000).

69. "Executive Outcomes implicated in recruiting mercenaries," *SABC News* (July 27, 2000). http://www.sabcnews.com/SABCnews/africa/central_africa/1,1009,2388,00.html

70. Correspondence with PMF executive, July 2000.

8. THE MILITARY CONSULTING FIRM: MPRI

1. Colum Lynch, "For U.S. Firms War Becomes a Business," *Boston Globe,* February 1, 1997.

2. David Shearer, *Private Armies and Military Intervention* (London: International Institute for Strategic Studies, Adelphi Paper no. 316, February 1998), p. 39. The difference in backgrounds is key. MPRI is primarily made up of retired senior-level personnel, most of whom would not be involved in a direct-combat role, even if they were still in the active duty military.

3. Steve Alvarez, "MPRI: A Private Military," *Stars and Stripes,* October 30, 2000.

4. Marco Mesic, "Croats Trained by Pentagon Generals," *Balcanica,* May 1996.

5. Paul De La Garza and David Adams, "Military Aid . . . From the Private Sector," *St. Petersburg Times,* December 3, 2000.

6. Ed Soyster quoted in Paul De La Garza and David Adams, "Military Know-How Finds Niche—And Some Critics," *St. Petersburg Times,* December 3, 2000.

7. John Donahue, *The Privatization Decision: Public Ends, Private Means* (New York: Basic Books, 1989), p. 218. It was generally known that MPRI would get the contract before the actual announcement was made. U.S. House of Representatives, "The Current Situation in Bosnia and the Former Yugoslavia and Preparations of U. S. Forces for Operation Joint Endeavor—Moliani-Levin Delegation," December 4, 1995.

8. Ken Silverstein, "Privatizing War," *The Nation,* July 7, 1998.

9. Interview, Sarajevo November 1996, July 1999.

10. Although still in this position in 1995, Sewall made several trips to Bosnia and Croatia, where many observers believed his team was providing the U.S.'s new allies with military advice, in violation of the UN embargo. MPRI was under suspicion at the time for aiding the Croat force. As a French commander commented on their visit to the former Yugoslavia, "If they are not involved in military planning, then what are they doing there? Are we supposed to believe Sewall and his people are tourists?" Silverstein, "Mercenary, Inc."

11. Military Professional Resources Incorporated (MPRI). Webpage: www.mpri.com.

12. Shearer, *Private Armies.*

13. Raymond Bonner, "War Crimes Panel Finds Croat Troops 'Cleansed' the Serbs," *New York Times,* March 20, 1999.

14. The site comes up as the third most popular site that mentions the firm.

15. Of interest, the firm's reaction has not been the standard denials of the allegations and legal action that most corporations take when challenged so publicly. Instead, it reportedly has focused on shutting down the site through electronic means and discovering the anonymous contributors. Interview with site administrator, July 2000. The interview was conducted over e-mail, through an "anonymyzer" program, to protect the identity of the interviewee.

16. Alvarez, *MPRI.* Deborah Avant, "Privatizing Military Training: A Challenge to U.S. Army Professionalism," in *The Future of the Army Profession,* ed. Don Snider (New York: McGraw Hill, 2002).

17. Marcia Triggs, "Army Contracts Out Recruiting," *Officer* 78, no. 3 (April 1, 2002).

18. Department of the Army *Contracting Support on the Battlefield.* FM 100–10–2. April 15, 1999; Department of the Army. *Contractors on the Battlefield.* FM 100–21. Washington: Headquarters. September, 1999.

19. "Operation Storm," *New York Review of Books,* October 22, 1998; Richard Holbrooke, *To End a War* (New York: Random House, 1998), see chapter on Washington Conference.

20. U.S. Senate, *U.S. Senate Select Committee Report on Iran/Bosnia Arms Transfers,* 1996. Available at http://www.parascope.com/articles/0197/bosnia.htm; Maud Beelma, "Dining with the Devil: America's 'Tacit Cooperation' with Iran in Arming the Bosnians," *APF Reporter* 18, no. 2 (1996); "Hypocrisy in Action: What's the Real Iran-Bosnia Scandal?" *New Yorker,* May 13, 1996.

21. David Isenberg, *Soldiers of Fortune Ltd.: A Profile of Today's Private Sector Corporate Mercenary Firms* (Center for Defense Information Monography, November 1997).

22. Shearer, *Private Armies,* 58.

23. Mesic, "Croats Trained by Pentagon Generals."

24. United Nations, "Report of the Monitors of European Union on Violations of Human Rights of the Serbs during and after Operation 'Storm,'" October 17, 1995. Available at http://www.aimpress.org/dyn/trae/archive/data/199510/51017–003–trae-zag.htm

25. Raymond Bonner, "U.S. Reportedly Backed British Mercenary Group in Africa," *New York Times,* May 13, 1998.

26. Interview with U.S. government official, Sarajevo, November 1996.

27. Roger Charles, a retired U.S. Marine colonel turned military researcher, as quoted in Silverstein, "Mercenary, Inc."

28. Quote from Paul Harris, "Bosnians Sign for U.S. Military Expertise," *Jane's Sentinel Pointer,* July 1996. See also, De La Garza, "Military Know-How," and "Operation Storm," *New York Review of Books,* October 22, 1998. Eager, 1995. Samantha Knight et al., "The Croatian Army's Friends," *U.S. News & World Report,* August 21, 1995, p. 41.

29. As quoted in Laura Silber and Alan Little, *Yugoslavia: Death of a Nation* (New York: Penguin Books, 1997), p. 357. This assessment is not surprising if *MPRI* was involved; its personnel were those who actually 'wrote' the textbook and ran the staff colleges.

30. As quoted in Juan Carlos Zarate, "The Emergence of a New Dog of War: Private International Security companies, International Law, and the New World Order," *Stanford Journal of International Law* 34 (Winter 1998): 75–156.

31. Halberstam, pp. 335–336.

32. Silverstein, "Mercenary, Inc."

33. De La Garza, "Military Know-How."

34. Zarate, "Emergence."

35. As quoted in Halberstam, p. 336.

36. In talks to congressional representatives, it was reported that " [Assistant] Secretary Holbrooke [had] suggested that a U.S. consulting firm, Military Professional Resources Incorporated [MPRI], of Alexandria, Virginia, might be selected to conduct the arm-and-train program. He did not reveal through what legal and other mechanisms this might be pursued." U.S. House of Representatives. *The Current Situation in Bosnia and the Former Yugoslavia and Preparations of U.S. Forces for Operation Joint Endeavor—Moliari-Levin Delegation,* Trip Report, December 11, 1995. This was long before either the contract competition with the other firms or even the Ankara Conference.

37. Interview with General William Boice, retired. Conducted in Sarajevo, November 7, 1996.

38. U.S. Department of State, transcript of Briefing by Ambassador Pardew, July 24, 1996.

39. Tammy Arbucki, "Building a Bosnian Army," *Jane's International Defense Review,* August 1997.

40. Interview conducted in Sarajevo, November 1996.

41. Thomas Valasek, "Bosnia: Five Years Later," *Defense Monitor,* December 2000.

42. As quoted in Bradley Graham, "Ex-GIs Work to Give Bosnian Force a Fighting Chance," *Washington Post,* January 29, 1997.

43. Stephen Hedges, "Out of D.C., Cheney Still Carried Clout," *Chicago Tribune,* August 10, 2000.

44. Stavros Tzimas, "U.S. Trains Both Camps in FYROM," *Kathimeini,* July 20, 2001. The Croat army accepted individuals of any nationality who were opposed to the Serbs and, thus had a high number of ethnic Albanians, angry over their treatment in Kosovo.

45. Yves Goulet, "MPRI: Washington's Freelance Advisors," *Jane's Intelligence Review,* July 1998.

46. Zarate, "Emergence of a New Dog."

47. EO felt that it was pressure from the U.S. government (and phone calls from President Clinton himself) that caused it to lose the contract, but a contributing factor was also Savimbi's refusal to sign the Lusaka accords until EO agreed to leave.

48. Shearer, *Private Armies,* 63.

49. "Generals Accused of Corruption: American Defense Firms Gives Up Angolan Contract." Jornal Digital (Portuguese online newspaper), October 25, 2000. Such off-budget bonuses are typical in Angolan business. According to the U.S. Department of the Energy, Angolan officials received $900 million in bonuses/payoffs last year from foreign oil companies.

50. Further information on ACRI is available at the U.S. military and State Department websites: http://www.eucom.mil/programs/acri/ and http://www.usinfo.state.gov/regional/af/acri/facto500.htm

51. Further information on ACSS is available at: http://www.africacenter.org/

52. Jason Sherman, "Arm's Length," *Armed Forces Journal International* (September 2000): 30.

53. Justin Brown, "The Rise of the Private-Sector Military," *Christian Science Monitor,* July 5, 2000.

54. On the Freedom House measures of freedom, Equatorial Guinea received the worst scores, tying with countries such as North Korea and Iraq. http://www.freedomhouse.org/ratings/index.htm. The country has also been prominently featured in reports by Amnesty International, the State Department World Report on Human Rights, and the UN Commission on Human Rights.

55. Brown, "Rise of the Private-Sector Military." Operations began later in 2000. MPRI was paid by the regime, which reportedly received the monies for the contract from Amerada Hess, Mobil Oil, and other big multinational corporations that have recently begun off-

shore drilling (and hence the need for a better coastal force). For more on the oil contracts, see Ken Silverstein, "U.S. Oil Politics in the "Kuwait of Africa," *Nation,* April 22, 2002. www.thenation.com

56. Steven Dudley, "Colombia Vows End To Abuses," *Washington Post,* July 22, 2000, p. 15.

57. De La Garza and Adams, "Military Aid . . . From the Private Sector."

58. Ibid.; interview with U.S. government official, June 2001.

59. Paul De La Garza, and David Adams, "Contract's End Hints of Colombia Trouble," *St. Petersburg Times,* May 13, 2001.

60. "L-3 Communications Announces Acquisition of MPRI," *Business Wire, July 18,* 2000.

61. Ibid., as quoted.

62. New contracts include work for the state of South Carolina on homeland security planning. "L-3 Communications Announces First Quarter 2002 Results," *Cambridge Telecom Report,* April 29, 2002.

9. MILITARY SUPPORT FIRM: BRS

1. As quoted in Tom Ricks and Greg Schneider, "Cheney's Firm Profited From 'Overused' Army," *Washington Post* (September 9, 2000): P. 6.

2. George Cahlink, "Army of Contractors," *Government Executive,* February 2002.

3. Tim Cross, "Logistic Support for UK Expeditionary Operations," *RUSI Journal,* (February 2000).

4. Corporate history from Halliburton website. http://www.halliburton.com/corp/whoweare/about_background.asp

5. Financial information about Halliburton (HAL) on www.etrade.com and Halliburton, *Halliburton 2000 Annual Report to* Investors, available at http://www.halliburton.com/corp/ir/ir.asp

6. Diana Henriques, "Mixed Reviews for Cheney in Chief Executive Role at *Halliburton,*" *New York Times,* August 24, 2000.

7. Ibid.

8. Dugger continues, "That was the turning point. He wouldn't have been in the running without Brown & Root's money and airplanes. And the 1948 election allowed Lyndon to become president." Ronnie Dugger as quoted in Robert Bryce, "The Candidate From Brown & Root," *Austin Chronicle,* August 25, 2000.

9. As quoted in Bryce, "Candidate From Brown & Root." For more on the LBJ link, see also Robert A. Caro, *The Path to Power* (New York: Vintage Books, 1990); Ronnie Dugger, *The Politician: The Life and Times of Lyndon Johnson* (New York: Norton, 1982).

10. Ricks and Schneider, "Cheney's Firm Profited from 'Overused Army.'"

11. As quoted in Stephen Hedges, "Out of D.C., Cheney Still Carried Clout," *Chicago Tribune,* August 10, 2000.

12. Karen Gullo, "Peacekeeping Helped Cheney Company," *Associated Press,* August 28, 2000.

13. Donald T. Wynn, "Managing the Logistics-Support Contract in the Balkans Theater," *Engineer,* July 2000. http://call.army.mil/call/trngqtr/tq4-oo/wynn.htm.

14. Wynn, "Managing the Logistical Support."

15. Nathan Hodge, "Brown & Root Poised to Win Base Work in Central Asia," *Defense Week,* April 29, 2002, p. 1.

16. As quoted in Ricks and Schneider, "Cheney's Firm Profited from 'Overused Army.'"

17. Interview with U.S. troops in Bosnia, August 1999. The author also enjoyed several lunches at the BRS-run dining facilities, including the best steak I had in Bosnia (the competition being admittedly weak).

18. General Accounting Office, "Contingency Operations: Army Should Do More to Control Contract Cost in the Balkans," NSDIAD-oo–225. October 6, 2000. http://www.gao.gov/; Gullo, "Peacekeeping Helped Cheney Company."

19. Larry Margasak, "Report on Cheney, Bathrooms," *Associated Press,* September 10, 2000. The firm cited the "cultural differences" in restroom behavior.

20. Scott Schonauer, "Hacker Sends Costly Virus to Brown & Root," *European Stars and Stripes*, February 7, 2001, p. 3.

21. Pratap Chatterjee, "Soldiers of Fortune," *San Francisco Bay Guardian*, May 6, 2002. www.sfbg.com/

22. *Halliburton 1999 Annual Report to Investors*. Available at http://www.halliburton.com/corp/ir/ir.asp

23. "Cheney, Halliburton Sued," CNN.com, July 9, 2002; "Halliburton Falls on SEC Probe," *CNN.com*, May 29, 2002.

24. Bryce, "Candidate from Brown & Root."

25. Terry Allen-Mills, "France's Scandal Trail Leads to U.S.," *Times*, December 31, 2000. http://www.sunday-times.co.uk/

26. General Accounting Office, "Contingency Operations: Opportunities to Improve the Logistics Civil Augmentation Program," GAO/NSIAD-97-63 (February 1997).

27. Bryce, "The Candidate from Brown & Root."

28. Ricks and Schneider, "Cheney's Firm Profited from 'Overused Army.'"

29. Ibid.

30. General Accounting Office, "Contingency Operations: Opportunities to Improve."

31. From Halliburton website. http://www.halliburton.com/BRS/brsss/ brsss_1199_balkansd.asp

32. Wynn, "Managing the Logistics-Support"; Gullo, "Peacekeeping Helped Cheney Company."

33. Bosnia, Croatia, Hungary; Wynn, "Managing the Logistics-Support."

34. Ibid.

35. Ibid.

36. Ibid. Many of these men and women who were not deployed would have had to been mobilized from National Guard and Reserve units, which would have made Congressional support even more difficult to obtain. This is discussed further in Part III.

37. Interview with PMF executive, June 2001.

38. General Accounting Office, Contingency Operations: Army Should Do More.

39. Hodge, 2002, p. 1.

40. Chris Hawley, "Contractor Aids U.S. Afghan Base," *Newsday*, October 6, 2002.

41. As Vice President Cheney noted on the campaign trail, "Over the last decade, commitments worldwide have gone up by 300 percent, while our military forces have been cut by 40 percent." As quoted in Ricks and Schneider, "Cheney's Firm Profited from 'Overused Army.'"

42. As quoted in Gullo, "Peacekeeping Helped Cheney Company."

43. Ibid.

44. *Halliburton 1999 Annual Report to Investors*.

45. "U.S. Firm to Retrieve Russian Sub," *Guardian*, October 3, 2000.

10. CONTRACTUAL DILEMMAS

1. John Donahue, *The Privatization Decision* (New York: Basic Books, 1989), 38.

2. Carl Clausewitz, *On War*, translated by Peter Paret (Princeton: Princeton University Press, 1976), 119.

3. *Privatization 1997: A Comprehensive Report on Contracting, Privatization, and Government Reform*. Reason Public Policy Institute, 11th Annual Report on Privatization 1997.

4. John D. Hanrahan, *Government By Contract* (New York: Norton, 1983), 115.

5. Ibid., 122.

6. However, prime contractors may use local or third country subcontractors as well as organic assets. Department of the Army, *Logistics: Army Contractors on the Battlefield*, Regulation 715–XX, January 31, 1999.

7. Donahue, *Privatization Decision*, 218.

8. Doug Brooks, "Write a Cheque, End a War: Using Private Military Companies to End African Conflicts," *Conflict Trends*, no. 6 (July 2000); Spicer, 1999.

9. David Shichor, *Punishment for Profit: Private Prisons/Public Concerns* (Thousand Oaks, Calif.: Sage Publications, 1995); AbdelFatau Musah and Kayode Fayemi, *Mercenaries: An African Security Dilemma* (London: Pluto Press, 2000).

10. General Accounting Office, "Contingency Operations: Opportunities to Improve the Logistics Civil Augmentation Program," GAO/NSIAD-97–63, February 1997.

11. General Accounting Office, "Contingency Operations: Army Should Do More to Control Contract Cost in the Balkans," NSDIAD-00–225, October 6, 2000. http://www.gao .gov/; Gregory Piatt, "GAO Report: Balkans Contracts Too Costly," *European Stars and Stripes*, November 14, 2000, p. 4.

12. Interview with U.S. government official, Sarajevo, July 1999. Unsurprisingly, similar issues regularly trouble clients working with the management consultant industry, the parallel to this sector. Interviews with management consultants, January 1999.

13. Shichor, *Punishment for Profit*, 122.

14. Interview with UNMIK personnel, summer 1999; O'Meara, "Dyncorp Disgrace." *Insight*, February 4, 2002.

15. Hanrahan, *Government By Contract*, 59.

16. General Accounting Office, "Contingency Operations: Army Should Do More.".

17. This may be in contravention of U.S. laws that forbid inappropriate contact of retired military officers with the current force, including working on any contracts that have anything to do with their previous organizations they just left, but no one has been prosecuted for it. Hanrahan, *Government by Contract*, 32.

18. Deborah Avant, "In Focus: Privatizing Military Training," *Foreign Policy In Focus* 5, no. 17 (May 2000). http://www.foreignpolicy-infocus.org/briefs/vol5/v5n17mil.html

19. Thomas J. Milton, "The New Mercenaries—Corporate Armies for Hire," Foreign Area Officers Association Journal, 1997.

20. The fact that industry employees do not have any union protection only underscores their dependence on the goodwill of firm management and the impetus to turn a profit. Shichor, *Punishment for Profit*, 56.

21. Donahue, *Privatization Decision*, 54.

22. Ashton Carter and John White, *Keeping the Edge* (Cambridge: MIT Press, 2001), 187.

23. Donahue, *Privatization Decision*, 105.

24. Jean Tirole, *The Theory of Industrial Organization* (Cambridge, Mass.: MIT Press, 1988), 29–49.

25. General Accounting Office, "Contingency Operations: Army Should Do More to Control Contract Cost in the Balkans." NSDIAD-00–225. October 6, 2000. http://www .gao.gov/

26. Interviews with a PMF employee and a U.S. government official, Sarajevo, July 1999.

27. Ibid.; Katie Merx, "Cop Fired From Kosovo Job," *Detroit News*, February 25, 2000.

28. As quoted in Kelly Patricia O'Meara, "Broken Wings," *Insight*, April 8, 2002. The RICO lawsuit was *Johnston v. DynCorp Inc., et al.* in the Texas' 17th District Court. After losing a similar case in Britain, involving the wrongful firing of another DynCorp "whistleblower," the company settled the Texas case. DynCorp, though, continues to deny any wrongdoing.

29. Kelly Patricia O'Meara, "Broken Wings," *Insight*, April 29, 2002.

30. In the BRS contract, two functions were partially taken over by U.S. military personnel and the other one contracted to another company. The only area that came under the original cost projection was just $3.5 million less and was based on a worst case scenario planning that did not occur and thus could not be billed for. General Accounting Office, "Contingency Operations: Opportunities to Improve the Logistics Civil Augmentation Program," GAO/NSIAD-97-63, February 1997; Piatt, "GAO Report: Balkans," 4; Alex Vines, "Mercenaries and the Privatisation of Security in Africa in the 1990s," in *The Privatisation of Security in Africa*, ed. Greg Mills and John Stremlau (Johannesburg: South Africa Institute of International Affairs, 1999), 62.

31. William Washington, "Subcontracting as a Solution, Not a Problem in Outsourcing," *Acquisition Review Quarterly* (Winter 1997): 79–86.

32. Avant, "In Focus: Privatizing Military Training"; see also Susan Gates and Albert Robert, "Comparing the Cost of DoD Military and Civil Service Personnel," *RAND Report,* MR-980-OSD (1998).

33. Duncan Showers, "Are We Ready to Fight and Win the Next War?" *Contractors on the Battlefield,* Air Force Logistics Management Agency, December 1999. General Accounting Office, "Outsourcing DoD Logistics: Savings Achievable But Defense Science Board's Projections Are Overstated," NSIAD-98-48, December 8, 1997.

34. James Murphy, "DoD Outsources $500m in Spare Parts Work," PlanetGov.com, September 29, 2000.

35. This was at the heart of Machiavelli's opposition to mercenaries.

36. Similarly, during the French and Indian War, the two sides employed one of the most clear-cut schemes for generating performance incentives among their hired Indian allies by offering piece rates, whereby a bounty was paid for human scalps. But, even this straightforward system failed to solve the principal-agent problem in the mercenary market. Doubts arose as to whether the scalps all came from the heads of enemies, or as "the scalp of a Frenchman was not distinguishable from the scalp of an Englishman, and could be had with less trouble." Francis Parkman, *France and England in North America* (New York: Library of America, 1983), 2:217.

37. United Nations, *Report of the Panel on United Nations Peace Operations,* A/55/305, S/2000/809, August 21, 2000.

38. Herbert Howe, "Global Order and Security Privatization," *Strategic Forum,* no. 140 (May 1998). In the Biafra war, Nigeria's hired air force failed to bomb Biafra's only airport, since their salaries were based on the months in service rather than results. Mallett described a similar phenomenon in the Middle Ages, "The state wanted quick and inexpensive victories; the condottieri wanted to make their living and save their skins." Michael Mallett, *Mercenaries and their Masters: Warfare in Renaissance Italy* (Totowa, N.J.: Rowman and Littlefield, 1974), 101–102.

39. Kevin Whitelaw, "The Russians Are Coming," *U.S. News and World Report,* March 15, 1999; Thomas Adams, "The New Mercenaries and the Privatization of Conflict," *Parameters,* (Summer 1999): p. 103–116. http://carlisle-www.army.mil/usawc/Parameters/99summer/adams.htm. The company sold Su-27 fighter planes, equivalent to the F-15, but also supplied the pilots, technicians, and ground control staff to operate them.

40. Gennady Charodeev, "Foreign Wars: Russian Generals Involved in a War between Ethiopia and Eritrea," *Izvestia,* May 26, 2000, p1, 4; Whitelaw, "The Russians Are Coming."; Greg Noakes, "Israeli Commandos' Congo Connection," *Washington Report on Middle East Affairs,* April/May 1994, p. 22. http://www.washington-report.org/backissues/0494/9404022.htm

41. As one Chechen rebel put it, "With money, anything's possible." "Russian Contract Soldiers in Chechnya Poor Quality, Often Quit," RFE/RL, October 2, 2000.http://www.russiatoday.com/news.php3?id=20534. "Arms, Money, and the Men: A Year of War in Chechnya," *Agence France Presse,* September 28, 2000. http://www.russiatoday.com/news.php3?id=204189

42. Corbus Claassens, as quoted in Marcia Lutyens, "Military Operations (ex VAT)," *Volkskrant* (Netherlands), February 17, 2001.

43. Nicholas Rufford and Pete Sawyer. "Death Crash and 'Secret UK Arms Deals,'" *Sunday Times,* November 19, 2000. http://www.sunday-times.co.uk/news/pages/sti/2000/11/19/stifgnafro2001.html
Again, this report is unconfirmed. The firms obviously vehemently deny his claim and have pursued legal action regarding its publication. The main claimant, a former employee of the firms, has since died in a car crash.

44. "British Firms Arming Sierra Leone Rebels," *London Sunday Times,* January 10, 1999. The firm also supplied rebel forces in Congo.

45. Avinash Dixit and Susan Skeath, *Games of Strategy* (New York: W. W. Norton, 1999), 259–263; James D. Morrow, *Game Theory for Political Scientists* (Princeton: Princeton University Press, 1994), chapter 9.

46. Anthony Mockler, *Mercenaries* (London: Macdonald, and Company 1969).

47. The fear of abandonment by hired forces was particularly felt in specialty areas that the rest of the force needed, such as, for example, that the French army refused to allow the Foreign Legion expand to artillery or cavalry units for fear of hamstringing the rest of its force. Douglas Porch, *The French Foreign Legion* (New York: Harper Collins, 1991).

48. J. Michael Brower, "Outsourcing at DOD: All It's Cracking People Up to Be?" *Military Review* 77 (November–December 1997): p. 67–68. http://wwwcgsc.army.mil/milrev/English/novdec97/insights.htm

49. Kathleen Melymuka, "Kaboom! The Field of IT Outsourcing Is Dotted with Land Mines," *Computerworld*, March 17, 1997. http://www.computerworld.com/cwi/story/0,1199,NAV47_STO1331,00.html

50. David Pugliese, "Canadian Troops Trapped in Shipping Dispute," *Ottawa Citizen*, July 25, 2000. http://www.ottawacitizen.com/national/000725/4506340.html Disturbingly, the U.S. Marines have since launched a similar contracted military transport system for forces in the Pacific.

51. GSG has since lost its business, but the rest of its former employees may be more happy to have made it out in one piece.

52. Stephen Zamparrelli, "Contractors on the Battlefield: What Have We Signed Up For?" Air War College Research report, March 1999.

53. Gordon Campbell, *Contractors on the Battlefield: The Ethics of Paying Civilians to Enter Harm's Way and Requiring Soldiers to Depend upon Them,* Joint Services Conference on Professional Ethics 2000, Springfield, Va., January 27–28, 2000.

54. Zamparrelli, "Contractors on the Battlefield?" 28.

55. In fact, in certain instances in the 1991 Gulf War, civilian contractor personnel walked off their jobs after chemical attack warnings. Ibid., 21; Maria Dowling and Vincent Feck, "Joint Logistics and Engineering Contract," *Contractors on the Battlefield* (Air Force Logistics Management Agency, December 1999).

56. Zamparrelli, "Contractors on the Battlefield?" 22.

57. Interview with PMF employee, June 2001.

58. Howard Michitsch, "Armed Forces Program Hits Snag," *Ottawa Citizen* August 25, 2001; Michael Evans, "Navy Dock Workers Threaten to Strike Over Privatisation Plans," *Times,* March 26, 2002.

59. John Keegan, *The First World War* (New York: Vintage Books, 1999), 239.

60. Zamparrelli, "Contractors on the Battlefield?" 7.

61. Department of the Army, *Logistics: Army Contractors on the Battlefield,* Regulation 715–XX, January 31, 1999.

62. Zamparrelli, "Contractors on the Battlefield?" viii.

63. Martin Van Creveld, *The Rise and Decline of the State* (Cambridge: Cambridge University Press, 1999), p. 317.

64. Zamparrelli, "Contractors on the Battlefield?" 18.

65. John Toland, *Battle: The Story of the Bulge* (New York: Bison Books, 1999).

66. "And from what I saw in Somalia . . . they could very easily have to throw down their wrenches and get off their laptops and pick up a weapon. We can't think it's just the Rangers or just the infantry that are going to fight the battles. It's going to be everybody." [Black Hawk Down] doesn't tell . . . how our cooks literally had to pick up their body armor and their weapons and go out to the city and fight as part to this force. It doesn't talk about the mechanics who had to go out and repair the vehicles that were virtually destroyed. It doesn't talk about all the communications guys who are working to get the communications up and running so all the different elements can speak to each other. Sgt. Eversmann, USA Army, as quoted in Franklin Fisher, "Somali Ranger Veteran Stresses Value of Support Troops," *Stars & Stripes,* April 03, 2001.

67. Campbell, *Contractors on the Battlefield: Ethics.*

68. Hanrahan, *Government by Contract,* 195. One former KGB spy called the private firm's security "a joke" and used access through one firm to steal U.S. military secrets.

69. Showers, "Are We Ready to Fight?"

70. Joseph Michels, "A Civil Sector Force Multiplier for the Operational Commander," *Global Thinking, Global Logistics,* Air Force Logistics Management Agency, December 1999.

71. Duncan Campbell, "Now Showing on Satellite TV: Secret American Spy Photos," *Guardian,* June 13, 2002.

72. Machiavelli, *Prince,* chapter 12.

73. Larry Taulbee, "Reflections on the Mercenary Option," *Small Wars and Insurgencies,* 9, no.2 (Autumn 1998): pp. 145–163.

74. Spicer, *Unorthodox Soldier,* 25.

75. William McNeill, *The Pursuit of Power* (Chicago: University of Chicago Press, 1982), p. 75.

76. Mockler, *Mercenaries,* 205. In fact, Mockler described revolt in these situations as near "inevitable."

77. Anthony Mockler, *The New Mercenaries* (London: Sidgewick & Jackson, 1985), 31.

78. "Eyewitnesses in Marten-Sho reported that a convoy consisting of approximately 150 mercenaries and accompanied by a Russian army unit was heading toward the village. When the units approached the village, a number of Russian attack helicopters approached and proceeded to fire on the mercenaries killing them all. The Russian army unit that accompanied the mercenaries, also took place in the attack and made sure no mercenary survived the incident. The coordination between the helicopters and ground units indicate that the attack was no accident." "Russia Betrays 150 Mercenaries," www.qoqaz.net, November 19, 2000. It must be noted that this is an unconfirmed report from Chechen sources.

79. Interview with PMF executive, February 2000.

80. Ibid.

81. Khareen Pech and Yusef Hassan, "Sierra Leone's Faustian Bargain," *Weekly Mail & Guardian,* May 20, 1997.

82. The business parallel is the recent rise of "consulting for equity," where the outside firm is paid in stock shares, rather than by traditional billing.

83. Chris Dietrich, "The Commercialisation of Military Deployment in Africa," *African Security Review* 9, no. 1 (January 2000).

84. Venter, "Market Forces."

85. Goulet, "Mixing Business With Bullets."

86. William Reno, *Warlord Politics and African States* (London: Lynne Rienner, 1998).

87. "Crude Awakening: The Role of the Oil and Banking Industries in Angola's Civil War and the Plunder of State Assets," a report by Global Witness, February 2000, available at http://www.oneworld.org/globalwitness/

88. Samuel Aoul et al. "Towards a Spiral of Violence?-The Dangers of Privatizing Risk Management in Africa," Memorandum, Working Group on Human Rights in Congo Development and Peace, Mining Watch Canada, February 2000.

89. "Crude Awakening."

90. The term is taken from the context of local service contracting. In this environment, "strategic privatization" is aimed at reducing the collective realm of big government versus "tactical privatization" aimed at reducing budget costs. PMFs obviously uses "strategic" in the military sense, but the idea of reducing an opponent's collective realm equally applies. Donahue, *Privatization Decision,* 136.

91. Reno, *Warlord Politics,* 36; and Michael Doyle, *Empires* (Ithaca: Cornell University Press, 1986).

92. William Reno, "Foreign Firms, Natural Resources, and Violent Political Economies," Social Sciences Forum (March 21, 2000). One such went to IDAS (International Defense and Security), a Belgian-Dutch company that obtained the rights to a diamond concession larger than Belgium in exchange for its security services. Aoul, "Towards a Spiral of Violence?" 2000.

93. Dinnen, 1997. *Challenging the State: The Sandline Affair in Papua New Guinea,* Australian National University Pacific Policy Paper 30, 1997. Likewise, in Congo Brazzaville, the Israeli

firm Levdan was awarded half of the shares of the Marine III oil production permit by the Lissouba government, whose military forces it coincidentally was training.

11. MARKET DYNAMISM AND GLOBAL SECURITY DISRUPTIONS

1. John Mearsheimer, "The False Promise of International Institutions," *International Security* 19, no.3 (Winter 1994, pp. 3–49.

2. For example, the simplified "state as microeconomic firm" model that neorealist theory uses to derive its findings. Kenneth Waltz, *Theory of International Relations* (New York: McGraw Hill, 1979); Richard D. Auster and Morris Silver, *The State as a Firm: Economic Forces in Political Development* (Boston: Martinus Nijhoff, 1979).

3. Jean-Michel Guéhenno, "The Impact of Globalisation on Strategy," *Survival* 40 (Winter, 2000, p. 6.

4. Greg Mills and John Stremlau, "The Privatisation of Security in Africa: An Introduction," *The Privatisation of Security in Africa*, ed. Greg Mills and John Stremlau (Pretoria: South Africa Institute of International Affairs, 1999, p. 13.

5. Jason Nisse, "Cash for Combat," *Independent*, November 21, 1999; Zarate, 1998. Juan Carlos Zarate, "The Emergence of a New Dog of War: Private International Security Companies, International Law, and the New World Order," *Stanford Journal of International Law* 34 (Winter 1998) pp. 75–156. One example is in Congo, where firms worked both for the Mobutu regime and the successor government of Joseph Kabila, Sr., despite U.S. support of rebel forces linked with Uganda and Rwanda. Another example is the support certain firms have offered to narcotics cartels.

6. Waltz, *Theory of International Relations*, p. 88. Such writers believe that the heart of national security is "[t]he maintenance of policy and behavioural autonomy—the minimization of external constraints on policy and behavior." Andrew L. Ross, "Arms Acquisition and National Security: The Irony of Military Strength," in *National Security in the Third World: The Management of Internal and External Threats*, ed. Edward E. Azar and Chun-in Moon, (Hants: Edward Elgar, 1988, p. 154.

7. Zarate, "Emergence." Indeed, the U.S. Air Force has even had to institute "stop-loss" programs to keep troops from exiting to join PMFs. Marni McEntee, "High Civilian Salaries Lure Away Many Security Troops," *European Stars and Stripes*, February 3, 2002.

8. Max Weber, *Theory of Social and Economic Organization*, translated by A. M. Henderson (New York: Free Press, 1964), p. 154.

9. Anthony Giddens, *A Contemporary Critique of Historic Materialism* (Berkeley: University of California Press, 1995, p. 121. As with Giddens's, other definitions of state sovereignty do not include the legitimacy aspect, for example Tilly's, which defines it as "controlling the principal means of coercion within a given territory." David Isenberg, *Soldiers of Fortune ltd.: A Profile of Today's Private Sector Corporate Mercenary Firms* (Center for Defense Information Monograph, November 1997), p. 1; Charles Tilly, *The Formation of National States in Western Europe* (Princeton: Princeton University Press, 1975), p. 638.

10. Janice Thomson, p. 12. *Mercenaries, Pirates, and Sovereigns: State-building and Extraterritorial Violence in Early Modern Europe* (Princeton: Princeton University Press, 1994), p. 12. Alexander Wendt, *Social Theory of International Politics* (New York: Cambridge University Press, 1999), 8–9. In post–Cold War conflict, antisocial market forces certainly affected socially defined relationships.

11. Thomson, *Mercenaries, Pirates*, 151.

12. Thucydides, *The History of the Peloponnesian War*. 431 B.C.E. Translated by Richard Crawley. Available at http://classics.mit.edu/Thucydides/pelopwar.html; Seyom Brown, "World Interests and the Changing Dimensions of Security," in *World Security: Challenges for a New Century*, ed. Michael Klare and Yogesh Chandrani (New York: St. Martin's Press, 1998), 2.

13. For example, Keohane emphasized that power is not very fungible in Robert Keohane, "Theory of World Politics," in *Neorealism and Its Critics*, ed. Robert Keohane (New York:

Columbia University Press, 1986). Others, such as Gilpin, differed. Robert Gilpin, *War and Change in World Politics* (Cambridge: Cambridge University Press, 1981).

14. Richard Rosecrance, *The Rise of the Virtual State: Wealth and Power in the Coming Century (New York:* Basic Books, 1999).

15. Barry Buzan, "Rethinking East Asian Security," in *World Security, ed. Klare and Chandari,* 103.

16. For other discussions of the fungibility of power, please see Robert Keohane, *International Institutions and State Power* (Boulder: Westview, 1989), esp. chaps. 4, 9, 10; David Baldwin, "Force, Fungibility, and Influence," *Security Studies* 8, no. 4 (summer 1999); Robert Art, "Force and Fungibility Reconsidered," *Security Studies* 8, no. 4 (Summer 1999).

17. Charles Smith, "Russian Migs in Sudan, *Newsmax.com,* January 4, 2002.

18. In contravention to the theoretic predictions of Waltz. See note 2.

19. Interview with PMF employee, March 2002.

20. Metz, *Armed Conflict in the 21st Century, The Information Revolution and Postmodern Warfare* (Strategic Studies Institute, U.S. Army War College, April 2000) http://carlisle-www .army.mil/usassi/ssipubs/pubs2000/conflict/conflict.htm. ix

21. Ibid, p. 19.

22. Alvin and Heidi Toffler, *War and Anti-War: Survival at the Dawn of the 21st Century* (New York: Little, Brown, 1993), p. 85.

23. "Russian Generals Behind Ethiopian Victory," *Izvestiya,* May 25, 2000; "Ethiopia-Eritrea: Eritrea Accuses Ethiopia of Using Mercenaries," *IRIN,* May 31, 2000.

24. As an Eritrean spokesperson noted, following a Russian-piloted Su-27 downing an Eritrean jet, "There are a lot of Russian advisers who are active. They are not just sitting at a desk." Charles Smith, "Wars and Rumors of Wars: Russian Mercenaries Flying for Ethiopia," *World Net Daily,* July 18, 2000, http://www.worldnetdaily.com/bluesky_smith_news/ 20000718_xnsof_russian_me.shtm. See also Thomas Adams, "Russians Fly for Both Sides in Horn of Africa," (1999).

25. Gennady Charodeev,"Foreign Wars: Russian Generals Involved in a War between Ethiopia and Eritrea," *Izvestia,* May 26, 2000, p. 1, 4; Smith, V; Peter Biles, "Bitter Foes," *World Today,* 56, no. 7 (July 2000); Kevin Whitelaw, "The Russians Are Coming," *U.S. News and World Report,* March 15, 1999.

26. Charodeev, "Foreign Wars," 1, 4.

27. In fact, former Soviet combat pilots are rapidly becoming dominant market players in Africa, displacing others primarily through their lower pay demands and less strict aircraft maintenance. As Joe Sala, a former Africa specialist in the U.S. State Department, notes, it almost appears that "if you don't speak Russian, you can't fly in Central Africa." Kevin Whitelaw, "The Russians Are Coming," *U.S. News and World Report,* March 15, 1999.

28. Rosalind Russell, "Macedonia Pounds Hills, World Urges Restraint," *Reuters,* March 24, 2001. Interview with U.S. military official, March 24, 2001.

29. Metz, *Armed Conflict* p. 14.

30. "Money nourishes war," or, as the French put it "Pas d'argent, pas de Suisses!" (No Money, No Swiss [mercenaries]!). Michael Howard, *War in European History* (London: oxford University Press, 1976), p. 38.

31. Immanuel Kant, *Perpetual Peace: A Philosophical Sketch* (1795). Available at http://www .mtholyoke.edu/acad/intrel/kant/kant1.htm

32. Jessica Matthews, "Power Shift: The Rise of Global Civil Society," *Foreign Affairs* 76, no. 1 (January/February 1997); Richard Rosecrance, "A New Concert of Powers," *Foreign Affairs* 71, no. 2, (Spring 1992); Dale Copeland, "Economic Interdependence and War," in *Theories of War and Peace: An International Security Reader,* ed. Michael Brown et al. (Cambridge: MIT Press, 1998).

33. See Carl von Clausewitz, *On War,* edited with an introduction by Anatol Rapoport (Middlesex: Penguin, 1968), p. 264. Also see John J. Mearsheimer, "Assessing the Conventional Balance: The 3:1 Rule and Its Critics," *International Security* 13, no. 4 (Spring 1989): pp. 54–89.

34. Westwood, 1995, Estimates are that it would require just 3–12 months advance notice for a capable firm to coordinate a conclusive information attack. In less than a month, it could enact a modest harassment attack.

35. "Top Science Advisers Calling For Higher Premium On Military Training," *Washington Post,* February 8, 2000, p. 1.

36. Richard Betts, *Surprise Attack* (Washington D.C.: Brookings Institution, 1982); Roberta Wohlstetter, *Pearl Harbor: Warning and Decision* (Stanford: Stanford University Press, 1962).

37. Jack L. Snyder, *The Ideology of the Offensive: Military Decision Making and the Disasters of 1914* (Ithaca: Cornell University Press, 1984); Stephen Van Evera, "The Cult of the Offensive and the Origins of the First World War," *International Security* 9, no. 1 (Summer 1984), pp. 58–107.

38. Randolph M. Siverson and Paul F. Diehl, "Arms Races, the Conflict Spiral, and the Onset of War," In *Handbook of War Studies,* ed. Manus I. Midlarsky (Boston: Unwin Hyman, 1989, pp. 195–218; Samuel Huntington, "Arms Races: Prerequisites and Results," in *Public Policy,* ed. Carl J. Friedric and Seymour E. Harris (Cambridge: Graduate School of Public Administration, 1958); Stephen Van Evera, *The Causes of War: Power and the Roots of Conflict* (Ithaca: Cornell University Press, 1999), esp. chaps. 2, 3.

39. Thomas Schelling, *Arms and Influence* (New Haven: Yale University Press, 1966), chaps. 2–4. See also Robert Jervis et al., *Psychology and Deterrence* (Baltimore: Johns Hopkins University Press, 1985).

40. James D. Fearon, "Rationalist Explanations for War," *International Organization* 49, no. 3 (Summer 1995, pp. 379–414.

41. For example, a U.S. official discussed how EO's "myth of invincibility" helped keep the peace in West Africa for a brief period. "U.S. Backs Role for Rebels in West Africa," *Washington Post,* October 18, 1999.

42. Brown & Root was the contractor for the destruction of Russian ICBMs, a task that the Russian central government was unable to perform.

43. Examples of work outlining patron-client balancing include: Barry Buzan, "People, States, and Fear: The National Security Problem in the Third World," in *Azar1988,* pp. 14–43; Stephen R. David, "Explaining Third World Alignment," *World Politics* 43, no. 2 (January 1991pp. 233–256; Jack S. Levy and Michael M. Barnett, "Alliance Formation, Domestic Political Economy, and Third World Security," *Jerusalem Journal of International Relations* 14, no. 4 (December 1992, pp. 19–40; Alexander Wendt and Michael Barnett, "Dependent State Formation and Third World Militarization," *Review of International Studies* 19, no. 4 (August 1993): 321–347.

44. Olav Stokke, "Aid and Political Conditionality: Core Issues and State of the Art," in *Aid and Political Conditionality, ed. Olav Stokke* (London: Frank Cass, 1995, p. 12.

45. Levy and Barnett, 1992.

46. Chris Spearin, "The Commodification of Security and Post-Cold War Patron Client Balancing," paper presented at the Globalization and Security Conference, University of Denver, Nov. 11, 2000.

47. Zarate, "Emergence."

48. Sean Dorney, *The Sandline Affair: Politics and Mercenaries and the Bougainville Crisis* (Sydney: ABC Books, 1998, p. 63.

49. Ibid., p. 229.

50. As quoted in Sinclair Dinnen, "Militaristic Solutions in a Weak States: Internal Security, Private Contractors, and Political Leadership in Papua New Guinea," *Contemporary Pacific* 11, no. 2 (Fall 1999, p.286. As explored in chapter 13, the contract did not work out as planned, but as a result of dynamics internal to the PNG military, rather than to external alliance dynamics.

51. Spearin, "Commodification."

52. Celeste Wallander and Robert Keohane, "Risk, Threat, and Security Institutions," in *Imperfect Unions: Security Institutions over Time and Space, ed.* Helga Haftendorn, Robert O. Keo-

hane, and Celeste A. Wallander (Oxford: Oxford University Press, 1999); Stephen Walt, *The Origins of Alliances* (Ithaca: Cornell University Press, 1990).

53. Buchizya Mseteka, "Angola Strained by War at Home and Abroad," *Reuters*, May 20, 1999.

54. Ambrose Evans-Pritchard, "EU force May Rent Ukraine Planes," *Electronic Telegraph*, February 14, 2001.

55. Toffler and Toffler, *War and Anti-War*, 85.

56. Khareen Pech, "South African Mercenaries in Congo," *Electronic Mail & Guardian*, August 28, 1998.

57. Yves Goulet, "MPRI: Washington's Freelance Advisors," *Jane's Intelligence Review*, July 1998.

58. All this while under indictment for stealing money from the Thai central bank. Brian Wood and Johan Peleman, *The Arms Fixers* (PRIO Report, March 1999).

59. John Horvath, "The Soros Effect on Central and Eastern Europe," *Telepolis*, June 1997. http://www.heise.de/tp/english/inhalt/te/1292/2.html

60. *A Force for Peace and Security*, Report from the Peace through Law Education Fund, 2002, p. 20.

61. Bruce Grant, "U.S. Military Expertise for Sale: Private Military Consultants as a Tool of Foreign Policy," *National Defense University Institute for National Security Studies, Strategy Essay Competition*, 1998, http://www.ndu.edu/inss/books/essaysch4.html.

62. Zarate, "Emergence."

63. Metz, *Armed Conflict*, p. 20; Westwood, "Military Information."

64. Interviews, Spring 1999.

65. Tim Spicer, *An Unorthodox Soldier: Peace and War and the Sandline Affair* (Edinburgh: Mainstream, 1999) p. 18.

66. Martin Van Creveld, *The Rise and Decline of the State* (Cambridge: Cambridge University Press, 1999, p. 406.

67. Zarate, "Emergence,"; "United Nations Commission on Human Rights," Report on the question of the use of mercenaries as a means of violating human rights and impeding the exercise of the right of peoples to self determination." 53rd Session, Item 7, Special Rapporteur, February 20, 1997, p. 90.

68. For example, this occurred in 1999 when the British Foreign Ministry had to step in to prevent Sandline from working with the KLA, blunting its claim to only be interested in working for states. Cullen 2000.

69. Stefaans Brummer, "SA Arms 'Stoke' the Burundi Fire," Weekly *Mail & Guardian*, December 5, 1997. Bernedette Muthien, *Corporate Mercenarism in Southern Africa*, Centre for Conflict Resolution Paper (South Africa), 1999.

70. Mohammad Bazzi, "British Say Islamic Group Taught Combat Courses in U.S.," *Newsday*, October 4, 2001; "'Holy War' Website Shut Down," *BBC Online*, October 4, 2001.

71. "Did 'Jihad' Arms Course visit U.S.?" MSNBC. Com, Dec. 27, 2001

72. U.S. Department of Justice, Office of the U.S. Attorney, Middle District of Pennsylvania, Press Release, September 30, 1998; http://www.fwop.org/news/fwoanws15A.html.

73. O'Brien, 1998; Andre Linard, "Mercenaries SA," *LeMonde Diplomatique*, August 1998, p. 31, www.monde-diplomatique.fr/1998/08/Linard/10806.html; Goodwin, 1997; Cullen, "Keeping the New Dog."; Arieh O'Sullivan, "Israeli Mercenaries in Congo May Face Fellow Israelis," *AP Worldstream*, February 3, 1994; Tim Kennedy, "Israeli Legislators Seek to Halt Export of Arms, Mercenaries to Congo," *Moneyclips*, Feb. February 24, 1994). The United Nations has also expressed its concern "at new unlawful international activities linking drug traffickers and mercenaries in the perpetration of violent actions which undermine the constitutional order of States." International Convention Against the Recruitment, Use, Financing and Training of Mercenaries, G.A. Res. A/44/34, U.N. GAOR, 44th Sess., 72nd mtg. 1989.

74. Goodwin, "Mexican Drug Barons."

75. "We have no particular inhibitions about going to the private sector if we can get good

and effective instruments," said the chairman of UNSCOM. "UN Hires Detective to Probe UNITA," *Globe and Mail (Toronto)*, April 19, 2001; Colum Lynch, "Private Firms Aid U.N. on Sanctions: Wider Intelligence Capability Sought," *Washington Post*, April 21, 2001. http://www.washingtonpost.com/wp-dyn/articles/A44304-2001Apr20.html

76. Lynch, "Private Firms Aid U.N." http://www.washingtonpost.com/wp-dyn/articles/A44304-2001Apr20.html; "The IMF's Intelligence Helper," *Intelligence Newsletter*, April 5, 2001.

77. Stephen Mbogo, "Mercenaries? No, PMCs," *West Africa Magazine*, no. 4244, September 18, 2000, p. 10-13.

78. Malan, 2000.

79. Jeffrey Lee, "Give a Dog of War a Bad Name," *Times*, London May 4, 1998.

80. Doug Brooks, "Write a Cheque End a War Using Private Military companies to End African Conflicts," *Conflict Trends*, no. 6, July 2000. http://www.accord.org.za/publications/ct6/issues6.htm. See also Jonathon Broder, "Mercenaries: The Future of U.N. Peacekeeping?" *Fox News*, June 26, 2000. Transcript available at http://www.foxnews.com/world/062300/un_broder.sml; Australian Broadcasting Corporation, "Dogs of War," *Lateline*, broadcast May 18, 2000. Transcript available at http://www.abc.net.au/lateline/archives/s128621.htm. The British Government also raised this plan in its Green Paper, House of Commons, *Private Military Companies: Options for Regulation*, HC 577, February 12, 2002.

81. Australian Broadcasting Corporation, "Dogs of War."

82. Mbogo, "Mercenaries? No, PMCs."

83. Brooks, "Hope for the Hopeless Continent" 2000; Howe, 1998; Mbogo, "Mercenaries? No, PMCs."

84. Doug Brooks, "Creating the Renaissance Peace," paper presented at Africa Institute's 40th Anniversary Conference, Pretoria, May 30, 2000.

85. M. Bradbury, *Aid Under Fire: Redefining Relief and Development Assistance in Unstable Situations. Wilton Park Paper*, supported by with DHA, ODI, and ActionAid, (London: HMSO, 1995).

86. Sean Greenaway and Andrew J. Harris, "Humanitarian Security: Challenges and Responses," paper presented at the Forging Peace Conference, Harvard University, March 13-15, 1998 p. 5.

87. Janice Stein, with Michael Bryans and Bruce Jones, *Mean Times: Humanitarian Action in Complex Political Emergencies—Stark Choices, Cruel Dilemmas*, (Toronto: University of Toronto on Program on Conflict Management and Negotiation, 1999).

88. James Fennell, "Private Security Companies: The New Humanitarian Agent," Presentation to the Conference on Interagency Co-ordination in Complex Humanitarian Emergencies, Cranfield University/Royal Military College of Science Shrivenham, U.K., October 19, 1999.

89. Howe, "Global Order."

90. Isenberg, "Soldiers of Fortune Ltd."

91. Center for Democracy and Development, *The Impasse in Sierra Leone*, www.cdd.org.uk/pubs/sierraleone.htm (accessed December 1999).

92. Brooks, "Hope for the 'Hopeless Continent.'"

93. Global Coalition for Africa and International Alert, "The Privatization of Security in Africa," conference report, Washington D.C. (March 12, 1999). http://www.gca-cma.org/esecurity.htm#0399

94. Tim Butcher, "UN Force Is Upstaged by British Expertise," *Telegraph*, May 12, 2000. http://www.telegraph.co.uk:80/et?ac=000291992355051&rtmo=QxHeeOeR&atmo=rrrrr Yas&pg=/et/00/5/12/wsie212.html; Malan, "Lean Peacekeeping."

95. Australian Broadcasting Corporation (ABC), "Sierra Leone—Soldiers of Fortune," ABC Documentary, producer Mark Corcoran, August 2000. Transcript at: www.abc.net/foreign

96. Isenberg, 1999; Toffler and Toffler, *War and Anti-War*, 229; Spicer, *Unorthodox Soldier*, 52.

97. Rubin, p. 55. After weeks of debate between member states, the UN finally considered sending a Canadian-led force, but it never deployed. Thousands of the Hutu refugees are thought to have been slaughtered in the aftermath.

98. Elizabeth Rubin, "Army of One's Own," *Harper's Magazine*, February 1997, p. 55.

99. Interview with PMF executive, April 2001. See also Mbogo, "Mercenaries? No, PMCs."; *Report of the Independent Inquiry into the Actions of the United National During the 1994 Genocide in Rwanda*, Igvar Karlson www.un.org (Dec. 15, 1999). The exact number of victims potentially saved by an intervention is, of course, open to debate. Alan Kuperman, "Rwanda in Retrospect," *Foreign Affairs* 79, no. 1 (January 2000pp. 94–118.

100. Spicer, *Unorthodox Soldier*, 233.

101. Mary Kaldor, *New and Old Wars* (Stanford: Stanford University, 1999), p. 10.

102. Jack Kelley "Safety at a Price: Military Expertise for Sale or Rent," *Pittsburgh Post-Gazette*, February, 2000.

103. As was seen with the Canadian elite forces in the Somalia operation, the potential for abuse by such forces is high.

104. David Shearer, *Private Armies and Military intervention*, International Institute for Strategic Studies, Adelphi Paper no. 316, February 1998. p. 70.

105. Peter Lock, "Military Downsizing and growth in the Security Industry in Sub-Saharan Africa." *Strategic Analysis* 22, no. 9 (December 1998).

106. Hedley Bull, *The Anarchical Society: A Study of Order in World Politics* (New York: Columbia University Press, 1977). p. 263.

107. United Nations Commission on Human Rights, "Report on the Question," 1997. See also David Francis, "Mercenary Intervention in Sierra Leone: Providing National Security of International Exploitation?" *Third World Quarterly* 20, no. 2 (Summer 1999, pp. 319–338.

108. Or, as Michael Grunberg, the director of Sandline, puts it, " The claim that it is recolonisation by big multinationals is bulls#*t." Lutyens, 2001. Marcia Lutyens, "Military Operations (ex VAT)," *Volkskrant* (Netherlands), February 17. 2001.

109. Michael Doyle, *Empires* (Ithaca: Cornell University Press, 1986).

110. As the UN special rapporteur continues, "Once a greater degree of security has been attained, the firm apparently begins to exploit the concessions it has received by setting up a number of associates and affiliates . . . thereby acquiring a significant, if not hegemonic, presence in the economic life of the country in which it is operating." As quoted in Dinnen, "Militaristic Solutions," 118. If the corporate dominance is just linked to market control and remains solely in the economic realm, then the proper description would be "emporialism," in which emporia (markets) are the targets, rather than imperialism. George Wilnius, *The merchant Warrior pacified* (New York: Oxford University Press, 1991), p. 5.

111. Scott Pegg, "Corporate Armies for States and State Armies for Corporations: Addressing the Challenges of Globalization and Natural Resource Conflict," paper prepared for delivery at the 2000 Annual Meeting of the American Political Science Association, Washington, D.C., August 31–September 3, 2000; "BP Accused of Backing 'Arms for Oil' Coup," *London Sunday Times*, March 26, 2000; Christian Aid, *The Scorched Earth: Oil and War in Sudan* (March 2001) http://www.christian-aid.org.uk/indepth/0103suda/sudanoil.htm; Alex Yearsly, "Oriental Timber Company Smuggles Weapons to RUF," Radio France International, May 10, 2001.

112. Palayiwa Millius, an advisor to the Sierra Leone peace negotiations, as quoted in McGrory, 1998. James Woods, a former U.S. Assistant Secretary of Defense, described the firms this way, "These enterprises could become stronger than some of the sovereign states they are hired to protect." As quoted in Diane Alden, "Soldiers R Us: The Corporate Military," *SpinTech*, September 12, 1999. Available at http://www.spintechmag.com/9909/da0999.htm

113. Lucy Sutherland, *The East India Company in Eighteenth-Century Politics*, (Oxford: Clarendon Press, 1979), p. 77.

114. Ian Douglas, "Fighting for Diamonds—PMCs in Sierra Leone." In Jakkie Cilliers and Peggy Mason, *Peace, Profit or Plunder? The Privatisation of Security in War-Torn African Societies*

(Pretoria: Institute for Security Studies, January 1999), pp. 175–200; Alex Vines, "The Business of Peace: 'Tiny' Rowland, Financial Incentives and the Mozambican Settlement." *Accord: An International Review of Peace Initiatives*, p. 78. http://www.c-r.org/acc_moz/contents_moz .htm.; Center for Democracy and Development *The Impasse in Siera Leone*, www.cdd.org .uk/pubs/sierraleone.htm, December, 1999. Also private correspondence with PMF employee, May 2000. Cullen, "Keeping the New Dogs"; Alex Vines, "Mercenaries and the Privatisation of Security in Africa in the 1990s," 1999, p. 78. Center for Democracy and Development, 1999. Also private correspondence with PMF employee, May 2000.

115. Metz, Steven. *Strategic Horizons: The Military Implications of Alternative Futures* (Strategic Studies Institute, U.S. Army War College, March 7, 1997, p. 21.

116. Thomson, *Mercenaries, Pirates*, 67.

117. See, for instance, Robert Cooper, *The Post Modern State and the World Order*. Demos paper no. 19 (1996); Stephen Korbin, "Back to the Future: Neomedievalism and the Postmodern Digital World Economy," *Journal of International Affairs* (Spring 1998, pp. 361–386; Phillip Cerny, "Neomedievalism, Civil War, and the New Security Dilemma: Globalisation as Durable Disorder," *Civil Wars* 1. no. 1 (Summer 1999); Barry Buzan, "From International System to International Society: Structural Realism and Regime Theory Meet the English School," *International Organization* 47 (Summer 1997, p. 327–352.

118. Steven Metz, *Armed Conflict* p., 13.

12. PRIVATE FIRMS AND THE CIVIL-MILITARY BALANCE

1. CIA World Factbook, "Papua New Guinea," 1999. Available at: www.cia.gov/cia/ publications/factbook/fields/languages.html

2. Tim Spicer, *An Unorthodox Soldier: Peace and War and the Sandline Affair* (Edinburgh: Mainstream, 1999), p. 155.

3. Juan Carlos Zarate, "The Emergence of a New Dog of War: Private International Security Companies, International Law, and the New World Order," *Stanford Journal of International Law* 34 (Winter 1998): 75–156.

4. Sinclair Dinnen, *Challenging the State: The Sandline Affair in Papua New Guinea*, Australian National University, Pacific Policy Paper 30, 1997.

5. However, when press reports broke, only the training aspects were publicly acknowledged. That a small group of cabinet ministers surreptitiously made the strategic decision to hire Sandline, possibly with their own personal financial incentives in mind, raises concerns about the firms and issues of government accountability. Dinnen, *Challenging the State*, p. 3.

6. Dinnen, *Challenging the State, p.* 123.

7. David Isenberg, *Soldiers of Fortune Ltd.: A Profile of Today's Private Sector Corporate Mercenary Firms*, Center for Defense Information Monograph, November 1997; David Shearer, *Private Armies and Military Intervention*, International Institute for Strategic Studies, Adelphi Paper no. 316, February 1998; and Peter Lewis Young, "Bougainville Conflict Enters Its Ninth Year," *Jane's Intelligence Review*, June 1997, are the primary sources of information on this episode.

8. Jonathon Carr-Brown, "Sandline 'Paid Bribe' to Win War Contract," *Sunday Times*, July 2, 2000. http://www.sundaytimes.co.uk/news/pages/sti/2000/07/02/ stinwenws01024.html

9. Dinnen, *Challenging the State*.

10. Anthony Regan, "Preparation for War and Progress Towards Peace," in *Challenging the State: The Sandline Affair in Papua New Guinea*, edited by Sinclair Dinnen, Australian National University, Pacific Policy Paper 30, 1997, p. 61.

11. Young, "Bougainville Conflict."

12. Spicer, *Unorthodox Soldier*, 167.

13. Regan, p. 67; and Ron May, "The Military Factor," in Dinnen, *Challenging the State*, 103.

14. Regan, "Wars of the Future . . . Today," 67.

15. Bill Standish, "Paradoxes in PNG," in Dinnen, *Challenging the State*, 75.

16. Spicer was charged with the illegal importation of cash and illegal possession of a firearm, a pistol, ironic in that he had just brought in 50 tons of weapons and been paid $18 million by the government for it. Spicer, *Unorthodox Soldier,* 184.

17. The interest alone was running at $5,000 a day. Simon Sheppard, "Soldiers for Hire," *Contemporary Review* (August 1999); Sebastien Berger, "Sandline Sues to Seize Nation's Assets," *Sunday Telegraph,* March 7, 1999.

18. Regan, "Wars of the Future . . . Today," 64.

19. Samuel Huntington, *The Soldier and the State: The Theory and Politics of Civil-Military Relations* (New York: Random House, 1957); ; Morris Janowitz, *The Professional Soldier: A Social and Political Portrait* (New York: Free Press, 1960). Peter D. Feaver, "The Civil-Military Problematique: Huntington, Janowitz, and the Question of Civilian Control," *Armed Forces and Society* 23, no. 2 (Winter 1996): 149–178; Samuel E. Finer, *The Man on Horseback: The Role of the Military in Politics* (New York: Praeger, 1962).

20. Stephen David, *Defending Third World Regimes from Coups d'Etat* (New York: University Press of America, 1985).

21. Charles Tilly, *Coercion, Capital, and European States, AD 990–1990* (Cambridge, Mass.: Blackwell, 1990): 213. See also Christopher Coker, *NATO, the Warsaw Pact, and Africa* (London: Macmillan Press, 1985).

22. Stephen David, *Third World Coups d'Etat and International Security* (Baltimore: Johns Hopkins University Press, 1987).

23. Isenberg, "Soldiers of Fortune Ltd."

24. Finer, *Man on Horseback,* 188.

25. Regan, "Wars of the Future . . . Today," 97.

26. Christopher Clapham, "Africa Security Systems: Privatisation and the Scope for Mercenary Activity," in *The Privatisation of Security in Africa,* ed. Greg Mills and John Stremlau (Johannesburg: South Africa Institute of International Affairs, 1999), 37.

27. Amos Perlmutter, *The Military and Politics in Modern Times* (New Haven: Yale University Press, 1977), 90–102.

28. This is one of the explanations for the PNG mutiny. Spicer, *Unorthodox Soldier,* 165.

29. Herbert Howe, "African Private Security," *Conflict Trends* no. 6 (July 2000). http://www.accord.org.za/publications/ct6/issue6.htm

30. Samuel Decalo, *The Stable Minority: Civilian Rule in Africa* (Gainesville: Florida Academic Press, 1998). Samuel Decalo, "Praetorianism, Corporate Grievances, and Idiosyncratic Factors in African Military Hierarchies," *Journal of African Studies* 2, no. 2 (Summer 1975): 247–73.

31. William Thompson, *The Grievances of Military Coup Makers* (Beverly Hills: Sage, 1973).

32. Herbert Howe, "African Private Security," *Conflict Trends,* no. 6 (July 2000). http://www.accord.org.za/publications/ct6/issue6.htm

33. Dinnen, *Challenging the State,* 2.

34. As a Colombian national guardsman near the Dyncorp base complained, "A Vietnam veteran does not subordinate himself to a Colombian police officer, and that's why there have been problems." Ignacio Gómez, "U.S. Mercenaries in Colombia," *Colombia Report,* July 16, 2000.

35. Douglas Porch, *The French Foreign Legion* (New York: Harper Collins, 1991), p. 245.

36. Ralston, *Importing the European Army* (Chicago: University of Chicago Press, 1990), 94.

37. Ibid., 174.

38. Interview with U.S. Defense Analyst, June 2001; Sherman, 2000; "Malu Counsels the Federal Government to Be Cautious of U.S. Aid Pledge to Military," *Vanguard,* January 22, 2001. Among the reports were that MPRI had also incurred the opposition of Nigerian General Victor Malu, by recommending reforms that threatened personal slush funds.

39. Howe, "Global Order and Security Privatization."

40. In the Solomon Islands in June 2000, the rumor spread that a force of Cuban fighters was being brought in. In a fashion similar to the army revolt in Sierra Leone, elements of the Solomon Islands Field Force allied themselves with local guerrillas to overthrow the civil-

ian regime. Ultimately, whether or not the reports of the hire were true (no evidence has proven them so), they were enough to spur a coup. "Rebels Shell Rivals from Australian Patrol Boat," *Age*, June 7, 2000. http://www.theage.com.au/breaking/0006/07/A44216–2000Jun7.shtml

41. Howe, "African Private Security."

42. Jendayi Frazer, "Sustaining Civilian Control: Armed Counterweights in Regime Stability in Africa," Stanford University Dissertation, March 1994; David Goldsworthy, "Civilian Control of the Military in Black Africa," *African Affairs* 80, no. 318 (January 1981): 49–74; Cynthia Enloe, *Ethnic Soldiers: State Security in Divided Societies* (Athens: University of Georgia Press, 1980).

43. Edward Luttwak, *Coup d'Etat: A Practical Handbook* (Cambridge, Mass.: Harvard University Press, 1968), p. 90.

44. William Reno, *Warlord Politics and African States* (London: Lynne Rienner, 1998).>

45. Yosi Walter, "Shadaq in the Congo," FBIS translation, *Tel Aviv Ma'ariv,* October 7, 1994, FBIS translation.

46. Huntington, *The Soldier and the State.*

47. Sherman, "Arm's Length," 30.

48. Perlmutter, *Military and Politics.* Finer, *Man on Horseback,* 25–28. Feaver, "Civil-Military Problematique": 149–178.

49. Frazer, "Sustaining Civilian Control,"; Huntington, *The Soldier and the State.*

50. Douglas Brooks, "The Business End of Military Intelligence: Private Military Companies," *Military Intelligence Professional Bulletin,* September 1999.

51. Elizabeth Rubin, "An Army of One's Own," *Harper's Magazine,* February 1997, p. 54.

52. Khareen Pech and David Beresford. "Africa's New-Look Dogs of War," *Weekly Mail & Guardian,* January 24, 1997.

53. Chris Dietrich, "The Commercialisation of Military Deployment in Africa," *African Security Review* 9, no. 1 (January 2000): 3–17.

54. Interviews with U.S. Army Officers, June 1998, July 2000. *British Security 2010,* Conference Proceedings Church House, Westminster, November 1995, p. 60.

55. Bruce Grant, "U.S. Military Expertise for Sale: Private Military Consultants as a Tool of Foreign Policy," National Defense University Institute for National Security Studies, Strategy Essay Competition, 1998. http://www.ndu.edu/inss/books/essaysch4.html

56. David King and Zachary Karabell, "The Generation of Trust: Public Confidence in the U.S. Military Since Vietnam," paper prepared for Visions of Governance in the 21st Century project (December 1999). http://www.ksg.harvard.edu/prg/king/gentrust.pdf,; Gallup Organization, "Military on Top, HMOs Last in Public Confidence Poll," Poll Release (July 14, 1999), available at http://www.gallup.com/poll/releases/pr990714.asp

57. Huntington, *The Soldier and the State,* p. 15.

58. Grant, "U.S. Military Expertise."

13. PUBLIC ENDS, PRIVATE MILITARY MEANS?

1. David Passage, *The United States and Colombia: Untying the Gordian Knot* (U.S. Army War College: Strategic Studies Institute, March 2000), 5. http://carlisle-www.army.mil/usassi/ssipubs/pubs2000.htm

2. Joshua Hammer and Michael Isikoff, "The Narco-Guerrilla War," *Newsweek,* August 9, 1999.

3. Paul De La Garza and David Adams, "Military Aid . . . From the Private Sector," *St. Petersburg Times,* December 3, 2000.

4. Niles Lathem, "America's Drug War Mercenaries," *New York Post,* April 29, 2001.

5. Steven Dudley, "Colombia Vows End To Abuses," *Washington Post,* July 22, 2000, p. 15; Nancy Dunne, "Dope Wars (Part II): Crackdown on Colombia," *Financial Times,* August 9, 2000; De La Garza and Adams, "Military Aid."

6. De La Garza and Adams, "Military Aid." The firm claims the need for both operational secrecy and contractual obligations.

7. "A Bill Before the U.S. Congress Would Prohibit the Use of Private Firms in the Fight Against Drugs," *Bogota Semana,* May 7, 2001.

8. Peter Gorman, "Ex-Navy Seals on Pay Per Kill Mission Plan Colombia's Mercenaries," *Narconews,* February 19, 2001.

9. Ted Robberson, "U.S. Launches Covert Program to Aid Colombia," *Dallas Morning News,* August 19, 1998; Ted Robberson, "Contractors Playing Increasing Role in U.S. Drug War"; De La Garza and Adams, "Military Aid"; Paul De La Garza and David Adams, "Military Know-How Finds Niche—And Some Critics," *St. Petersburg Times,* December 3, 2000.

10. Daniel Burton-Rose and Wayne Madsen. "Governments of, by, and For the Corporations: Corporate Soldiers," *Multinational Monitor* 20, no. 3 (March 1999). Available at: http://www.essential.org/monitor/mm1999/mm9903.07.html#rose

11. Juan O. Tamayo, "U.S. Civilians Taking Risks in Drug War for Colombia," *Miami Herald,* February 22, 2001.

12. In fact, pilots acknowledge that the twin propeller OV-10 is not very good for aerial fumigation, as air turbulence resulting from its design does not allow the herbicide to fulfill its purpose and is instead blown into a scatter and dissipates it. Salisbury, 1998; Ignacio Gómez, "U.S. Mercenaries in Colombia," *Colombia Report,* July 16, 2000.

13. Jeremy McDermott, "U.S. Crews Involved in Colombian Battle," *Scotsman,* February 23, 2001. Also reported in Juan Tamayo, "Colombian Guerrillas Fire on U.S. Rescuers," *Miami Herald,* February 22, 2001.

14. Tamayo, "Colombian Guerrillas Fire on U.S. Rescuers.".

15. Ibid. DynCorp also reportedly lost two pilots while flying operations against Peruvian guerrillas. Ken Silverstein, "Mercenary, Inc.?" *Washington Business Forward,* April 26, 2001.

16. Dunne, "Dope Wars."

17. "Colombian Rebels Threaten U.S. Civilian "Mercenaries," *Reuters,* April 4, 2001.

18. As quoted in Jared Kotlet, "Americans Work in Danger Zone in Colombia," *Associated Press,* February 25, 2001.

19. These procedures are implemented by the Department of State's Office of Defense Trade Controls (ODTC) under the Arms Export Control Act and the International Traffic in Arms Regulation. Bruce Grant, "U.S. Military Expertise for Sale: Private Military Consultants as a Tool of Foreign Policy," National Defense University Institute for National Security Studies, Strategy Essay Competition, 1998. http://www.ndu.edu/inss/books/essaysch4.html

20. Ibid.

21. As was noted by David Isenberg of the industry's increasing activity during the Clinton Administration, "The administration likes it because it avoids the prospect of creating a furor if [something goes wrong]," as quoted in Justin Brown, "The Rise of the Private-Sector Military," *Christian Science Monitor,* July 5, 2000. http://www.csmonitor.com/durable/ 2000/07/05/f-p3s1.shtml

22. Mark Thompson, "Generals for Hire," *Time,* January 15, 1996.

23. General Accounting Office, "Contingency Operations: Opportunities to Improve the Logistics Civil Augmentation Program," GAO/NSIAD-97-63 (February 1997); Donald T. Wynn, "Managing the Logistics-support Contract in the Balkans Theater," *Engineer,* July 2000. http://call.army.mil/call/trngqtr/tq4-00/wynn.htm

24. Theodore Lowi, "Making Democracy Safe for the World: On Fighting the Next War," in *American Foreign Policy: Theoretical Essays,* ed. John G. Ikenberry (New York: Harper Collins, 1989), pp. 258–292.

25. Grant, "U.S. Military Expertise."

26. "Colombian Rebels Threaten."

27. General Peter Jones, retired, interview in Sarajevo, November 11, 1996.

28. This description is ironic in that at the time Croatia's own army was a client of MPRI. Croatian Foreign Press Bureau, *Daily Bulletin,* July 15, 1996.

29. Gennady Charodeev, "Foreign Wars: Russian Generals Involved in a War between Ethiopia and Eritrea," *Izvestia,* May 26, 2000, pp. 1, 4.

30. Stephaans Brummer, "Investing in the Bibles and Bullets Business," *Weekly Mail & Guardian,* September 16, 1994.

31. "More Weasel Words," *London Times,* October 22, 2000. http://www.sunday-times.co .uk/news/pages/sti/2000/10/22/stinwcldro1002.html

32. Raymond Bonner, "War Crimes Panel Finds Croat Troops 'Cleansed' the Serbs," *New York Times,* March 20, 1999.

33. William Arkin, "the Underground Military," *Washington Post,* May 7, 2001..

34. Christopher Marquis, "Inquiry on Peru Looks at a C.I.A. Contract," *New York Times,* April 28, 2001. http://www.nytimes.com/2001/04/28/world/28PLAN.html

35. Thompson, "Generals for Hire."

36. Duncan Campbell, "War on Error: A Spy Inc. No Stranger to Controversy," *Center for Public Integrity Report,* June 12, 2002.

37. Grant, "U.S. Military Expertise."

38. Silverstein, "Mercenary, Inc.?"

39. As quoted in Hanrahan, 1983, p. 317.

40. Grant, "U.S. Military Expertise."

14. MORALITY AND THE PRIVATIZED MILITARY FIRM

1. Elizabeth Rubin, "An Army of One's Own," *Harper's Magazine,* February 1997.

2. David Shearer, *Private Armies and Military Intervention,* International Institute for Strategic Studies, Adelphi Paper no. 316, February 1998, op. 71; Tim Spicer, *An Unorthodox Soldier: Peace and War and the Sandline Affair* (Edinburgh: Mainstream, 1999), p. 24.

3. David Shichor, *Punishment for Profit: Private Prisons/Public Concerns* (Thousand Oaks, Calif.: Sage, 1995), p. 67.

4. Jeremy Black, ed., *European Warfare: 1453–1815* (London: Macmillan, 1999).

5. Abdel-Fatau Musah and Kayode Fayemi, *Mercenaries: An African Security Dilemma* (London: Pluto, 2000); Xavier Renou, "Promoting Destabilization and Neoliberal Pillage: The Utilization of Private Military Companies for Peacekeeping and Peace Enforcement Activities in Africa," paper presented at ISA/APSA International Security Conference, Denver, November 2000.

6. Rubin, "An Army of One's Own." The same contract pilots were later filmed apparently firing randomly with rockets and machine guns at a village where rebels from the Revolutionary United Front (RUF) were believed to be hiding. Fran Abrams, "British Officer Advised Gunship Killers," *The Independent,* September 7, 2000. http://wwww.independent. co.uk/news/world/Africa/2000–09/afuko70900.shtml

7. Alex Vines, "The Business of Peace: 'Tiny' Rowland, Financial Incentives, and the Mozambican Settlement," *Accord: An International Review of Peace Initiatives* (1999). http:// www.cr.org/acc_moz/contents_moz.htm

8. With a destructive power comparable to low-yield nuclear weapons, in the understatement of the U.S. Defense Intelligence Agency (DIA), "the kill mechanism [which uses a fuel-infused blast to rupture lungs] against living targets is unique and unpleasant." Because the "shock and pressure waves cause minimal damage to brain tissue . . . it is possible that victims of FAEs are not rendered unconscious by the blast, but instead suffer for several seconds or minutes while they suffocate from ruptured lungs." (1993 DIA report quoted in Human Rights Watch, "Backgrounder on Russian Fuel Air Explosives." http://www.hrw.org/press/ 2000/02/checho215b.htm, accessed March 20, 2000.

9. Interview with former firm employee, summer 1999.

10. Anthony Daniels, "There's Nothing We Can Do to Help Sierra Leone," *Sunday Telegraph,* September 3, 2000. http://www.dailytelegraph.co.uk:80/ dt?ac=002830376029449& rtmo=lnFnQAot&atmo=HHHH22NL&pg=/00/9/3/d001.html

11. Among the SOA's graduates are notorious dictators Manuel Noriega and Omar Torrijos of Panama, Leopoldo Galtieri and Roberto Viola of Argentina, Juan Velasco Alvarado of Peru, Guillermo Rodriguez of Ecuador, and Hugo Banzer Suarez of Bolivia. Lower-level SOA graduates participated in human rights abuses that include the assassination of Archbishop Oscar Romero and the El Mozote massacre of 900 civilians. These individuals may be noto-

rious exceptions among the school's thousands of graduates, but their careers certainly benefited by their association with its top-level military training. School of the America's Watch, http://www.soaw.org/

12. Bruce Grant, "U.S. Military Expertise for Sale: Private Military Consultants as a Tool of Foreign Policy," National Defense University Institute for National Security Studies, Strategy Essay Competition, 1998. http://www.ndu.edu/inss/books/essaysch4.html

13. Chris Stephen, "KLA Trains Refugees to Recapture Border Territory," *Irish Times,* April 7, 1999.

14. Christian Jennings, "Private U.S. Firm Training Both Sides in Balkans," *Scotsman,* March , 2001. http://wwww/thescotsman.co.uk/world.cfm?id+51340

15. "Das Doppelspiel der Amerikaner," *Der Spiegel,* July 30, 2001. http://www.spiegel.de/ spiegel/0,1518,147569,00.html

16. Jeffrey Herbst, "The Regulation of Private Security Forces," in *The Privatisation of Security in Africa,* ed. Greg Mills and John Stremlau (Pretoria: South Africa Institute of International Affairs, 1999), p. 121. A parallel is in the profession of defense lawyers, who range from those working for those clients that they truly believe are innocent to those specializing in aiding known criminals.

17. Global Coalition for Africa, *African Social and Economic Trends,* Annual Report 1999/ 2000.

18. "Rogue Wave-Rogue Trader: Financial Storms Heading Towards the U.S. Economy," *Financial Sense On-Line,* October 26, 2000. http://www.financialsense.com/series2/rogue .htm

19. "Who Is Yair Klein and What Is He Doing in Colombia and Sierra Leone?" Democracy NOW! Program, *Pacifica Radio,* June 1, 2000; *Colombia Bulletin* 3, no. 1 (Spring 1998).

20. Damien Lilly, "From Mercenaries to Private Security Companies: Options for Future Policy Research," *International Alert* brief (November 1998).

21. Juan Carlos Zarate, "The Emergence of a New Dog of War: Private International Security Companies, International Law, the New World Order," *Stanford Journal of International Law* 34 (Winter 1998): 75–156.

22. Samia Aoul et al., "Towards a Spiral of Violence? The Dangers of Privatizing Risk Management in Africa," memorandum, Working Group on Human Rights in Congo, Development and Peace, Mining Watch, February 2000.

23. Antony Barnett, "Anger at Kosovo Mines Contract: Firm Accused of Human Rights Abuses Wins Million-Pound Government Deal," *Observer,* May 7, 2000. http://www.observer .co.uk/uk_news/0.7903,218247,00.html; Partap Chatterjee, "Mercenary Armies and Mineral Wealth, *Covert Action Quarterly* (Fall 1997).

24. Ken Penhaul, "Americans Blamed in Colombia Raid," *San Francisco Chronicle,* June 15, 2001; Phil Stewart, "U.S. Pilots Summoned in Colombian Bombing Probe," *Reuters,* June 14, 2001; T. Christian Miller, "A Colombian Town Caught in a Cross-fire," *Los Angeles Times,* March 17, 2002.

25. Brian Wood and Johan Peleman, *The Arms Fixers,* PRIO Report, March 1999; ; "Mercenaries and Arms Dealers in the Post-Cold War World: Interview with Ken Silverstein," *Connection,* August 11, 2000. Transcript available at: http://www.theconnection.org/archive/ 2000/08/0811a.shtml

26. Wood and Peleman, "The Arms Fixers," p. 9; Alejandro Bustos, "Critics of Plan Colombia Denounce Washington's 'Secret War' in South America," *Vancouver Province,* June 18, 2001.

27. Peter Fabricius, "Private Security Firms Can End Africa's Wars Cheaply," *Saturday Star* (Johannesburg), September 23, 2000.

28. Robert Capps, "Outside the Law," *Salon,* June 28, 2002; http://archive. salon.com/ news/feature/2002/06/26/bosnia/; Antony Barnett, "British Firm Accused in Sex Scandal," *Guardian,* July 29, 2001. Indeed, the British tribunal that ruled against DynCorp in the case of Kathryn Bolkovac, an employee who was demoted and then fired after she reported the sex crimes within its international police force contract in Kosovo, was especially troubled. In

the words of Charles Twiss, the tribunal chairman, "We have considered DynCorp's explanation of why they dismissed her and find it completely unbelievable. There is no doubt whatever that the reason for her dismissal was that she made a protected disclosure and was unfairly dismissed." Sava Radovanovic, "The Seamy Side of Peacekeeping: Whistle-Blower Vindicated," *Associated Press,* August 11, 2002.

29. Patrick J. Cullen, Keeping the New Dog of War on a Tight Lease," *Conflict Trends,* no. 6 (July 2000). http://www.accord.org.za/publications/ct6/issue6/htm.

30. "Guns for Hire Again," *Africa Confidential,* November 23, 2001.

31. Cullen, "Keeping the New Dog of War."

32. Jeffrey Herbst, "The Regulation of Private Security Forces."

33. Philip Winslow, "Why Africa's Armies Open Arms to Elite Fighters from South Africa," *Christian Science Monitor,* October 19, 1995, p. 1.

34. Cullen, "Keeping the New Dog of War."

35. Doug Brooks, "Creating the Renaissance Peace," paper presented at Africa Institute's 40th Anniversary Conference, May 30, 2000, Pretoria; ; Doug Brooks, "Write a Cheque, End a War: Using Private Military Companies to End African Conflicts," *Conflict Trends,* no. 6 (July 2000). http://www.accord.org.za/publications/ct6/issue6/htm.

36. Interview with PMF executive, June 2001. That the executive was not with the firm Control Risks heightened his credibility.

37. Cullen, "Keeping the New Dog of War."

38. Spicer, *Unorthodox Soldier,* p. 18.

39. Lilly, "From Mercenaries."

40. Interview with firm executive, February 2001.

41. Jason Nisse, "Cash for Combat," *Independent,* November 21, 1999.

42. "Why We Help Where Governments Fear to Tread," *Sunday Times,* May 24, 1998.

43. Spicer, *Unorthodox Soldier,* p. 159. *Peta Thorycroft, "Mobutu Couldn't Afford SA Mercenaries," Weekly Mail & Guardian,* July 18, 1997.

44. Spicer, *Unorthodox Soldier,* p. 50.

45. Nisse, "Cash For Combat."

46. William Hartung, "Deadly Legacy Update: U.S. Arms and Training Programs in Africa," World Policy Institute Documents, March 22, 2001.

47. Ashton Carter and John White, *Keeping the Edge* (Cambridge: MIT Press, 2001), p. 176.

48. Legitimacy arises from the consent of the people to the sovereign to provide security. But, if another gives consent, there is no reason for their consent in turn. The "location of sovereign judgment" argument illustrates why subcontracting security does not provide the legitimacy indirectly. Whereas sovereignty is centralized to avoid conflicts, in subcontracting conflicts of interests (particularly if private) are inherent. Thomas Hobbes, *The Leviathan* (1651), chapter 30. Available at http://www.orst.edu/instruct/phl302/texts/hobbes/leviathan-contents.html

49. John Hoffman, *Beyond the State* (Cambridge, Mass.: Polity Press, 1995), p. 78.

50. As quoted in Jack Kelley, "Safety at a Price: Military Expertise for Sale or Rent," *Pittsburgh Post-Gazette,* February 15," 2000.

51. Hoffman, *Beyond the State,* p. 83; Michael McManus, *From Fate to Choice: Private Bobbies, Public Beats* (Aldershot, Eng.: Avebury, 1995), p. 11.

52. Indeed, an estimated 8–10 million were killed during the private rule of Belgian Congo. Adam Hochschild, *King Leopold's Ghost: A Story of Greed, Terror, and Heroism in Colonial Africa* (New York: Houghton Mifflin, 1999); Christopher Clapham, *Africa and the international System: The Politics of State Survival* (Cambridge: Cambridge University Press, 1996), p. 26.

53. Blaine Harden, "Africa's Gems: Warfare's Best Friend, *New York Times,* April 6, 2000.

54. Peter Lock, "Military Downsizing and Growth in the Security Industry in SubSaharan Africa," *Strategic Analysis* 22, no. 9 (December 1998).

55. Alex Vines, "The Business of Peace: 'Tiny' Rowland, Financial Incentives and the Mozambican Settlement," *Accord: An International Review of Peace Initiatives,* 1998.

56. Martha Huggins, "Armed and Dangerous," Americas.Org, November 2000. http://www.americas.org/News/Features/200011_Private_Security/index.asp

57. Edward Blakely and Mary Snyder, *Fortress America: Gated Communities in the United States* (Washington, D.C.: Brookings Institution Press, 1997), p. 24.

58. Shearer, *Private Armies and Military Intervention,* p. 13.

15. CONCLUSIONS

1. "The important reason for the decline of PMCs like *EO* is that the market for privatizing war foundered on the problem of legitimacy in the eyes of the international community. The careful efforts of PMCs to overcome the negative view of mercenaries were ultimately unsuccessful." Kim Nossal, "Bulls to Bears: The Privatization of War in the 1990s," in *War, Money, and Survival,* ed. Gilles Carbonnier (Geneva: ICRC, February 2000). "At the turn of the century, it would appear as if PMCs have lost their competitive edge in Africa . . . Companies such as Executive Outcomes seem to have been marginalised by market forces." Chris Dietrich, "The Commercialisation of Military Deployment in Africa," *African Security Review* 9, no. 1 (January 2000).; See also David Isenberg, *Soldiers of Fortune Ltd.: A Profile of Today's Private Sector Corporate Mercenary Firms,* Center for Defense Information Monograph, November 1997..

2. Christopher Clapham, "Africa Security Systems: Privatisation and the Scope for Mercenary Activity," in *The Privatisation of Security in Africa,* ed. Greg Mills and John Stremlau (Pretoria: South Africa Institute of International Affairs, 1999). Jeffery Herbst, "The Regulation of Private Security Forces," in *The Privatisation of Security in Africa,* ed. Greg Mills and John Stremlau (Pretoria: South Africa Institute of International Affairs, 1999), p. 123; Gumisai Mutume, "Private Military Companies Face Crisis in Africa," *InterPress Service,* December 11, 1998..

3. "Are Private Security Forces Sometimes Preferable to National Military Forces?" Conference Notes, *Fiftieth Anniversary Symposium of the Moore Society on International Law,* University of Virginia, February 24, 2001.

4. Herbst, "The Regulation of Private Security Forces," p. 126.

5. Thomas Adams, "The New Mercenaries and the Privatization of Conflict," *Parameters* (Summer 1999): 103–116. http://carlisle-www.army.mil/usawc/paramaters/99summer/adams.htm

6. Donald T. Wynn, "Managing the Logistics-Support Contract in the Balkans Theater," *Engineer* (July 2000). http://call.armly.mil/call/trngtr/tq4–00/wynn.htm

7. Doug Brooks and Hussein Solomon, "From the Editor's Desk," *Conflict Trends,* no. 6 (July 2000). http://www.accord.org.za/publications/ct6/issue6/htm

8. Kenneth Waltz, *Theory of International Relations* (New York: McGraw Hill, 1979), pp. 76–77 and 127–28. Also see João Resende-Santos, "Anarchy and the Emulation of Military Systems: Military Organization and Technology in South America, 1870–1914," *Security Studies* 5, no. 3 (Spring 1996): 193–260.

9. "The very existence of such companies has boosted demand," United Nations Commission on Human Rights, Report on the question of the use of mercenaries as a means of violating human rights and impeding the exercise of the right of peoples to self determination." 57th Session, Item 7, Special Rapporteur, January 2001.

10. Isenberg, "Soldiers of Fortune, Ltd."

11. Global Coalition for Africa and International Alert, "The Privatization of Security in Africa," Conference Report, Washington, D.C., March 12, 1999. http://www.gca-cma.org/esecurity.htm#0399

12. Sarah Lunday, "Firms Join Security Drive," *Charlotte Observer,* February 13, 2002.

13. Jimmy Burns, "Corporate Security: Anxiety Stirred by Anti-Western Sentiment," *Financial Times,* April 11, 2002.

14. James Des Roches, spokesmen for Pentagon's Defense Security Cooperation Agency, as quoted in Esther Schrader, "U.S. Companies Hired to Train Foreign Armies," *Los Angeles Times,* April 14, 2002.

15. Rick Scavetta, "Brown & Root to Begin Making Improvements to Uzbekistan Base," *European Stars and Stripes,* May 2, 2002. BRS also took over the main U.S. bases in Afghanistan at Bagram and Khandahar.

16. P. W. Singer and Anja Manuel, "A New Model Afghan Army," *Foreign Affairs* 81, no. 4 (July 2002): 44–59; Schrader, "U.S. Companies Hired to Train Foreign Armies."

17. David Leppard, "Mercenaries Chase 20 Million Prize for the Head of Bin Laden," *Sunday Times,* September 30, 2001; Paul Bedard, "A Bounty Hunt for Bin Laden Yields heads, Ears," *U.S. News and World Report,* July 29, 2002.

18. U.S. House of Representatives HR 3076, "The September 11 Marque and Reprisal Act of 2001," submitted by Rep. Ron Paul, October 10, 2001. Poll results reported at www .techcentralstateion.com/defense.asp, September 22, 2001.

19. Global Coalition for Africa, *African Social and Economic Trends,* Annual Report 1999/ 2000.

20. Elizabeth Rubin, "An Army of One's Own," *Harper's Magazine,* February 1997.

21. Examples include Ronald Coase, "The Nature of the Firm," *Economica* 4 (1937): 386–405; Thrain Eggertson, *Economic Behavior and Institutions* (New York: Cambridge University Press, 1990); Douglass C. North, *Institutions, Institutional Change, and Economic Performance* (New York: Cambridge University Press, 1990); Roland Vaubel and Thomas Willett, *The Political Economy of International Organizations* (Boulder, Colo.: Westview Press, 1991); "War, Chaos, and Business: Modern Business Strategy," Kettle Creek Corporation Report, 2001.

22. Such as EO's support of elections in Sierra Leone. Similarly, the argument has been made that certain firms have expanded into the humanitarian sphere, for example by offering demining services, driven not by traditional profit or military motives, but rather as an indirect path to gaining respectability for their firms. William Reno, *Warlord Politics and African States* (London: Lynne Rienner, 1998); Antony Barnett, "Anger at Kosovo Mines Contract: Firm Accused of Human Rights Abuses Wins Million-Pound Government Deal," *Observer,* May 7, 2000. http://www.observer.co.uk/uk_news/0,6903,218247,00.html.

23. Stephen Zamparelli, "Contractors on the Battlefield: What Have We Signed Up For?" Air War College Research Report, March 1999.

24. Susan Davidson, "Where Is the Battle-line for Supply Contractors?" U.S. Air Force Air Command and Staff College Research Report, April 1999.

25. General Accounting Office, "Contingency Operations: Army Should Do More to Control Contract Cost in the Balkans," NSDIAD-00–225, October 6, 2000. http://www.gao .gov

26. Jamie Wilson and Kevin Maguire, "American Firm in Bosnia Sex Trade Row Poised to Win MoD Contract," *Guardian,* November 29, 2002.

27. "Outsourcing 2000," *Fortune,* May 29, 2000, pullout section.

28. Stephen Newbold, "Competitive Sourcing and Privatization: An Essential USAF Strategy," *Contractors on the Battlefield,* Air Force Logistics Management Agency, December 1999.

29. R. Philip Deavel, "Political Economy of Privatization for the American Military," *Air Force Journal of Logistics* 22, (Summer 1998): 3–9. Available online at http://www.il.hq.af.mil/ aflma/lgj/vol22_no2_6aug_web_order.pdf

30. Interview with U.S. Air Force contracting officer, June 2002.

31. Zamparrelli, "Contractors on the Battlefield," 37.

32. Wynn, "Managing the Logistics-Support."

33. Joseph Michels, "A Civil Sector force Multiplier for the Operational Commander," *Global Thinking, Global Logistics* (Washington: Air Force Logistics Management Agency, December 1999).

34. Doug Brooks and Hussein Solomon, "From the Editor's Desk."

35. Private correspondence, September 2000.

36. Greg Mills and John Stremlau, "The Privatisation of Security in Africa: An Introduction," in *The Privatisation of Security in Africa,* ed. Greg Mills and John Stremlau (Pretoria: South Africa Institute of International Affairs, 1999), 14.

37. The ITAR regimes are available at http://www.pmdtc.org/reference.htm

38. Avant, 2000.

39. These procedures are implemented by the Department of State's Office of Defense Trade Controls (ODTC) under the Arms Export Control Act and the International Traffic in Arms Regulation. Bruce Grant, "U.S. Military Expertise for Sale: Private Military Consultants as a Tool of Foreign Policy," National Defense University Institute for National Security Studies, Strategy Essay Competition, 1998. http://www.ndu.edu/inss/books/essaysch4.html

40. As quoted in Russell Miller, *The East Indiamen* (New York: Time-Inc., 1980).

41. These include "Private Military Companies-Independent or Regulated?" Sandline White Paper, March 1998, available at http://www.sandline.com/site/index.html; Herbert Howe, "Global Order and Security Privatization," *Strategic Form*, no. 40 (May 1998); ; Isenberg, *Soldiers of Fortune Ltd.*; Doug Brooks, "Write a Cheque, End a War Using Private Military Companies to End African Conflicts"; Stephen Mbogo, "Mercenaries? No, PMCs," *West Africa Magazine*, September 18, 2000, pp. 10–13; Global Coalition for Africa and International Alert, "The Privatization of Security in Africa," Conference Report, Washington, D.C., March 12, 1999. http://www.gca-cma.org/esecurity.htm#0399

42. Brooks and Solomon, "From the Editor's Desk."

43. Alex Vines, "The Business of Peace: 'Tiny' Rowland, Financial Incentives, and the Mozambican Settlement," *Accord: An International Review of Peace Initiatives.* http://www.c-r.org/acc_moz/contents_moz.htm.
For example, the proposed IPOA code of conduct is a well-intentioned first measure.

44. Avant, "In Focus: Privatizing Military Training."

45. Ibid.

46. The full text of the law is available at http://www.feds.com/basic_svc/public_law/106–523.htm

47. Global Coalition for Africa and International Alert, "Privatization."; Anne-Marie Slaughter, "The Real New World Order," *Foreign Affairs* (September 1997).

48. A green paper is a policy paper that discusses the issues but makes no formal recommendations. "Private Military Companies: Options for Regulation," House of Commons, February 12, 2002.

49. Paul Waugh, "Mercenaries as Peacekeepers Plan Under Fire," *Independent*, February 14, 2002.

50. This is an amended approach of that suggested by Mills and Stremlau, *Privatisation of Security in Africa*, p. 19.

51. Mbogo, "Mercenaries? No, PMCs."

52. Martin Van Creveld, The Rise and Decline of the State *(Cambridge: Cambridge University Press,* 1999), p. 429.

POSTSCRIPT: THE LESSONS OF IRAQ

1. P. W. Singer, "Iraq Can Wait till Phase 1 Done," *Baltimore Sun*, March 19, 2002.

2. T. Christian Miller, "Contractors Outnumber Troops in Iraq," *Los Angeles Times*, July 4, 2007, p. 1.

3. Bernd Debusmann, "In Outsourced U.S. Wars, Contractor Deaths Top 1,000,"*Reuters*, July 3, 2007.

4. Cam Simpson and Aamer Madhani, U.S. Cash Fuels Human Trade, *Chicago Tribune*, October 9, 2005.

5. William Matthews, "JCS Nominee Is Warned: Crack Down on Contractors." *Defense News*, August 6, 2007, p. 14.

6. Matt Kelley, "Largest Iraq Contract Rife With Errors," *USA Today*, July 17, 2007.

7. Ibid.

8. Major General George Fay and Lieutenant General Anthony Jones, U.S. Army "Investigation of Intelligence Activities at Abu Ghraib," 2004. Available http://news.findlaw.com/hdocs/docs/dod/fay82504rpt.pdf.

9. David Phinney, "Marines Jail Contractors in Iraq," CorpWatch.com, June 7, 2005.

10. Robert Young Pelton, "Blackwater Contractor Kills Vice President's: Green Zone Shooting Just One of Many Industry 'Dirty Secrets' Iraqslogger.com, February 8, 2007; "In Iraq, a Private Realm of Intelligence Gathering," *Washington Post,* July 1, 2007; Sean Raymont, "'Trophy' Video Exposes Private Security Contractors Shooting Up Iraqi Drivers," *Telegraph,* Nov. 26, 2005; Tom Jackman, "U.S. Contractor Fired On Iraqi Vehicles for Sport, Suit Alleges," *Washington Post,* November 17, 2006; A20.

11. For further on this, please see P. W. Singer, "Frequently Asked Questions on the UCMJ Change and Its Applicability to Private Military Contractors," January 12, 2007, available at http://pwsinger.com/commentary_070112.html; Congressional Research Service, "Private Security Contractors in Iraq: Background, Legal Status, and Other Issues," updated June 21, 2007; available at http://www.fas.org/sgp/crs/natsec/RL32419.pdf.

12. Kathleen Schalch, "KBR Drivers Say They Risked Their Lives to Pad Profits," National Public Radio, *Morning Edition,* June 8, 2004.

13. Matt Kelley, "Record Cases in Contract Probe; Crackdown Aims at 'Second Insurgency,'" *USA Today,* August 15, 2007.

14. Renae Merle, "Government Short Of Contracting Officers: Officials Struggle to Keep Pace With Rapidly Increasing Defense Spending," *Washington Post,* July 5, 2007, Pg. E8.

15. Roxana Tiron, "Watchdog Group: Government Awards Contracts Despite Firms' Misconduct," *The Hill,* July 19, 2007.

16. "Testimony of General Barry R. McCaffrey (USA, Ret.), Adjunct Professor of International Relations, United States Military Academy, Before The House Armed Services Committee," *PRNewswire-USNewswire,* July 31, 2007.

17. GAO, *Rebuilding Iraq: Actions Still Needed to Improve the Use of Private Security Providers,* GAO-06-865T June 13, 2006, available at: http://www.gao.gov/docdblite/details.php?rptno=GAO-06-865T.

18. As quoted in "Contractors in Spotlight as Shootings Add Up," *Charlotte Observer,* September 11, 2005, p. 6a.

19. Bill Sizemore, "Escort Offers 'Services' to Private Military Contractors in Iraq," *Virginian-Pilot,* August 3, 2007.

20. Major General George Fay and Lieutenant General Anthony Jones, U.S. Army "Investigation of Intelligence Activities at Abu Ghraib," 2004. Available http://news.findlaw.com/hdocs/docs/dod/fay82504rpt.pdf.

21. P.W. Singer, "Humanitarian Principles, Private Military Agents: Some Implications of the Privatized Military Industry for the Humanitarian Community" in Humanitarian Policy Group, *Resetting the Rules of Engagement: Trends and Issues in Military–Humanitarian Relations,* February 2006. Download at http://www.brookings.edu/views/articles/singer20060307.htm.

22. For further on this episode, please see Robert Young Pelton, *Licensed to Kill,* New York: Crown, 2006.

23. As quoted on Nathan Hodge, "Revised US Law Spotlights Role of Contractors on Battlefield." *Jane's Defense Weekly,* January 10, 2007, p. 10.

24. As quoted in William Matthews, "Contractor Crackdown: Civilian Contract Employees Can Now Be Prosecuted under the UCMJ," *Armed Forces Journal,* February 2007, http://www.armedforcesjournal.com/2007/02/2471808.

25. P. W. Singer, "The Law Catches Up to Private Militaries, Embeds," *DefenceTech,* January 3, 2007, available at http://www.defensetech.org/archives/003123.html.

Bibliography

"A Bill before the U.S. Congress Would Prohibit the Use of Private Firms in the Fight against Drugs." *Bogota Semana,* May 7, 2001.

Abrams, Fran. "British Officer Advised Gunship Killers." *The Independent,* September 7, 2000. http://www.independent.co.uk/news/World/Africa/2000-09/afuk070900.html

Adams, James. *The Next World War.* New York: Simon & Schuster, 1998.

Adams, Thomas. "The New Mercenaries and the Privatization of Conflict." *Parameters* (Summer 1999): 103–116. http://carlisle-www.army.mil/usawc/Parameters/99summer/adams.htm

"African Peacekeeping 'Could Be Privatized.'" Ananova.com, September 26, 2000. http://www.ananova.com/news/story/sm_68734.html

Air Force Field Manual 1-1: Basic Aerospace Doctrine of the United States Air Force. Washington D.C.: U.S. Government Printing Office, 1992.

Alden, Diane. "Soldiers R Us: The Corporate Military." *SpinTech,* September 12, 1999. http://www.spintechmag.com/9909/da0999.htm.

Allen-Mills, Terry. "France's Scandal Trail Leads to US." *The Times.* December 31, 2000. http://www.sunday-times.co.uk/

Alvarez, Steve. "MPRI: A Private Military." *Stars and Stripes,* October 30, 2000. http://www.stripes.com/servlet/News/ViewArticle?articleId=100033570&buildId=100033587

"America's 100 Fastest-Growing Companies." *Fortune,* September 6, 1999.

Aning, Emmanuel Kwesi. "Africa's Security in the New Millennium: State or Mercenary Induced Stability?" *Conflict Trends,* no. 6 (July 2000). http://www.accord.org.za/publications/ct6/issue6.htm

Aoul, Samia, et al. "Towards a Spiral of Violence?—The Dangers of Privatizing Risk Management in Africa." Memorandum, Working Group on Human Rights in Congo, Development and Peace, Mining Watch Canada, February 2000.

Arbucki, Tammy. "Building a Bosnian Army." *Jane's International Defense Review,* August, 1997.

"Are Private Security Forces Sometimes Preferable to National Military Forces?" Conference Notes, Fiftieth Anniversary Symposium of the Moore Society on International Law, University of Virginia, February 24, 2001. http://www.law.virginia.edu/lawweb/lawweb2.nsf/0aee13661173471f852566cc007da682/8ee7d0a8c4dc5fb685256a1e0050c18f?OpenDocument&Highlight=0,Moore,society

Arkin, William. "The Underground Military." *Washington Post,* May 7, 2001. http://washingtonpost.com/wp-dyn/articles/A44024-2001May4.html

Armorgroup—Company Brief. Armorgroup Marketing Presentation, received February 2000.

Armor Holdings. "Armor Holdings, Inc., Reports Record Third Quarter Operating Results of $0.22 Per Diluted Share before Merger and Integration Charges and Other Unusual Expenses." *PRNewswire,* November 14, 2000.

———. "IBNet Announces Joint Marketing Agreement with Armorgroup." Armorgroup press release, April 7, 2000. www.armorholdings.com

———. "Proxy Statement: Annual Meeting of Stockholders to Be Held on June 15, 2000." Company report, June 2000.

"Arms, Money, and the Men: A Year of War in Chechnya." *Agence France Presse,* September 28, 2000. http://www.russiatoday.com/news.php3?id=204189

Arnold, Guy. *Mercenaries.* London: St. Martin's Press, 1999.

Art, Robert. "Force and Fungibility Reconsidered." *Security Studies* 8, no. 4 (Summer 1999).

Art, Robert J., and Robert Jervis, eds. *International Politics: Anarchy, Force, Political Economy, and Decision Making.* Glenview, Ill.: Scott Foresman, 1985.

Aston, Trevor, ed. *Crisis in Europe, 1560–1660.* London: Routledge & Kegan Paul, 1965.

Auster, Richard D., and Morris Silver. *The State as a Firm: Economic Forces in Political Development.* Boston: Martinus Nijhoff, 1979.

Australian Broadcasting Corporation. "Dogs of War." *Lateline,* broadcast May 18, 2000. Transcript available at http://www.abc.net.au/lateline/archives/s128621.htm

———. "Sierra Leone—Soldiers of Fortune." Australian Broadcasting Corporation Documentary. Producer Mark Corcoran. August 2000. Transcript at www.abc.net/foreign

Avant, Deborah. "From Mercenaries to Citizen Armies: Explaining Change in the Practice of War." *International Organization* 54, no. 1 (Winter 2000).

———. "In Focus: Privatizing Military Training." *Foreign Policy in Focus* 5, no. 17 (May 2000). http://www.foreignpolicy-infocus.org/briefs/vol5/v5n17mil.html

———. "The Market for Force: Exploring the Privatization of Military Services." Paper prepared for discussion at the Council on Foreign Relations Study Group, the Arms Trade and the Transnationalization of the Defense Industry: Economic versus Security Drivers, 1999.

Azar, Edward E., and Chun-in Moon, eds., *National Security in the Third World: The Management of Internal and External Threats.* Hants: Edward Elgar, 1988.

Baldwin, David. "Force, Fungibility, and Influence." *Security Studies* 8, no. 4 (Summer 1999).

Barnett, Antony. "Anger at Kosovo Mines Contract: Firm Accused of Human Rights Abuses Wins Million-Pound Government Deal." *Observer,* May 7, 2000. http://www.observer.co.uk/uk_news/0,6903,218247,00.html

Bates, Robert. *Prosperity and Violence.* New York: Norton, 2001.

Bayley, C. C. *Mercenaries for the Crimea: The German, Swiss, and Italian Legions in British Service, 1854–56.* Montreal: McGill-Queens University Press, 1977.

———. *War and Society in Renaissance Florence: The "De Militia" of Leonardo Bruni.* Toronto: University of Toronto Press, 1961.

Bedard, Paul. "A Bounty Hunt for Bin Laden Yields Heads, Ears." *U.S. News and World Report,* July 29, 2002.

Beelma, Maud. "Dining with the Devil: America's 'Tacit Cooperation' with Iran in Arming the Bosnians." *APF Reporter* 18, no. 2 (1996).

Bender, Bryan. "Defense Contracts Quickly Becoming Surrogate Wariors." *Defense Daily*, March 28, 1997, p. 490.

Berger, Sebastien. "Sandline Sues to Seize Nation's Assets." *Sunday Telegraph*, March 7, 1999.

Berman, Eric. *Re-Armament in Sierra Leone*. Small Arms Survey Occasional Paper 1, December 2000.

Betts, Richard. *Surprise Attack*. Washington, D.C.: Brookings Institution, 1982.

Biles, Peter. "Bitter Foes." *The World Today* 56, no. 7 (July 2000).

Binmore, Kenneth, and Larry Samuelson. "An Economist's Perspective on the Evolution of Norms." *Journal of Institutional and Theoretical Politics* 150, no. 1 (1994).

Bisseker, Claire. "Africa's Military Time Bomb." *Johannesburg Financial Mail*, December 11, 1998.

Black, Jeremy, ed. *European Warfare: 1453–1815*. London: Macmillan, 1999.

Blakely, Edward, and Mary Snyder. *Fortress America: Gated Communities in the United States*. Washington, D.C: Brookings Institution Press, 1997.

Bonn International Center for Conversion (BICC). *An Army Surplus—The NVA's Heritage*. BICC Brief no. 3, 1997. *www.bicc.de/weapons/brief*

Bonner, Raymond. "U.S. Reportedly Backed British Mercenary Group in Africa." *New York Times*, May 13, 1998.

———. "War Crimes Panel Finds Croat Troops 'Cleansed' the Serbs.' *New York Times*, March 20, 1999.

Bowe, Christopher. "Agency Aims to Swell the Ranks." *Financial Times*, August 10, 2000.

Boxer, C. R. *Jan Compagnie in Oorlog en Vrede*. London: Heinemann Educational Books, 1979.

Boyne, Sean. "The White Legion: Mercenaries in Zaire." *Jane's Intelligence Review*, June, 1997.

"BP Accused of Backing 'Arms for Oil' Coup." *London Sunday Times*, March 26, 2000.

Bradbury, M. *Aid Under Fire: Redefining Relief and Development Assistance in Unstable Situations*. Wilton Park Paper, supported by with DHA, ODI, and ActionAid, London: HMSO, 1995.

"Britain Uses Agency to Recruit for Military." *Reuters*, March 12, 2001.

"British Firm Is Offering Shipping Companies the Services of Up to 300 ex-British Army Gurkhas to Combat Piracy, Particularly in Asia." *Reuters*, February 24, 2000.

"British Firms Arming Sierra Leone Rebels." *London Sunday Times*, January 10, 1999.

"British-Russian Security Venture." *Intelligence Newsletter*, no. 304, January 30, 1997.

British Security 2010. Conference Proceedings Church House, Westminister, November 1995.

Broad, William. "Private Ventures Hope for Profits on Spy Satellites." *New York Times*, February 10, 1997, p. 1.

Broder, Jonathon. "Mercenaries: The Future of U.N. Peacekeeping? *Fox News*, June 26, 2000. Transcript available at http://www.foxnews.com/world/062300/un_broder.sml

Brooks, Douglas. "The Business End of Military Intelligence: Private Military Companies." *Military Intelligence Professional Bulletin,* September 1999.

Brooks, Doug. "Creating the Renaissance Peace." Paper presented at Africa Institute's 40th Anniversary Conference, May 30, 2000, Pretoria.

——. "Hope for the 'Hopeless Continent': Mercenaries." *Traders: Journal for the Southern African Region* no. 3 (July–October 2000).

——. "Messiahs or Mercenaries?" *International Peacekeeping* 7, no. 4 (2000): 129–144.

——. "Write a Cheque, End a War: Using Private Military Companies to End African Conflicts." *Conflict Trends,* no. 6 (July 2000). http://www.accord.org.za/publications/ct6/issue6.htm

Brooks, Doug, and Hussein Solomon. "From the Editor's Desk." *Conflict Trends,* no. 6 (July 2000). http://www.accord.org.za/publications/ct6/issue6.htm

Brower, J. Michael. "Outland: The Vogue of DOD Outsourcing and Privatization." *Acquisition Review Quarterly, no. 4 (Fall 1997).* Available online http://www.dsmc.dsm.mil/pubs/arq/97arq/browe.pdf

——. "Outsourcing at DOD: All It's Cracking People Up to Be?" *Military Review.* Vol. 77, November–December 1997): 67–68. http://wwwcgsc.army.mil/milrev/english/novdec97/insights.htm

Brown, Justin. "Internet Challenges Old Assumptions About Spying." *Christian Science Monitor.* April 6, 2000.

——. "The Rise of the Private-Sector Military." *Christian Science Monitor,* July 5, 2000. http://www.csmonitor.com/durable/2000/07/05/f-p3s1.shtml

Brown, Michael, et al., eds. *Theories of War and Peace: An International Security Reader.* Cambridge: MIT Press, 1998.

Brummer, Stephaans. "Investing in the Bibles and Bullets Business." *Weekly Mail & Guardian,* September 16, 1994.

——. "SA Arms 'Stoke' the Burundi Fire." *Mail & Guardian,* December 5, 1997.

Bryce, Robert. "The Candidate from Brown & Root." *Austin Chronicle,* August 25, 2000.

Bull, Hedley. *The Anarchical Society: A Study of Order in World Politics.* New York, Columbia University Press, 1977.

Burns, Jimmy. "Corporate Security: Anxiety Stirred by Anti-Western Sentiment." *Financial Times,* April 11, 2002.

Burton-Rose, Daniel, and Wayne Madsen. "Governments of, by, and forr the Corporations: Corporate Soldiers." *Multinational Monitor* 20, no. 3 (March 1999). http://www.essential.org/monitor/mm1999/mm9903.07.html#rose.

Business Executives for National Security Tooth to Tail Commission. "After Kosovo: Operation 'Restore Balance.'" Update no. 33, May 25, 1999. www.bens.org/pubs

——. "Defense Department Headquarters—Too Many Chiefs, Not Enough Warriors." Update no. 7, November 14, 1997. www.bens.org/pubs.

Butcher, Tim. "UN Force Is Upstaged by British Expertise." *The Telegraph,* May 12, 2000. http://www.telegraph.co.uk:80/et?ac=000291992355051&rtmo=QxHeeOeR&atmo=rrrrrYas&pg=/et/00/5/12/wsie212.html

Cahlink, George. "Army of Contractors." *Government Executive,* February 2002.

Campbell, Gordon. *Contractors on the Battlefield: The Ethics of Paying Civilians to En-*

ter Harm's Way and Requiring Soldiers to Depend upon Them. Joint Services Conference on Professional Ethics 2000. Springfield, Virginia, January 27–28, 2000.

"Canadian, Anglo-Italian Firms to Train UK Navy." *Reuters,,* July 25, 2000. http://ca.dailynews.yahoo.com/ca/headlines/ts/story.html?s=v/ca/20000725/ts/canada_navy_col_1.html

"Can Anybody Curb Africa's Dogs of War" *The Economist,* January 16, 1999.

Carbonnier, Gilles. *War, Money, and Survival.* Geneva: ICRC, February 2000.

Caro, Robert A. *The Path to Power.* New York: Vintage Books, 1990.

Carr-Brown, Jonathon. "Sandline 'Paid Bribe' to Win War Contract." *The Sunday Times,* July 2, 2000. http://www.sundaytimes.co.uk/news/pages/sti/2000/07/02/stinwenws01024.html

Carter, Ashton, and John White. *Keeping the Edge.* Cambridge: MIT Press, 2001.

Center for Democracy and Development *The Impasse in Sierra Leone.* www.cdd.org.uk/pubs/sierraleone.htm. December 1999.

Cerny, Philip. "Neomedievalism, Civil War and the New Security Dilemma: Globalisation as Durable Disorder." *Civil Wars* 1, no. 1 (Summer 1999).

Charodeev, Gennady. "Foreign Wars: Russian Generals Involved in a War between Ethiopia and Eritrea." *Izvestia,* May 26, 2000): 1, 4.

Chatterjee, Partap. "Mercenary Armies and Mineral Wealth." *Covert Action Quarterly* (Fall 1997).

Christian Aid. *The Scorched Earth: Oil and War in Sudan.* March 2001. http://www.christian-aid.org.uk/indepth/0103suda/sudanoil.htm

Cilliers, Jakkie. "Book Review: Sean Dorney, *The Sandline Affair—Politics and Mercenaries and the Bourgainville Crisis,* ABC Books, Sydney, 1999, and Mary-Louise O'-Callaghan, *Enemies Within—Papau New Guinea, Australia, and the Sandline Crisis: The Inside Story,* Doubleday, Netley, 1999." *African Security Review* 9, no. 1 (February 2000).

Cilliers, Jakkie, and Peggy Mason. *Peace, Profit or Plunder? The Privatisation of Security in War-Torn African Societies.* Pretoria: Institute for Security Studies. January 1999.

"CIS Pilots Fight in Ethiopia." *Izvestia,* May 23, 2000, p. 4.

Clapham, Christopher. *Africa and the International System: The Politics of State Survival.* Cambridge: Cambridge University Press, 1996.

Coase, Ronald. "The Lighthouse in Economics." *Journal of Law and Economics* 17 (October 1974): 357–376.

——. "The Nature of the Firm." *Economica* 4 (1937): 386–405.

Cohen, Roger. "After Aiding Croatian Army, U.S. Now Seeks to Contain It." *New York Times,* October 28, 1995, p. 5.

Collier, Paul, and Anke Hoeffler. "Greed and Grievance in Civil War." *World Bank Policy Research Paper,* no. 2355, May 2000.

"Colombian Rebels Threaten U.S. Civilian 'Mercenaries.'" *Reuters,* April 4, 2001

The Commission on America's National Interests. *America's National Interest,* July 2000.

Conetta, Carl, and Charles Knight. *Defense Sufficiency and Cooperation: A U.S. Military Posture for the Post-Cold War Era.* Project on Defense Alternatives Briefing Report 9, March 1, 1998.

Contamine, Phillipe. *War in the Middle Ages.* New York: Basil Blackwell, 1984.

Copetas, Craig. "It's Off to War Again for Big U.S. Contractor." *Wall Street Journal,* April 4, 1999, p. A21.

"Corporate Security: Risk Returns." *The Economist,* November 20, 1999.

Correy, Stan. "The Business of Cybersecurity—the War Against Privacy?" Australian Broadcasting Corporation, August 20, 2000. http://www.abc.net.au/rn/talks/bbing/s167110.htm

Croatian Foreign Press Bureau. *Daily Bulletin,* July 15, 1996.

Cross, Tim. "Logistic Support for UK Expeditionary Operations." *RUSI Journal,* February 2000.

"Crude Awakening: The Role of the Oil and Banking Industries in Angola's Civil War and the Plunder of State Assets." A report by Global Witness. February 2000. Available at http://www.oneworld.org/globalwitness/

Cullen, Patrick J. "Keeping the New Dog of War on a Tight Lease." *Conflict Trends,* no. 6 (July 2000). http://www.accord.org.za/publications/ct6/issue6.htm

Daley, Paul. "Civilians May Form Special Reserve." *The Age* (Melbourne), April 28, 2000. http://www.theage.com.au/.

David, Stephen R.. *Defending Third World Regimes from Coups d'Etat.* New York: University Press of America, 1985.

——. "Explaining Third World Alignment." *World Politics* 43, no. 2 (January 1991): 233–256.

——. *Third World Coups d'Etat and International Security.* Baltimore: Johns Hopkins University Press, 1987.

Davis, James W., Jr. "Correspondence: Taking Offense at Offense-Defense Theory." *International Security* 24, no. 3 (Winter 1998/99).

Deavel, R. Philip. "Political Economy of Privatization for the American Military." *Air Force Journal of Logistics* 22 (Summer 1998): 3–9. http://www.il.hq.af.mil/aflma/lgj/vol22_no2_6aug_web_order.pdf

Decalo, Samuel. "Praetorianism, Corporate Grievances and Idiosyncratic Factors in African Military Hierarchies." *Journal of African Studies* 2, no. 2 (Summer 1975): 247–273.

——. *The Stable Minority: Civilian Rule in Africa.* Gainesville: Florida Academic Press, 1998.

De La Garza, Paul, and David Adams. "Contract's End Hints of Colombia Trouble." *St. Petersburg Times,* May 13, 2001.

——. "Military Aid . . . From the Private Sector." *St. Petersburg Times,* December 3, 2000.

——. "Military Know-How Finds Niche—And Some Critics." *St. Petersburg Times,* December 3, 2000.

Delbruck, Hans. *History of the Art of War: Within the Framework of Political History.* Westport, Conn.: Greenwood Press, 1975.

Diamond, Hohn. "Wary U.S. Offers Little Help in Sierra Leone Crisis." *Chicago Tribune,* May 18, 2000.

Dietrich, Chris. "The Commercialisation of Military Deployment in Africa." *African Security Review* 9, no. 1 (January 2000).

Dinnen, Sinclair. *Challenging the State: The Sandline Affair in Papua New Guinea.* Australian National University, Pacific Policy Paper 30, 1997.

——. "Militaristic Solutions in a Weak State: Internal Security, Private Contractors, and Political Leadership in Papua New Guinea," *The Contemporary Pacific* 11, no. 2 (Fall 1999).

Dixit, Avinash, and Susan Skeath, *Games of Strategy*. New York: Norton, 1999.

Donahue, John. *The Privatization Decision: Public Ends, Private Means*. New York: Basic Books, 1989.

Dorney, Sean. *The Sandline Affair: Politics and Mercenaries and the Bougainville Crisis*. Sydney: ABC Books, 1998.

Doswald-Beck, Louise. "Implementation of International Humanitarian Law in Future Wars." *Navy War College Review* (Winter 1999). www.nwc.navy.mil/press/Review/1999/winter/art2–w99.htm

Dowling, Maria, and Vincent Feck. "Joint Logistics and Engineering Contract." *Contractors on the Battlefield*. Air Force Logistics Management Agency. December 1999.

Doyle, Michael. *Empires*. Ithaca: Cornell University Press, 1986.

Dudley, Steven. "Colombia Vows End to Abuses." *Washington Post*, July 22, 2000, p. 15.

Duffield, Mark. "Internal Conflict: Adaptation and Reaction to Globalisation." *The Cornerhouse*. Briefing 12, 1999. http://cornerhouse.icaap.org/briefings/12.html

Duffy, Andy. "SA Mercenaries Working for the UN." *Electronic Mail & Guardian,* July 17, 1998.

Dugger, Ronnie. *The Politician: The Life and Times of Lyndon Johnson*. New York: Norton, 1982.

Dunne, Nancy. "Dope Wars (Part II): Crackdown on Colombia." *The Financial Times*, August 9, 2000.

Eggertson, Thrain. *Economic Behavior and Institutions*. New York: Cambridge University Press, 1990.

Enloe, Cynthia. *Ethnic Soldiers: State Security in Divided Societies*. Athens: University of Georgia Press, 1980.

"Ethiopia Eritrea: Eritrea Accuses Ethiopia of Using Mercenaries." *IRIN*, May 31, 2000.

Evans-Pritchard, Ambrose. "EU Force May Rent Ukraine Planes." *The Electronic Telegraph*, February 14, 2001.

"Ex-SAS Men in Secret Rescue." *New Zealand Herald*, March 9, 2000. http://www.nzherald.co.nz

Fabricus, Peter. "Private Security Firms Can End Africa's Wars Cheaply." *Saturday Star* (Johannesburg), September 23, 2000.

Farah, Douglas. "Cartel Hires Mercenaries to Train Security Forces." *Washington Post*, November 4, 1997.

Fearon, James D. "Rationalist Explanations for War," *International Organization* 49, no. 3 (Summer 1995): 379–414.

Feaver, Peter D. "The Civil-Military Problematique: Huntington, Janowitz, and the Question of Civilian Control." *Armed Forces and Society* 23, no. 2 (Winter 1996): 149–178.

Feigenbaum, Harvey, and Jeffrey Henig. "Privatization and Political Theory. *Journal of International Affairs* 50, Winter 1997, p. 338–57.

Fennell, James. "Private Security Companies: The New Humanitarian Agent." Presentation to the Conference on Interagency Co-ordination in Complex

Humanitarian Emergencies, 19 October 1999 at Cranfield University/Royal Military College of Science Shrivenham, UK.

Finer, S. E. *The Man on Horseback: The Role of the Military in Politics.* New York: Praeger, 1962.

Fisher, Franklin. "Somali Ranger Veteran Stresses Value of Support Troops." *Stars & Stripes.* April 3, 2001.

Fisher-Thompson, Jim. "French General Details Renewed Commitment to Africa." *USIS.* June 3, 1999. http://www.eucom.mil/programs/acri/usis/99jun03.htm

"Foreign Special Operations Forces." *Special Warfare: The Professional Bulletin of the John F. Kennedy Special Warfare Center and School* 11, no. 2, Spring, 1998.

Forsythe, Frederick. *The Dogs of War.* NY: Bantam, 1974.

Fox, Robert. "Fresh War Clouds Threaten Ceasefire: Secret U.S. Military Advice Helps 'Cocky' Croats Push Towards Eastern Slavonia." *Sunday Telegraph.* October 15, 1995.

Francis, David. "Mercenary Intervention in Sierra Leone: Providing National Security or International Exploitation?" *Third World Quarterly* 20, no. 2, April 1999.

Frazer, Jendayi. Sustaining Civilian Control: Armed Counterweights in Regime Stability in Africa. Stanford University Dissertation, March 1994.

Friedric, Carl J., and Seymour E. Harris, eds. *Public Policy.* Cambridge: Graduate School of Public Administration, 1958.

Gallup Organization. "Military on Top, HMOs Last in Public Confidence Poll," Poll Releases July 14, 1999. http://www.gallup.com/poll/releases/pr990714.asp

Garner, Jay M. "The Next Generation of Threat to US Military Superiority . . . 'Asymmetric Niche Warfare'." *Phalanx* 30, no. 1, March 1997.

Garrett, Geoffrey, and Barry Weingast. "Ideas, Interests, and Institutions." In Goldstein, Judith and Robert Keohane. *Ideas and Foreign Policy.* Ithaca: Cornell University Press, 1993.

General Accounting Office. "Contingency Operations: Army Should Do More to Control Contract Cost in the Balkans." NSDIAD-00-225. October 6, 2000. http://www.gao.gov/

——. "Contingency Operations: Opportunities to Improve the Logistics Civil Augmentation Program." GAO/NSIAD-97-63. February 1997.

——. "Outsourcing DoD Logistics: Savings Achievable But Defense Science Board's Projections Are Overstated." NSIAD-98-48, December 8, 1997.

"Generals For Hire." *Serbia Bulletin,* March 1996 edition.

Giddens, Anthony. *A Contemporary Critique of Historic Materialism.* Berkely: University of California Press, 1995.

Gill, Stephen. "Globalisation, Market Civilisation, and Disciplinary Neoliberalism." *Millennium* 24, no. 3 (Winter 1995).

Gilligan, Andrew. "Inside Lt. Col. Spicer's New Model Army." *Sunday Telegraph,* November 22, 1998.

Gilmour, Bob. "St. Albert Officer to Lead Forces' First Private Contract on Overseas Mission." *The Edmonton Journal,* July 6, 2000.

Gilpin, Robert. *War and Change in World Politics.* Cambridge: Cambridge University Press, 1981.

Glaser, Charles L., and Chaim Kaufmann, "What Is the Offense-Defense Balance and Can We Measure It?" *International Security* 22, no. 4 (Spring 1998): 44–82.

Global Coalition for Africa. *African Social and Economic Trends*. Annual Report 1999/2000. www.gca-cma.org

Global Coalition for Africa and International Alert. "The Privatization of Security in Africa." Conference Report, Washington, D.C., March 12, 1999. http://www.gca-cma.org/esecurity.htm#0399

Goldsworthy, David. "Civilian Control of the Military in Black Africa." *African Affairs* 80, no. 318 (January 1981): 49–74.

Gómez, Ignacio. "U.S. Mercenaries in Colombia." *Colombia Report*, July 16, 2000.

Goodenough, Patrick. "Are Guns-for-Hire the Answer in Sierra Leone?" CNSNews.com, May 11, 2000. http://www.cnsnews.com/ViewGlobal.asp?Page=b.html

Goodpaster, Andrew. *When Diplomacy Is Not Enough*. Report to the Carnegie Commission on Preventing Deadly Conflict, July 1996.

Goodwin, Christopher. " Mexican Drug Barons Sign Up Renegades from Green Berets." *Sunday Times*, August 24, 1997.

Gorman, Peter. "Ex-Navy Seals on Pay Per Kill Mission Plan Colombia's Mercenaries." *Narconews*, February 19, 2001.

Goulet, Yves. "DSL: Serving States and Multinationals." *Jane's Intelligence Review*, June 1, 2000.

Goulet, Yves. "Mixing Business with Bullets." *Jane's Intelligence Review*, September 1997.

———. "MPRI: Washington's Freelance Advisors." *Jane's Intelligence Review*, July 1998.

Graham, Bradley. "Ex-GIs Work to Give Bosnian Force a Fighting Chance." *Washington Post*, January 29, 1997.

Grant, Bruce. "U.S. Military Expertise for Sale: Private Military Consultants as a Tool of Foreign Policy." National Defense University Institute for National Security Studies, Strategy Essay Competition. 1998. http://www.ndu.edu/inss/books/essaysch4.html.

Gray, Chris. *Postmodern War: The New Politics of Conflict*. New York: Guilford, 1997.

Greenaway, Sean, and Andrew Harris. *Humanitarian Security; Challenges and Responses*. Paper presented to Forging Peace Conference, Harvard University, March 1998.

Griffith, G. T. *The Mercenaries of the Hellenistic World*. Groningen: Boom's Boekhuis, 1968.

Gullo, Karen. "Peacekeeping Helped Cheney Company." *AP*, August 28, 2000.

Guéhenno, Jean-Michel. "The Impact of Globalisation on Strategy," *Survival* 40 (Winter 2000).

Haftendorn, Helga, Robert O. Keohane, and Celeste A. Wallander. *Imperfect Unions: Security Institutions over Time and Space*. Oxford: Oxford University Press, 1999.

Haldon, John. *Warfare, State, and Society in the Byzantine World 565–1204*. London: UCL Press, 1999.

Halliburton. *Halliburton 1999 Annual Report to Investors*. http://www.halliburton.com/corp/ir/ir.asp

Hammer, Joshua, and Michael Isikoff. "The Narco-Guerrilla War." *Newsweek*, August 9, 1999.

Hanrahan, John D. *Government By Contract*. New York: Norton, 1983.

Harden, Blaine. "Africa's Gems: Warfare's Best Friend." *New York Times*, April 6, 2000.

Harris, Paul. "Bosnians Sign for U.S. Military Expertise." *Jane's Sentinal Pointer,* July 1996.

Hartung, William. "Deadly Legacy Update: U.S. Arms and Training Programs in Africa." World Policy Institute Documents, March 22, 2001.

Hedges, Stephen. "Out of D.C., Cheney Still Carried Clout." *Chicago Tribune,* August 10, 2000.

Held, David, Anthony McGrew, David Goldblatt, and Jonathan Perraton. *Global Transformations: Politics, Economics, and Culture.* Stanford,Calif.: Stanford University Press, 1999.

Heller, Joseph. *Catch-22.* New York: Scribner, 1961.

Henriques, Diana. "Mixed Reviews for Cheney in Chief Executive Role at Halliburton." *New York Times,* August 24, 2000.

Henry, Ryan, and C. Edward Peartree. "Military Theory and Information Warfare." *Parameters* (Autumn 1998): 121–135.

Hobbes, Thomas. *The Leviathan.* 1651. http://www.orst.edu/instruct/phl302/texts/hobbes/leviathan-contents.html

Hochschild, Adam. *King Leopold's Ghost: A Story of Greed, Terror, and Heroism in Colonial Africa.* New York: Houghton Mifflin, 1999.

Hoffman, John. *Beyond the State.* Cambridge: Polity, 1995.

Holbrooke, Richard. *To End a War.* New York: Random House, 1998.

Homer-Dixon, Thomas. "Environmental Scarcities and Violent Conflict: Evidence from Cases." *International Security* 19, no. 1 (Summer 1994): 5–40.

Horvath, John. "The Soros Effect on Central and Eastern Europe" *Telepolis* (June 1997). http://www.heise.de/tp/english/inhalt/te/1292/2.html

House of Commons. *Private Military Companies: Options for Regulation.* HC 577, February 12, 2002.

Howard, Michael. *War in European History.* London: Oxford University Press, 1976.

Howe, Herbert. "African Private Security." *Conflict Trends,* no. 6 (July 2000). http://www.accord.org.za/publications/ct6/issue6.htm

——. *Ambiguous Order: Military Forces in African States.* Boulder, Colo.: Lynne Rienner, 2001.

——. "Global Order and Security Privatization." *Strategic Forum,*no. 140 (May 1998).

——. "To Stabilize Tottering African Governments." *Armed Forces Journal International,* November 1996.

Huie, William. *Can Do! The Story of the Seabees.* New York, E. P. Dutton, 1944.

Human Rights Watch, "Backgrounder on Russian Fuel Air Explosives." http://www.hrw.org/press/2000/02/checho215b.htm, March 20, 2000.

Human Rights Watch. *Landmine Monitor: Africa Report.* 1999. http://www.hrw.org/hrw/reports/1999/landmine/WEBAFR1.html

Huntington, Samuel. *The Soldier and the State; The Theory and Politics of Civil-Military Relations.* New York: Random House, 1957.

"Hypocrisy in Action: What's the Real Iran-Bosnia Scandal?" *The New Yorker,* May 13, 1996.

"I Could Tell You, But I'd Have to Kill You: The Cult of Classification in Intelligence." *Stratfor.com.* Weekly Global Intelligence Update, September 18, 2000. www.stratfor.com

Ignatieff, Michael. *The Warrior's Honor: Ethnic War and the Modern Conscience.* New York: Henry Holt, 1998.

Ikenberry, G. John, ed. *American Foreign Policy: Theoretical Essays.* New York: Harper Collins, 1989.

"The IMF's Intelligence Helper." *Intelligence Newsletter,* April 5, 2001

"Improving the Combat Edge through Outsourcing." *Defense Viewpoint* 11, no. 30, March 1996.

Irish, Jenny. *Policing for Profit.* ISSS Monograph Series, no. 39, 1999.

Isenberg, David. "Have Lawyer, Accountant, and Guns, Will Fight: The New, Post-Cold War Mercenaries." Paper prepared for International Studies Association Convention, February 19, 1999.

Isenberg, David. "The New Mercenaries." *Christian Science Monitor,* October 13, 1998, p. 19.

——. *Soldiers of Fortune Ltd.: A Profile of Today's Private Sector Corporate Mercenary Firms.* Center FOR Defense Information Monograph, November 1997.

"It's Not Just Governments That Make War and Peace Now." *New York Times,* November 28, 1998.

"It's Off to War Again for Big U.S. Contractor. " *Wall Street Journal,* April 14, 1999, p. A21.

Jackson, Robert H. *Quasi-states: Sovereignty, International Relations, and the Third World.* New York: Cambridge University Press, 1990.

Janowitz, Morris. *The Professional Soldier: A Social and Political Portrait.* New York: Free Press, 1960.

Jennings, Christian. "Private U.S. Firm Training Both Sides in Balkans." *The Scotsman,* March 2, 2001. http://www.thescotsman.co.uk/world.cfm?id=51340

Jervis, Robert. "Cooperation Under the Security Dilemma." *World Politics* 30, January 1978.

Jervis, Robert, et al. *Psychology and Deterrence.* Baltimore: Johns Hopkins University Press, 1985.

Jones, Trevor, and Tim Newburn. *Private Security and Public Policing.* Oxford: Clarendon Press, 1998.

Kaiser, David. *Politics and War.* Cambridge: Harvard University Press, 1990.

Kaldor. Mary. *New and Old Wars.* Stanford, Calif.: Stanford University Press, 1999.

Kant, Immanuel. *Perpetual Peace, A Philosophical Sketch.* 1795. Available at http://www.constitution.org/kant/perpeace.htm

Kaplan, Robert. "The Coming Anarchy." *Atlantic Monthly,* February 1994.

Katzenstein, Peter, ed. *The Culture of National Security: Norms and Identity in World Politics.* New York: Columbia University Press, 1996.

Keegan, John. "The Warrior's Code of No Surrender." *U.S. News & World Report,* January 23, 1995, p. 47.

Kelley, Jack. "Safety at a Price: Military Expertise for Sale or Rent." *Pittsburgh Post-Gazette,* February 15, 2000.

——. " Safety at a Price: Security Is a Booming, Sophisticated, Global business." *Pittsburgh Post-Gazette.* February 13, 2000.

Kemp, Kenneth W., and Charles Hudlin. "Civilian Supremacy over the Military: Its Nature and Limits." *Armed Forces and Society* 19, no. 1 (Fall 1992).

Kennedy, Tim. "Israeli Legislators Seek to Halt Export of Arms, Mercenaries to Congo." *Moneyclips,* February 24, 1994.

Keohane, Robert. *International Institutions and State Power.* Boulder, Colo.: Westview, 1989.

———, ed. *Neorealism and Its Critics.* New York: Columbia University Press, 1986.

Kiernan, V. G. "Foreign Mercenaries and Absolute Monarchy." In *Crisis in Europe 1560–1660, ed. Trevor Aston, 117–140.* London: Routledge & Kegan Paul, 1965.

King, David, and Zachary Karabell, "The Generation of Trust: Public Confidence in the U.S. Military Since Vietnam." Paper prepared for Visions of Governance in the 21st Century project. December 1999. http://www.ksg.harvard.edu/prg/king/gentrust.pdf,;

Klare, Michael. "The Kalashnikov Age." *Bulletin of the Atomic Scientists* 55, no. 1 (January/February 1999). http://www.bullatomsci.org/issues/1999/jf99/jf99klare.html

Klare, Michael, and Yogesh Chandrani. *World Security: Challenges for a New Century.* New York: St. Martin's Press, 1998.

Knight, Samantha, et al. "The Croatian Army's Friends." *U.S. News & World Report,* August 21, 1995, p. 41.

Kohn, Richard. "Out of Control: The Crisis in Civil-Military Relations." *The National Interest,* no. 35 (Spring 1994): 3–17.

Kohn, Richard. "An Exchange on Civil-Military Relations." *The National Interest,* no. 36 (Summer 1994): 23–31.

Korbin, Stephen. "Back to the Future: Neomedievalism and the Postmodern Digital World Economy." *Journal of International Affairs* (Spring 1998): 361–386.

Kotlet, Jared. "Americans Work in Danger Zone in Colombia." *AP,* February 25, 2001.

Krause, Keith, and Michael Williams. "Broadening the Agenda of Security Studies: Politics and Methods." *Mershon International Studies Review* 40 (October 1996).

Kuperman, Alan. "Rwanda in Retrospect." *Foreign Affairs* 79, no. 1, January 2000. pp. 94–118.

"L-3 Communications Announces Acquisition of MPRI." *Business Wire,* July 18, 2000.

Lane, Frederic C. *Profits from Power: Readings in Protection Rent and Violence Controlling Enterprises.* Albany: SUNY Press, 1979.

Langley, Lester, and Thomas Schoonover. *The Banana Men: American Mercenaries and Entrepreneurs in Central America, 1880–1930.* Lexington: University Press of Kentucky, 1995.

Lathem, Niles. "America's Drug War Mercenaries." *New York Post,* April 29, 2001.

Latzko, David A. "The Market for Mercenaries." Paper presented at the Eastern Economic Association Meetings, Crystal City, Virginia, April 4, 1997.

Leander, Anna. "Global Ungovernance: Mercenaries, States, and the Control over Violence." Copenhagen Peace Research Institute Working Paper, 2002.

Lee, Jeffrey. "Give a Dog of War a Bad Name." *The Times,* May 4, 1998.

Lesser, Ian. *Countering the New Terrorism.* Santa Monica: RAND Corporation, 1999.

Levy, Jack S., and Michael M. Barnett, "Alliance Formation, Domestic Political Economy, and Third World Security," *Jerusalem Journal of International Relations* 14, no. 4 (December 1992): 19–40.

Lieber, Keir. "Grasping the Technological Peace: The Offense Defense Balance and International Security." *International Security* 25, no. 1 (Summer 2000): 179–206.

Lilly, Damien. "From Mercenaries to Private Security Companies: Options for Future Policy Research." *International Alert* brief, November 1998.

Linard, Andre. "Mercenaries SA." *LeMonde Diplomatique.* August 1998, p. 31. www.monde-diplomatique.fr/1998/08/Linard/10806.html

Little, Robert. "American Civilians Go Off to War, Too." *Baltimore Sun,* May 26, 2002.

Lizza, Ryan. "Sierra Leone, the Last Clinton Betrayal." *New Republic,* July 2000. http://www.tnr.com/072400/lizza072400.html

Lock, Peter. *Illicit Small Arms Availability.* Third International Berlin Workshop. Consolidating Peace through Practical Disarmament Measures and Control of Small Arms—From Civil War to Civil Society, Berlin, July 2–5, 1998. http://www.ssaa.org.au/berlinwksp.html

——. "Military Downsizing and Growth in the Security Industry in SubSaharan Africa." *Strategic Analysis* 22, no. 9 (December 1998).

Lowe, Christian. "Navy, Marine Corps Consider Privatizing Some Aerial Refueling." *Defense Week* August 21, 2000, p. 1.

——. "Services Look to Contractors to Fly 'Adversary' Aircraft." *Defense Week,* September 25, 2000, p. 1.

Lubold, Gordon. "Privatization Means Fewer Corps Cooks." *Marine Corps Times,* January 8, 2001, p. 9.

Luttwak. Edward. *Coup d'Etat: A Practical Handbook.* Cambridge: Harvard University Press, 1968.

——. "Towards Post-Heroic Warfare." *Foreign Affairs* 74, no. 3 (May/June 1995).

Lutyens, Marcia. "Military Operations (ex VAT)." *Volkskrant* (Netherlands), February 17, 2001.

Lynch, Colum. "For U.S. Firms War Becomes a Business." *Boston Globe,* February 1, 1997.

——. "Private Firms Aid U.N. on Sanctions: Wider Intelligence Capability Sought." *Washington Post,* April 21, 2001. http://www.washingtonpost.com/wp-dyn/articles/A44304–2001Apr20.html

Lynn-Jones, Sean M. "Offense-Defense Theory and Its Critics." *Security Studies* 4, no. 4, Summer 1995): 660–691.

MacDonnell, Hector. *The Wild Geese of the Antrim MacDonnells.* Dublin: Irish Academic Press, 1999.

Machiavelli, Niccolò. *The Prince.* 1515. Translated by W. K. Marriott. http://www.constitution.org/mac/prince12.htm

Malan, Mark. "Lean Peacekeeping Turns Mean: Crisis and Response in Sierra Leone." Paper presented to ISS security seminar, South Africa, May 18, 2000.

Malan, Mark, and Jakkie Cilliers. *Mercenaries and Mischief: The Regulation of Foreign Military Assistance Bill.* Institute for Security Studies Occasional Paper No 25, September 1997.

Mallett, Michael. *Mercenaries and their Masters: Warfare in Renaissance Italy.* Totowa, N.J.: Rowman and Littlefield, 1974.

Mandel, Robert. "The Privatization of Security." *Armed Forces & Society* 28, no. 1 (Fall 2001): 129–152.

Mandelbaum, Michael. "Is Major War Obsolete?" *Survival* 40 (Winter 1998): 35–47.

Margasak, Larry. "Report on Cheney, Bathrooms." AP, September 10, 2000.

Marley, Anthony D. "Problems of Terminating Wars in Africa," *Small Wars and Insurgencies* 8, no. 3 (Winter 1997).

Marquis, Christopher. "Inquiry on Peru Looks at a C.I.A. Contract." *New York Times*, April 28, 2001. http://www.nytimes.com/2001/04/28/world/28PLAN.html?pagewanted=print

Martin, Brendan. *In the Public Interest.* London: Zed Books, 1993.

Matthews, Jessica Tuchman. "Power Shift: The Rise of Global Civil Society," *Foreign Affairs* 76, no. 1 (January/February 1997).

——. "Redefining Security," *Foreign Affairs* (Spring 1989): 163–177.

Mbogo, Stephen. "Mercenaries? No, PMCs." *West Africa Magazine*, September 18, 2000): 10–13.

McDermott, Jeremy. "U.S. Crews Involved in Colombian Battle." *The Scotsman*, February 23, 2001.

McGreal, Chris. "Sierra Leone Peace Force Accused of Sabotage." *The Guardian*, August 20, 2000. http://www.guardianunlimited.co.uk/international/story/0,3604,366353,00.html

McGrory, Daniel, and Nicholas Woods. "Soldiers for Sale." *London Times*, May 9, 1998. www.the-times.co.uk/cgi-bin/Backissue.

McKirk, Jan. "Drug Sub in Andes Linked to Russians." *The Independent*, September 10, 2000.

McManus, Michael. *From Fate to Choice: Private Bobbies, Public Beats.* Aldershot, Eng.: Avebury, 1995.

McNeill, William. *The Pursuit of Power.* Chicago: University of Chicago Press, 1982.

Mearsheimer, John. "The False Promise of International Institutions." *International Security* 19, no. 3, (Winter 1994): 3–49.

Melymuka, Kathleen. "Kaboom! The Field of IT Outsourcing Is Dotted with Land Mines." *Computerworld*, March 17, 1997. http://www.computerworld.com/cwi/story/0,1199,NAV47_STO1331,00.html

Merx, Katie. "Cop Fired from Kosovo Job." *Detroit News*, February 25, 2000.

Mesic, Marco. "Croats Trained by Pentagon Generals." *Balcanica*, May 1996.

Metz, Steven. *Armed Conflict in the Twenty-first Century: The Information Revolution and Postmodern Warfare.* Strategic Studies Institute, U.S. Army War College. April 2000. http://carlisle-www.army.mil/usassi/ssipubs/pubs2000/conflict/conflict.htm

——. *Refining American Strategy in Africa.* U.S. Army War College, Strategic Studies Institute. April 2000. http://carlisle-www.army.mil/usassi/ssipubs/pubs2000.htm

——. *Strategic Horizons: The Military Implications of Alternative Futures.* Strategic Studies Institute, U.S. Army War College. March 7, 1997.

Michels, Joseph. "A Civil Sector Force Multiplier for the Operational Commander." *Global Thinking, Global Logistics.* Air Force Logistics Management Agency. December 1999.

Midlarsky, Manus I., ed. *Handbook of War Studies.* Boston: Unwin Hyman, 1989.

Miller, Russell. *The East Indiamen.* New York: Time-Incorporated, 1980.

Millett, Allan R. *The American Political System and Civilian Control of the Military: A Historical Perspective.* Columbus: Mershon Center of the Ohio State University, 1979.

Mills, Greg, and John Stremlau, eds. *The Privatisation of Security in Africa.* Pretoria: South Africa Institute of International Affairs, 1999.

Milton, Thomas J. "The New Mercenaries—Corporate Armies for Hire." *Foreign Area Officers Association Journal* (1997).

Mockler, Anthony. *Mercenaries.* London: Macdonald, 1969.

———. *The New Mercenaries.* London: Sidgewick & Jackson, 1985.

"More Weasel Words." *London Times,* October 22, 2000. http://www.sundaytimes .co.uk/news/pages/sti/2000/10/22/stinwcldro1002.html

Morrow, James D. *Game Theory for Political Scientists.* Princeton: Princeton University Press, 1994.

Moskos, Charles, and F. Wood, eds. *The Military: More Than Just a Job?* Washington, D.C.: Pergamon Brassey's, 1988.

Mseteka, Buchizya. "Angola Strained by War at Home and Abroad." *Reuters,* May 20, 1999.

"Mueller, John. "The Common Sense." *The National Interest* (Spring 1997).

Murphy, James. "DoD Outsources $500m in Spare Parts Work." PlanetGov.com, September 29, 2000.

Musah, Abdel-Fatau, and Kayode Fayemi. *Mercenaries: An African Security Dilemma.* London: Pluto Press, 2000.

Mutume, Gumisai. "Private Military Companies Face Crisis in Africa." *InterPress Service,* December 11, 1998.

Myers, Laura. "Pentagon's Computers Fail Hired Hackers' Test." *Seattle Times,* April 17, 1998.

Myers, Steven. "U.S. Spy Sub Said to Record Torpedo Blast Aboard Kursk." *New York Times,* August 29, 2000. http://www.nytimes.com/library/world/europe/ 082900russia-sub.html

Nathan, Adam, and Michael Prescott. "Gurkhas Called Up to Fill Army Ranks." *Sunday Times* (UK), June 11, 2000.

Neild, Robert. "Expose the Unsavory Business behind Cruel Wars." *International Herald Tribune,* February 17, 2000.

Newbold, Stephen. "Competitive Sourcing and Privatization: An Essential USAF Strategy." *Contractors on the Battlefield.* Air Force Logistics Management Agency. December 1999.

Nisse, Jason. "Cash for Combat." *The Independent,* November 21, 1999.

Noakes, Greg. "Israeli Commandos' Congo Connection." *Washington Report on Middle East Affairs* (April/May 1994): 22. http://www.washington-report.org/ backissues/0494/9404022.htm

North, Douglass C. *Institutions, Institutional Change, and Economic Performance.* New York: Cambridge University Press, 1990.

Nossal, Kim. "Bulls to Bears: The Privatization of War in the 1990s." In *War, Money and Survival,* ed. Gilles Carbonnier. Geneva: ICRC, February 2000.

"NSA Head: Tech Weakness Makes U.S.Vulnerable." CNN.com, February 12, 2001.

O'Brien, Kevin. "Military-Advisory Groups and African Security: Privatised Peacekeeping." *International Peacekeeping* 5, no. 3 (Autumn, 1998): 78–105.

——. "PMCs, Myths, and Mercenaries: The Debate on Private Militaries Companies." *RUSI Journal* (February 2000).

O'Connell, Robert L. *Of Arms and Men: A History of War, Weapons, and Aggression.* New York: Oxford University Press, 1989.

Ohmae, Kenichi. *The End of the Nation State: The Rise of Regional Economies.* New York: Free Press, 1995.

O'Meara, Kelly. "Dyncorp Disgrace." *Insight,* February 4, 2002.

"100 Fastest-Growing Companies" *Fortune,* September 2000. http://www.fortune.com/fortune/fastest/csnap/0,7130,45,00.html

"Operation Storm." *New York Review of Books,* October 22, 1998.

Ormrod, David. *The Reign of Edward II.* New Haven: Yale University Press, 1990.

O'Sullivan, Arieh. "Israeli Mercenaries in Congo May Face Fellow Israelis." *AP Worldstream,* February 3, 1994.

"Outsourcing 2000." *Fortune,* May 29, 2000, pullout section.

Parke, H. W. *Greek Mercenary Soldiers: From the Earliest Times to the Battle of Ipsus.* Oxford: Oxford University Press, 1933.

Parker, Andrew, and Francesco Guerrera. "Ex-Soldiers Find There Is Money to Be Made Out of Wars." *Financial Times,* April 17, 2001.

Parkman, Francis. *France and England in North America.* New York: Library of America, 1983.

Passage, David. *The United States and Colombia: Untying the Gordian Knot.* U.S. Army War College, Strategic Studies Institute. March 2000. http://carlisle-www.army.mil/usassi/ssipubs/pubs2000.htm

Pech, Khareen. "South African Mercenaries in Congo." *Electronic Mail & Guardian,* August 28, 1998.

Pech, Khareen, and David Beresford. "Africa's New-Look Dogs of War." *Weekly Mail & Guardian,* January 24, 1997.

Pech, Khareen, and Yusef Hassan. "Sierra Leone's Faustian Bargain." *Weekly Mail & Guardian,* May 20, 1997.

Pegg, Scott. "Corporate Armies for States and State Armies for Corporations: Addressing the Challenges of Globalization and Natural Resource Conflict." Paper prepared for delivery at the 2000 Annual Meeting of the American Political Science Association, Washington, D.C., August 31–September 3, 2000.

Penhaul, Karl. "Americans Blamed in Colombia Raid." *San Francisco Chronicle.* June 15, 2001, URL: http://www.sfgate.com/cgi-bin/article.cgi?file=/c/a/2001/06/15/MN219178.DTL.

Perlmutter, Amos. *The Military and Politics in Modern Times.* New Haven: Yale University Press, 1977.

Peters, Ralph. "The New Warrior Class." *Parameters* 24 (Summer 1994).

Piatt, Gregory. "GAO Report: Balkans Contracts Too Costly." *European Stars and Stripes,* November 14, 2000, p. 4.

Piening, Christopher. *Global Europe: The European Union in World Affairs.* New York: Lynne Rienner, 1997.

Porch, Douglas. *The French Foreign Legion.* New York: Harper Collins, 1991.

Porter, Gareth, "Environmental Security as a National Security Issue." *Current History* 94, no. 592 (May 1995): 218–222.

Posen, Barry. "Nationalism, the Mass Army, and Military Power. *International Security* 18, no. 2 (Summer 1993).

Power, Samantha. "The Croatian Army's Friends." *U.S. News and World Report,* August 21, 1995, p. 41.

Priest, Dana. "Special Alliances: The Pentagon's New Global Entanglements." *Washington Post,* July 12, 1998.

"Princes of Private U.S. Intelligence." *Intelligence Newsletter,* February 8, 2001.

"Private Military Companies—Independent or Regulated?" Sandline "White Paper," March 1998. http://www.sandline.com/site/index.html

Privatization 1997: A Comprehensive Report on Contracting, Privatization, and Government Reform. Reason Public Policy Institute, 11th Annual Report on Privatization 1997.

Privatization '98. Reason Public Policy Institute, 12th Annual Report on Privatization and Government Reform, 1998.

Pugliese, David. "Canadian Troops Trapped in Shipping Dispute." *The Ottawa Citizen,* July 25, 2000. http://www.ottawacitizen.com/national/000725/4506340.html

Pugliese, David. "Canadians Turn to Private Firms for EW Training, Combat Support." *The Ottawa Citizen,* September 7, 2000.

Pugliese, David. "Hire Mercenary Peacekeepers: General." *The Ottawa Citizen,* April 6, 1998.

"Puntland Elders Oppose British Maritime Firm's Plans to Set Up Base." *BBC Summary of World Broadcasts,* July 29, 2000.

Quetteville, Henri. "French Mercenary 'Is Behind Nudist Coup.'" *The Electronic Telegraph* (UK), August 11, 2000. http://www.telegraph.co.uk/et?ac=0032721 89007435&rtmo=fqqlvrMs&atmo=gggggDVK&pg=/et/00/8/11/wnude11.html

"RAF Puts Refuel Job on Market." *London Times,* December 22, 2000.

Ralston, David. *Importing the European Army.* Chicago: University of Chicago Press, 1990.

Rangel Suarez, Alfredo. "Parasites and Predators: Guerrillas and the Insurrection Economy of Colombia." *Journal of International Affairs* 53, no. 2 (Spring 2000): 577–601.

Rathmell, Andrew. "The Privatisation of Intelligence: A Way Forward for European Intelligence Cooperation." *Cambridge Review of International Affairs* 11, no. 2 (Spring 1998): 199–211.

Raum, Tom. "Wars Rage in Third of World Nations." Associated Press, December 30, 1999.

"Rebels Shell Rivals from Australian Patrol Boat." *The Age, June 7, 2000.* http://www.theage.com.au/breaking/0006/07/A44216-2000Jun7.shtml

Redlich, Fritz. *The German Military Enterpriser and His Work Force: A Study in European Economic and Social History.* Wiesbaden: Franz Steiner Verlag Gmbh, 1964.

Rees, Philip. "Colombia-Drug Wars." BBC, November 11, 2000. http://www.abc.net.au/foreign/2000/ep2-10.htm#lead

Regan, Tom. "Wars of the Future . . . Today." *Christian Science Monitor,* June 24, 1999.

Reno, William. "Foreign Firms, Natural Resources, and Violent Political Economies." *Social Science Forum,* March 21, 2000.

Reno, William. *Warlord Politics and African States.* London: Lynne Rienner, 1998.

Renou, Xavier. "Promoting Destabilization and Neoliberal Pillage: The Utilization of Private Military Companies for Peacekeeping and Peace Enforcement Activities in Africa." Paper presented at ISA/APSA International Security Conference, Denver, November 2000.

Resende-Santos, João. "Anarchy and the Emulation of Military Systems: Military Organization and Technology in South America, 1870–1914," *Security Studies* 5, no. 3 (Spring 1996): 193–260.

Ricks, Tom, and Greg Schneider. "Cheney's Firm Profited From 'Overused' Army." *Washington Post,* September 9, 2000, p. 6.

"Risky Returns: Doing Business in Chaotic and Violent Countries." *The Economist,* May 20, 2000.

Robberson, Ted. "Contractors Playing Increasing Role in U.S. Drug War." *Dallas Morning News,* February 27, 2000.

——. "Shedding Light on a Dark War." *Dallas Morning News,* May 3, 2001. http://www.dallasnews.com/world/355876_andean_03int.A.html

——. "U.S. Launches Covert Program to Aid Colombia." *Dallas Morning News,* August 19, 1998.

Robbins, Christopher. *Air America: The Story of the CIA's Secret Airlines.* New York: G. P. Putnam's Sons, 1979.

Rosecrance, Richard. "A New Concert of Powers," *Foreign Affairs* 71. no. 2 (Spring 1992).

Rosecrance, Richard. *The Rise of the Virtual State: Wealth and Power in the Coming Century.* New York: Basic Books, 1999.

Rothbard, Murray. *For a New Liberty: The Libertarian Manifesto.* New York: Macmillan, 1978.

Rubin, Elizabeth. "An Army of One's Own." *Harper's Magazine,* February 1997.

Rufford, Nicholas, and Pete Sawyer. "Death Crash and 'Secret UK Arms Deals'." *Sunday Times,* November 19 2000. http://www.sunday-times.co.uk/news/ pages/ sti/2000/11/19/stifgnafro2001.html

Russell, Rosalind. "Macedonia Pounds Hills, World Urges Restraint." *Reuters,* March 24, 2001.

"Russia Betrays 150 Mercenaries." www.qoqaz.net, November 19, 2000.

"Russian Contract Soldiers in Chechnya Poor Quality, Often Quit." RFE/RL, October 2, 2000. http://www.russiatoday.com/news.php3?id=205234

"Russians Fly for Both Sides in Horn of Africa." *London Times,* February 19, 1999.

"Russian Generals behind Ethiopian Victory." *Izvestiya,* May 25, 2000.

Sadowski, Yahya. *The Myth of Global Chaos.* Washington, D.C.: Brooking Institution, 1998.

Saint, Steven. "NORAD Outsources." *Colorado Springs Gazette,* September 1, 2000.

Scammell, G. V. *The English Trading Companies and the Sea.* London: Trustees of the National Maritime Museum, 1982.

Schelling, Thomas. *Arms and Influence.* New Haven: Yale University Press, 1966.

Schemo, Diana Jean. "Oil Companies Buy an Army to Tame Colombia's Rebels." *New York Times,* August 22, 1996.

Schonauer, Scott. "Hacker Sends Costly Virus to Brown & Root." *European Stars and Stripes,* February 7, 2001, p. 3.

Schoneich, Martin. "Fighting Crime with Private Muscle: The Private Sector and Crime Prevention." *African Security Review* 8, no. 5 (May 1998).

Schrader, Esther. "U.S. Companies Hired to Train Foreign Armies." *Los Angeles Times,* April 14, 2002.

Sclar, Elliott. *Selling the Brooklyn Bridge: The Economics of Public Service Privatization.* New York: Twentieth Century Fund, 1999.

"Securicor to Acquire Gray Security Services." *London Stock Exchange Regulatory News Service,* September 15, 2000.

Sennett, Richard. *The Fall of Public Man.* New York: Alfred A. Knopf, 1977.

"Serb Snatched by Rogue NATO Bounty Hunter." *The Sunday Times,* July 23, 2000. www.Sunday-times.co.uk

Shearer, David. *Private Armies and Military Intervention.* London: International Institute for Strategic Studies, Adelphi Paper no. 316, February 1998.

Sheppard, Simon. "Soldiers for Hire." *Contemporary Review,* August 1999.

Sheridan, Michael. "Briton Quits Indonesia over 'Psych War' Claims." *Sunday Times,* August 6, 2000. http://www.Sunday-times.co.uk/news/pages/sti/2000/08/06/stifgnasio2001.html

Sherman, Jason. "Arm's Length." *Armed Forces Journal International* (September 2000): 30.

Sherwell, Phillip, and Julius Strauss. "Nigerian Troops in Sierra Leone Are Kept Waiting for Wages." *London Sunday Telegraph,* June 18, 2000.

Shichor, David. *Punishment for Profit: Private Prisons/Public Concerns.* Thousand Oaks, CA: Sage Publications, 1995.

Showers, Duncan. "Are We Ready to Fight and Win the Next War?" *Contractors on the Battlefield.* Air Force Logistics Management Agency, December 1999.

"Sierra Leone: Briefing on the Civil War." *IRIN,* May 31, 2000.

Silber, Laura, and Alan Little. *Yugoslavia: Death of a Nation.* New York: Penguin Books, 1997.

Silverstein, Ken. "Mercenary, Inc.?" *Washington Business Forward,* April 26, 2001.

——. "Privatizing War." *The Nation,* July 7, 1998.

Singer. P. W. "Caution: Children at War." *Parameters* 31 (Winter 2001): 40–56.

Singh, Jasit. *Light Weapons and International Security.* New Delhi: Institute for Defense Studies and Analysis, 1995.

Slaughter, Anne-Marie. "The Real New World Order." *Foreign Affairs* (September 1997).

"Small But Victorious War." *Izvestiya,* May 31, 2000.

Smith, Adam. *The Wealth of Nations.* 1776. http://www.socsci.mcmaster.ca/~econ/ugcm/3ll3/smith/wealth/wealbko5

Smith, Charles. "Russian MIGs in Sudan." *Newsmax.com,* January 4, 2002.

——. "Wars and Rumors of Wars: Russian Mercenaries Flying for Ethiopia." *World Net Daily,* July 18, 2000. http://www.worldnetdaily.com/bluesky_smith_news/20000718_xnsof_russian_me.shtm

Smith, Richard. *Mercenaries and Mandarins: The Ever-Victorious Army in Nineteenth Century China.* Millwood, N.Y.: KTO, 1978.

Snyder, Jack L. *The Ideology of the Offensive: Military Decision Making and the Disasters of 1914.* Ithaca, N.Y.: Cornell University Press, 1984.

"Soldier of Fortune—The Mercenary as Corporate Executive." *African Business,* December 1997.

South African Institute of International Affairs. "Private Security: Phantom Menace or Evil Empire?" *Intelligence Update,* May 11, 2000.

"South Africa-Nigeria: Military Relationship." *IRIN,* April 18, 2000.

Spearin, Christopher. "The Commodification of Security and Post-Cold War Patron-Client Balancing: New Actors, New Objectives, and New Consequences." ISA/APSA International Security Conference, Denver, November 2000.

Spicer, Tim. *An Unorthodox Soldier: Peace and War and the Sandline Affair.* Edinburgh: Mainstream, 1999.

Stein, Janice, with Michael Bryans and Bruce Jones. *Mean Times: Humanitarian Action in Complex Political Emergencies—Stark Choices, Cruel Dilemmas.* Toronto: University of Toronto Program on Conflict Management and Negotiation, 1999.

Stephen, Chris. "KLA Trains Refugees to Recapture Border Territory." *Irish Times,* April 7, 1999.

Stokke, Olav, ed., *Aid and Political Conditionality.* London: Frank Cass, 1995.

Sullivan, Kevin. "Tequila Shooters Take Aim at Cactus Rustlers." *Washington Post,* August 11, 2000. http://washingtonpost.com/wp-dyn/articles/A5683-2000Aug10.html

Sun Tzu. *The Art of War.* Translated by Samuel Griffith. New York: Oxford University Press, 1971.

Sutherland, Lucy. *The East India Company in Eighteenth Century Politics.* Oxford: Clarendon Press, 1979.

Taibel, Paul. "Outsourcing & Privatization of Defense Infrastructure." Business Executives for National Security Report, 1998. Available at http://www.bens.org/pubs/outsrce.html.

Tamayo, Juan O. "Colombian Guerrillas Fire on U.S. Rescuers." *Miami Herald,* February 22, 2001.

———. "U.S. Civilians Taking Risks in Drug War for Colombia." *Miami Herald,* February 26, 2001.

Taulbee, Larry. "Myths, Mercenaries and Contemporary International Law." *California Western International Law Journal* 15, no. 2 (Spring 1985): 339–363.

———. "Reflections on the Mercenary Option." *Small Wars and Insurgencies* 9, no. 2 (Autumn 1998): 145–63.

Taylor, Kate, and Terry J. Gander. "Mine Clearance in Cambodia." *International Defense Review,* February 1, 1996, p. 5.

Taylor, Paul, "The European Community and the State: Assumptions, Theories, and Propositions." *Review of International Studies* 17 (1991): 109–125.

"The Thatcher Revolution." *The Economist.* September 21, 1996, p. 8.

Thom, William. "The African Military: Problems and Prospects." *Africa Digest* 18, no. 2, (September 1995): p. 8.

———. "Africa's Security Issues through 2010." *Military Review.* Headquarters, Department of the Army. Professional Bulletin 100–99–5/6,Vol. 80, no. 4, July–August 2000. http://www-cgsc.army.mil/milrev/English/JulAug00/thom.htm

Thompson, Mark. "Generals for Hire." *Time,* January 15, 1996.

Thompson, William. *The Grievances of Military Coup Makers.* Beverly Hills: Sage, 1973.

Thomson. Janice. *Mercenaries, Pirates, and Sovereigns: State-building and Extraterritorial Violence in Early Modern Europe.* Princeton, N.J.: Princeton University Press. 1994.

Thorycroft, Peta. "Mobutu Couldn't Afford SA Mercenaries." *Weekly Mail & Guardian,* July 18, 1997.

Thucydides. *The History of the Peloponnesian War, 431 B.C.* Translated by Richard Crawley. Available at http://classics.mit.edu/Thucydides/pelopwar.html.

Tickler, Peter. *The Modern Mercenary*. London: Thorsons, 1987.

Tilly, Charles. *Coercion, Capital, and European States, A.D. 990–1990*. Cambridge, Mass.: Blackwell, 1990.

———. *The Formation of National States in Western Europe*. Princeton, N.J.: Princeton University Press, 1975.

Tirole, Jean. *The Theory of Industrial Organization*. Cambridge: MIT Press, 1988.

Toffler, Alvin, and Heidi Toffler. *War and Anti-War: Survival at the Dawn of the Twenty-first Century*. New York: Little, Brown, 1993.

Toland, John. *Battle: The Story of the Bulge*. New York: Bison Books, 1999.

"Top Science Advisers Calling for Higher Premium on Military Training." *Washington Post*, February 8, 2000, p. 1.

Toro, Juan. "Colombia Militia Enjoys Support." AP, September 6, 2000.

Tracey, James, ed. *The Rise of Merchant Empires*. New York: Cambridge University Press, 1990.

Transano, Vincent. "History of the Seabees." Naval Historical Center, accessed Nov. 2000. http://www.history.navy.mil/faqs/faq67-1.htm

Traub, James. "The Worst Place on Earth." *New York Review of Books*, June 29, 2000. http://www.nybooks.com/nyrev/WWWfeatdisplay.cgi?20000629061F

Tuck, Christopher. "'Every Car or Moving Object Gone': The ECOMOG Intervention in Liberia." *African Studies Quarterly* 4, no. 1 (February 2000). http://web.africa.ufl.edu/asq/v4/v4i1a1.htm

"$2.4 Billion Needed for Pentagon Computer Security." UPI, September 13, 2000.

"UK Outlines Revised Plans to Privatise Defence Research." *Jane's Defence Weekly*, March 26, 2000. http://www.janes.com/defence/editors/uk_plans.html

Ulbrich, Jeffrey. "French No Longer Africa Gendarmes." AP, May 23, 2001.

Ullman, Richard H., "Redefining Security," *International Security* 8, no. 1 (Summer 1983): 129–153.

United Nations. Report of the Expert of the Secretary-General, Graça Machel, "Impact of Armed Conflict on Children." Document A/51/306 & Add 1. August 26, 1996. gopher://gopher.un.org:70/00/ga/docs/51/plenary/A51–306.

———. Report of the Monitors of European Union on Violations of Human Rights of the Serbs during and after Operation "Storm." October 17, 1995. available at http://www.aimpress.org/dyn/trae/archive/data/199510/51017-003-trae-zag.htm

———. *Report of the Panel on United Nations Peace Operations*. A/55/305, S/2000/809. August 21, 2000.

———. "Transcript of Press Conference By Secretary General Kofi Annan at UN Headquarters on 12 June, 1996."

United Nations Commission on Human Rights. "Report on the question of the use of mercenaries as a means of violating human rights and impeding the exercise of the right of peoples to self-determination, submitted by the Special Rapporteur of the Commission on Human Rights." 51st Session, Item 106, August 29, 1995.

———. "Report on the question of the use of mercenaries as a means of violating human rights and impeding the exercise of the right of peoples to self determination." 53d Session, Item 7, Special Rapporteur, February 20, 1997.

———. Report on the question of the use of mercenaries as a means of violating human rights and impeding the exercise of the right of peoples to self determination. 57th Session, Item 7, Special Rapporteur, January 2001.

United Nations Development Programme. UN Human Development Index 22000, available at http://undp.org/hdr2000/english/HDR2000.html

"UN Hires Detective to Probe UNITA." *Globe & Mail,* April 19, 2001.

"US Backs Role for Rebels in W. Africa." *Washington Post,* October 18, 1999.

U.S. Department of the Army. *Contracting Support on the Battlefield.* FM 100-10-2. April 15, 1999.

———. *Contractors on the Battlefield.* FM 100–121. Washington: Headquarters. September 1999.

———. *Logistics: Army Contractors on the Battlefield.* Regulation 715–XX, January 31, 1999.

U.S. Department of State. *Transcript of Briefing by Ambassador Pardew,* July 24, 1996.

"U.S. Firm to Retrieve Russian Sub." *The Guardian,* October 3, 2000.

U.S. House of Representatives. *The Current Situation in Bosnia and the former Yugoslavia and Preparations of U.S. Forces for Operation Joint Endeavor—Moliari-Levin Delegation,* Trip Report, December 11, 1995.

U.S. Senate. U.S. Senate Select Committee Report on Iran/Bosnia Arms Transfers. 1996. Available at http://www.parascope.com/articles/0197/bosnia.htm

Valasek, Thomas. "Bosnia: Five Years Later." *Defense Monitor,* December 2000.

Van Bergen Thirion, C. J. "The Privatisation of Security: A Blessing or a Menace?" South African Defence College Paper, May 1999.

Van Creveld, Martin. *The Rise and Decline of the State.* Cambridge: Cambridge University Press, 1999.

———. *Supplying War: Logistics from Wallenstein to Patton.* Cambridge: Cambridge University Press. 1977.

Van Evera, Stephen. *The Causes of War: Power and the Roots of Conflict.* Ithaca, N.Y.: Cornell University Press, 1999.

———. "The Cult of the Offensive and the Origins of the First World War." *International Security* 9, no. 1 (Summer 1984): 58–107.

———. "Hypotheses on Nationalism and War," *International Security* 18, no. 4, (Spring 1994): 5–39.

———. "Offense, Defense, and the Causes of War." *International Security* 22, no. 4, (Spring 1998): 5–43.

Van Vauuren, Ian. "The Changing Nature of Warfare: Implications for Africa." *African Security Review* 7, no. 1 (January 1998).

Vaubel, Roland, and Thomas Willett. *The Political Economy of International Organizations.* Boulder, Colo.: Westview Press, 1991.

Venter, Al J. "Market Forces: How Hired Guns Succeeded Where the United Nations Failed." *Jane's International Defense Review,* March, 1998.

———. "Out of State and Non State Actors Keep Africa Down." *Jane's Intelligence Review* 11, May 1, 1999.

———. "Sierra Leone's Mercenary War." *Jane's International Defense Review,* November, 1995.

———. "U.S. Forces Guard Angolan Oilfields." *Weekly Mail & Guardian,* October 10, 1997.

Vines, Alex. "The Business of Peace: 'Tiny' Rowland, Financial Incentives and the Mozambican Settlement." Accord: An International Review of Peace Initiatives. http://www.c-r.org/acc_moz/contents_moz.htm.

Von Clausewitz, Carl. *On War.* Edited with an introduction by Anatol Rapoport. Middlesex, Eng.: Penguin, 1968.

Walker, R. B. J. "Genealogy, Geopolitics, and Political Community." *Alternatives* 13 (January 1988).

Wall, Robert. "Army Leases 'Eyes' To Watch Balkans." *Aviation Week & Space Technology,* October 30, 2000, p. 68.

Walt, Stephen. *The Origins of Alliances.* Ithaca, N.Y.: Cornell University Press, 1990.

Walter, Yosi. "Shadaq in the Congo." *Tel Aviv Ma'ariv,* October 7, 1994, FBIS translation.

Waltz, Kenneth. *Theory of International Relations.* New York: McGraw Hill, 1979.

"War, Chaos, and Business: Modern Business Strategy." Kettle Creek Corporation briefing, 2001. http://www.belisarius.com/

Washington, William. "Subcontracting as a Solution, Not a Problem in Outsourcing." *Acquisition Review Quarterly* (Winter 1997): 79–86.

Watson, Francis. *Wallenstein: Soldier under Saturn.* London, Appleton-Century, 1938.

Weber, Max. *Theory of Social and Economic Organization.* Translated by A. M. Henderson, New York: Free Press, 1964.

Weiner, Myron, ed. *International Migration and Security.* Boulder, Colo.: Westview Press, 1993.

Weinstein, Jeremy M. "Africa's 'Scramble for Africa': Lessons of a Continental War." *World Policy Journal* 17, no. 2 (Summer 2000).

Wendt, Alexander. *Social Theory of International Politics.* New York: Cambridge University Press 1999.

Wendt, Alexander, and Michael Barnett, "Dependent State Formation and Third World Militarization." *Review of International Studies* 19, no. 4 (August 1993): 321–347.

Westwood, Chris. "Military Information Operations in a Conventional Warfare Environment." Air Power Studies Centre Paper, Number 47, 1995. www.defense.gov.au/apsc/publish/paper47.htm

Whitelaw, Kevin. "The Russians Are Coming." *U.S. News and World Report,* March 15, 1999.

Wilkins, Mira, ed. *The Free-Standing Company in the World Economy, 1830–1996.* Oxford: Oxford University Press, 1998.

"William Shawcross Interviewed by Jennifer Byrne." Australian Broadcasting Corporation, August 29, 2000. Transcript available at http://www.abc.net.au/foreign/interv/shawcross.htm

Wilnius, George. *The Merchant Warrior Pacified.* New York: Oxford University Press, 1991.

Wohlstetter, Roberta. *Pearl Harbor: Warning and Decision.* Stanford: Stanford University Press, 1962.

Wood, Brian, and Johan Peleman. *The Arms Fixers.* PRIO Report, March 1999.

"The World War Web?" *The Industry Standard,* February 12, 1999.

Wynn, Donald T. "Managing the Logistics-Support Contract in the Balkans Theater." *Engineer,* July 2000. http://call.army.mil/call/trngqtr/tq4–oo/wynn.htm

Xenophon. *Anabasis.* English translation by Carleton L. Brownson. Cambridge: Harvard University Press, 1922.

Yakov, Valery, "Russia's 'Wild Geese'—Or, An Evening with a Mercenary." *Current Digest of the Post-Soviet Press*, May 5, 1993.

Yearsly, Alex. "Oriental Timber Company Smuggles Weapons to RUF." *Radio France International*, May 10, 2001.

Yocherer, Greg. "Classic Battle Joined." *Military History* (February 2000). http://www.thehistorynet.com/MilitaryHistory/articles/2000/02002_cover.htm

Young, Crawford. "The African Colonial State Revisited." *Governance* 11, no. 1 (January 1998): 101–120.

Young, Peter Lewis. "Bouganville Conflict Enters Its Ninth Year." *Jane's Intelligence Review*, June, 1997.

Zamparrelli, Stephen. "Contractors on the Battlefield: What Have We Signed Up For?" Air War College Research report, March 1999.

Zarate, Juan Carlos. "The Emergence of a New Dog of War: Private International Security Companies, International Law, and the New World Order." *Stanford Journal of International Law* 34 (Winter 1998): 75–156.

Index